Walking in Grace

2022 Daily devotions to draw you closer to God

Formerly *Daily Guideposts*

Guideposts

Copyright © 2022 by Guideposts. All rights reserved.

This book, or parts thereof, may not be reproduced, stored in a retrieval system, or transmitted in any form or by any means, electronic, mechanical, photocopying, recording or otherwise, without the written permission of the publisher.

Walking in Grace is a registered trademark of Guideposts.

Acknowledgments

Every attempt has been made to credit the sources of copyrighted material used in this book. If any such acknowledgment has been inadvertently omitted or miscredited, receipt of such information would be appreciated.

Scripture quotations marked (CEV) are taken from *Holy Bible: Contemporary English Version.* Copyright © 1995 American Bible Society.

Scripture quotations marked (CSB) are taken from *The Christian Standard Bible.* Copyright © 2017 by Holman Bible Publishers. Used by permission.

Scripture quotations marked (ESV) are taken from the *Holy Bible, English Standard Version.* Copyright © 2001 by Crossway Bibles, a division of Good News Publishers. Used by permission. All rights reserved.

Scripture quotations marked (GNT) are taken from the *Holy Bible, Good News Translation.* Copyright © 1992 by American Bible Society.

Scripture quotations marked (GW) are taken from *GOD'S WORD Translation.* Copyright © 1995 by God's Word to the Nations. Used by permission of Baker Publishing Group.

Scripture quotations marked (ICB) are taken from *The Holy Bible, International Children's Bible®.* Copyright © 1986, 1988, 1999, 2015 by Tommy Nelson™, a division of Thomas Nelson. Used by permission.

Scripture quotations marked (KJV) are taken from the *King James Version of the Bible.*

Scripture quotations marked (MSG) are taken from *The Message.* Copyright © 1993, 1994, 1995, 1996, 2000, 2001, 2002 by Eugene H. Peterson.

Scripture quotations marked (NASB) are taken from the *New American Standard Bible.* Copyright © 1960, 1962, 1963, 1968, 1971, 1972, 1973, 1975, 1977, 1995 by the Lockman Foundation. Used by permission.

Scripture quotations marked (NIV) are taken from *The Holy Bible, New International Version.* Copyright © 1973, 1978, 1984, 2011 by Biblica, Inc. Used by permission of Zondervan. All rights reserved worldwide. zondervan.com

Scripture quotations marked (NKJV) are taken from *The Holy Bible, New King James Version.* Copyright © 1982 by Thomas Nelson, Inc.

Scripture quotations marked (NLT) are from the *Holy Bible, New Living Translation.* Copyright © 1996, 2004, 2007 by Tyndale House Foundation. Used by Permission of Tyndale House Publishers Inc., Carol Stream, Illinois 60188. All rights reserved.

Scripture quotations marked (NRSV) are taken from the *New Revised Standard Version Bible.* Copyright © 1989 by the Division of Christian Education of the National Council of the Churches of Christ in the United States of America. Used by permission. All rights reserved.

Scripture quotations marked (NRSVCE) are taken from *New Revised Standard Version Bible: Catholic Edition.* Copyright © 1989, 1993 National Council of the Churches of Christ in the United States of America. Used by permission. All rights reserved worldwide.

Scripture quotations marked (Tanakh) are taken from *Tanakh: A New Translation of the Holy Scriptures according to the Traditional Hebrew Text.* Copyright © 1985 by the Jewish Publication Society. All rights reserved.

Scripture quotations marked (TLB) are taken from *The Living Bible.* Copyright © 1971 by Tyndale House Publishers, Wheaton, Illinois 60187. All rights reserved.

Scripture quotations marked (TPT) are taken from *The Passion Translation.* Copyright © 2016 by Broadstreet Publishing Group, Savage, Minnesota. All rights reserved.

Cover and interior design by Müllerhaus
Cover photo by Shutterstock
Monthly page opener photos by Pixabay (p. 1, 35, 66, 133, 167, 301, 335, 368) and Unsplash (p. 100, 200, 234, 268)
Indexed by Kelly Anne White
Typeset by Aptara, Inc.

Printed and bound in the United States of America
10 9 8 7 6 5 4 3 2 1

Dear friend,

We welcome you with joy to a new volume of *Walking in Grace 2022*, the daily devotional book that has become a touchstone for so many on their faith journey. If this is your first time reading *Walking in Grace*, welcome. We're so glad to have you! And if you're a longtime, devoted reader of *Daily Guideposts*, welcome to *Walking in Grace*, an alternate title to *Daily Guideposts*. This volume is filled with more of the heartfelt, inspiring devotions you have come to know and love.

The theme for this year's book is "The Lord Is Near" based on Psalm 145:18: "The Lord is near to all who call on him, to all who call on him in truth." Within, our forty-nine writers show how, amidst the brokenness of this world, they experienced God's ongoing redemption and miraculous love, as they called upon Him daily and found Him so very near.

In Psalm 145, David tells us the Lord is "filled with unfailing love," that He "always keeps his promises," and that He "helps the fallen." These words were a balm to us and our writers this year as we walked faithfully with God, called upon Him, and drew near to His heart.

For some writers, it was a year of letting go, saying goodbye, or experiencing loss. Others enjoyed new blessings and gifts, forgiveness and reconciliation, joy and laughter. Yet all share stories of rejoicing in every circumstance, as they saw God's nearness and faithfulness, His hand guiding, blessing, delighting, and comforting them.

Pablo Diaz tells of moving from New York to Florida and how God's plan was evident throughout that journey; Erika Bentsen delights us with an endearing story about friendship that happens to include a lot of s'mores; Vicki Kuyper reflects on how God's unconditional love guides her in life, especially in being a grandmother; Sabra Ciancanelli shares an unlikely and beautiful story about being comforted in her grief by a goose; God uses something as simple as laundry to help Ashley Kappel experience and teach gratitude to her daughter; Jon Sweeney is surprised by a reminder of God's hope when he gets a second bag of chips with his lunch; Julia Attaway experiences the power of prayer and hope of God's love as she prays for family friends; and Rick Hamlin tells us how he can sing the Lord's praises after his mother's passing, among many more stories.

This year, we are pleased to welcome three new writers, Jerusha Agen, Jenny Keller, and Shirley Raye Raymond. And we are filled with gratitude as we say a fond farewell to beloved writer Elizabeth Sherrill, who is retiring from *Walking in Grace* after many years as a contributor. She will be missed! While Sharon Foster and Bill Giovannetti are not featured in this year's book, we hope to welcome them back next year.

This volume has six special series for you to enjoy. Stephanie Thompson takes you along as she learns and experiences more about prayer than she thought possible in "Praying Together." Ginger Rue shares humorous and delightful stories—and spiritual lessons—in a series about her dog, Cookie. Debbie Macomber reflects on the many times she has seen God's fingerprints on her life, evidence of His goodness and provision. From a convent in Italy to a small church in Massachusetts to a pristine lake in New Hampshire, Gail Thorell Schilling will take you on a tour of many "Sacred Spaces" where she has experienced God's presence. Carol Knapp uses her gifts and passion for the Bible as she plumbs Scripture for her series "Wisdom's Delights." Logan Eliasen will spend Holy Week with us as he travels to a friend's wedding. And Lynne Hartke remembers Christmases past and present in her Advent series.

Wherever you find yourself in your faith walk, we're so glad you're here, ready to embark on a journey of drawing closer to God's goodness, mercy, and love. We pray God's richest blessings upon you this year as you call upon Him, knowing He'll be near in every moment.

Faithfully yours,
Editors of Guideposts

P.S. We love hearing from you! We read every letter we receive. Let us know what *Walking in Grace* means to you by emailing DailyGPEditors@guideposts.org or writing to Guideposts Books & Inspirational Media, 100 Reserve Road, Suite E200, Danbury, CT 06810. You can also keep up with your *Walking in Grace* friends on facebook.com/DailyDevofromGP.

January

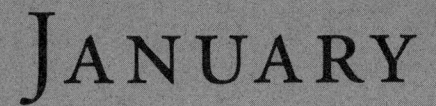

*You are near, O Lord,
And all Your commandments
are truth.*

—Psalm 119:151 (NKJV)

New Year's Day, Saturday, January 1

PRAYING TOGETHER: New Year, New Revelation

See, I am doing a new thing! Now it springs up; do you not perceive it? I am making a way in the wilderness and streams in the wasteland.
—Isaiah 43:19 (NIV)

New Year's Day, 8:00 a.m.—my favorite morning of the year. With my husband and teenage daughter still sleeping, I have a rare moment to myself. Sitting in the stillness of my home office, I hold a steaming cup. I savor the opportunity to reflect on the year behind me and the one ahead.

I'm a goal-setter, so making resolutions is something I relish. As I do each year, I methodically make my list: lose weight, exercise daily, write a novel, have a consistent quiet time, clean every room in our house of clutter. I love setting goals! New beginnings hold such promise.

Pleased with my New Year's list, I turn to last year's resolutions to see how I fared: lose twenty pounds (accomplished by summer's end, before regaining ten over the holidays); exercise three to four times a week (success); awaken a half-hour earlier to pray (ugh, such a fail); write a novel (worked on it for a week, then abandoned it); deep-clean every room (does thinking about it each day count?).

I flipped the pages two years back. You guessed it—the list of changes I'd planned to implement into my life looked pretty much the same. I checked resolutions from previous years. Even five years ago, it was the same! I've been setting identical goals over and over again, only to watch them fade into the winter gloom.

Like a champagne cork popping across the room, it hit me. I might like making resolutions, but I don't like keeping them!

Lord, I want this year to be different. Help me to find the new beginning I crave by setting resolutions that I'll actually keep.
—Stephanie Thompson

Digging Deeper: Job 8:7; Proverbs 16:1–9; Jeremiah 29:11

Sunday, January 2

PRAYING TOGETHER: Only One Resolution

One thing I ask from the LORD, this only do I seek: that I may dwell in the house of the LORD all the days of my life, to gaze on the beauty of the LORD and to seek him in his temple. —Psalm 27:4 (NIV)

Irritation bubbled up that New Year's Day when I discovered that my beloved resolution-making activity had been a sham for all these years. I was still cogitating about my resolutions when my family and I walked into church the next day. After we found seats, I saw the sermon topic: resolutions. *Great*, I thought. *Another reminder of how I've fallen short.*

Our pastor confided that he liked making New Year's resolutions too. I sat forward in my chair. He paced away from the pulpit and shared his secret: Instead of making a list of them like I did, he made only one resolution a year. He'd done this for the past twenty-five years. His one-resolution-a-year habit had therefore grown into an arsenal of twenty-five life changes because he had concentrated on adding only one new behavior at a time.

He then divulged the most important resolution he'd ever made—his first, in fact—which was now a lifelong habit: praying with his spouse.

Out of the corner of my eye, I peeked at my husband sitting on the other side of our daughter. We'd been married seventeen years. We prayed before meals, but I think Pastor was talking about something more meaningful.

Michael traveled for work. Our schedules were different. These days, we passed like two ships in the night. But more than that, I didn't know if Michael would want to commit to a daily prayer time with me.

An unmistakable flutter inside my chest confirmed that I needed to pursue this. But would Michael agree? Would he help me make and keep this one resolution?

Lord, give me courage to ask a question that might result in a no. Prepare Michael's heart if this is to be.
—Stephanie Thompson

Digging Deeper: Luke 10:4–42; Philippians 3:12–14

Monday, January 3

I have given you an example to follow: do as I have done to you.
—John 13:15 (TLB)

Every morning I walk across the street to our huge neighborhood pool where I swim alone for twenty-five minutes before joining the water aerobics class. I love that I get to exercise for a total of about two hours every morning and chat with my women friends. Before I leave the house, I have to remember five things: my towel, my key to the pool gate, my water shoes, my sun hat, and my sunglasses. Five things. I'd forget one or two if I wasn't in the habit of asking myself, "Do you have the five things?" before I walk out the door.

Same thing goes for church. I need four things for that: my reading glasses, my church contribution envelope, a small notebook, and a pen in my purse, just in case the priest says something during the homily that I specifically want to remember and ponder later.

Every week, when I run down my list of things to remember to take out the door, either to the pool or to church, I also try to remember to prepare my heart. I tell myself, "No gossiping at the pool. Be nice to that woman who talks too loud and interrupts the class with her loud laughing." At church I have to remind myself to stop thinking about what so-and-so is wearing and stop fuming over the fact that the air-conditioning is too cold again.

The older I get, the more lists and reminders become a part of my life. But the best lists are the ones that keep me squared away with Jesus, whether I'm in church or at the pool or anywhere else.

Jesus, bless all those I come in contact with and help me bless them by being as much like You as I can muster today.
—Patricia Lorenz

Digging Deeper: Galatians 5:22–24; 2 Thessalonians 3:11–16

Tuesday, January 4

WISDOM'S DELIGHTS: Wisdom of Knowing Jesus
All things have been handed over to Me by My Father, and no one knows who the Son is except the Father, and who the Father is except the Son, and anyone to whom the Son wills to reveal Him. —Luke 10:22 (NASB)

Letters and words are lifelong friends. But numbers have always been something of a mystery. Over a period of months after seeing the number 22 appear again and again, I finally wondered if I should be paying attention. What a surprise during prayer to receive a nudge to look at Bible verses numbering 22! In my Scripture reading, I began noting these verses—excited for how God would speak His wisdom and truth to me through them.

Luke 10:22 follows a spontaneous exclamation of joy from Jesus. He has sent seventy of His followers ahead to the towns He plans to visit to prepare the people for His coming. To tell them, "The kingdom of God has come near you." (v. 9) They return thrilled with their success.

Jesus praises His heavenly Father that it is not the "wise and intelligent" (v. 21) who are willing to believe He is sent from God—but humble folk who would not be considered worthy of recognition by those in positions of authority in that day.

Then comes the breathtaking affirmation that only Jesus knows the Father—and that He is willing to make Him known among humankind. My heart leaps. God is knowable through the life of Jesus. So I feel a hunger to read what the Bible says about Him—every word and action, every assurance, every promise—and to make them my own. Because they are for me. And for all who believe.

Jesus, the greatest wisdom I can desire is intimacy with God through You.
—Carol Knapp

Digging Deeper: John 17:3, 26; Ephesians 1:17, 3:19;
Colossians 1:15

Wednesday, January 5

And call upon me in the day of trouble: I will deliver thee, and thou shalt glorify me. —Psalm 50:15 (KJV)

Years ago, right out of college, I met a woman who told me she had lost everything in a house fire. Not one belonging was spared. Thankfully, she lived alone, didn't have pets, and wasn't home at the time. She leaned in and confided, "I was devastated, but now I can honestly say it was the best thing that ever happened to me." At the time, I was struggling to find a job, and this woman, a friend of a friend, a stranger, had given me the wisdom of her experience.

Fast forward to last week, when my husband was laid off. I went for a walk, looking for any silver lining to grasp onto, and this woman and her story came back to me.

"At the time I felt so lost," I remembered the woman say. "But you have no idea how freeing it is to start over. It's a gift. Starting over is always a gift."

So now, as my husband and I go through the process of letting go of what we had and embracing our current situation, I hold onto the trust that in every bit of difficult news, there is a chance, as hard as it might seem, to rethink it as an opportunity—a chance for something new.

Dear Lord, help me to take upsetting news in stride, to be thankful for life's thorns and storms, hoping that one day I may look back and see them as blessings in disguise.
—Sabra Ciancanelli

Digging Deeper: Psalm 86:7; Isaiah 40:29; 2 Corinthians 12:9

Feast of the Epiphany, Thursday, January 6

Holy, holy, holy is the Lord God Almighty. —Revelation 4:8 (NIV)

By the time Epiphany rolls around, my Christmas spirit is usually on the wane. I've been looking with anticipation to the nativity for more than a month already, starting on that first Sunday of Advent. By now, Christ has been born in a manger. The shepherds have kept their watch. There have been many silent nights. And the tree needles are all over the floor.

Today is the day we celebrate the arrival of wise men from the east who came to see for themselves if the promise of a Messiah had come true.

It reminds me of my old neighbor Bill. Bill had been raised a deer hunter by his father, and went hunting every season for more than a half century, until one quiet early dawn when, sitting in his blind up in an oak tree, Bill was stunned to see a magnificent elk stroll into the clearing. Bill didn't have an elk-hunting license, but it wouldn't have mattered. He told me that he couldn't have pulled the trigger anyway. He was awed down to his wool socks. And he never hunted anything again.

This Epiphany (the word means "revelation") I am going to follow Bill's lead and look past the tree—whose needles are falling—to focus on the crib, where the Lord brings me to silent awe.

*Jesus—Friend, Lord, Teacher, Savior—I wonder at
what You've done for me!*
—Jon M. Sweeney

Digging Deeper: Psalm 33:8; Revelation 4:1–3

Friday, January 7

Because of the L<small>ORD</small>'s great love we are not consumed, for his compassions never fail. They are new every morning; great is your faithfulness.
—Lamentations 3:22–23 (NIV)

More than thirty years ago, as I prepared to be a bride, my friend Darlene and I had a complicated falling-out. The cause of the argument has become hazy over the years, but our friendship came to a sudden stop. I replaced her as my maid of honor and severed all ties. But I never stopped thinking about her and wondering if we would ever reconcile.

We had a few mutual friends, and over the years, I would ask them how she was doing and whether she was happy. Despite our departure from each other, I wanted the best for her. About a decade later, when I moved to a town not far from where she was living, I saw a mention in the local newspaper about her nephew and instinctively dialed her phone number from memory. I hoped she wouldn't answer, but she did. We traded semi-awkward pleasantries, spoke politely, and then went our separate ways again. While I wanted to reconnect, I didn't have the courage to make the suggestion.

Later I learned that her mother passed away. I immediately recalled that when my mother had died—years before my wedding—Darlene was one of the first people to just sit with me and let me cry. I'd never forgotten that gesture and knew that I wanted to offer some sort of solace to her as well.

At her mother's wake, we shared a strong embrace. It had been thirty years since we had seen each other, and so much had changed. But it seemed like a perfect time to make things new again.

> *Lord, I thank You for the ability to begin again. Your mercy and grace are never-ending, and I am forever grateful.*
> —Gayle T. Williams

Digging Deeper: Isaiah 43:18–19; 2 Corinthians 5:17

Saturday, January 8

Behold, I will do a new thing.... —Isaiah 43:19 (KJV)

We live in an old wooden two-story house built in 1845 on the highest hill in Macon, Georgia. From the vista of our front porch, much of the saga of American history has been glimpsed by families whose names now recede in time. For the past twelve years, we have enjoyed sharing in this evolving story.

Several weeks ago I uncovered a treasure in the backyard. It is a buried trove of old, hand-shaped, red clay bricks formed by long-forgotten craftsmen and masons. Over time, I unearthed two hundred bricks and have washed and stacked them. Now I am deciding how to preserve and use them.

I admit I am a bit crazy to be so excited about old bricks that are bruised and chipped. But there is something about the quest to discover and preserve lost relics, images, and stories that fascinates me. I have intuited that God is also delighted to find "old bricks," like many of us are, and restore us to useful purpose. We may be cracked and chipped and stained by the chapters of life, but our usefulness and character may be just beginning. God can restore purpose for our present day in every season of our life.

Dear God, throughout my life, use me to accomplish
and fulfill Your purposes. Amen.
—Scott Walker

Digging Deeper: Job 12:12; Psalm 92:2–14; Proverbs 16:31

Sunday, January 9

SACRED SPACES: Chiavari, Italy

So, what shall I do?... I will sing with my spirit, but I will also sing with my understanding. —1 Corinthians 14:15 (NIV)

The heavy front door at Casa Rosmini, the convent bed-and-breakfast where I am staying in Chiavari, Italy, doesn't budge.

"Bottone nero!" pipes the tiny nun in the reception.

Ah, the black button! I press it, and the door glides open. The dear lady grins and bobs in acknowledgment. For two days now, the Sisters and I have managed to communicate in my meager Italian and their equally limited English. Mercifully, their hospitality and loving smiles convey more than words. But this morning, I overslept for the service in the convent's chapel. As I hurry to the Basilica Cattedrale de Nostra Signora dell'Orto (Cathedral of Our Lady of the Garden), just down the street, I look forward to the familiar rites.

My eyes adapt to the dim interior of the cavernous church, its Baroque sanctuary extravagantly encrusted in gold and hung with paintings. In the sparse congregation, no one speaks or looks at me. The service begins, but even with a program I cannot follow it. The melodic Italian language is incomprehensible. In what should be my inclusive faith community, I feel like a stranger.

Suddenly, the organ swells. The "Celtic Alleluia"! I learned it years ago in Wyoming. As I join in the singing, the melody evokes other Christian communities where I've sung it: in Boston, in New Hampshire, in France. And now in Italy. No longer a stranger, I feel drawn into the sacredness of this place, this community of believers. Both here and at the convent, though our languages differ, our spirits are one.

Lord of All, how beautifully You connect me to my brothers and sisters in Christ.
—Gail Thorell Schilling

Digging Deeper: Psalm 117; Matthew 18:20; Ephesians 4:4–6

Monday, January 10

They were longing for a better country—a heavenly one. Therefore God is not ashamed to be called their God, for he has prepared a city for them.
—Hebrews 11:16 (NIV)

I am not a native New Yorker, but I consider the city my home. I came here from Michigan via graduate school in New Haven, Connecticut. I was born in Havertown, Pennsylvania, and have lived in New Mexico and New Jersey. Still, I've lived in New York longer than all those places put together. So yes, I consider myself a New Yorker.

My first winter here saw the blizzard of '83, when the city ground to a halt under nearly twenty inches of snow. I was here for the Wall Street crash of '87 and another devastating blizzard in '96. I was here on September 11, 2001, when terrorists struck the World Trade Center, and in August 2003, when a massive blackout left most of Manhattan, including our Chelsea neighborhood, without power for several steamy days. I remember the city reeling after the Great Recession hit in 2008 and the flooding after Superstorm Sandy in 2012, just as the economy was coming back.

"Boy, you guys really go through it," my sister back in Michigan recently said, the subtext being, "Boy, you are really crazy to live there." Not at all. I wouldn't live anywhere else, though I admit New York isn't for everyone.

Through all those crises, New Yorkers prayed. We may not be part of the Bible Belt, but there are over two thousand churches within our city limits, plus mosques, synagogues, temples, and hundreds of daily twelve-step meetings.

New York is, at heart, a praying place, populated by people of faith who put our city in God's hands through thick and thin. Maybe that's why I love it here. We are a city of God.

Lord, thank You for watching over our beautiful city and over people like me who have come to call it home.
—Edward Grinnan

Digging Deeper: 2 Timothy 4:16–18; Revelation 21:1–4

Tuesday, January 11

Do nothing from selfish ambition or conceit, but in humility count others more significant than yourselves. —Philippians 2:3 (ESV)

I was walking up to the grocery store when I saw a woman at the entrance struggling to get her walker over the curb. As she struggled, I paused. I wanted to help her, but I hesitated.

Would I be intruding on her personal space? What if my help made her uncomfortable, as she wanted the dignity of doing it herself? What if she had a friend or family member close by, already ready to help her out?

In the thirty seconds that I stood there thinking, hesitating, another woman came up behind her and said, "My name is Maria. Let me help you." She grabbed the woman's bags, helped her up the curb, and walked next to her into the store.

For the next half hour as I shopped, I saw Maria. Maria selflessly walked through the entire store with the woman—walking slowly, helping her grab cans from shelves and pick the perfect peaches. Maria never left her side.

I have no idea what Maria's plans were for that day, but I do know that she gave them up to help the woman who needed help. Immediately, without hesitating.

I had paused. And if I am honest with myself, even if I had jumped in to help the woman over the curb, I probably would have helped her up and then moved on to finish my shopping. I don't think I would have stayed with her the entire shopping trip.

But Maria did.

And I hope that next time, I will be like Maria.

Jesus, give me the humility and patience to jump in to help anytime someone needs help. Help me not to pause, not to hesitate, but instead to be Your hands and feet.
—Erin MacPherson

Digging Deeper: 2 Corinthians 9:8; Philippians 2:5–8

Wednesday, January 12

For I was hungry and you gave me food, I was thirsty and you gave me drink, I was a stranger and you welcomed me. —Matthew 25:35 (ESV)

"Look, Mom! A chickadee!" my daughter called, pointing to the bird feeder outside our window. We'd been enjoying learning about the feeder's many visitors. In particular, we'd wondered how such diminutive creatures could weather central Alaska's long, frigid winters. From our bird book, we discovered that, to stay warm, chickadees sometimes burn through as much as ten percent of their body's fat reserves in one night! The following day—if enough food is available—they pack on the same amount of fat in preparation for the next night.

Knowing this, we'd been diligent about making sure our feeder never ran out of seeds. It felt good helping God feed His "birds of the air."

But this morning, as I watched the birds flit between the feeder and the snow-covered spruce trees, my thoughts turned to those humans left outside, without shelter, food, or safety. To the world's refugees—of whom Jesus had been one—fleeing violence. The homeless. The marginalized. The trafficked, lost, and abused. There was so much desperate need in the world.

What could I possibly do to make a difference?

But I looked again at the chickadees on our feeder, whose coming night would be easier, thanks to the seeds we put out. God is aware I cannot fix the world. Yet His call to action remains: "Share your bread with the hungry, shelter the oppressed and the homeless, clothe the naked when you see them."

In the face of staggering odds, He compels me to be moved, to do something. To act.

Lord, I understand now that by focusing on my feelings of being overwhelmed, I've been focusing on myself. Help me see others' needs as I believe You do—personally, individually, and with an open heart.
—Erin Janoso

Digging Deeper: Luke 14:12–14; James 1:22–27

Thursday, January 13

The harvest is plentiful, but the laborers are few; therefore ask the Lord of the harvest to send out laborers into his harvest.
—Matthew 9:37–38 (NRSV)

I was teaching a class titled Writing to God when one student asked, "What do you think heaven is like?" It led to quite a discussion. It's an important question for Christians who are as focused on reaching the Lord in the next world as on doing His work in this one.

I had to think about my own answer. When envisioning the Lord, I usually perceive a great, mighty light. But how do I see heaven? At that moment, He gave me a glimpse. I gazed at the women in the class, all my age or older, all worn with their own cares and the world's sorrows and everything else that made them seek out a class on writing to the Father. In the eyes of one woman, who often smiled even as she dedicated her life to a church outreach ministry while struggling to pay her bills, I saw heaven. I also saw heaven in the worry lines of another woman's forehead as she prepared to make a ten-hour drive in the middle of winter to visit a sick friend. I saw heaven in the determined optimism of a third woman who was single and had found the courage to move into an assisted-living facility.

I realized in that God-given moment that "seeing" heaven, at least from here on earth, may be simply seeing others the way He sees us: broken, struggling, hopeful, challenged—and beautiful.

Father, when earth seems so far from heaven, let me see it and all who are in it with Your eyes.
—Marci Alborghetti

Digging Deeper: Psalm 84; John 3:31

Friday, January 14

For you created my inmost being; you knit me together in my mother's womb. I praise you because I am fearfully and wonderfully made; your works are wonderful, I know that full well. —Psalm 139:13–14 (NIV)

Every January, when the *Daily Guideposts* submission deadline is announced, I go into a panic. This year's deadline was April 3, when my students are writing longer pieces, my grammar students are struggling, and my midsemester grades are due. In addition, my daughter Charlotte was getting married in February.

"This deadline's scary," I told my editor, and she obligingly, unexpectedly extended it to after finals. What a blessing!

In March, though, as always, ideas for devotionals started flinging themselves at me. Soon after Charlotte's wedding, I had several drafted. Apparently, the habit of writing about God's work in my life in March is so securely embedded in my brain that I can't *not* write about it.

That's the way of habits. They're unconscious. Our bodies just do them.

As a sufferer of PTSD (post-traumatic stress disorder), I'm habitually triggered on the anniversary of an assault I suffered one December in grad school. End-of-semester activities, Christmas carols, and scents of pine and cinnamon tell my body it's that time of year, and suddenly I'm struggling. My therapist once said my body's instinctive reactions to the attack—such as playing possum during the attack and being unable to remember key parts afterward—had protected me. It occurred to me that my Christmastime triggers caused me to operate that way too. And once I became aware of that, my triggers became reminders to grieve my losses and to celebrate and praise God for my survival.

Likewise, the unconscious habit of my mind to write about God in March, during my most stressful time of year, is evidence of God's presence in my life. He created me—indeed, He created all of us—to be creatures of habit. Just as spring follows winter, year upon year, God ensures that I will return, despite everything, to Him.

Thank You, God, for the evidence of Your abiding presence in me.
—Patty Kirk

Digging Deeper: Psalm 13, 40

Saturday, January 15

BLESSED BY ONE SWEET COOKIE: Closer Encounters
So then let us pursue what makes for peace and for mutual upbuilding.
—Romans 14:19 (ESV)

The other day during her walk, my dog, Cookie, raised her hackles and barked fiercely at a scary presence. "What is it, girl?" I asked, then turned to see that Cookie was protecting me from…my neighbor's leaf blower. He'd left it sitting on his lawn. I couldn't convince Cookie that the leaf blower was harmless until I took her over for a closer look.

Upon inspection, Cookie realized she could let her guard down and relax. When my neighbor came back and I explained what we were doing, he joked that I should teach Cookie how to use the machine and thus put her energy to good use!

I walked along, chuckling at my silly pup, but then I thought again about an incident that had been bothering me for days. A woman had taken offense at a comment I'd made and had upbraided me in front of a large group of people. I'd certainly meant no offense and had thought I was just making a lighthearted joke, but she had seen it differently. I asked a friend who'd witnessed the incident if I'd been out of line. "No," my friend replied. "Her response was sharp and rude." Other witnesses agreed that the lady was "just that way." And yet I couldn't put it out of my mind.

Cookie had gotten up close and seen things differently; maybe I could too. I thought the circumstances in this woman's life had left her bitter. Maybe she stayed on guard to protect herself. I wrote a sincere note, apologizing for having offended her. She never responded, but I felt much better. And with that burden lifted, I could turn my attention to more important matters—like teaching Cookie how to use that leaf blower.

Father, let the Holy Spirit teach me to see more clearly.
—Ginger Rue

Digging Deeper: Proverbs 12:16; Ephesians 4:32

Sunday, January 16

PRAYING TOGETHER: Just Ask

Again, truly I tell you that if two of you on earth agree about anything they ask for, it will be done for them by my Father in heaven.
—Matthew 18:19 (NIV)

As I got ready for bed, our minister's sermon replayed in my mind. He had shared that he concentrates on only one resolution each new year and is thus able to keep it. Those resolutions then became twenty-five lifelong habits. His first and best resolution, he'd said, was praying with his spouse.

I wanted to replicate his idea, but reasons why it wouldn't work bombarded me: Michael traveled during the week. I was preoccupied with our daughter until bedtime. Michael didn't like "churchy" activities.

I worried that my husband wouldn't want to commit. That he'd say no. Or, worse, that he'd say yes to appease me. It would become drudgery. We'd quit. I'd be resentful.

Maybe I should pick another resolution. Just because it worked for our pastor didn't mean it would work for us. Truth be told, we rarely connected on a deeper level. I plucked up my courage.

Michael was watching television. I scooted next to him on the couch.

"What would you think about praying together each day?" I tried to be nonchalant, but the quiver in my voice betrayed me.

Michael smiled. "That's a great idea!" He grabbed my hand.

We bowed our heads. Awkward silence.

"I'll start," I said. I praised God for the idea to pray together. I thanked Him for Michael's willingness. I prayed for family members, friends, and those who were sick. Michael added his petitions. We said "amen" and hugged.

Holy chills ran down my spine. Praying together, I felt closer to God and my husband too.

Thank You for showing me, Lord, that the best resolution is one that brings me closer to You.
—Stephanie Thompson

Digging Deeper: Ecclesiastes 4:9–12; Acts 1:14

Martin Luther King Jr. Day, Monday, January 17

All the believers... had everything in common. They sold property and possessions to give to anyone who had need. —Acts 2:44–45 (NIV)

Perhaps surprisingly—because I'm an African American—my first impression of Martin Luther King Jr. was that of an intellectually gifted middle-class preacher whose life bore little resemblance to mine. A Mississippi girl who'd worked as a maid from age twelve into adulthood, I saw little kinship between me and this well-versed minister-scholar. But as I observed his actions, I recognized the unveiling of something far exceeding intellectual prowess: a godly man fixated on the needs of all.

In one edition of King's book *Where Do We Go From Here: Chaos or Community?*, Vincent Harding links Dr. King's vision to a quote from Thomas Paine: "We have the power to begin the world over again"—a wonderfully idealistic statement that captures King's core. Likely best known for the words "I have a dream," King boldly declares that "brotherhood [would one day] be the *condition* of man, not the *dream* [italics added]." In order to begin the world anew, he believed, we must be anchored together by a strong sense of commitment to the worth of every human being, no matter the race or class.

In the book of Acts, community isn't defined by proximity but by the needs of one's fellow man, and though the Jerusalem converts couldn't have known it then, the Holy Spirit would eventually deposit their community spirit far and abroad.

Jesus's blood offers the only real way to begin again—a miracle He performs for each repentant believer. But He left it to the hearts of people like the Reverend Dr. Martin Luther King Jr., and to you and me, to extend the power of the cross through compassion for all.

*Jesus, help me never to forget that what
I do affects so many more than me.*
—Jacqueline F. Wheelock

Digging Deeper: John 13:34–35;
1 Thessalonians 3:12; 2 Thessalonians 1:3

Tuesday, January 18

Whoso putteth his trust in the Lord shall be safe.
—Proverbs 29:25 (KJV)

"No brakes! No brakes!" my father roars in his superhuman voice. Loud squeals and laughter follow as the runaway wagon speeds down the hill, sending him and his grandchild headlong into the lake. As they tumble about in the warm water, a cry fills the summer air: "Do it again, Pa, let's do it again!"

And so I was raised. My father had a unique way of teaching a daughter bravery, daring, and grit. Having quit school in the ninth grade to work and see his sisters through college, he lacked the ability to "wax eloquently." He was a teacher of another kind. Setting me up on a high branch, he'd say, "Jump to me." Tossing me off the end of the pier, he'd say, "Swim." I jumped, I swam. And my response was always the same: "Do it again, Daddy. Do it again!"

He always caught me, was always swimming beside me, was always where I needed him to be.

His lessons continued. Gripping the steering wheel of a straight-shift car, stopped on the rim of a hill, he would say, quite casually, from the passenger's seat, "Drive." I didn't always succeed on the first try, or the second, whether it was driving a straight shift, raising children, running a charity, or even cooking a complicated dish. But I've always jumped in and weathered life's ups and downs and sideways and ended up "safe," just as my daddy promised.

These years later, I see the same promises reflected in the way our Father in heaven raises us to become our best, brave selves. "Jump," He says, on the edge of every challenge. And when we do, He's always there to catch us.

Let's do it again, Father. Let's do it again!
—Pam Kidd

Digging Deeper: Psalm 116:16; Mark 4:40; 2 Timothy 1:7

Wednesday, January 19

Like arrows in the hand of a warrior, So are the children of one's youth. Happy is the man who has his quiver full of them!
—Psalm 127:4–5 (NKJV)

Faith, the oldest of our three adult daughters, sent the following family text: "Mom & Dad: Did you guys intentionally make home a place for us to be weird? Or did you accept that we were going to be weird no matter what?"

This may seem like an odd text until you realize that Faith's premise is correct: all three sisters are, um, *quirky*, and each in her own way. Over the years, many incredulous parents have said to me, "Those are *your* kids?" Yep—the one wearing a tutu and cowboy boots to kindergarten? Mine. The one barreling down a black-diamond mountain with no idea how to ski, let alone how to stop? Yes. The one talking to a maple tree? Ahhh...yeah. Also mine.

My wife, Sandee, responded to Faith's text first: "Absolutely. Weird as you wanted to be, as long as you weren't rude or mean."

I, however, did not respond—too choked up with memories. Truth is, I sometimes played the heavy—squelching their personalities, reining in their craziness. Looking back, I don't know why. They turned out to be smart, lovely, compassionate young women—and still a bit odd.

When I was contemplating parenthood all those years ago, these were not the kids I had envisioned—and thank God for that. "We cannot form our children on our own concepts," said Goethe. "We must take them and love them the way God gives them to us."

Lord, thank You for all of Your blessings—especially Faith, Hope, and Grace, my manna from heaven, who taught me to be a better parent.
—Mark Collins

Digging Deeper: Genesis 15:5; Mark 10:14

Thursday, January 20

Above all, keep loving one another earnestly, since love covers a multitude of sins. —1 Peter 4:8 (ESV)

Even from my writing room, I can tell by the way my teenage son Samuel opens the front door and walks into the kitchen that things are different from when he left this morning. We had a disagreement over a plan for his future and didn't know how to close the chasm. Morning had birthed a rush of dueling opinions, hostile attitudes, and sharp words—my son's and mine. Hours later, my soul is still stinging.

"Mom, can you help me, please?" he calls.

I leave my writing room and find him in the kitchen with a paper napkin pressed into his palm. He's bleeding.

"I fell in the school parking lot," he says. "The ice was sharp. I think it's deep."

We go to the bathroom, and he pulls the napkin away. I hold his hand under the tap and let water spill over his wound. There's a zigzag of a cut. It's not deep, but his hand is pebbled with tiny bits of gravel.

And the process begins: the painful process of removing what will fester and cause further pain.

As I wash his hand, I remember newborn fingers that curled around mine. I think about the warm, little boy hand that once fit the flesh of my palm like a seed. Back then, we'd lived and learned and walked and talked about Jesus until His love was the language of our days.

But now we're quiet until nearly the end. Then Sam finally speaks as the water over his wound runs clear.

"I love you, Mom."

"I love you too."

I still don't know what the future will bring, but we are restored. We'll keep loving each other, and the flow of forgiveness will make us clean.

> *Lord, thank You for love that gives grace. Amen.*
> —Shawnelle Eliasen

Digging Deeper: Jeremiah 31:3; 1 John 4:19

Friday, January 21

Those who wait for the LORD shall renew their strength, they shall mount up with wings like eagles.... —Isaiah 40:31 (NRSV)

For the last few years of my mom's life I used to tell her that I had a secret prayer for her. "Mom, when the time comes—and I don't wish for it to come anytime soon—but when it comes, I pray that you get a direct flight."

She liked that idea. No long stay in a hospital, no lingering illness, no back-and-forth with dozens of doctors and medical specialists. Mom had always been blessed with good health. Those last two years she still lived at home with help from a wonderful caregiver who came in during the day. Then at age ninety-three, she was hit with flulike symptoms that landed her in the hospital. The diagnosis: pneumonia. I immediately flew out to California to see her.

That was a Tuesday. On that Thursday—what turned out to be her last day—all four of us kids stood around her hospital bed while a minister from her church read her favorite passage—"the one about eagles' wings," as she put it. We sang the song about eagles' wings and then she turned to me and quietly said, "I'm going to the Lord's house soon."

Later that night, when none of us were there, we got a call from the hospital. Mom had died a little after ten o'clock.

One of the difficulties of such a direct flight is that it can leave those of us left behind on the tarmac staring at the sky, struggling with an unexpected sense of loss. What I take comfort in is how God's love shimmered through all of those years of Mom's love for us, our prayers answered.

Thank You, God, for answering prayers. Help me, now, to know Your presence in all Your answers.
—Rick Hamlin

Digging Deeper: 1 Thessalonians 5:16; 1 John 5:14

Saturday, January 22

Whoever has two coats must share with anyone who has none; and whoever has food must do likewise. —Luke 3:11 (NRSV)

One wintry day, I chopped potatoes and onions for soup. Then I realized my recipe made twice as much soup as our family of four would eat. And potato soup doesn't freeze well.

A question popped into my head. *Who else would enjoy this soup?* Was that God's voice? Or my imagination? I poured the vegetables into a pot and adjusted the heat. A name dropped into my thoughts. *Eileen.* She was a friend from church with small children and parents in declining health. Maybe some soup would cheer her up.

Hesitantly, I dialed her number. "Hi, Eileen, I'm making potato soup. Would you like some?" During her extended silence, I formulated several ways to assure her that she didn't have to accept my offer.

Eileen asked, "How did you know that's my favorite soup?"

I grinned. "I *didn't* know, but God did!" Her laughter sounded delighted.

Another blustery day, I made a large pot of chicken vegetable soup. This time I prayed right away, "Lord, if someone needs this soup today, please let me know."

As the soup simmered, my thoughts drifted to my neighbor. I picked up my phone. "Hi, Toni. I'm making chicken soup. Would you like some?" She paused. I held my breath.

Toni's first words made me smile. "How did you know we were sick?" She and her little girl had been curled up on the couch all day, and chicken soup, she said, sounded perfect.

I replied cheerfully, "I *didn't* know, but God did!"

Dear Lord, Thank You for Your persistent nudges. You offer joy to my friends and me! I will keep listening.
—Leanne Jackson

Digging Deeper: Proverbs 8:32–35; Matthew 25:37–40

Sunday, January 23

He that followeth me shall not walk in darkness... —John 8:12 (KJV)

In the movie *Wall Street*, Michael Douglas plays an investment villain who makes the case that selfishness is a natural part of financial prosperity. He won an Oscar for his portrayal. A memorable quote from the movie is "Greed...is good."

I was fifteen when I first saw the movie. Already, I had my sights set on the investment business, but here was a stark portrayal of men choosing money over ethics. Darkness over light.

My goal was somewhat different. As that fifteen-year-old, I saw investing as a way to help people. People like my minister dad. People who spend their lives working hard and doing good but who lack money management and investment skills.

I'm grateful that *Wall Street* embedded itself in my head, with its glaring choice of good versus bad and light versus dark. The truth is there. We all know that there are those willing to use others, even ruin individual lives, for personal gain.

Greed, however, is sneakier than outright theft, cheating, and dishonesty. Greed has a way of landing on my shoulder and whispering, "You earned it. Why not keep it for yourself?"

Greed is not my friend. It reminds me that there is a reason Jesus warns about the dangers of loving money. And a reason my father's sermons often pointed out the difficulty of recognizing our own greed.

"People don't really tithe ten percent anymore," greed whispers as I hold my tithe card.

I write a number on the card. "Very generous," I tell myself. "No one knows it's not ten percent." No one except God and me. Greed...is *not* good. I scratch out that number and write a new one.

Dear God, keep me aware when temptations like greed make their way into my life. Help me to remember the joy of true generosity.
—Brock Kidd

Digging Deeper: Proverbs 16:8; Matthew 16:26; John 3:19

Monday, January 24

PRAYING TOGETHER: My Husband's Heart
I pray that your love will overflow more and more, and that you will keep growing in knowledge and understanding. —Philippians 1:9 (NLT)

Praying with my husband was proving to be the easiest resolution I'd ever made. No counting calories, sweating at the gym, or berating myself for not cleaning places I preferred to ignore. All I did to keep this resolution was to call Michael before bedtime when he was working out of town on weekdays. On weekends at home, he'd plop down beside me after the nightly newscast. We'd close our eyes, thanking, praising, and petitioning heaven. I liked having a specific reason to connect, but I wasn't convinced that one resolution could change much for me. It seemed too easy.

"Ready to pray?" Michael called me at bedtime. He was on the road that week.

I sat on the edge of my bed and bowed my head. After thanking God for our blessings, Michael prayed for wisdom about a situation at work. He worried what a possible outcome could mean for his job. He was deeply concerned how it might affect our family. His voice quivered as he talked to God.

I never knew. Hearing the pressure he shouldered as sole provider surprised me. We'd been married almost two decades, but I never imagined he felt this anxiety. We'd been on a conveyor belt of busyness for so many years that Michael and I rarely made time to go deep with our feelings, thoughts, or fears.

I had expected my resolution to bring me closer to God. Praying with Michael was bringing me a new understanding of my husband too.

Thank You, Lord, that praying together is easy and enlightening. Like those overlooked spaces I'd rather not clean, help me not to overlook the thoughts and feelings of those I love.
—Stephanie Thompson

Digging Deeper: Ephesians 4:2–3; Philippians 4:6

Tuesday, January 25

If you then, though you are evil, know how to give good gifts to your children, how much more will your Father in heaven give the Holy Spirit to those who ask him! —Luke 11:13 (NIV)

I waited for the phone call. It wasn't because I needed thanks for the gift I'd sent my best friend of fifty years. I just wanted to know a porch pirate hadn't absconded with the "just because I'm thinking of you" goodie that I'd ordered online and had delivered to her door.

How do you show your love and appreciation for someone who has stood by you through the awkwardness of middle school and the drama of high school? Through the horrors of wearing ugly bridesmaids gowns in each other's weddings? Through raising kids, and experiencing marital struggles, money problems, and menopause? I chose a gift of Thai iced tea. The last time we were together, I'd introduced her to the lovely blend of black tea, spices, coconut milk, and good old-fashioned sugar. It reminded me of her—sweet, with a little spice!

When I texted Michele to see if my gift had arrived, she responded, "Well, I was kinda confused as to why you'd send me little green army men in yoga poses." How many belly-laugh emojis can you add to one text-message response?

Obviously, there had been a mix-up with the order. But my first thought (right after *I need to straighten this out!*) was *That's exactly how I feel about prayer!* I'll pray for a friend's healing or a freelance job to pay an unexpected bill and sometimes wind up with what feels a bit like "yoga Joes." How often I forget that prayer is a conversation and not a catalog order. It's sharing my heart with the One who created it and accepting that He always knows best. After all, God is God—and I am not.

Dear Lord, I want Your will to be my deepest desire and most consistent prayer.
—Vicki Kuyper

Digging Deeper: Psalm 5:3; Isaiah 55:8–9; Luke 11:1–12

Wednesday, January 26

For his invisible attributes, namely, his eternal power and divine nature, have been clearly perceived, ever since the creation of the world, in the things that have been made. —Romans 1:20 (ESV)

I sometimes wish I had a camera with me when people find out how much I love winter. Their reactions range from surprise to an expression that clearly reveals they are questioning my sanity. While there are other people in this world who, like me, favor winter above all other seasons, it seems we're in the minority.

I love the times, though, when people ask me why I enjoy winter so much. Mostly because then I get to tell them about one of the most wondrous evidences of the awesome character of our God—snow.

Nothing moves me more to worship my Creator than huge, fluffy flakes falling in silence and cloaking our world in a blanket of white, sparkling perfection. When I catch these flakes in my gloved hand, I stare at them in wonder.

Each tiny flake is a work of art more stunning and intricate than anything I could ever imagine. Each flake is unique from the others, and each one shouts to the heavens that our God is an artist like no other. That He loves beauty more than we do. That we are surrounded by evidences of His glory and power that can inspire and encourage us if we'll only look closely.

So, throughout winter, I strive to keep my eyes open to the reminders all around me of the amazing God I serve. The season truly does bring a winter wonderland—a world full of the wonders of my Father, Who has made me, in His eyes, even more beautiful than snow.

Remind me, Father, to look for the beauty You weave into every day of my life. Help me to pause to worship and be grateful.
—Jerusha Agen

Digging Deeper: Psalm 19:1, 29:2

Thursday, January 27

And the woman said to Elijah, "Now I know that you are a man of God, and that the word of the Lord in your mouth is truth."
—1 Kings 17:24 (ESV)

Truth can sometimes be a mirror. One winter night, my five-year-old son, Jacques, was particularly reluctant to go to sleep, so I suggested he tell me a story instead of me telling him one. Jacques started, "Once upon a time, there was an old lady named Mommy."

As I giggled, my initial thought was *Am I?*

"Old" is usually based on perspective. If Jacques's perspective was a mirror that night, I *am* old. Jacques's story was innocent, and I received the truth he told in that way. As a parent, I hope Jacques always speaks truth without hesitation.

I suspect that as Jacques grows older, however, his truth may need courage to articulate. Jacques's truth may become tempered by others, by society, or by his relationships. His truth will also change from observation to lived faith. One of the gravest responsibilities as believers in Christ is to name and declare our own truth in Him. Speaking truth in the name of Christ is not always simple or easy. It often takes courage and resolve.

As I encourage Jacques to speak and own truth in these early years, I hope he learns to speak truth even when it may not always be what others want to hear. This takes courage. After all, sometimes the truth really is "There was an old lady named Mommy."

Lord God, You are the ultimate truth. May my words and actions tell truth rooted in Your love and in Your mercy. Give me courage to always reside in the truth of Your Word.
—Jolynda Strandberg

Digging Deeper: Psalm 25:5; John 4:24

Friday, January 28

I am my beloved's and my beloved is mine. —Song of Solomon 6:3 (ESV)

I sat across from my husband in the booth at the Mexican restaurant we'd chosen for lunch. We were engulfed in our own worlds—he was answering emails, and I was mindlessly scrolling through social media. We barely glanced at each other while we waited for our meals. It was ironic, since the reason for our lunch date was to spend more time together.

With our work schedules, personal obligations, and the children, we'd become more like roommates sharing a house than spouses sharing a life. After nearly fifteen years of marriage, the familiarity of it all had caused our relationship to grow stagnant. Our time together needed to be renewed and refreshed if we wanted to enjoy the intimacy we once shared.

"Phones in the middle of the table," I suggested. He silently agreed, reaching across the table for my hand.

As my husband and I made eye contact, I felt my heart fill with hope. From that moment, the Lord pressed onto my heart the truth that if I made our marriage a priority, within time the love and intimacy wouldn't just return to the way it had been, but would flourish beyond my expectations.

And that's exactly what's happened. Even while balancing the hectic lifestyle that comes from raising three children, we have been intentional about spending time together in weekly brunch or lunch dates. Our mornings begin with whispered prayers. We no longer feel like roommates trudging through life on two separate paths. Rekindling our love and friendship has put us back on the journey of a meaningful life together.

Lord, thank You that my marriage can be a reflection of Your relationship with Your children. When hectic days steal our time, help us to reconnect with one another so our love never grows dim.
—Tia McCollors

Digging Deeper: Proverbs 19:14, 31:10;
1 Corinthians 13:4–7; 1 Peter 3:7, 4:8

Saturday, January 29

But he giveth more grace. Wherefore he saith, God resisteth the proud, but giveth grace unto the humble. —James 4:6 (KJV)

I didn't set out to become the poster child for opioid addiction. When I wrote my story about my harrowing OxyContin withdrawal, I figured few folks would be interested. Then I went to buy a vehicle, and as I rummaged through my purse for my wallet, the salesman across the desk said, "I read your story about your addiction to those opioids."

It was a good fifteen seconds before I could even find the wherewithal to raise my head, let alone face him. I started to say, "Actually, I was prescribed that medication for uncontrolled pain. I took it only as directed. And mine was a physical tolerance, not really an addiction."

But then I remembered another Roberta. The one who, during withdrawal, developed horrible gastrointestinal distress and soiled her friend's gorgeous bathroom.

Truth was, two years after the fact, I still harbored pride. Even after the embrace of grace-gifts from God and human angels. Grace that literally saved my life and led to complete freedom from the pain that had plagued me for half a century. Grace that reached down and swooped me up and has never let me go.

My eyes and the salesman's met. His were filled with amazing compassion. "That took tremendous courage, Roberta," he said. "Both to live it and to tell it."

Suddenly, I saw my journey anew. Yes, my opioids were recommended by the medical profession, but my dependence and withdrawal were the same as those of any drug addict. The only difference was that *I* had been the recipient of loving care and prayer, of open-arms hospitality.

My story isn't over, Lord. Go with me as I visit the streets of my city, where folks as desperate as I was are longing for You.
—Roberta Messner

Digging Deeper: 2 Chronicles 30:9; Romans 3:24; Ephesians 2:8; Hebrews 4:16

Sunday, January 30

Help the weak, be patient with everyone.
—1 Thessalonians 5:14 (NASB)

I am running late for a speaking engagement at a country church. The old asphalt road is all hills and curves, and I am stuck behind a dilapidated dump truck, going forty miles per hour. Miles and miles go by, with nowhere for me to pass. My blood pressure is rising, and my face is hot.

This driver is clearly not in a hurry. His elbow is casually draped out the window, and he is leisurely smoking a cigar. Not once does he even glance in his rearview mirror.

I rehearse what I would like to say to him: "You know, there are other people on this road who might need to get somewhere a little faster."

At long last, the truck slows and signals a right turn. I take a deep breath and ready myself to lunge forward.

The truck turns, and suddenly I see why he was driving so slowly. In front of him was a wee little car, with a wee little woman at the wheel. As I pass her, I can see that she looks frightened, straining through thick eyeglasses to see over the steering wheel.

I sail ahead, feeling a bit sheepish about my impatience. I have been reminded that people sometimes behave the way they do because something is slowing them down: perhaps physical handicap, private grief, or just deep anxiety about the road ahead.

I need to make allowances for people who are struggling. After all, some days I move pretty slowly myself.

Forgive me, Lord, when I expect too much out of the people around me.
—Daniel Schantz

Digging Deeper: Psalm 37:7; Ecclesiastes 7:8

Monday, January 31

I am the LORD. I have called you for a righteous purpose, and I will hold you by your hand. —Isaiah 42:6 (CSB)

This morning, when I happened upon this Isaiah 42 verse, I read it repeatedly. I was more familiar with the scriptural image in Psalm 31:15 of God holding my "times," or maybe even myself, in His hand, which seemed so oversized that I could hardly imagine it.

I'd missed this more relatable take—God holding my hand. Like my mom, walking me to the bus stop on my first day of kindergarten. Like my older brother, coaxing me, fatigued and faltering, down a steep glen. "See that next berm? Come. I think you can make it that far." Like my sister, comforting me on the night of Mom's stroke.

Like a reminder as recent as yesterday, on a birthday whose fulsome numbers mocked my fantasy—that I'm "forever young." My celebration started as my Sundays always do—by attending church. This time I accompanied and sat between two neighbor girls, both happy to share my day. As hymns sometimes do, a song set me crying, a lilting "Alleluia, alleluia." The girls noticed and fussed, "What's wrong?" *I don't know,* I shrugged. "Maybe my birthday" and "It's okay," I said.

In the next few moments, I absorbed a jumble of emotions: nostalgia, yearning, gratitude, hope. Then toward the end of the service, the younger girl stood at the end of the aisle, reaching for my hand, guiding me forward to the railing for Communion and its age-defying grace.

Lord, whatever this year brings my way, take hold of my hand.
—Evelyn Bence

Digging Deeper: Psalm 138

January

THE LORD IS NEAR

1 _____

2 _____

3 _____

4 _____

5 _____

6 _____

7 _____

8 _____

9 _____

10 _____

11 _____

12 _____

13 _____

14 _____

15 _____

January

16 _____

17 _____

18 _____

19 _____

20 _____

21 _____

22 _____

23 _____

24 _____

25 _____

26 _____

27 _____

28 _____

29 _____

30 _____

31 _____

February

*And when you draw close to God,
God will draw close to you.*

—James 4:8 (TLB)

Tuesday, February 1

PRAYING TOGETHER: When I Don't Know How to Pray

Likewise the Spirit helps us in our weakness; for we do not know how to pray as we ought, but that very Spirit intercedes with sighs too deep for words. —Romans 8:26 (NSRV)

A young relative was making bad choices. We didn't know all the details, but his grades had dropped, and he was rebellious and defiant at home—not keeping his room clean or doing household chores.

Michael and I were stymied. This boy had been a fun-loving, happy child. Did he have a learning disability? An emotional problem? Depression or anxiety issues? Was he being bullied or peer-pressured at school? Using drugs or alcohol?

His mother confided that he'd recently made friends with someone who had a poor reputation. The situation disturbed me greatly. We had already been praying for him for a couple of weeks, but nothing had changed, and I was discouraged. When Michael called that evening I switched my phone to speaker, sat on the bed, and hugged my knees. I didn't know what, or how, to pray. *Lord, reach him!*

Michael asked that this young man would be strong and make right choices.

Then it was my turn. *Lord, I don't know how to pray.* I took a deep breath. When I exhaled, bold words tumbled out of my mouth: "If it's Your will, remove this negative influence from his life."

The blunt idea surprised me, but it became my prayer mantra. A week later, we discovered that the student who had been a bad influence was sent to a long-term, out-of-state reform academy.

Our young relative still had challenges, so we continued to keep him in prayer. But now, even when I did not know how or what to pray, I knew, thankfully, the Holy Spirit did.

> *God, thank You for answered prayers and for interceding when I can't find the words to pray.*
> —Stephanie Thompson

Digging Deeper: Proverbs 22:6; Isaiah 58:11; John 14:20

Wednesday, February 2

Show me your ways, LORD, teach me your paths. Guide me in your truth and teach me, for you are God my Savior, and my hope is in you all day long. —Psalm 25:4–5 (NIV)

The weather is a hassle to many folks—too hot, cold, windy, whatever they don't like about it. But you won't hear weather complaints from me. I live on a ridgetop and have a three-hundred-sixty-degree view of the valley below, sky above, and mountains in the distance. Most days, the sun shines on my little piece of earthly paradise. When it doesn't, I enjoy watching clusters of gray clouds float through the trees as rain showers come my way.

The most spectacular views occur in the cooler months, on those rare days when the ground is warmer than the air and the temperature difference deposits a thick layer of fog between the ridges. By early morning, it settles to the valley floor and covers everything except the tallest peaks in a fluffy meringue. From my hilltop vantage point, what appears to be a sea of frosted glass spreads from my yard to the next ridge, looking like a solid walkway across a wide expanse. At least one cup of coffee is required to sweep away my morning brain fog and make me focus on the truth—the frosted-glass floor is an illusion covering the valley underneath.

Each time I observe this unique weather phenomena, I thank God for lifting me out of the fluff this world wants us to believe is solid ground. Every day I thank Him for providing me a better path to walk in life—one built on His truth, illuminated by His light, covered in His love, and lined with eternal hope in Him.

Lord, show us the way to Your solid ground and give us the wisdom to walk it daily with You.
—Jenny Lynn Keller

Digging Deeper: Psalm 40:2, 119:105; John 14:6

Thursday, February 3

Are not all angels ministering spirits sent to serve those who will inherit salvation? —Hebrews 1:14 (NIV)

I left work after six that overcast winter evening. It was already darkish. Highway construction had squashed the two lanes into a curvy path between orange cones. The road was almost invisible against the oncoming headlights, so I drove slower than the forty-five-mile-per-hour construction-zone limit.

Without warning, a road worker stood before me. I skidded to a stop just inches from him. He didn't move or even flinch. He just gestured angrily at his sign and the looming machine about to cross.

I shared this story with my husband when I got home. How there'd been no warning this monster truck was about to cross. How the lined-up headlights of oncoming cars—stopped by another imperceptible flagman—had backlit this man, his sign, those cones, making them all just vaguely darker shapes in the darkness already all around. How the man seemed angry at me, when it was his crew's fault, not mine, that I hadn't seen him. How I'd almost killed him.

Days later, rage still sizzled through me. I stopped at the site to confront the crew about their dereliction of duty, but they waved me down the road to another crew, who just looked at me with confusion.

I have post-traumatic stress disorder, which converts even near-traumas into inescapable wrath and horror. It wasn't until weeks later that I was able to realize the truth of the situation: I *hadn't* killed that man. Surely an angel, or God Himself, had stood near me or that man, near us both, and kept the invisible worst from happening.

Thank You, Lord, for all the disasters You protect me from that I don't even know about!
—Patty Kirk

Digging Deeper: Acts 12:1–18

Friday, February 4

Even though I walk through the darkest valley, I will fear no evil, for you are with me; your rod and your staff, they comfort me.
—Psalm 23:4 (NIV)

My son, Henry, and I love to watch scary movies. We have our own spots on the couch and a routine: make popcorn, grab our favorite blankets, turn the lights off, then press Play.

We can tell in the first five minutes if the movie is going to be any good. If the acting is terrible, we abandon it and find something else. We talk a lot about writing, direction, camera angle. Henry is a master at knowing how something could have been better.

He hates the "jump scare," where the director builds suspense only to have the danger be a cat meowing or a family member coming around a corner. According to Henry, jump scares are pointless and they ruin your trust in the movie.

But the last time we settled down to watch a movie, I couldn't get my mind off a worry. I had been waiting for an important document to come in the mail that was missing in transit. Even with special tracking, it had become lost. That night, no matter how hard I tried or what was happening in the movie, my mind kept creating upsetting what-ifs.

"How come you're only half watching?" Henry asked. "It's good, Mom, watch!"

The next day I was up early, hoping the document would come, when in the middle of doing dishes it hit me: I was just as bad as a jump scare, making tension over nothing.

Dear Lord, when I'm worried, guide me to imagine best-case scenarios as I leave the outcome of the situation in Your hands through prayer.
—Sabra Ciancanelli

Digging Deeper: Luke 12:22; John 14:4

Saturday, February 5

Do not close your ears to my cry for relief. —Lamentations 3:56 (NIV)

My "Group of Six" sends texts almost daily. We've known each other since our kids were preschoolers. We homeschooled in the same co-op, and now our kids range from being in high school to being finished with college. We have prayed for each other's families for two decades.

Yesterday morning, our before-work chat turned to young adults who had strayed from their faith. There are many, even among these faithful families.

"I think we need a new prayer," my friend Mary Ellen texted wryly. "Something like, 'Lord, we New York City moms think You need to speak louder to these kids. But please keep it shy of seeming like a hallucination!'"

We all hit the heart emoji. She'd nailed it, as usual.

After work, I slipped into the church near my office for some quiet time. I silently populated the pew, name by name, with the twenty-one children from my Group of Six families. *I bring these young people to You, Lord*, I prayed, naming each one, *in the only way I know how: with my heart.*

I spent half an hour before the Lord on their behalf. I prayed for each, summing up my time with a silent plea that today, they would hear His voice and would not harden their hearts.

> *Jesus, whisper Your love loudly to those who have rejected You. Or maybe shout. I want them to love You as I do.*
> —Julia Attaway

Digging Deeper: Psalm 95:7–8

Sunday, February 6

But seek first his kingdom and his righteousness, and all these things will be given to you as well. —Matthew 6:33 (NIV)

Recently, my husband, Don, and I attended a sixtieth wedding anniversary reception for longtime friends from Texas. We had a joyful reunion and were blessed with wonderful fellowship and a moving tribute to the love of Christ and family.

But there's a backstory; we almost didn't go. The reception had been on Super Bowl Sunday, and I'd wanted to watch every second of the game. After all, it had been fifty years since the Kansas City Chiefs (my favorite team) had had the chance to win the national championship.

"I'll send a card and regrets," I told Don when we received the invitation. "They won't really miss us."

Don was incredulous. "You want to watch TV instead of attending a real-life milestone celebration?"

Well, yes, I did, although it was embarrassing to admit. And it brought other troublesome choices to mind. Just that week, I'd missed a meeting to watch my favorite basketball team play. And during my Bible study, I had surreptitiously checked my phone for sports scores—three times. I wasn't a sports fan. I was a sports fanatic.

"God, please help me reorder my priorities," I whispered. Then I checked "yes" on the invitation reply card.

Since then, I've been working on being just a fan. With God's help, I'm cutting down on sports viewing and staying off my phone when I'm with other people.

And the Super Bowl? I watched the last quarter and cheered loudly when the Chiefs rallied from twenty-four points down to win. It was thrilling, but it paled in comparison to the wonderful day we had with our friends.

Heavenly Father, help me let go of anything that takes Your place in my life.
—Penney Schwab

Digging Deeper: Deuteronomy 5:7; Luke 10:41–42

Monday, February 7

PRAYING TOGETHER: Anytime, Anywhere Prayers
Ask and it will be given to you; seek and you will find; knock and the door will be opened to you. —Matthew 7:7 (NIV)

My husband and I had been praying together every night now for several months. We'd settled into a familiar routine. Whoever was ready for bed first would ask, "Want to pray?" And then Michael always started because my lengthy prayers irritated him. I was equally annoyed that his prayers seemed rushed. These days, praying together sometimes felt like another chore. Not holy and special as it did when we began.

It was also during this time that Michael had been shopping for a car. After looking for months, he test-drove one that he liked, but the mileage and price were high for a used car. It wasn't perfect, but it was the best he'd seen so far. He decided to make an offer.

We pulled into the dealership. Michael was nervous. "What if it's not the one?" he asked, as we sat in the parking lot.

I suggested we pray. Maybe my idea irritated him or maybe he was nervous, but Michael blurted out, "God, is this the car for us? Amen."

I glared at him, then flippantly prayed, "Lord, show Michael if he should buy this car. Give him a sign."

He drove it again, and we made an offer. The salesman took the price to his boss. We waited so long for him to come back that we sat down at a table in the open-air showroom. Finally, an employee drove the car we wanted into the showroom and parked it right in front of Michael. A steady drip from the undercarriage caught Michael's attention. Had he not been sitting in that chair and had the car not pulled up in front of him, we wouldn't have known.

Weeks later, Michael found the perfect car with low miles for thousands of dollars less.

Lord, thank You for signs and for teaching me that
You answer short, long, and flippant prayers all the same.
—Stephanie Thompson

Digging Deeper: 1 Samuel 10:7; Isaiah 38:7

Tuesday, February 8

And the Lord God formed man of the dust of the ground, and breathed into his nostrils the breath of life... —Genesis 2:7 (NKJV)

The mountains glistened with fresh snow as I walked toward the pasture, calling out in a singsong voice, "Good morning!" My horse nickered and my mule honked as they ran to the fence to greet me. But as I swung the gate open, SkySong, my thirteen-hundred-pound white horse, blocked my way.

I cocked my head to the side. Then in wonder, I stopped. In the crisp air, steam slowly poured from his nostrils as he stuck his face directly in mine. His nostrils quivered as he gently inhaled the steam from my breath. A tear rolled down my cheek as we stood, face-to-face, sharing the intimacy of each other's breath of life.

The breath of life. What an incredible gift from God.

It was something I'd never given much thought to until I was in an ICU family waiting room and became friends with a patient named Emily. The married, middle-aged mother had slowly paced the hallways throughout the day. The hospital was her temporary home while she waited for donor lungs so she could live. Throughout the weeks that I was there, I would be sure to pop into her room to visit. Each time I left, I thanked God for the ability to breathe easily. Months later, I celebrated when I heard that she had come through surgery and was able to breathe.

And now, while rubbing SkySong's favorite spot on his forehead, I marveled at the beauty of breath and gave God thanks.

Lord, thank You for stopping me and reminding me to give You intimate time. Teach me to be grateful for what You have given me. Amen.
—Rebecca Ondov

Digging Deeper: Psalm 100, 147

Wednesday, February 9

When you lie down, you will not be afraid; when you lie down, your sleep will be sweet. —Proverbs 3:24 (NIV)

When Beau was about two and a half, we all finally started sleeping relatively soundly, and definitely taking it for granted. So when a mystery virus woke him at 3:00 a.m. two nights in a row, Brian and I turned into zombies.

The third night, somewhat delirious, I climbed the steps to take my place: prone on the floor beside his bed, where I could shush and soothe him as he whined in his sleep. But that was not to be.

"Mama, I want you carry me up," he said. And, instead of arguing, I did. I picked up my boy, all thirty pounds of his sweaty, jammied, sleepy mass, and took him upstairs, where I cuddled him in the baby rocker. As I rocked him, he fell into a sweet slumber, snoozing peacefully in my arms.

My elbow tingled. My aging knees ached in the cross-legged position I'd picked. But here, in this holy moment, I got a gift. I've always known you never know when your "lasts" will take place. Your last time to pick up your child, the last time to wash their hair, the last time they'll run to you open-armed at school pickup.

My children had never been snuggle sleepers; they preferred to be swaddled, tucked, and patted in the security of their own elephant-patterned sheets. So to be given the moment to stare into his face, pray over him, and see the purity of Jesus in his sweet baby face was a gift.

I long for moments when the line between heaven and earth fades, where I can see the other side from over here. And that night, I felt like I got a chance.

Lord, thank You for giving me moments to dwell in Your holy place within my own house. The space between heaven and earth grows thin, and I am renewed.
—Ashley Kappel

Digging Deeper: Psalm 3:5, 121:3–4

Thursday, February 10

You, Lord, preserve both people and animals. How priceless is your unfailing love, O God! —Psalm 36:6–7 (NIV)

Tarby, my beautiful golden chow, died unexpectedly on February 10. She was thirteen. The previous day, she'd seemed fine—begging for treats, trotting to the barn and back with my husband, Don, and napping on the porch. I was shocked and heartbroken but thankful she hadn't suffered.

Tarby had entered my life and heart as a two-month-old ball of fur, her tail wagging so hard I thought it would fall off. I hadn't wanted a dog, but she was a gift from our children and I couldn't say no. She became my daily walking companion, ranging far out in the fields, running four miles while I walked two. At age ten, she still walked with me, but not as far or fast. Like most farm dogs, she preferred to be outdoors or in her bed in the garage. However, she hated loud noises, so she spent thunderstorms, July Fourth, and weather extremes in the house. She was gentle with the grandchildren, and they vied for the honor of being Tarby's favorite.

Don and I dug a grave and buried her at the edge of the backyard. This spring I'll plant marigolds on the grave, because Tarby loved to lie among them.

A friend sent a sympathy card that read, "Hope it comforts you to know that you gave your pet a good home on earth." The words helped, and they also gave me an idea. Because so many dogs need homes, my next dog will be from a shelter. Giving an unwanted dog a home is the best thing I can do to honor Tarby's life. I think she would agree!

Thank You, Lord, that I loved and was loved by a good dog. Amen.
—Penney Schwab

Digging Deeper: Ecclesiastes 3:1–4; Romans 8:28

Friday, February 11

Then God said, "Let lights appear in the sky to separate the day from the night. Let them be signs to mark the seasons, days, and years."
—Genesis 1:14 (NLT)

I feel like I'm living inside a snow globe this morning in Colorado, with big, fluffy flakes floating to the ground. This month we are close to setting an all-time record for February snowfall, and many people are complaining. Not me! I like the white blanket that covers up February's normally brown ground and the coziness inside as we turn on the fireplace, even in the morning.

I confess: I'm a weather junkie.

"Why?" my non-weather junkie husband, Lynn, asks. "You can't do anything about the weather."

"But you can shape your expectations for the day," I tell him. "Decide what to have for dinner (chili tonight!), be more prepared to enter into small-talk weather conversations."

So we coexist in a house where he likes to turn off the news before the weather report, while I say, "No! Wait! I want to hear it!"

When I discovered the weather app on my phone, I was thrilled. Not only could I find hour-by-hour predictions for changing weather in our area, but I also could check the weather that faraway family and friends were experiencing. For instance, when I saw the "heavy rain all day long" icons for Phoenix, where my granddaughter was playing an outdoor soccer tournament, I could text my sympathy to her.

I like that the ever-changing weather, good or bad, always takes place within God's never-changing creation of days and nights; sun, moon, and stars; sunrises, sunsets, and seasons. And I like to know, always, that February's snow prepares the brown ground to grow green in springtime.

Creator God, the changing weather shapes our days in both good and hard ways, but I'm thankful for the unchanging rhythm of days and nights and sunshine You created.
—Carol Kuykendall

Digging Deeper: Leviticus 26:4; 2 Timothy 4:2

Saturday, February 12

Start children off on the way they should go, and even when they are old they will not turn from it. —Proverbs 22:6 (NIV)

My darling twelve-year-old great-niece Alexis and I have a tradition. A few days before Valentine's Day, we get together so we can make cards for her classmates and other dear ones. Alexis has special needs, and her huge heart results in some of the sweetest love notes ever.

This year, on February 12, we drove to a nearby Starbucks and claimed the long table by the window. Armed with cardstock, colorful retro valentines, stickers, glitter, and glue, we got to work. When we had completed the last valentine on her list, a guy walked in. "Alexis!" he bellowed. "What are *you* doing here?"

Alexis giggled, then leaned into me, her brown hair brushing my ear. She whispered that she wanted to give this friendly man, Mike, a valentine. I cautioned her, saying that we only had enough for the people on her list and that if she gave an extra one away, someone would be left out.

Alexis hates leaving anyone out. But insistence filled every fiber of her being. "Mike!" she fairly shouted. She stretched her hand in his direction, her dark eyes dancing. Alexis signed Mike's card, "Love! Alexis," and hurried to the chair where he now sat, sipping a hot drink.

When Alexis returned to our card-making table, I asked her who Mike was. "Church Awana," she said smiling, referring to the club she attends, where kids learn how to know, love, and serve Jesus. "He gives me punch and tells me Jesus is in my heart."

Oh, Lord Jesus, I thank You for Sunday school teachers, Vacation Bible School and Awana workers, nursery devotees, and other laborers in Your field who point children to You.
—Roberta Messner

Digging Deeper: Deuteronomy 6:6–7; 3 John 1:4

Sunday, February 13

He answered, "Love the Lord your God with all your heart and with all your soul and with all your strength and with all your mind; and, Love your neighbor as yourself." —Luke 10:27 (NIV)

Our church revised its twenty-year-old mission statement this year. The mission had needed updating—it was too long for me to memorize. But the motto of the old mission, *To Be Christ's Light,* I never forgot. Inspired by it for years, I didn't want that piece of the old to disappear.

Luckily, with each component of the new mission (italicized below), came three action questions to use as daily measures in living out our faith and being Christ:

Connecting All to Christ. Would others know that I follow Jesus if they spent time with me today? Did I thank God today? Did I extend Christ's kindness today?

To Become Healthy in God. Did I actively seek ways to grow spiritually today? Did I obey the teachings of Jesus today? Did I open my life to be changed by Christ today?

And Courageous in Love. Did I see every person as a child of God today? Did I make someone's life better today? Was Christ my priority as I used my time, talents, and treasures today?

In a small-group study series on applying the measures, we started each discussion with the question "How have you been living the measures so far?" One person told about finding and calling a high school friend he hadn't talked to in years. Another member shared how she had reacted with kindness rather than frustration to an annoying restaurant server.

Today, I sent out cards of encouragement, which I wouldn't have otherwise thought to do. And I became grateful for the new mission and daily measures, which have inspired many to take more intentional actions in trying to be Christ's light.

Dear Lord, thank You for new ways that draw us to grow in You and share Your Love! Amen.
—John Dilworth

Digging Deeper: Matthew 28:19; Luke 6:31

Monday, February 14

PRAYING TOGETHER: United in Christ
Though one may be overpowered, two can defend themselves. A cord of three strands is not quickly broken. —Ecclesiastes 4:12 (NIV)

I was mad. And hurt. My husband had spoken carelessly that morning, and I took offense. He apologized, but I wouldn't let go of my resentment. I busied myself in the office the rest of the day to avoid him.

Now it was bedtime. I didn't want to break my resolution, but I didn't want to pray with my husband, either. I crawled between the covers. Michael was still in the living room watching TV. I scrolled Facebook, waiting to see if he'd initiate. Moments later, he stood in the doorway.

"Wanna pray?"

I nodded.

Michael didn't mention the misunderstanding to God. Instead, he thanked Him for bringing us together all those years ago, for giving us a wonderful life.

My turn. Guilt covered me. I felt like a child who had wasted the day sulking. I asked God to forgive me. We said, "Amen." I asked Michael to forgive me too.

When we had married, Michael and I dubbed ourselves "Team Thompson." It was the two of us against the world. We vowed to stand together. United. Always.

Then complications of life crowded in—job stress, disagreements, financial burdens, a child who was now a teen—and Team Thompson needed another player: a holy expert, available 24/7.

In praying to God each day, we rejoiced over prayers answered and wisdom gained as we grew in our love and understanding for each other. I also learned that it was impossible to stay angry with someone with whom I was praying.

Lord, thank You for being the glue that binds us together in all circumstances. May we intentionally include You in our lives each day.
—Stephanie Thompson

Digging Deeper: Song of Solomon 2:10–12; Ephesians 4:2–3, 4:26–27

Tuesday, February 15

Are not two sparrows sold for a penny? Yet not one of them will fall to the ground outside your Father's care. —Matthew 10:29 (NIV)

Julee called to say that something was wrong with Gracie. I rushed home, praying Gracie would greet me with her usual exuberance. Instead, she moved tentatively, leaned into my leg, and looked up at me imploringly. She was in pain.

Julee said our vet thought Gracie might have strained a muscle. "She prescribed pain pills and said to watch her for a few days." Julee's eyes were red with tears.

Gracie is a high-energy, athletic creature, graceful as the wind, and it was possible that she simply tweaked something. I grew more worried when Gracie refused to climb the stairs to the second floor.

Julee ladled a measure of warm homemade chicken noodle soup into Gracie's bowl. "This always makes her feel better," she said.

I watched Gracie until it was bedtime. I climbed the stairs, hoping she would follow. Gracie just sat on the landing, her eyes pleading and plaintive before she drooped her head and I disappeared into the bedroom.

A minute later, I reappeared at the top of the stairs, holding my pillow and a blanket. Gracie raised her head. Her tail wagged slowly at the sight of my bedding. She understood I was coming down to sleep with her. She knew she would be safe. That's all she needed from me. That's all so many animals need from us humans. To know that we are there for them, just as they are so often there for us.

I pulled Gracie's bed next to the couch, and we settled in for the night. She gave a satisfied sigh. In the morning we both felt better, and in a few days she was running like the wind again.

Father, You brought Gracie into my life to help teach me to be a better human. I think it's working.
—Edward Grinnan

Digging Deeper: Genesis 1:24–26; Luke 14:5–6

Wednesday, February 16

Sing to Him, sing psalms to Him; Talk of all His wondrous works!
—1 Chronicles 16:9 (NKJV)

"Grandma, please tickle my back," my grandson Logan begged. When Logan had come to live with us, he was only three years old. Chuck and I had begun a bedtime ritual with him of getting on our knees and saying our prayers. Afterward, we would kiss him good night, but sometimes I stayed and gently ran my fingers over his back as he went to sleep. The back-tickling routine became a bonding tradition for us.

While I tickled, I sang songs that I had sung to him while taking him on walks in the stroller when he had been a toddler. These songs were old childhood tunes from church, like "Jesus Loves Me," "Jesus Loves the Little Children," "Every Day with Jesus," and so on. Then I ended with the fun song "Itsy, Bitsy Spider," tickling him with the "spider," as my fingers ran all over his back.

Even though Logan is ten years old now, he still loves to have his back tickled when he goes to bed. I sometimes wondered if those "Jesus songs," as he used to call them, meant anything to him or if he was too old for such songs. Then recently, I heard the old hymn "How Great Thou Art." That evening, when I tickled Logan's back, the hymn was fresh on my mind, so I sang it. Surprisingly, he really liked the song and asked me to sing it again.

The next night, when I went through my back-tickling repertoire, I wrapped it up with our traditional "Spider" song. Then Logan asked me to sing the *new* song.

"What new song?" I asked, then realized it was "How Great Thou Art." I said, "But I already sang the last song."

"No, from now on, I want that new song to be the last song," he said.

Lord, thank You for the blessing of sharing Your truth in song.
—Marilyn Turk

Digging Deeper: Proverbs 22:6; James 5:13

Thursday, February 17

The Lord is my shepherd. I shall not want. —Psalm 23:1 (Tanakh)

My friend Susan was asking everyone at the sisterhood meeting, "What's on your bucket list?"

I hadn't thought about that before. I knew there was a movie about bucket lists, but I hadn't seen it. All of the women at the meeting took some time to think about the question, and I was grateful it hadn't been asked on Shabbat. One of the Sabbath prohibitions is about making prayers of petition, and it's often referred to as the "Don't ask God for anything on Shabbos" rule. The thinking of the rabbis seemed to be that if we were asking for something, that meant we were conscious of what we didn't have. On the Sabbath, we are only supposed to be thankful for our blessings, and that left out the yearning of petitionary prayer.

I looked around at the other women in the group, and they were all busily writing lists. My own pad was still blank.

Susan called time at five minutes and wanted us to read our lists. Travel figured very strongly: Paris, Machu Picchu, the Galapagos Islands, a Mediterranean cruise. Family was another quite popular theme: a grandchild graduating from college, becoming a great-grandmother, watching a granddaughter get married. When I was the only one who hadn't said anything, Susan looked at me. I was trying hard to come up with something, but my mind seemed to be as blank as my pad. Finally I sighed and said, "I got nothing."

And then it hit me. I really had everything. Anything I wanted to see or do, all of those things had been accomplished. My journeys now were inward, and they were always new to me. My family life was unexpectedly richer than I'd ever thought I wanted. I felt such gratitude that I suddenly thought, *It might as well be Shabbat after all.*

You have embarrassed me with a full, rich life, my Source of Blessings.
—Rhoda Blecker

Digging Deeper: Judges 18:10; Psalm 116:12

Friday, February 18

I will betroth you to me in faithfulness and love, and you will really know me then as you never have before. —Hosea 2:20 (TLB)

After my husband, Jack, died I was going through his papers and discovered he had saved every card and note that I ever gave him. On our fifth wedding anniversary, I'd made him a card and written the following:

Top ten reasons I love you: 10. You enjoy traveling like I do. 9. You are slow to anger. 8. You don't care if I do things with my friends and family on my own. 7. You're a great card player. 6. You don't swear or smoke. 5. You are a wonderful sleep partner. 4. You're always willing to do most anything I organize. 3. You're always willing to help me with anything. 2. You are kind and soft-spoken. 1. You are very loving and affectionate.

At the bottom of the card, I wrote, "I hereby renew our marriage vows for another twenty-five years." Of course I didn't know at the time that I'd only have twenty-one more months with my hunka hunka burnin' love, but I'm sure glad I shared my feelings with him when I did.

These days I send text messages to my four kids and nine grands, giving them two or three reasons why I love them and am proud of them. It doesn't take a lot to build up someone's self-esteem, and positive words can only make their world dazzle.

Jesus, as You walked the Holy Land teaching the religion of love, You cradled everyone in Your loving arms. Help me to do the same.
—Patricia Lorenz

Digging Deeper: 2 Samuel 1:22–27; Psalm 17:7–8; Titus 3:4–8

Saturday, February 19

SACRED SPACES: Roadside Shrines, Greece
One who is faithful in a very little is also faithful in much...
—Luke 16:10 (ESV)

Situated in the Aegean Sea, the Greek island of Tinos is home to about eight thousand people and, incredibly, one thousand churches. The most famous is the grand Church of Panagia Evangelistria, a pilgrimage site that the faithful crawl to on hands and knees. Other blue-domed family churches as small as gardening sheds dot this rocky landscape scoured by the wind. But the shrines that most intrigued me were about the size of country mailboxes on posts by the side of the road. My traveling companion, Liz, and I first noticed them while aboard a local bus that groaned up the switchbacks of Tinos.

It wasn't until we visited the Peloponnese that we could closely examine one. On a narrow, paved path in Nafplio, between the cliffs and the sea, we found a wooden box about as big as a bird feeder on a pedestal. It featured a pitched roof and one glass side facing the path. Inside, a tiny oil lamp the size of a tea light flickered, illuminating a faded photograph of a young man. Icons and dried flowers completed the miniscule memorial.

I later learned that these shrines mark a place of death, thanksgiving, or respite. Had someone fallen from the eight-hundred-foot cliff here or died at sea? Or was this shrine meant to be a place of rest on the trek to the beaches? I would never know. I only knew that some nameless person had remembered another. Back home, I commemorate differently: I bring lilacs to my parents' graves and pray for deceased loved ones for a year following their deaths.

Perhaps, then, even more sacred than the tiny shrine is the perpetual devotion of the person who tends it.

Father God, thank You for those who are faithful in love. May I be likewise.
—Gail Thorell Schilling

Digging Deeper: Lamentations 3:20; Matthew 5:4; John 13:34

Sunday, February 20

Lift up a song for Him who rides through the deserts, Whose name is the LORD, *and exult before Him.* —Psalm 68:4 (NASB)

I often begin my day with a walk—any time of year. This particular morning, feeling especially cheerful, I composed little songs to God for all the sights and sounds I was experiencing. Since it was the end of February in a northern clime, I tossed in a song for the chill in the air.

There was a melody for the mist clinging in the pines on the mountainsides. For the Canada geese honking along the river. The ravens calling overhead. The mountain jay scolding. I looked up in the tree to see the jay, and there on another branch sat a robin. My first of the year. I added a robin tune in my song for God's creation.

When I'd finished walking, I claimed my bench, in its location beneath an upper deck, to gaze over the valley. I wasn't there long before a distinctive odor drifted my way. A skunk! Not about to sing that song, I scurried inside.

Indoors, I opened Facebook, and there was a memory of this day six years earlier. The post read, "Today, care for my mom has been exhausting. The strength I have for this—on this last howling February night—is not my own. 'Be strong and of good courage for I am with you.' (That's a God quote from Joshua 1:9)."

I was struck immediately by the difference in these two days, years apart. One so joyful and the other so draining. But on that day with my mother—worn out from giving end-of-life care—I'd also had a song. A great aria of God's strength pouring into me to enable this act of love for her.

In every season—where God is sought—there is a song.

My Songmaker, let me hear Your music.
—Carol Knapp

Digging Deeper: Psalm 59:16–17, 104:33; Acts 16:25

Presidents' Day, Monday, February 21

And let us not grow weary of doing good, for in due season we will reap, if we do not give up.—Galatians 6:9 (ESV)

Jacques, my five-year-old son, jumped into the car after school. He was wearing a headband hat made of construction paper. It was black, and I couldn't figure out why he would have made a pilgrim's hat at school in February. He was quick to correct me by saying, "It's Abraham Lincoln's hat; we learned about Presidents' Day today." I delved a little deeper and found that he knew Presidents' Day celebrated the birthdays of two great leaders: George Washington and Abraham Lincoln.

I paused and thought about how all our nation's leaders, past and present, often face impossible decisions and unprecedented critique. Being a national leader is tough, and it requires a great deal of grace and discernment. After all, had George Washington failed, there would be no United States of America. If Abraham Lincoln had been unable to unite our nation, America as we know it would not exist. Such leadership decisions, which affect each and every American, present and future, happen daily.

On Presidents' Day, we remember great sacrifices made for the sake of our nation by leaders who provide examples of commitment, courage, and duty. And as citizens, we can support our nation's leaders by lifting them up in prayer. May we all know the power of being active participants in our government by praying for our leaders' strength, courage, and discernment.

Dear Father, surround our leaders with Your grace and protection as they govern our great nation for the betterment of us all.
—Jolynda Strandberg

Digging Deeper: Isaiah 41:8–10; Hebrews 13:7–9

Tuesday, February 22

The LORD is my strength and my shield; My heart trusted in Him, and I am helped; Therefore my heart greatly rejoices, And with my song I will praise Him. —Psalm 28:7 (NKJV)

I squint into the wind-driven snow as I limp out on a badly sprained foot to feed the animals. A snowflake finds a gap in my scarf, and I cringe. I could rattle off a few choice words about the pain and the weather, but a memory of Grandpa jumps in the way.

Grandpa had homesteaded in Montana as a boy. They winter-fed their stock with a team of horses pulling a sled—the coldest job in the world, according to Grandpa. Years later they got a tractor to pull the sled, which made feeding much faster, but just as cold. Then they got a farm truck with windows to block the wind. When they upgraded to a truck with a heater, Grandpa couldn't imagine such luxury could exist.

But always for Grandpa, there was song. Hardship was a way of life back then. But hard times didn't harden his heart. A man of deep faith, Grandpa faced every challenge and every blessing, too, with music. If he could sing, it wasn't so bad. And it wasn't so bad if he could sing.

"You can complain, Erika," Grandpa once said, "but it doesn't stop the wind. Just sing along with what's going on around you." Finding rhythm in the throb of my foot, I begin tentatively. How did that song go that Grandpa taught me? Concentrating on the words diverts the focus from my discomfort. By the time I finish feeding, I am laughing and belting out "Mockin' Bird Hill" at the top of my lungs.

You're right, Grandpa. This really isn't so bad.

> *Lord, help me focus on the tempo in the tempest.*
> *As long as I have a choice, I choose joy.*
> —Erika Bentsen

Digging Deeper: Psalm 32:11, 35:9, 98:4, 105:3

Wednesday, February 23

God does not play favorites. —Romans 2:11 (GW)

"Will Baby Taylor look like us?" It sounded like a simple question, but what my granddaughters were really asking their newly pregnant mother was "If the baby has white skin like you, instead of black skin like us, will you love her more?"

Even from an early age, Lula and Shea have been very vocal about how the color of their skin differs from that of my son and daughter-in-law, who adopted them out of the foster care system three years ago. Although I was excited to welcome another grandchild into the family, I was wary of the transition that this new baby's five- and seven-year-old siblings were going to have to make.

But one thing I wasn't worried about was being tempted to play favorites. How could I? Lula is Lula. Shea is Shea. And the yet-to-be-welcomed Taylor would be a wholly new adventure in love. If it's "fruitless" comparing apples to oranges, how much less sense does it make to compare one grandchild to another?

If becoming a grandmother has taught me anything (other than how patience truly is a virtue), it's that love is both a gift and a choice. My love for all four of my grandchildren, and the one I've yet to meet, flows freely—with the same wildly wonderful power as rivers in a storm. But I choose how to channel that love through the words I speak and the actions I take. With God's unconditional love to guide me—and to reassure me that I, too, am chosen and cherished—I pray that each of my grandchildren will come to fully understand how worthy of love they truly are.

Dear Lord, please take my imperfect love and make it more like Yours.
—Vicki Kuyper

Digging Deeper: 1 Samuel 16:7; John 15:12;
Romans 12:9–10; James 2:1

Thursday, February 24

I will be glad and exult in you; I will sing praise to your name, O Most High. —Psalm 9:2 (NRSV)

I knew I wanted to sing at my mom's memorial service. The question was, what song would it be, and would I be able to sing it without dissolving into tears? You can't really sing when you're crying.

I kept thinking back to how Mom would indulge my love for music by letting me sit next to her on the piano bench as she played songs from the Rodgers & Hammerstein songbook. Hadn't I sung one of those songs at Dad's memorial only eight years earlier—"No Other Love"—because it was one of his favorites?

It was harder to focus on any one of Mom's favorites because there were so many. Maybe something from *The Sound of Music,* because that was the first musical she ever took me to see. What would be appropriate for a memorial service? "Climb Ev'ry Mountain" had those great lyrics and that line "till you find your dream." Wasn't Mom always encouraging the four of us to pursue our dreams, just like she did with my love of music and singing?

That was it. I wanted to honor her love of music and how she had shared it with me and how we had shared it together. It had to be some song that the whole congregation could sing together, so that way, at least when I started choking up with tears, they could help.

They did. We did. I began by telling them how Mom would sit next to me on the piano bench, playing things from *The Sound of Music.* Then I said, "Let's all sing 'Do-Re-Mi...' *Doe, a deer, a female deer....*"

We sing Your praises, Lord, because You make our hearts sing.
—Rick Hamlin

Digging Deeper: Psalm 68:6, 71:23; Acts 16:25

Friday, February 25

GOD'S FINGERPRINTS: He Gives Us Hope and a Future

"For I know the plans I have for you," declares the Lord, "plans to prosper you and not to harm you, plans to give you hope and a future."
—Jeremiah 29:11 (NIV)

I recently met with a high school friend who has spent most of his career in computer technology.

When I asked Dan how he'd gotten into this line of work, he had a funny story. After graduating from high school in the mid-1960s, he heard about a test being offered at the local community college over something called the computer. This was in the infancy of such technology. He took the test on a fluke, and the professor later called Dan to urge him to take the class, as he'd aced the test. Dan signed up for the two-year program, which was five hours a day. It launched his career.

Only after he'd graduated did his professor tell him that he'd told everyone in the class that they'd aced the test. In fact, the teacher himself had been only one chapter ahead of the class, as the technology was so new.

After hearing his story, I commented that God had had His fingerprints all over Dan's entry into the world of computers. Hearing myself, I realized how often God had His fingerprints on my life too—on all our lives. I certainly didn't need to look far to recognize incidents that could not have been an accident.

Dear Lord, Your fingerprints on my life have left indelible marks, and for that I will always be grateful.
—Debbie Macomber

Digging Deeper: Proverbs 16:9; Jeremiah 18:5–6

Saturday, February 26

[God's mercies] are new every morning; great is your faithfulness.
—Lamentations 3:23 (ESV)

This winter I discovered a new pastime: crossword puzzles printed in the daily newspaper. I find them challenging, even difficult. I nailed only one in three months—on a Monday, when they're easiest.

What's so frustrating: my mistake on one word can shut down a whole section—gridlock. Sometimes I can reconsider, backtrack, and revise. But sometimes I just have to give up, walk away, and admit that the task is beyond me. I switch off the light and go to bed. Even so, I always anticipate the next day's challenge.

Today's demanding puzzle is full of false starts, cross-outs, and rewrites. And I'm still stuck. There's no point in my giving it more attention. It's time to move on.

On the weekend, I often review recent challenges. And this evening, after doing so, I was mentally setting the week to rest when the Spirit nudged me to frame my *examen* in a crossword-type grid. Was there a time when one mistake brought a whole segment of life to a standstill? (When eating too much watermelon mucked up my digestion.) Where did minor adjustments loosen a logjam? (When I had to tear out a seam on a sewing project.) Where did more time and effort help me find a solution? (When clearing off my dresser and unearthing a favorite lost earring.) When was it time to say, "That's it!"? (When trimming bushes, I had to step back. Enough!)

The questions brought clarity, especially as I turned the insights over to God.

Lord, I trust that You have guided my steps this week. Now I turn a calendar page and address a new challenge, with anticipation of renewed grace.
—Evelyn Bence

Digging Deeper: Philippians 3:13–16

Sunday, February 27

Many plans are in a man's heart, But the counsel of the LORD will stand.
—Proverbs 19:21 (NASB)

I was on the road playing music and, somehow, I'd shown up at the church three weeks early. (In my defense, I've never claimed organization as my strong suit). Still, the pastor was a friend and happy to see me.

We had a beautiful night of worship. Later, the room slowly emptied. A man approached and introduced himself as Kevin. I was surprised to see tears in his eyes. It was a struggle for him to speak. But when he finally did, the story was beautiful.

"A year ago, I had major heart failure," he said. "I was told I was terminal. For months, I couldn't even move. I was waiting to die." He picked up one of my books. "Every night my wife would read me a chapter out of this. God ministered so much comfort to me."

"But you're here now," I finally managed to say. "What happened?"

He smiled. "God is merciful!"

We talked long, and I thanked him deeply for telling me his story. And I *did* feel thankful. But I felt something else too—a healthy dose of conviction. You see, I'd spent a good portion of the drive that day praying about my own problems and reminding God that bills were due.

His answer? A slap on the back of my head. *Buck, when did you get the idea any of this was about you?*

Kevin and I both knew it had been God ministering to him, and not my temporal words. And God didn't have to let me hear Kevin's testimony. In fact, I didn't deserve to hear it at all. But He did. And had I not been three weeks early, I probably wouldn't have. An accident? I don't think so.

My calendar is lousy, but God's is perfect.

Lord, forgive me. My agenda is earthly, but Yours is eternal.
—Buck Storm

Digging Deeper: Psalm 100:5; Proverbs 16:9; Hebrews 11:6

Monday, February 28

The Father of mercies and God of all comfort, who comforts us in all our affliction, so that we may be able to comfort those who are in any affliction, with the comfort with which we ourselves are comforted by God. —2 Corinthians 1:3–4 (ESV)

I prayed silently as I talked with a young woman from church, asking God for words of comfort to give her during her time of grief. I had received a referral to contact her, as she was needing financial help for her mother's funeral expenses. My role at church involves reaching out to people in need of financial, emotional, or spiritual support. Oftentimes, I have not met the other person, but after talking with them in person or by phone, I usually feel an instant heart connection. This time was no different.

As she shared her story, my mind returned to 2015, the year I lost my parents. In late 2014, my seventy-seven-year-old mother, who had suffered from congestive heart failure, had taken a turn for the worse. After she'd spent several weeks in the hospital, my eighty-year-old father became extremely ill, seemingly overnight. After surgery, physical therapy, and the prognosis that he would most likely leave the hospital in a wheelchair, he died suddenly from a heart attack. The stress of my mother's illness and his own had taken a toll. Three weeks later, my strong-minded but weak-bodied mother passed away.

Revisiting my own grief following my parents' deaths helped me enter into the young woman's grief. I had walked the thorny path she now found herself on. I encouraged her to allow herself space to mourn—in the midst of hospital bills, funeral plans, and burial arrangements. And by God's grace, through the comfort He had shown me, I was able to comfort this sweet young lady.

Lord, You never waste pain, so help us comf
with the comfort You have gi
—Carla Hendricks

Digging Deeper: Psalm 86:17; Isaiah 51.

February

THE LORD IS NEAR

1 _____

2 _____

3 _____

4 _____

5 _____

6 _____

7 _____

8 _____

9 _____

10 _____

11 _____

12 _____

February

15 _____

16 _____

17 _____

18 _____

19 _____

20 _____

21 _____

22 _____

23 _____

24 _____

25 _____

26 _____

27 _____

28 _____

March

*But as for me, how good it is to be near God!
I have made the Sovereign LORD my shelter,
and I will tell everyone about
the wonderful things you do.*

—Psalm 73:28 (NLT)

Tuesday, March 1

There is a time for everything, and a season for every activity under the heavens. —Ecclesiastes 3:1 (NIV)

"What are you going to do with these?" My husband, Chuck, pointed to the overflowing basket of papers.

"I need to sort and file them."

"When do you think you'll do that?" *In other words, why am I procrastinating?*

I sighed and picked up the basket. I'd put this chore off long enough.

I sorted the pile into stacks. Expired coupons went in the trash. Old notices about our grandson Logan's school events were also discarded. But his assorted homework papers and tests—what to do with them? When Logan had started kindergarten, I'd kept almost everything he did. I couldn't possibly throw away his early attempts to draw or write. But as he got older, there were too many papers to keep, and my attachment to them diminished.

Then there were the pictures—the latest class pictures and team pictures—too many to put on the refrigerator or to frame, but they had to be saved. As I filed them with his previous pictures, I could see how Logan had changed over time. His cute little cherub face had transformed into a little boy's face, each year marking a new level of maturity.

Where had the time gone? For seven years, Logan had lived with us. How had he changed right under my nose? Soon he'd finish elementary school and then move on to middle school. He'd also move out of our house and into a home with his father, who was ready to be a full-time parent.

Over the years, Chuck and I had prayed for this time to come. Now the time had arrived, and the years had evaporated into memories. Once again, God had answered our prayers.

Lord, help me accept this change, knowing Your timing is perfect.
—Marilyn Turk

Digging Deeper: Psalm 75:2; Ecclesiastes 3:11

Ash Wednesday, March 2

Have mercy on me, O God, according to your unfailing love; according to your great compassion blot out my transgressions. —Psalm 51:1 (NIV)

Gray sky hung heavily over Central Park, leafless branches still dripping from an early morning rain. I began my forty-minute walk to the office, feeling slightly less drab than the weather. Lost in thought, I passed under stately trees and beside huge rocks etched by glaciers, unmoved by their beauty. I emerged alongside one of the drives that winds through the park. A jogger passed, heading the opposite way. There was an odd smear on her forehead. It took a moment to process.

Oh! Ash Wednesday! I remembered. I'd prayed Psalm 51 that morning and going to church was on my agenda, but I'd still half forgotten the date. Curious, I began to look more closely at the people passing by. Sure enough, another runner whizzed by, a dark cross etched on his brow. Then came a bicyclist with a normal forehead. Soon I had spied a dog walker, a young mom, and an elderly man, all with ashy crosses. There weren't tons of people—it *was* only 8:15 a.m.—yet each one made me happy. Christians! Christians willing to be publicly identified as such.

By noon, the sun had emerged, and I headed to a church near my office. The pews were packed with hundreds of people, the mood solemn and quiet. Later, as the congregation dispersed, each of us with a visible sign of repentance, people on the street did double takes, wondering what was going on. I walked back to the office, elated and ridiculously happy each time I saw a brow with an ashy cross, knowing that person had not only asked for forgiveness but also been granted it.

Jesus, if You must, drive me to sackcloth and ashes so I may taste the forgiveness Your sacrifice has offered me.
—Julia Attaway

Digging Deeper: Psalm 51:3–6

Thursday, March 3

When I tried to figure it out, all I got was a splitting headache....
Until I entered the sanctuary of God. Then I saw the whole picture...
—Psalm 73:16–17 (MSG)

"Cemetery Land Reclamation Project" read the US Army Corps of Engineers sign. Six-feet-high chain-link fencing stretched the length of the parking lot. Yellow caution tape, two forest-green dumpsters, and "Danger—Do Not Enter" signs cluttered the covered walkway leading up to my favorite West Point café. My morning routine seemed in jeopardy.

Yet when I rounded the walkway, I spotted a construction worker exiting the shop, java in hand. Gratified, I entered.

Inside, West Point cadets readied for class. A department head, seemingly focused on the business of the day, sipped a latte. Two mothers attended to babies in strollers. And three grizzled-looking hard-hat workers appeared to be on break.

Favorite baristas graciously filled my order. I savored the Hearty Blueberry Oatmeal and decaf latte with pleasure and good cheer. The morning was blessed.

Similarly, all too often throughout the week, national and global events disrupt my daily routine and seem to frustrate and confuse me. Troublesome headlines dash my hopes or a letdown too easily occurs. Then I enter our Cornwall Presbyterian Church. Whether for choir practice, a Lenten or Advent Taizé service, or Sunday morning worship, I'm in a sanctuary, a place of refuge.

Fellowship occurs. Stability returns. The Lord is near. And I am blessed.

Almighty God, enable me to continue to find shelter in Your holy temple, and a grace-filled perspective for the day ahead. Amen.
—Kenneth Sampson

Digging Deeper: Psalm 23:6, 27:4

Friday, March 4

WISDOM'S DELIGHTS: Wisdom of Forgiveness

Jesus said to him, "I do not say to you, up to seven times, but up to seventy times seven." —Matthew 18:22 (NASB)

Peter, one of the twelve disciples, asks Jesus how many times he must forgive someone for a personal offense. Thinking generously, he suggests, "Up to seven times?"

Jesus doesn't give the answer Peter expects: He says "seventy times seven," which is telling Peter not to even count the times he forgives. Jesus then tells a story about a compassionate king who forgave a man a large debt he couldn't possibly repay. In turn, that man showed no mercy toward another who owed him much less. The king became angry when he heard this and rescinded his kindness toward the man. Jesus cautions his disciples that this is what will happen "if each of you does not forgive his brother from your heart." (v. 35)

God—on Whose repeated forgiveness I depend—requires that I do the same for others and that they do the same for me. Not grudgingly, but from a sincere heart.

I don't know where I would be without God's mercy extended to me through Jesus, Who gave His life so I might be forgiven. Some years back, I engaged in behavior that hurt everyone who knew me. I knew it was also hurting the God Who loved me—but I kept on. Until one day, I called out to Him in agony. He did not abandon me but rescued and forgave me—and in time, He brought me healing forgiveness from those I'd betrayed.

Withholding forgiveness hurts everybody.

Some are not going to ask for it; they do not even know they've offended. Yet even from the cross, Jesus called for His Father to forgive those who were crucifying Him, saying, "Father, forgive them; for they do not know what they are doing." (Luke 23:34, NASB)

Forgiveness is a wisdom near to the heart of God.

Lord, only from You comes power to forgive.
—Carol Knapp

Digging Deeper: Micah 7:18–19; Matthew 6:9–15; Colossians 3:13

Saturday, March 5

In all your ways submit to him, and he will make your paths straight.
—Proverbs 3:6 (NIV)

Olivia was so close to riding her bike. She could push, glide, coast, and pedal. But while she had the coordination to get going and stay going, she couldn't find her confidence.

For months, she'd suit up in her bike gloves and helmet and loop endlessly, teetering back and forth on her toes. At bedtime, we'd pray for her to master bike-riding, a huge deal in the life of a six-year-old.

I'd like to say that, immediately after that, she pushed off down our hill and rode until dawn, but life isn't like the movies. For a week straight, Brian did sprints up and down our street, balancing, correcting, and encouraging her with every step. Then suddenly, she just went.

At dinner that night, we shared our highs and lows. "My high is riding my bike. It's just such a free feeling," she said, nailing the exact moment of liberty she experienced as she pedaled away.

I think God must often see us like this: content to wobble along, unaware of how much freedom is available to us with just a little confidence and an extra push. The times I have struggled hardest are also the ones when I looked to myself first, a lesson I'm afraid I have had to learn again and again. Turns out, overcoming human nature isn't like riding a bike; it's more like lassoing a unicorn.

These days, Olivia pedals freely, working on her tight turns and getting ready to race her cousins during our annual vacation. And my prayers for her—that she always seek His help first and find the strength inside herself when she needs it—continue to come true.

May I always find my strength and confidence in You, Lord.
Help me learn when I need to spread my wings and fly.
—Ashley Kappel

Digging Deeper: Joshua 1:9; Psalm 139:13–16; Philippians 4:13

Sunday, March 6

SACRED SPACES:
Philips Brooks House, Cambridge, Massachusetts

And ye shall seek me, and find me, when ye shall search for me with all your heart. —Jeremiah 29:13 (KJV)

How many different churches had I visited the year I was twenty-three? Eight? Ten? More? Yet none had reassured me of God's presence. I kept searching.

By the time I found Phillips Brooks House on the Harvard University campus, the folk Mass was well underway. From the doorway, I saw about fifty students seated on chairs or cross-legged on the floor. The celebrant officiated at what appeared to be a card table covered in a hand-embroidered cloth.

Musicians clustered around a piano included a man with a red twelve-string guitar and a woman with long hair holding a wooden recorder. When they eased into the soulful refrain of what I would later learn was a Taizé chant, I aimed for an empty spot on the floor, carefully stepped over the worshippers, and sat. The woman to my right beamed a welcome and offered to share her songbook. We sang together. The celebrant's message tugged at my conscience yet gave me hope. The entire community joined hands for prayers. Yes, God's grace infused this ordinary room.

I did not know then that the smiling woman and I would still be friends more than fifty years later. Nor could I have imagined that I would marry the fellow with the red guitar, that the celebrant would officiate at our wedding, or that the woman on the recorder would be my bridesmaid. I only knew that the warm welcome, the simplicity of the entire liturgy, the intense faith in this congregation, had touched my soul. I had finished seeking for now. I was home.

Lord, help me to trust where You lead, especially when I don't know the way.
—Gail Thorell Schilling

Digging Deeper: Psalm 63:1; Isaiah 55:6; Amos 5:4; Matthew 7:7

Monday, March 7

Train up a child in the way he should go; even when he is old he will not depart from it. —Proverbs 22:6 (ESV)

I am teaching my son to drive. Of all the parenting challenges, fears, and worries, this stage is off-the-charts hard for me. Maybe it is because I was in a near-fatal car accident when I was sixteen, so I know the dangers of teenage driving firsthand. But my guess is every parent knows what I'm going through. It's like the first day of kindergarten all over again—only it's worse.

Solomon is a quick study. His first try, he backs out of the driveway more easily than I imagined. And having him at the wheel is a bittersweet mixed bag of blessings and fears so huge I can barely contain myself in the passenger seat. I grip the armrest hard.

"Relax, Mom," he says.

I try. My husband and I take turns with the lessons, and I investigate teaching-to-drive tips on the internet. And as the days progress and his skills increase, my tension eases. I remember back to when Solomon entered preschool and I asked my sister how you let go of worrying so much. "How do you trust they'll be okay?"

"You just have to," she said. "It feels terrible the first few times, but you'll see—the more you trust, the more you let go, the easier it gets. There really isn't an alternative. You trust. Just trust."

God, of all of life's lessons, letting go is one of the hardest for me. When my heart feels torn and I want nothing more than to hold on tight, help me to release my grip and to trust that You have it all in Your control.
—Sabra Ciancanelli

Digging Deeper: Matthew 7:11; Philippians 1:6

Tuesday, March 8

God decided in advance to adopt us into his own family by bringing us to himself through Jesus Christ. This is what he wanted to do, and it gave him great pleasure. —Ephesians 1:5 (NLT)

When Hurricane Irma pounded Florida's lower Keys years ago, we hesitated about whether to keep our reservations there for several months later. With wind gusts of 165 miles per hour, my family's favorite vacation destination took a beating. What wind didn't tear apart, the tidal surge washed away. The devastation was so severe that residents weren't allowed into the area for two weeks, when roads and utilities were repaired enough for limited use.

After getting assurance that our rental unit was livable, we went in hopes of helping with cleanup and doing our small part to boost the local economy. Despite the area resembling a war zone, with mangled boats tossed far from the water and roofless houses on every street, we found optimistic residents making do with what remained and occasionally having fun with it.

A great example was their approach to cleaning up the waterways and wildlife reserves. Every refrigerator removed from canals and mangrove thickets was put up for adoption and went to the highest bidder, who immediately donated the dangerous eyesore to the recycling center. The money aided cleanup efforts.

As I watched a dive team ready a hefty unit for hoisting out of a canal, I thought about how much their recovery process mirrored what God offers us. When life rips us apart, blows us to places we never intended to go, and dumps us in a location far from where we should be, God stands ready and willing to rescue, adopt, and restore. Nothing can separate us from His healing love.

Lord, thank You for being a loving father who is compassionate, gracious, slow to anger, and abounding in love and faithfulness. Grant us the wisdom to seek You when we've lost our way.
—Jenny Lynn Keller

Digging Deeper: Psalm 86:15; Romans 8:16

Wednesday, March 9

To everything there is a season, A time for every purpose under heaven.
—Ecclesiastes 3:1 (NKJV)

I come from a long line of Irish fatalists. (Is the glass half empty or half full? Neither—it's *all* empty... and give me back my glass.) Thanks to prayer and much internal work, I have rehabbed myself back to the ranks of the merely morose.

Not surprisingly, Ash Wednesday has special meaning for me. No matter your health or wealth, this cheerful verse is literally written on your forehead: "Remember that you are dust and that to dust you shall return." It's just the kind of stark reminder that we Debbie Downers need to gird ourselves for a long penance.

Each year I promise to give up something for Lent but rarely succeed. Mostly I ruminate throughout this season of reflection, pondering my slim chance of ever joining the Choir Invisible. At least that's how Lent begins. But that's not the end of it—"it" being Lent *or* life. It ends with Easter, where nothing is all empty except the tomb. Even a stalwart pessimist such as myself must acknowledge this joyful answer to the eternal question, this tock to answer the tick of our mortal clock.

This year, in addition to the traditional Easter service followed by the traditional brunch followed by the even more traditional nap, I'll be humming a song. Nope, not "Easter Parade," but a snippet from singer-songwriter Jim White: "For those who dwell on disaster/Let sorrow be their master...."

Lord, if I am to give up something, let me give up the sorrow of Lent for the joy of the empty tomb. No doubt sorrow will find me again, but there's time enough for that, and time for every season under heaven.
—Mark Collins

Digging Deeper: Ecclesiastes 3:17; Romans 8:38–39

Thursday, March 10

Therefore, as God's chosen people, holy and dearly loved, clothe yourselves with compassion, kindness, humility, gentleness and patience.
—Colossians 3:12 (NIV)

It was a horrible weather day. The temperature was just above freezing and the north wind was howling at thirty miles per hour. My husband, Don, and I had been in Garden City, fifty miles from home, for Don's medical test and some shopping. Before leaving town, we stopped for lunch at a favorite café. Because of the wind, I waited to shut my car door until Don got out and shut his.

We took our time eating. When I stepped out of the café, I gasped: my car door was wide open. I ran out and had begun searching through the car, checking on our purchases from the day, when a pleasant female voice said, "Don't worry, no one touched anything." I looked up to see a young woman in the car next to mine. "I didn't want to shut the door and risk locking you out," she continued, "so I decided to watch until someone came back."

She brushed off my thanks. "You'd have done the same," she said with a smile.

No, I wouldn't have done the same—at least not with a smile. My impatient self would have begrudged the forty-five minutes we'd been in the café. Hadn't I rolled my eyes earlier that morning when a salesclerk had taken a personal call before ringing up my purchase? And I'd complained twice about the two-hour wait for Don's ten-minute test.

I may never conquer my tendency toward impatience. But now when I'm tempted to respond to irritating situations with impatience, the words "You'd have done the same" come to mind. Most of the time, I take a deep breath, calm down, and do my best to follow that advice.

Lord Jesus, let me look for opportunities to pass on the many gifts of patience and kindness that I have received.
—Penney Schwab

Digging Deeper: Isaiah 63:7; 2 Peter 1:5–8; 1 John 3:18–19

Friday, March 11

So let us not grow weary in doing what is right, for we will reap at harvest time, if we do not give up. —Galatians 6:9 (NRSV)

I have an old friend who remembers being a really good soccer player in school. He was a starter all through high school and then played on his university team. But I use the phrase "really good" purposefully, because my friend is always quick to say that he was never a "star."

This is one of his warm memories about playing the sport: When the guys were choosing sides, all through his youth, he was always one of the first they picked for a team. Why? Because the ones who really were the "stars" knew that my friend was happy and content (and really quite good) at passing the ball.

They would pick him quickly, over the others, precisely because they knew that he wasn't trying to be the star of the team. He wasn't as happy trying to score as he was at trying to make the great pass to the scorer.

What a great lesson my friend's experience provides for how a Christian should lead!

"Servant-leader" is a phrase we hear and often don't comprehend; his is an example of how it works in daily life. A servant-leader helps other people score. A servant-leader thrives on making the great pass and even on seeing cheers for the one who scores. A servant-leader doesn't need praise from the crowd but knows that the good he does is seen in heaven.

Teach me to lead and not follow, Lord, and teach me to lead in the ways You've shown us.
—Jon M. Sweeney

Digging Deeper: John 3:27–30; Romans 12:1–8

Saturday, March 12

When you are disturbed, do not sin; ponder it on your beds, and be silent. —Psalm 4:4 (NRSV)

Saturday afternoon, a neighbor girl called and begged, "Please come over and help me build a Lego bus. I tried, but it fell apart. It's too *complicated*." I hesitated. She continued. "Not the whole kit, just a little."

I went, intending to stay half an hour. But following precise instructions to connect one brick to another—it's complicated, indeed. My coaching didn't prevent false starts.

"Oops, something's not right," I said more than once. "Let's go back four or five steps and set things aright."

In an hour, we'd completed only one of three decks. Even so, we celebrated with a high five.

"Stay longer," she said. "Help me finish!"

We'd both become invested in the project. We built a second deck. We stopped when her mom served her a sandwich. Before I knew it, I'd been with her nearly four hours. The model bus wasn't perfect; the hinge to swing the door open was "locked" shut. Some of the passengers hadn't boarded. But the three-story wonder was framed and rolling.

"It's finished. Look!" She carried her treasure over to show her family and then walked toward her bedroom. "I'll take a picture," she announced, reaching for the doorknob.

I heard the crash and then saw the hundreds of Legos strewn across the parquet. She gasped. I groaned. Our eyes met and mourned.

Uncharacteristically, she didn't lash out, and she dismissed my offer to help. She picked up the wreckage, then sighed deeply as she walked me to the front door. Her parting words caught me off guard. I'll remember them the next time my day implodes: "I'm going to take a break. I'll try again tomorrow."

A new day brings a new perspective on life. Thank You,
Lord, for this overnight, transitional grace.
—Evelyn Bence

Digging Deeper: Psalm 4; Lamentations 3:19–24

Sunday, March 13

By his great mercy he has given us a new birth into a living hope through the resurrection of Jesus Christ from the dead. —1 Peter 1:3 (NRSV)

I looked at the bulletin board with some surprise. It was in what we still called "the boys' room," although our two boys were now adults and hadn't lived there for years. What was missing from the board though?

Oh, yes, now I realized. The two crosses I'd woven together from palm fronds after a Palm Sunday service a couple of years ago. Or maybe it was our son, Tim, who had pinned them there even before then. I'd taken them down myself just weeks ago and dropped them by church before Ash Wednesday. They would be burned, along with the other old palm fronds saved from Palm Sunday, their ashes used to mark people with the sign of the cross.

Now here we were in the middle of Lent, in that wilderness period when the promise of Easter feels as though it can't come soon enough. Outside looked gloomy; spring was slow in coming. The crocuses were pushing up, but the golden forsythia now shivered in a cold rain. There were even predictions of light snow. Some spring this was.

Maybe this is what Lent is all about, I thought. Finding God in the in-between times of life, seeing how He might be present in a veritable absence.

Was it my imagination, or was there a faded shadow of those crosses on that bulletin board, a mark of where they had been? I stepped closer and looked. Yes, there was—just the faintest outline. Loss and a presence, marked together at once.

We don't usually say "Happy Lent," but I wanted to say it now. What about Easter not coming soon enough? It was always here; I just had to look closer.

Lord, in those down times when I feel lost and alone, let me know of Your presence. It's always there.
—Rick Hamlin

Digging Deeper: Matthew 20:17–19; Acts 4:3

Monday, March 14

Be anxious for nothing.... And the peace of God...will guard your hearts and your minds in Christ Jesus. —Philippians 4:6–7 (NASB)

I consider myself a positive person, but some mornings I wake up fighting off the anxiety that seems to have lain in wait for me while I slept. This morning was one of those mornings. I went downstairs to feed Gracie, telling myself not to turn on the news.

My angst was only amplified by the return of the robin, the one who had harassed our house and car all last spring. He was at it again, flinging himself at my windows. It drives me and Gracie crazy. "You're a bird dog," I say to her. "Do something!" But she only paced, worry on her face.

I called our vet clinic and asked Dr. June for help. "What do I do about this crazy bird?"

"This is nesting season, so he's back," Dr. June said. "He sees his reflection and thinks he sees an enemy. Close your curtains and hang a towel over the mirror. That should stop it."

I'd give it a try, but I was prepared for another siege. But something else she said stayed with me. What the robin took to be his enemy was really just his own reflection.

Am I the same way? I think my anxiety is something prompted by the uncertainties of the day. Yet those are external factors. My fears and worries are internal. And too often my worries occupy the space where God's love and grace can abide.

Yes, I sometimes wake up troubled by a troubled world, but I also wake up to a loving God Who has lain in wait for me while I slept.

Thankfully, the robin's campaign was brief this year. Maybe he had learned his lesson. Maybe I had too.

God of love and protection, in an uncertain world,
You are the only certainty.
—Edward Grinnan

Digging Deeper: Isaiah 41:10; Matthew 6:25–34

Tuesday, March 15

But when you give alms, do not let your left hand know what your right hand is doing, so that your alms may be done in secret; and your Father who sees in secret will reward you. —Matthew 6:3–4 (NRSVCE)

I don't like the phrase "God loves a cheerful giver." It makes me feel like a failure. Even though I volunteer, my heart isn't always in it, and I wonder if that makes my gift less worthy in His eyes.

I don't have this dilemma when I give money or goods. I feel cheerful donating cash to help solve a problem or bath towels to comfort someone in a homeless shelter. But giving my time sometimes makes me less than cheerful.

I felt this way last week on my way to take fresh fruit to the shelter. It was the next-to-last stop in a long day, and I still had to grocery-shop afterward.

I slogged through a cold drizzle into the shelter, lugging fruit and a sodden attitude. Both shelter managers hugged me, as residents cleared space on a table. I grabbed plastic gloves and started parceling out grapes while a line formed. I was greeted, thanked, hugged again. Some folks caught me up on their latest news, good and bad. I exchanged several "God blesses." As I got ready to leave, a new resident asked to speak with me. Shaken and worried, she wept in my arms, and we prayed.

Walking back to the car, I can't say that I felt cheerful. But I did feel loved. And loving.

Father, Thank You for encouraging me as I do Your work.
—Marci Alborghetti

Digging Deeper: Matthew 2:9–11; Galatians 6:9

Wednesday, March 16

"For I know the plans I have for you," declares the LORD, *"plans to prosper you and not to harm you, plans to give you hope and a future."*
—Jeremiah 29:11 (NIV)

I crunched through knee-deep snow toward a bucket hanging from a birch tree in our yard. *Why hadn't I worn boots instead of sneakers?* I thought, as snow soaked my socks. Even though our calendar said it was nearly springtime, this scene was still decidedly winter.

But yesterday, my daughter had gone on a field trip to a local birch-syrup cooperative. They'd loaned each interested kid a metal tree tap. She'd come home so excited, and we'd dutifully drilled the little hole in the tree, placed the tap, and hung her five-gallon bucket. I'd tried not to let my doubt show. It was hard to believe we'd get much from this leafless, winter-bound tree.

Yet.

Drip. Drip. Drip.

Something *was* happening! I lifted the bucket's lid and peeked inside. It was already half full! And the clear, waterlike sap was running from the tap at such a rate that it would not be long before the bucket was brimming.

To my eyes, this tree looked like it was still fully locked in winter's embrace. But just under its bark, God was working, readying it for the spring that, despite appearances, really was right around the corner.

I thought about a few of the chronic struggles in my own life. As I fitted the lid back onto the sap bucket, I realized I'd been thinking about them all wrong. I cannot know the seasons that are to come in my life. But God can and does, and—just like with this tree—He knows the work I must do and to be ready when it's time.

Thank You, God, for the reminder of how Your perfect timing is at work in the world and in my life.
—Erin Janoso

Digging Deeper: Romans 8:26; Hebrews 13:20–21

St. Patrick's Day, Thursday, March 17

I am the LORD who practices steadfast love, justice, and righteousness in the earth. For in these things I delight, declares the LORD.
—Jeremiah 9:24 (ESV)

My niece Haddie is an Irish step dancer.

If you've never seen Irish step dancing, you should. It's absolutely beautiful—dancers with quick feet, lots of rhythm, and stunning costumes.

Those costumes—called "solo dresses" in the Irish dance world—are also elaborate. Most of these dresses are custom-made for dancers in Ireland, where they are hand-cut, carefully stitched, and then embellished with tiny rhinestone crystals to make them sparkle.

Last year, after many months of saving, searching, and waiting, Haddie got her first solo dress. It was turquoise with soft cream and navy swirls and thousands of green and blue crystals.

Once the dress was perfect, Haddie carefully packed it up in a waterproof dress bag to fly to a dance competition. On the way home, because it was so bulky and cumbersome to carry, she decided to check the bag.

Big mistake.

For three days, we all fretted and worried and prayed and pleaded with the airline to find the one-of-a-kind, irreplaceable, priceless dress.

Now you're probably thinking I'm going to start pontificating about storing up treasures in heaven and not in crystal-bound dresses, which is important. But in this case, we learned not about treasure but about trust.

The airline found that dress a week later, but in the interim, as we waited and prayed, we learned something more valuable: that even if the dress had disappeared, we were okay. Covered in Jesus's steadfast love and peace.

Lord, thank You for Your peace that is more delightful, shinier, and better than crystals. Amen.
—Erin MacPherson

Digging Deeper: Mark 11:20–25; John 7:38

Friday, March 18

BLESSED BY ONE SWEET COOKIE:
Enthusiasm for Others

Love each other with genuine affection, and take delight in honoring each other. —Romans 12:10 (NLT)

"You know, if Cookie were a person, she'd be you," I joked with my friend Brent one day.

Fittingly enough, I'd met Brent at the dog park a few years ago. He often brings his rescue, Rocky, to play there. It took me a while to learn Brent's real name, because for the longest time, I just called him Mayor. He seemed to know everyone at the park by name, and everyone liked him, so I thought of him as the unofficial dog park mayor.

Brent laughed when I told him he was the human version of Cookie (he laughs at pretty much everything), but they do have a strong trait in common: an enthusiasm for others. Brent's enthusiasm takes the form of learning everyone's name and stories (and remembering them), greeting everyone with a big smile, and never being in too big a hurry to have a conversation. Cookie's enthusiasm involves running up to people so fast and jumping on them so hard that she frequently knocks them into next week! (We're working on that.)

While I can be as friendly as the next person, I'm naturally introverted and feel drained after too much interaction with others. And I can find myself getting so caught up in my own agenda that I often don't take as much interest in other people as I should. Cookie, and human friends like Brent, remind me to work on that—to take joy in others' company. Minus knocking them down, of course.

Father, help me to love like Jesus does.
—Ginger Rue

Digging Deeper: Galatians 5:22; 2 Thessalonians 1:3

Saturday, March 19

You make known to me the path of life; you will fill me with joy in your presence, with eternal pleasures at your right hand. —Psalm 16:11 (NIV)

It was almost the end of winter, and I'd been obsessively checking the height of my boys over the past few months.

They didn't know it yet, but when they topped fifty-four inches, I planned to buy season passes to my favorite amusement park, Six Flags. At fifty-four inches, they could ride the extreme roller coasters, and only then would a season pass be worth the money.

My oldest son stood up straight against the loft bedpost, where I'd marked their heights since the ages of three and four. I placed the ruler on top of his head and marked it with a pencil—fifty-four exactly! I measured my youngest, who was shooting up fast. He was closer to fifty-five!

I ran to my computer and purchased the passes, then shouted, "We're going to Six Flags to ride your very first extreme roller coaster!"

We spent the next few weeks watching videos of the rides, and soon we were on a bus to the park itself! I could barely contain my excitement as we stood in line at my favorite ride in the park, Nitro. We even waited the extra time to ride in the first car.

Our backs pressed against the seats as we slowly went up the steep hill. Suddenly we were at the top, looking down at the world—and then we were flying. I lifted my arms in the air with each drop and turn, and the boys did the same. They were screaming joyfully, a sound that filled my heart with so much happiness.

As a mother, I've enjoyed introducing my boys to the world, but as we soared through the air on this particular day, I knew that our excitement of exploring adventures together had just begun.

Lord, thank You for new experiences and adventures!
—Karen Valentin

Digging Deeper: Ecclesiastes 11:9; Psalm 118:24

Sunday, March 20

For he hath said, I will never leave thee, nor forsake thee.
—Hebrews 13:5 (KJV)

A darling child with long brown hair captured my attention. She sat in the pew in front of me next to her doting grandma and fumbled with her phone. *She'd been better off in Kiddie Care,* I thought. Oh, she was quiet enough, but she sure wasn't paying any attention to the Sunday morning worship service. Pastor Chuck had been talking about how God was with us always, even during the difficult waiting moments, when we thought nothing was happening in our lives.

When the time came for greeting one another, the little girl turned around to face me. She had the biggest brown eyes. She stretched a tiny hand toward mine and smiled. "I'm Kaylee," she announced boldly. "He's *with* you while you're waiting."

I was so astonished, I nearly gasped. *Where did* that *come from?*

My thoughts traveled back to a conversation I'd recently had with a renowned geriatrician. Dr. Shirley Neitch and I were discussing how patients with dementia will sometimes be unaware of their surroundings, then have a lucid period where they pray or praise Jesus. Dr. Neitch explained that it all stemmed from early memories when, as itty-bitty things, they heard the Word, sang hymns, and fellowshipped with other believers.

It never leaves them. Ever. Even when earthly memory fails.

He will never leave us or forsake us. I'd heard that explored in countless sermons my entire life. But that tiny girl with the eyes that reached my heart put a face on the promise. Kaylee might have been fiddling with a phone in child's play. But she was also hiding the words of Jesus in her heart, where they would never leave her.

Remind me of Your forever-and-ever promises, Lord.
—Roberta Messner

Digging Deeper: Deuteronomy 31:6; Joshua 1:9; Matthew 28:20

Monday, March 21

Accept one another, then, just as Christ accepted you, in order to bring praise to God. —Romans 15:7 (NIV)

As a member of my church's ministry EMBRACE (Encouraging Multitudes by Raising Affection, Concern, and Empathy), I frequently make calls to first-time guests to thank them for visiting and to invite them to return.

The calls aren't always successful: Many people don't even answer, because they don't recognize my telephone number. Some, when reached, think that I'm an annoying telemarketer and quickly hang up. It's discouraging at times, but it's important to let visitors know that we are grateful that they chose to visit our church—even if they don't hang on the phone long enough to hear me say that.

One recent call I made, however, was quite different. It was to Tonya, who had attended for her grandson's baptism. She was excited to receive my call and thanked me many times for being part of a church that had meant so much to her daughter-in-law and her family. I began to bring the call to a close by asking Tonya if she had any concerns that she would like us to pray about.

"No, honey," Tonya said. "Is there anything I can pray about for *you*?" I was dumbstruck. In the four years that I had been making these calls, no one had ever offered to pray for me. I asked Tonya to pray for the church's forthcoming plans to erect a new building. She immediately joined me in prayer about that, and then prayed for my family, for me, and for our church overall, and my tears just flowed.

These phone calls aren't easy for me to make, but after this call to Tonya, I completely understood their value.

Dear Lord, let us reach out to others to show the very same agape love that You so willingly share with Your flock.
—Gayle T. Williams

Digging Deeper: Galatians 6:2; Philippians 2:3

Tuesday, March 22

I praise you because I am fearfully and wonderfully made; your works are wonderful, I know that full well. —Psalm 139:14 (NIV)

"In your big blue eyes I see intense fragility and all your love for me, how perfect life can be...." I woke from a deep sleep with those words flowing through my mind. *Yes! That was it!*

Those were the lyrics to the second verse of a song I'd written over thirty years ago as a lullaby to my first daughter. I had tried to sing it earlier that day to her daughter—my seven-month-old-granddaughter—as I put her down for a nap. I'd remembered most of it, but when I'd come to the second verse, there had been a gap I'd just hummed through. Try as I might, I couldn't remember the words. But they came to me that night at about 2:00 a.m., waking me from slumber.

This same thing has happened to me many times. I laughingly envision a little man inside my head, frantically searching through file cabinets of memories until he victoriously extracts the right one and waves it aloft, calling out, "Here it is!"

How astounding God made our brains. To think that every experience I've ever had is stored in detail somewhere deep inside is mind-boggling. Sometimes that little man locates it quickly. Other times he takes a little longer. Sometimes he can't seem to find it at all and eventually gives up. But I feel confident it's still there, influencing me in some way in my current thinking, reactions, fears, delights, and more.

Yes, Lord, Your creation is utterly incredible and amazing. I am in awe.
—Kim Taylor Henry

Digging Deeper: Psalm 104:24, 106:1–2, 111:1–3

Wednesday, March 23

Be strong and courageous, and do the work. Do not be afraid or discouraged, for the LORD God, my God, is with you…
—1 Chronicles 28:20 (NIV)

I had a familiar bad dream last night.

I was hosting a dinner for my table of moms in our church's MOPS (Mothers of Preschoolers) group, where I am a mentor. (True to a point. That dinner was two days away.) In my dream, all six moms showed up at the door at the same time, excited to spend an evening around a table specially set for them, with a unique menu I'd already shared with them. (The menu part is true too.) But here's the bad part. I totally forgot they were coming until I opened the door. The table wasn't set. I had no food ready. So now what did I do? I made a bad choice. I tried to act like a spontaneous person who lets my guests help me make dinner. But when I opened the refrigerator, it was totally empty. And then the electricity went off.

I forced myself awake, out of my bad dream, but didn't sleep well the rest of the night.

Then in the sunlight of a new morning, I knew why I'd had this dream. When I'm overwhelmed by the preparation necessary for an upcoming commitment, I sometimes fall into a familiar pattern of procrastinating. So now what? I know the answer starts with prayer.

I prayed out loud as I marched around the kitchen with my second cup of coffee. Then I turned on some praise music. Finally, I sat down with paper and pencil, checked my recipes, and began to make a detailed grocery list for the food I needed for the dinner party.

Several hours later, the necessary food filled the near-empty refrigerator. *Whew! Progress!*

Lord, in the light of day, I can see that the positive power of a bad dream is the prompt to pray.
—Carol Kuykendall

Digging Deeper: Proverbs 19:15; Lamentations 3:22–23

Thursday, March 24

Then shall the dust return to the earth as it was: and the spirit shall return to God who gave it. —Ecclesiastes 12:7 (KJV)

"Oh my goodness," I say, as I catch myself in the mirror. "My earth suit is melting."

Ah, yes, it's true. Though I don't usually take time to dwell on it, the skin on my face and neck, ever so slightly, like a slow-burning candle, creeps down. Though smiling sort of keeps things at an even keel, I can't possibly smile all the time. So I simply accept the inevitable "melt."

"Oh, well," I say to myself as I jump into the day, "I won't need this earth suit forever anyway."

And to my way of seeing things, it does make sense. I seemed to have been sucked into this body with my first breath, and it's been the vehicle to make my way through life ever since. I feel a keen responsibility to maintain it as best I can. Eating healthfully, exercising, taking long walks, appreciating beauty, and talking often to the Father are all ways to stay "tuned up."

But I've always had a sense that I'm just a temporary resident of this earth form. You surely know the feeling. Gazing out a window, kicking through fall leaves, showing kindness, loving simply—they are all moments when our spirit flies free from this old earth suit and hovers ever close to the face of God.

A spirit "hath not flesh and bones" (Luke 24:39 KJV), so as the years pass by, and my earth suit grows more wobbly, I hope I can always remember that the "suit" is not who I am. I am hope, belief, joy flying free, a spirit on my way back home, where our Father waits.

Father, on the day I ditch my earth suit, spread Your arms and welcome me home.
—Pam Kidd

Digging Deeper: Psalm 22:26; 1 Corinthians 15:44

Friday, March 25

And my God will supply all your needs according to His riches in glory in Christ Jesus. —Philippians 4:19 (NASB)

My husband had called during my workday, telling me he had "some news." I prayed as I walked downstairs to meet him, bracing for the bad news I could feel coming my way. A few minutes later I was face-to-face with him. With glassy eyes and a shaky voice, he said, "I lost my job today." He shared a few more details. I grabbed his hand, closed my eyes, and prayed a prayer of hope, faith, and trust in God.

As my husband drove off, the reality of his job loss sank in, and fear threatened to overtake me. We have four kids, a mortgage, and several monthly expenses. With my part-time ministry position, he is the major breadwinner in our family. I had no idea how we would manage our family's financial needs.

Over the next week, I processed and prayed. I began to share the news—first with my sisters, then with close friends, and lastly with coworkers. One day when I was feeling low, I spoke to the Father without formality. "Lord, this is so hard. Could You please throw me a bone here?"

In less than an hour, my supervisor called with additional ministry needs—needs that would require more work hours from me and, therefore, a more substantial paycheck. The next day, one of my sisters sent me fifty dollars. A few days later, my other sister sent a hundred and fifty dollars. A day later, I opened my mail and found a reimbursement check for an overpaid medical bill.

Through all of this, I heard God's voice. He had heard my prayer. He cared for me and my family. He loved me still. And He would supply all my needs.

Dear Lord, please help us to worry less, to pray more, and to trust You always.
—Carla Hendricks

Digging Deeper: Psalm 23:1; Matthew 6:25–34

Saturday, March 26

From him the whole body, joined and held together by every supporting ligament, grows and builds itself up in love, as each part does its work.
—Ephesians 4:16 (NIV)

I'd never cared about the purpose and daily habits of bees until I had one stage a takeover of my back deck. It arrived daily, zipping and fluttering around for three to four hours. Its presence prevented me from enjoying my normal cup of green tea outside on chilly mornings or escaping to read a novel in solitude. In annoyance, I attempted to get rid of it through swatting and, eventually, insect repellant, but neither worked. Even when the bee disappeared, it eventually returned minutes later.

When I researched to find out when I'd be able to reclaim the deck as my own, I discovered that my daily visitor was most likely doing its job. Although I couldn't identify its specific species, I discovered that one thing was consistent among all bees—they have jobs. And they all stick to their assigned duties, each doing its part. Among an extensive list, jobs can range from being queen bee to being queen attendant, forager, nurse, cleaner, guard, or architect.

Watching the bee safely through my kitchen window was a constant reminder that I have meaningful parts to play in life too. I'm not a health-care worker, but I can volunteer to donate blood. I'm not as gifted as my aunt at preparing dinner for large groups of people, but if a potluck needs to be organized, I'm the woman for the job. And I may not deliver eloquent sermons to large congregations, but the power of my written words has strengthened the faith of others.

Lord, let my focus be clear and my work for Your people be diligent.
—Tia McCollors

Digging Deeper: Psalm 133:1; Proverbs 27:17; Ecclesiastes 4:9–12; 1 Corinthians 12:25–27

Sunday, March 27

He has made everything beautiful in its time. He has also set eternity in the human heart; yet no one can fathom what God has done from beginning to end. —Ecclesiastes 3:11 (NIV)

"There is poetry inside all of us," said one who had never in her life written a line of verse worth the paper and ink.

Admittedly, I was a bit carried away that spring as I looked upon a newly greened tree bending to the wind, causing me to personify it and elevate it to the status of William Wordsworth. Though Solomon says in Ecclesiastes 3, "He has made everything beautiful in its time," I was not gifted to determine whether poetry was hidden in that sapling. Solomon's announcement, however, found in that same verse—proclaiming that God has "set eternity in the human heart"—enlightened me to a divine truth.

As a believer, I often struggle with how to spread the gospel. I wonder if the moment is right or if a bumbling effort might yield a permanent turnoff. But remembering that God has already set eternity in the hearts of mankind—that God Himself has placed within us a flicker of wonder about future existence—can be a powerful motivator toward the telling of His goodness.

Being rebuffed can be disappointing, even humiliating. But to be assured that the object of our attention was born with the need to know God ("a mysterious longing which nothing under the sun can satisfy, except God," according to Ecclesiastes 3:11, AMP), and to see that need flare into hope, vanquishes the threat of rejection.

How rewarding it is to watch eternity bloom in the human heart! The way of salvation has already been prepared. All I have to do is point God's children in the right direction and let the Holy Spirit do the rest.

Father God, help me trade the shackles of intimidation
for the courage of the cross.
—Jacqueline F. Wheelock

Digging Deeper: Psalm 14:1; John 10:28–29

Monday, March 28

For we are his workmanship, created in Christ Jesus for good works, which God prepared beforehand, that we should walk in them.
—Ephesians 2:10 (ESV)

The woman poured out her story, her heart in bits and pieces, each sliver more terrible to hear than the last.

I sat across from her at a Bible study I lead for inmates at the county jail. Yet in that moment, I didn't feel like an adequate leader. I was stunned in the face of the nightmare she'd lived through as a child. During my time of service at the jail, I'd heard a great many tales of woe, but never had I met someone who had been through such horrific trauma.

What could I say? Why in the world did the Lord send me to help this woman? I'm not a psychologist or social worker. I'm not a brilliant theologian.

Yet I opened my mouth and words came out. True words about God's role in suffering. About the comfort we have in His sovereignty, justice, and grace.

Believing these truths, the student lit with a tearful smile as she embraced the hope set before her.

Often when I set out to teach this Bible study, feelings of inadequacy overwhelm me. Honestly, for many things in my life, I feel unequipped, unskilled, or simply not good enough.

But then God gently reminds me I am His workmanship. I am equipped for the good works He calls me to do because He created me for them and them for me. All I have to do is walk with God through each day, confident He will provide all I need to accomplish His work.

Lord, help me to remember You chose and equipped me for the task at hand, not because of anything good in me, but because of everything good in You.
—Jerusha Agen

Digging Deeper: 2 Timothy 3:16–17; Hebrews 13:20–21

Tuesday, March 29

May my meditation be pleasing to him, as I rejoice in the LORD.
—Psalm 104:34 (NIV)

A friend told me about his conversation with the mayor of our city. The mayor had mentioned that he rose daily at 4:00 a.m. to pray and read the Bible. The story stuck with me. I had struggled to establish a time for daily prayer and devotional reading. I would start reading the Bible, fall behind, and find myself starting again weeks or months later.

Sometime after hearing the story about the mayor, finding myself restarting again, I decided to try getting up early to read a copy of *Daily Guideposts* that I had been given. Soon, I was waking up eager to read the daily devotions. Before long, I added prayer and later Bible reading.

As my responsibilities increased, my days started earlier and so did my quiet time. This time is now the most important hour of my day. I come away energized by new insight and grounded in God's presence to deal with the day.

Then recently I came across this quote from John Wesley: "O begin! Fix some part of every day for private exercises. You may acquire the taste which you have not: what is tedious at first will afterwards be pleasant…read and pray daily…give it time and means to grow."* If I had read Wesley's words long ago, I don't know if they would have inspired me to stick with my initial attempts to read and pray. But I do know that the mayor's story helped me find that mornings work best for me. And the wisdom and faith treasures I found reading *Daily Guideposts* kept waking me early and inspiring me to more prayer and Bible reading.

Dear Jesus, thank You for teaching us to do as You did to take time apart to pray! Amen.
—John Dilworth

Digging Deeper: Joshua 1:8; Psalm 77:12, 119:148

---

*James C. Miller, Gospel of Luke (Franklin, TN: Seedbed Publishing), 2019, ix.

Wednesday, March 30

He will take care of the helpless and poor when they cry to him; for they have no one else to defend them. —Psalm 72:12 (TLB)

After Jack died, I didn't attend any grief-share meetings at church. One reason I didn't go was because they were held at the same time as my water aerobics class, and there was no way I was going to miss that.

Instead, I stepped into a new world—that of being a volunteer ambassador at the big, beautiful Tampa airport. Two or three days a month, you'll find me sitting at a big desk in baggage claim, answering all kinds of questions from jolly travelers, excited to be in Florida. Some are getting ready to head to the cruise terminal for a weeklong Caribbean adventure. Others are ready to dip into our glorious Gulf of Mexico and relax for a week.

Instead of sitting around thinking about all the things I used to do with Jack and wallowing in widow misery, I decided to surround myself with people who need my help to ease the stress of travel. When I jump up to point to the four-story escalator that will take travelers to the tram that will take them to the car rental center, I'm happy because I know my directions and smiles are making their day easier.

I joke around with the passengers, give the kids free pencils with rubber airplanes on the ends, and sometimes let travelers use my cell phone if their batteries have died. All I know is I am joyful every minute I am helping a passenger. And after a day at the airport, when I go home to my condo, it doesn't seem lonely at all.

Lord, thank You for the grace to step out of my aloneness and into the throngs of people who need a smiling face to send them on their way.
—Patricia Lorenz

Digging Deeper: Isaiah 41:10; Matthew 11:28–30;
1 Thessalonians 5:14–16

Thursday, March 31

A new heart also will I give you, and a new spirit will I put within you.
—Ezekiel 36:26 (KJV)

It's been a hard winter—rainy, cold, dark. But now, spring is teasing with the first purple crocus pushing through a crusty dusting from a forgotten snow. A veil falls across the woods on the horizon, brought by the softness of barely discernible baby buds.

But I am holding back. Maybe I'm waiting for blooming dogwoods to lift my spirit?

On my early morning walk, I stop and study the first green carpeting the meadow. I see tiny wildflowers barely discernible in fresh grass. In the woods, the first trillium poke through the leaves. To be sure, new life is everywhere. So why do I feel disconnected, like I no longer fit into God's amazing scheme?

Ahead is my "praying tree." A place I often stop on my walks to connect with things unseen. I first bonded with this tree when I noticed, some years ago, that someone had carved their initials inside a heart on its trunk. But, sadly, a storm had ripped a huge limb from the tree and left it hanging, grinding into the bark, making short work of the heart. Each day, I brought whatever I could find to wedge between the limb and the tree trunk. Saving the heart seemed important.

Then one day, a small miracle: a tree trimer had removed the broken limb. The heart is safe. I stop now and stroke the soft moss that grows on the tree. And there it is. How can I believe it? A handprint has somehow formed in the bark just above my head. Hesitantly, I lift my hand and find a perfect fit. God promised a "new heart, a new spirit," and once again, He has delivered in a totally unexpected way.

Okay, God, You've astonished me once more. Thank You.
—Pam Kidd

Digging Deeper: Numbers 14:21; Isaiah 49:13

March

THE LORD IS NEAR

1 _____

2 _____

3 _____

4 _____

5 _____

6 _____

7 _____

8 _____

9 _____

10 _____

11 _____

12 _____

13 _____

14 _____

15 _____

March

16 _____

17 _____

18 _____

19 _____

20 _____

21 _____

22 _____

23 _____

24 _____

25 _____

26 _____

27 _____

28 _____

29 _____

30 _____

31 _____

April

Oh, how abundant is your goodness, which you have stored up for those who fear you. . . .

—Psalm 31:19 (ESV)

Friday, April 1

Come out of the ark, you and your wife and your sons and their wives.
—Genesis 8:16 (NIV)

This morning the weatherman displayed the week-ahead calendar, and every single square showed rain. Even now, there was a downpour outside. I mopped the kitchen floor of my dog's dirty paw prints. No matter how hard we tried to avoid tracking in mud, dirty floors seemed to be one certainty of spring.

I had moved onto the rest of my least favorite chores—emptying the large kitty litter pans and scrubbing the outside of the kitchen trash pail—when my thoughts turned to the ark and Noah's wife. Exactly who was this nameless woman of extraordinary patience, courage, and perseverance?

I wonder what it must have been like on the ark. I wonder how Noah's wife coped when she looked out and saw no sun. Where did she find hope? When the second dove came back and she knew the end was in sight, how did she feel? Did she worry about what they would find after the storm?

My own housekeeping challenges were nothing compared to the difficulties and devastation she experienced, yet I was inspired by her strength and fortitude, and her ability to endure the trip and start over. It had once bothered me that she was not named, but now I realize that, perhaps, it's because she is meant to represent mothers of families everywhere—because she holds hope and cares for those she loves.

Dear Lord, when I feel tired of cleaning up after a household of kids and cats and a dog in an exceptionally muddy spring, guide me to see that the abundance of dirt reflects a house of blessings.
—Sabra Ciancanelli

Digging Deeper: Genesis 6; Galatians 6:5

Saturday, April 2

Cast all your anxiety on him because he cares for you. —1 Peter 5:7 (NIV)

Standing in Disney World, we got the text; our flight home had been canceled. We'd already checked our bags that morning, which was great in that it let us make fun plans to have lunch at the Dino restaurant, but terrible in that we'd have to go to the airport to rebook.

We made it to the airport with three worn-out kids and about two hundred fellow passengers trying to rebook. Everyone was tense and, frankly, my kids became anxious. "What are we going to do?" they asked. "How will we get home?"

I pulled them away from the chaos to get their attention. "Guys," I said, "we are fine. The airline booked us a new flight tomorrow, they gave us a room in a hotel, and we can eat dinner in the airport. We'll be back home before work or camp even starts, and we even have our jammies and our toothbrushes." I continued, "Basically, all we got was a bonus night of vacation with each other." We said a prayer that we'd soon be safely in our jammies, and then we headed back into the fray.

The kids got more excited when they realized the airport food court had a huge fish tank. As they chased the fish, my husband, Brian, and I talked. There's a reason we call trips with children "travel" and not "vacation"; they're work! But these are the chances we get to teach our kids about faith and flexibility.

That night, as we blessed our food, we prayed that the other travelers would make it home safely, that the pilots would get a good night's sleep, and that we would enjoy the extra time together as a family.

Lord, thank You for the minor trials and inconveniences You bring to me, so that I may teach my children to come to You in all times.
—Ashley Kappel

Digging Deeper: Proverbs 15:1–3

Sunday, April 3

... They are no longer two, but one flesh. —Mark 10:8 (NIV)

Marrying a ranch girl comes with an addendum of fine print on the wedding license—namely, about livestock and where they reside. That said, when my new husband, Randy, came home to find a bull calf in the kitchen—granted, it was a hopelessly small newborn, and it was extremely cold outside—he wasn't as enthusiastic as I would have hoped. Although Randy had raised steers in the past, he firmly believed that cattle belonged outdoors. Not surprisingly, he was fundamental in helping me find another home for the bottle-fed orphan within the week.

The night little Hamish went to another loving home, despite Randy taking me out for a lavish "forgive me" dinner, my tears were abundant. *Lord, why do Randy and I have to be so different?*

But over the next few months, I did have to admit, grudgingly, that the TLC Hamish received from his new family far exceeded the attention I could have given him. My selfish prayers matured to *Lord, help me consider our needs before my wants.*

A year later, Randy called from Swan Lake, where he'd been working. "A rancher has just found a premature calf, and they don't have time to help her as much as she'll need. Do you want her?"

"What if she's in the kitchen for a week?" I asked, holding my breath.

"She's a beautiful heifer," was Randy's reply.

"I'm on my way."

> *Lord, thank You for joining me with this incredible man.*
> *Let our good qualities blend as we grow closer to each other.*
> —Erika Bentsen

Digging Deeper: Genesis 2:24; Ephesians 5:1, 25

Monday, April 4

And he said to them, "Come away by yourselves to a desolate place and rest a while." —Mark 6:31 (ESV)

The tree was dead, its branches brittle and bare. Heartsick, I thought back to the previous summer, when our whole family had gathered here at my grandmother's beloved off-the-grid home to plant the little maple in her memory. We'd interred her ashes around its roots and imagined it growing big and strong, sharing the legacy of Nanny's strength and resilience with future generations. But it hadn't even survived its first winter.

Nanny's life had been filled with struggle, but this place had been her refuge. And it was where she shared with her children, and—later—her grandchildren, the renewal she always found when she was loose in the wilds of God's creation. To me, as a kid, the meadows, woods, and creek of Nanny's camp felt like heaven on earth.

But two summers ago, we'd lost Nanny. And now her memorial tree was gone too. Dejected, I sank to my knees. And that's when I saw them. Tiny, green maple leaves, hiding among the weeds at the tree's base. A closer look revealed little shoots pushing up from the dead tree's roots. I laughed out loud. Of course!

Over and over again, life had cut Nanny down. But again and again, fortified by the strength she'd found here, she'd fought back and overcome. I looked over to where my six-year-old daughter played with her cousin in the meadow. Thanks to Nanny, they would grow up knowing—as I had, and my mom before me—the peace that could be found in God's wild places. I smiled down at the little maple shoots, grateful. Nanny's legacy was alive and well.

The restorative power of Your creation is a precious gift, God. Thank You.
—Erin Janoso

Digging Deeper: Genesis 1:31; Job 14:7; Luke 5:16

Tuesday, April 5

Now, our God, we give you thanks, and praise your glorious name.
—1 Chronicles 29:13 (NIV)

I open the window to let spring rush inward, but it's a letdown. I miss the rich scent of my deep purple lilacs and the songs of the birds that nested near the stone patio of our old house.

We moved over a year ago, and I'm still homesick. It doesn't help that our Victorian, straight across the Mississippi from where we live now, hasn't sold.

I take the broom from the closet and begin to sweep the spoils of family breakfast: crumbs of toast, a Cheerio, a curl of bacon the dog missed. When I sweep under our antique cabinet, I see the pumpkin on the bottom shelf. It's been around since fall.

Years ago, when our boys were small, November meant a construction paper tree on the dining room door. The boys wrote expressions of gratitude on red and gold paper leaves, and attached them to the tree. Last year, though, we used a Sharpie marker and wrote what we were thankful for on this pumpkin. Soon it was scripted with things we were grateful for: Music. Bonfires. Soup. Swim team. The handwriting varied on this garland of gratitude, the outflow of my family of seven souls.

"Wow!" My thirteen-year-old, Gabriel, comes around the corner and sees me studying the pumpkin. "That thing's lasted like crazy. Is it drying out? Maybe it's not a pumpkin. Maybe it's a gourd."

I don't know. But I lift it from the shelf and place it on the center of the table again. It provides the simple truth that grumbling and gratitude can't share the same space.

Spying vacant strips of orange between lines of words on the pumpkin, I root through a drawer for my marker.

Yes, I need to be in a different place.

Lord, forgive me when grumbling lives where gratitude should. Amen.
—Shawnelle Eliasen

Digging Deeper: Psalm 69:30, 100:4–5

WALKING IN GRACE

Wednesday, April 6

WISDOM'S DELIGHTS:
The Wisdom of Finding Security in God

And He said to His disciples, "For this reason I say to you, do not worry about your life...." —Luke 12:22 (NASB)

Jesus tells a story of a rich man who kept enlarging his barns for his crops and other possessions. With his future comfort assured, life is one big party. But he hadn't planned on life ending. Jesus calls him foolish, asking "...now who will own what you have prepared?" (Luke 12:20 NASB) and then closes the story with "So is the man who stores up treasure for himself, and is not rich toward God." (Luke 12:21 NASB)

Thousands are gathered, listening to His teaching. Many are barely getting by. They have walked miles in dusty, worn-out sandals. They yearn for the security the rich man felt with his overflowing barns.

Jesus tells them what they have never heard—working to get more of earth's temporary comforts is an empty pursuit. Instead, He says, seek God's kingdom first, and He will meet their life's basic needs.

While we don't have barns, my husband and I rent two storage units for which monthly fees add up to a sizable annual sum. I admit to feeling uncomfortable with this. This amount could multiply the kingdom of God. It could help support a homeless shelter. Or fund a human trafficking rescue program. Reduce someone's medical bills. Add to food bank shelves. The list is long.

We share a home with multiple families, and we have limited space. But I know I could consolidate our storage. I'm continually being challenged not to accrue "stuff" and to be generous with what I have.

Fortunately, I can look to Jesus, Who demonstrated how God's kingdom invests in others. He traveled light and understood that lasting things aren't things at all.

> *Lord, instead of worrying about life's temporal inventory, help me to look to the richness of seeking and sharing Your kingdom.*
> —Carol Knapp

Digging Deeper: Jeremiah 9:23–24; Romans 14:17

Thursday, April 7

Do not lay up for yourselves treasures on earth, where moth and rust destroy... —Matthew 6:19 (ESV)

April. Tax time. Render unto Caesar. Why am I not better organized? Why did I wait this long? It's enough to make me tear my hair out. Every year. So really, I have no one to blame but myself. And all these confusing government forms, of course.

The other night I was trying to find documentation for the charitable donations I'd made that year. Could I deduct contributions to my twelve-step home group? I had no receipts. You just drop what you can afford in the basket. In fact, it is perfectly allowable to take money out of the basket if you are really in need, though I have never seen anyone do it.

While I was grappling with this issue, I suddenly remembered my father's approach to charitable donations. He never deducted them on his taxes. Charity was about giving freely, but a tax deduction was receiving something in return for giving. For him that tainted the spirit of giving.

Not that he thought the tax code should be overhauled to exclude this deduction. It just wasn't something he was personally comfortable with. I, on the other hand, had always been comfortable with it. In fact, I hadn't thought about it much...until now.

I stared at all the papers and receipts scattered across my desk. Did I feel the same way? My father was not a rich man and neither am I, but I'm certainly in a position to help others with minimal sacrifice. I can afford to give without expecting a rebate from Uncle Sam, can't I? And besides, my twelve-step program had literally saved my life.

So this year at least, I chose to follow my father's lead. I gave freely as I have received freely. And I had a little less work to do on my tax forms.

*Help me, Lord, to give from my heart, to love
my brothers and sisters as You love us.*
—Edward Grinnan

Digging Deeper: Proverbs 23:4–5; Luke 12:20–21, 32–34

Friday, April 8

And when your children ask you, "What do you mean by this rite?" you shall say, "It is the Passover sacrifice to the LORD, because He passed over the houses of the Israelites in Egypt." —Exodus 12:26–27 (Tanakh)

In the past, I'd always gone to Dan and Debbie's Seder on the first night of Passover, bringing the hard-boiled eggs (because they knew better than to ask me to cook anything). But this year that tradition would not take place, because Debbie had passed away the week before the holiday. That meant my only "official" Seder would be on the second night, when the synagogue held its group Seder for everyone.

The second-night community Seder was always fun, and I looked forward to attending it every year. I shared a table there with good friends, some of whom I would only see at Pesach (Passover). Some years we would spend so much time catching up with one another that the Seder went by almost before we noticed it.

Tonight as the Seder swept by, the question "Why is this night different from all other nights?" landed with a thud and brought me up short. Clearly, this Passover night needed to be different from all the others. But it didn't really feel that way to me. Yet what did deliverance from slavery really mean on a night when the kids were racing around and the rabbi seemed to be officiating over a room where people were talking to one another instead of paying attention?

Once I started thinking about that, I became aware that I was being shown what freedom really meant—gathering together, without fear, without compulsion, without repression, in a group filled with love for one another. The form of the Seder might have been slapdash, but its meaning had never been clearer to me.

> *Dear God, thank You for freeing us to celebrate You with one another and with a jolly good time!*
> —Rhoda Blecker

Digging Deeper: Exodus 12:14; Deuteronomy 6:21

Saturday, April 9

And all these blessings shall come upon you and overtake you, because you obey the voice of the LORD your God. —Deuteronomy 28:2 (NKJV)

My five-year-old son had been counting down the days until the annual community Easter egg hunt held the weekend before Easter. And now that day had finally arrived! He lined up with the other children in his age group, their eyes wide with anticipation for the start of the Easter egg hunt.

The group stretched behind the imaginary line in the vast field of the church, their oversized baskets hooked in their hands. The pastor began the countdown, and at the sound of *"Go!"* nearly a hundred pair of little feet bolted across the grass.

Truthfully, they didn't have to run far—no more than ten yards—before reaching the clusters of colorful plastic eggs that were well within their sight and grasps. My son, however, passed the crowd and ran farther than the rest. I beckoned him back, pointing to all of the eggs he was missing. Undeterred, he yelled back, "Mom, all the good stuff is back here!" Once he reached a suitable spot, he fell to his knees and stuffed his basket with eggs until they spilled over the brim. His blessings overflowed.

I experience that same childlike excitement when God blesses me beyond my expectations. Many times such blessing has been the result of following His voice and daring to go beyond the crowd. Times when I stepped outside my comfort zone and received a blessing fashioned just for me—like my son said, the "good stuff."

Thank You, Lord, for calling me out of my comfort zone. Following Your voice will always lead me to an abundant life, even more than I imagined.
—Tia McCollors

Digging Deeper: Deuteronomy 28:6; Psalm 32:8; Isaiah 30:21; John 10:27

Palm Sunday, April 10

A LIVING HOPE: The Goodness of My Savior

Then they brought it to Jesus, and after throwing their clothes on the colt, they helped Jesus get on it. —Luke 19:35 (CSB)

It's late on a Sunday night. I sit at my desk and flip a pen between my fingers. A blank sheet of paper sits in front of me.

It has been months since Kendall asked me to officiate his wedding. Now the wedding is days away, and I still haven't written the ceremony. Every time I press pen to paper, the same doubts rise in my mind. *What do I, a single man, know about marriage? How can I speak credibly on something I have no experience with?*

In an attempt to quiet the doubts, I set down my pen and open my Bible. I find myself in Luke, reading the passion story. I've read it dozens of times. But this time, I read it with a fresh perspective. I see the Passion Week as a long-awaited wedding: Since the fall of Adam and Eve, sin had separated humanity from a holy God. At the cross, humanity was cleansed and joined with him. And at the center of this cosmic wedding was Christ.

It was Palm Sunday, and Christ was walking down the aisle, approaching Jerusalem. His posture was exactly as a spouse's should be: humble, riding on a donkey rather than a steed; gentle, coming as an intercessor rather than a warrior; and selfless, heading toward a cross rather than a throne.

Although I have never been married, I have been united with God through Christ. I have personally experienced Christ's humility, gentleness, and selflessness—all traits that are essential to a successful marriage. And I am more than qualified to speak about the goodness of my Savior.

Jesus, thank You for saving me and for showing me how to live.
—Logan Eliasen

Digging Deeper: Ephesians 5:25–26; Philippians 2:5–8

Monday, April 11

And God said, "Let the earth sprout vegetation, plants yielding seed, and fruit trees bearing fruit in which is their seed, each according to its kind, on the earth." And it was so. —Genesis 1:11 (ESV)

I love eating things that grow wild—wherever I may be living. That means blackberries and goose plums here in Oklahoma, and fennel and mussels when I lived in Laguna Beach, California. When I weed, I save dandelions to eat as wilted salad or sautéed with garlic. This year, I became obsessed with poke, a wasteland plant that grows person-tall in spring everywhere I've lived. I have harvested masses of its sumptuous tender leaves to eat immediately and freeze for later.

People say poke is poisonous unless harvested young and boiled multiple times, pouring off the water each time. But I just preboil it once, the way my mom and mother-in-law used to, and usually eat it as they did, either scrambled with eggs or doused with pepper vinegar alongside corn bread and beans. This year, I used it in everything, inventing such low-brow delicacies as poke lasagna: green poke pasta layered with Béchamel and tomato sauces and more poke. Oh, man! My Instagram followers went wild.

Why this sudden mania for a weed I've eaten since childhood? I wondered as I gathered yet another load. I'm not food-insecure. Even if I were, soon my garden would offer up spinach and chard, greens I also love that don't require parboiling. Perhaps it was just my frugality.

Then, suddenly, I knew why. Poke—so prolific, so ubiquitous, so insistently green that it stays bright even after a long boiling—is the perfect antidote to the dearth of winter. Of all the plants that push themselves up from the drab, hard dirt every spring, none more clearly says, "Hush, now. I'm here, walking beside you in the cool of the day. I will provide."

Father God, thank You for nature's reminders of Your presence!
—Patty Kirk

Digging Deeper: Genesis 1–2

Tuesday, April 12

A LIVING HOPE: God's Glory and Majesty

Some of the Pharisees from the crowd told him, "Teacher, rebuke your disciples." He answered, "I tell you, if they were to keep silent, the stones would cry out." —Luke 19:39–40 (CSB)

I kick off my shoes at the door. My roommate Craig looks up from the book he is reading.

"Can you start loading the Jeep?" I ask.

"Sure thing," he says. "We can be out of here in half an hour."

"Perfect," I say. I loosen my tie as I dash up the stairs. I've put in a full day at work, but I'm overflowing with energy. By dawn, Craig and I will be in Colorado.

Our trip has two purposes: I will be officiating my friend Kendall's wedding in Denver. And Craig and I have planned a camping trip in the Rockies.

I trade my suit for jeans and a tee. Then I grab my prepacked duffel bag. Soon, the Jeep is full and our journey begins.

Craig and I are excited as I merge onto the interstate. We talk as I drive. Slowly, night drifts across Iowa's fields. Our conversation slows, then halts. Craig has fallen asleep.

Several hours later, I stop at a gas station and wake him. We switch places. Craig leads us across dark Nebraskan plains as I drift in and out of consciousness.

We continue trading shifts into the early hours. The novelty of the trip has worn thin—But so has the night. As I drive, light begins to peer from behind me. And what lies in front of me is breathtaking.

I shake Craig awake. He swipes at his eyes. Then he sees them. Mountains. We marvel in silence, and then Craig speaks.

"How can anyone see mountains and not know there is a God?"

I stare at peaks drenched in daybreak. And I have no answer.

Father, thank You for revealing Your glory.
Let Your praises never leave my lips.

—Logan Eliasen

Digging Deeper: 2 Samuel 22:50; 1 Chronicles 16:23–31

Wednesday, April 13

Be ready to do whatever is good. —Titus 3:1 (NIV)

In elementary school, I donned a Girl Scout uniform. Did I sell cookies? The memory is vague.

But I clearly remember the motto. With fellow Scouts, I learned the lesson well: "Be prepared"—mostly for hardship. How to cook an egg on a tin-can burner. How to make a bedroll from quilts. How to make a sling—or was it a tourniquet?—from a towel. Similarly, at home, my parents instilled in me a spiritual vigilance to be ready for God-knows-what, maybe even a warning of biblical proportion: to "seek shelter" like Noah or "store up" like Joseph in Egypt.

Even now I'm prepared—and ready—for unexpected adversity. I keep a well-stocked pantry and use a nonelectric can opener. Since 9/11—more than twenty years ago—I've rarely let my dashboard gas gauge slip below half full. (What if I need to evacuate in a hurry?)

But was there more to the lessons that I'd missed? The Girl Scout website includes a "Be prepared" explanation dated a decade before I joined up: "A Girl Scout is ready to help out wherever she is needed." And in the back of my dad's King James Bible, I recently made a new discovery: "Be ready to do every good work."

I let the scripture seep into my spirit. Yesterday I phoned a friend who lives alone. She sounded—sleepy? Sick? "Are you okay?" I asked.

"My back went out—in pain," she admitted.

Here and now, "I'll pray for you" seemed hollow. On the other hand, I didn't much want to drive clear across town. Just then, the apostle's admonition kicked in. I offered something specific: "Can I go to a drugstore for you?"

"I've taken something; it should take effect soon." She paused. "But I really appreciate your offer. Thank you."

Lord, prepare my heart to respond in Your good will to needs set before me.
—Evelyn Bence

Digging Deeper: Titus 3:4–9, 13–14

Maundy Thursday, April 14

A LIVING HOPE: Forgiven by Christ

Simon Peter said to Him, "Lord, then wash not only my feet, but also my hands and my head." —John 13:9 (NASB)

I shift my stance and adjust my backpack straps. My friend Craig and I are at the head of our trail.

"This is crazy," Craig says. "I can't believe we're camping in the Rocky Mountains."

"Other people have taken this trail." I point at the tramped snow in front of us.

"Then they were crazy too," Craig says, but I know he's grinning beneath the layers covering his mouth.

We begin our mountain ascent. The path is slick and winding. Half a mile in, we pass a pair of hikers heading back toward the trailhead.

Another mile up, and the trail is different now. Only a few sets of footprints press into the snow. But soon even those prints halt, and the trail is marked only by a gap in the foliage.

"It looks like we've got this mountain to ourselves," Craig says.

I nod, breathing heavily. The air is thin but clean. Stripped of impurities.

Soon we pause to rest. I take in my surroundings. Tall pines and strong boulders, all softened with a gentle covering of snow.

"Everything here is pristine," I say. And as my breathing slows, I come to a new understanding. "I think this is what it is like to be forgiven by Christ."

"What do you mean?" Craig asks.

"Every imperfection here is covered with purity. The blemishes of humanity have been removed. God's intended order is restored."

We are quiet. Words sink in while feet are still. Then we resume our venture into God's creation, and I whisper a prayer.

Lord, thank You for covering my mistakes with Your perfection.
—Logan Eliasen

Digging Deeper: Psalm 51:7; Isaiah 1:18

Good Friday, April 15

A LIVING HOPE: Reconciled to God
We are punished justly, for we are getting what our deeds deserve. But this man has done nothing wrong. —Luke 23:41 (NIV)

My friend Craig and I broke camp at dawn, but that was not early enough. The road from Estes Park to Denver is a twisting one, and the drive is slower than I anticipated.

"You can still make it to the wedding rehearsal on time." Craig shields his eyes from the morning sun. "Maybe."

My foot presses deeper into the gas pedal.

"*Maybe* isn't good enough," I say.

Cliffs and valleys pass peripherally. Then we round a bend. The wild landscape becomes a small town. Homes and shops blink by. And red and blue lights flash behind me. *No, no, no!* My foot switches from gas pedal to brake, and I park my vehicle while time slips by.

An officer approaches. "Do you know how fast you were driving?"

My mind floods with possible responses: ignorance, denial, or persuasion. But I knew there were rules. And I had broken them.

"Too fast," I say.

"Fifteen over," the officer says. "I'm sorry, but I have to write you a ticket."

I pass him my license and registration, and he returns to his car.

"I should have noticed the speed limit," Craig says.

"No," I say. "It was my responsibility to follow the law."

As I await the ticket I have earned, I think about how I have done much worse. I am flawed and sinful. But I am not the one who paid the penalty for my sins. Christ took the punishment in my place. The perfect One redeemed the lawbreaker. And because of Him, I can stand blameless before a holy God.

The officer returns. And as I accept the ticket, I thank Christ for accepting the weight of my sins.

Jesus, thank You for taking my punishment upon Yourself.
—Logan Eliasen

Digging Deeper: Isaiah 53:5; 2 Corinthians 5:21

Holy Saturday, April 16

A LIVING HOPE: Times of Waiting

The women who had come with him from Galilee followed along and observed the tomb and how his body was placed. Then they returned and prepared spices and perfumes. And they rested on the Sabbath according to the commandment. —Luke 23:55–56 (CSB)

My friend Kendall and I sit in folding chairs. We both wear suits. Kendall's tie is tight. So is his jaw.

Outside, people are gathering for Kendall's wedding. He has prepared for this day for over a year. Now he is drumming his fingers on his knee.

"It's going to be fine," I say. "You are ready for this."

Kendall exhales. "I feel adrift," he says. "I am a doer. I like taking action. I have never been any good at waiting."

I nod, understanding what Kendall means. I know how hard it is to wait. Kendall is waiting for his bride to walk down the aisle. For years, I've been waiting for mine to walk into my life.

"It's difficult to wait," I say. "Waiting means acknowledging events aren't under our control."

I put my hand on Kendall's shoulder.

"But waiting doesn't mean events are out of control," I say. "Because, ultimately, God is in control."

Kendall ruminates. His face begins to relax. "Can you pray with me?"

I move my chair across from Kendall's. We each bow our heads in submission. And we each trust God in our times of waiting.

Father, help us to trust in You while we wait.
—Logan Eliasen

Digging Deeper: Psalm 130:5–6; Lamentations 3:25

Easter Sunday, April 17

A LIVING HOPE: The Promise of Faithful, Forever Love

So Peter and the other disciple started for the tomb. Both were running, but the other disciple outran Peter and reached the tomb first.
—John 20:3–4 (NIV)

I scramble up stone, making my way along whatever serves as a trail. Footings are loose.

It is my last morning in Colorado. During this trip, I've camped on mountains and hiked in valleys. I've celebrated the marriage of two friends. I've learned more about who I am and who God is.

But in twenty-four hours, I will be back in my office. I will no longer explore wilderness. I will sit in a chair with four wheels.

So today, I carry a heaviness. And a question: *What happens next?*

As the early sunlight warms my neck, I think of another man who grappled with the same question. Peter.

Peter had followed Jesus Christ across Judea. He had seen the power of the promised Messiah. Then, in less than a day, everything changed. His savior was murdered. His faith was shaken. The disciple of God once again became a fisherman.

What happens next?

Everything. A report of a disappearing body. A burning, gasping run to a tomb. Folded linens and wrappings. Peter's story had only begun.

On the quietest of Sundays, Christ had shattered the bonds of death. He reunited sinful humanity to a holy God. And he rolled back the stone and redeemed Peter, the rock on whom He had chosen to build His church.

For Peter, the best was yet to come.

I know the same is true for me. The faithful God Who brought me to this place will accompany me back home. And I can't wait to see what He has in store for me there.

Jesus, thank You for the cross and the empty tomb. And thank You that my relationship with You will continue for eternity.
—Logan Eliasen

Digging Deeper: Deuteronomy 31:8; Philippians 1:4–6

Easter Monday, April 18

A LIVING HOPE: Christ's Light in the Darkness

He also said to them, "This is what is written: The Messiah will suffer and rise from the dead the third day, and repentance for forgiveness of sins will be proclaimed in his name to all the nations, beginning at Jerusalem." —Luke 24:46–47 (CSB)

In the early hours of the morning, my journey draws to its close. My Jeep is pointed eastward, Colorado is far behind me, my friend Craig has fallen asleep in the passenger seat, and I am alone with my thoughts.

Outside, the night smothers Iowa's cornfields. After the grandeur of the Rockies, the rows seem simple and predictable.

This is my home. But I have never felt more out of place.

The boy inside me feels stifled by the familiar. I want to experience and explore. And this does not seem like the place to do those things.

I drive on through the darkness. Soon, I reach my exit. I recognize the street I turn onto; I know which department stores line it.

"What am I doing here?" I whisper. But, as my words break silence, I realize I'm asking the wrong question.

"What can I do here?" I whisper.

I don't need an answer. I already know.

Here, in Iowa, I have relationships with people I care about. Here, Jesus has provided me with opportunities to share His love with others. Here, I can be Christ's light in the darkness.

And I can't think of a greater adventure than that.

Lord, help me to share Your gospel with the world.
And help me begin at home.
—Logan Eliasen

Digging Deeper: Matthew 10:6–7; Acts 1:8

Tuesday, April 19

I sought the LORD, and he answered me, and delivered me from all my fears. —Psalm 34:4 (NRSVCE)

We'd just come home after spending a wonderful Lent and Easter at a terrific church in New Hampshire. April here in Connecticut was raw; spring was not cooperating. The few pathetic daffodils I saw on my walk seemed to wonder if they'd poked up out of the earth too early.

I felt ragged, too, missing New Hampshire and not sure New London still felt like home. I trudged along, realizing this was more than just the blues. After having been away for so long, I wasn't sure I made a difference here anymore. A new pastor had made changes at our church that contrasted sharply with the vibrancy of our New Hampshire experience. Now I wasn't sure that I belonged.

By the end of my walk, I felt as gray as my surroundings. I wondered if it was God's will that we spend more time in New Hampshire.

The next day, after work, my husband, Charlie, said, "You didn't mention that you saw so many folks on your walk yesterday."

I looked blankly at him.

"Over coffee today, Reid said he was so happy to see you on your usual route; he called his wife to tell her things were back to normal. That reminded Sue that she had clothes she wanted us to bring to the shelter." He continued, "Then at work, Cathy said as soon as she saw you, she decided she needed to start walking again. Then Mike called, wondering when we'd be back at the shelter."

The weather was still gray when Charlie and I took a walk that day. But the daffodils looked much sturdier, more hopeful of the coming warmth.

> *Father, thank You for reminding me that there are many ways to do Your work.*
> —Marci Alborghetti

Digging Deeper: Ecclesiasticus 1:1–10; 1 Thessalonians 4:1–2, 9–12

Wednesday, April 20

Not that I have already obtained this or am already perfect, but I press on to make it my own, because Christ Jesus has made me his own.
—Philippians 3:12 (ESV)

Wresting the wheel of our Subaru wagon to the left and then quickly right again, I gunned the engine up the hill, not daring to slow down. It'd gotten warm quickly this spring, and the melting snow had transformed our half-mile long driveway into a sloppy, squelchy mess. Staying on the driveway's high points was an effort worth making though. The muddy ruts were deep, and I'd learned the hard way that getting sucked in wasn't great for the vulnerable undercarriage of the car.

A thought pricked at my mind: *Funny how essential it feels to protect the car's well-being. What about your own?*

Over the past year, I'd been trying to form a handful of healthier routines. Going to the gym had been on my to-do list today, but time had run short, and here I was coming home without having worked out. Last night I'd meant to write in my gratitude journal, but sleep was more tempting. And the quiet writing time I liked to include in my morning routine? Yeah, my snooze button had been winning that contest lately. *Tomorrow,* I'd tell myself as my eyes closed for five more minutes. It apparently required no effort at all to get pulled back into the ruts of my old habits. Ruts that lead me away from, rather than toward, my God-given, possibility-filled potential.

Positive change is hard. It takes work. But as I pulled the car—still in one piece—into the garage, having successfully navigated the mud for one more day, I knew it was work worth doing.

Thank You for Your gift of potential, God. I pray to You for the strength and endurance to not get stuck in ruts, to look for the opportunities You present to me.
—Erin Janoso

Digging Deeper: Hebrews 10:36, 12:1

Thursday, April 21

You make my life pleasant, and my future is bright. —Psalm 16:6 (CEV)

While peeling a carrot, I glanced out the window at the thick gray clouds of spring and groaned. The clouds seemed to mirror my mood. With each stroke of the peeler, I pecked at myself about opportunities I'd missed and things I should have done. After chopping the carrots and adding them to the pot of soup, I heard the peeping of the four baby chicks I'd just purchased. To keep them warm, I'd placed them in a horse's dry water tank in my entryway.

Four yellow fuzz balls curled under the infrared heat lamp. When they heard me walk over, they stood and stretched. On their heads, three had black stripes; the fourth had a small black dot, perfectly centered. As they awoke, they looked at one another. And then the three with striped heads, one by one, pecked at the black dot, as if to remove it from the fourth chick's head. I giggled. "Hey, chicks, that dot doesn't come off." But they didn't listen. Each time they strutted past Dot, they pecked it in the head.

"Silly birds. There are some things you can't change." And when I said that, it was as if I were talking to myself.

Gray days can be gloomy for me, and oftentimes I peck at myself all day. Like the dot, there are things I can't change. Like the past. And the weather. But I can create sunshine in my day. So that's exactly what I did. The rest of the afternoon, instead of focusing on things I'd done wrong, I chose to think about God's promises and the things I had done right.

And eventually, the chicks gave up on trying to remove Dot's dot too.

Thank You, Lord, for Your promises that make my future look bright.
—Rebecca Ondov

Digging Deeper: Psalm 37:37; Proverbs 23:17–18

Friday, April 22

My roots spread out to the waters, with the dew all night on my branches, my glory fresh with me, and my bow ever new in my hand.
—Job 29:19–20 (ESV)

I'm a plant killer. I love plants, but I kill them. It happens every spring—wildflowers blooming, trees covered in green leaves, stores full of summery flowers, and I get the urge to try again. This year, it was fifty dollars' worth of pansies and daisies to fill the pots on my porch.

My husband wasn't thrilled about it. "You're just wasting money!"

"This time, they'll survive!"

Over the next few weeks, I lovingly cared for them, moving them into the sunlight each morning, faithfully watering them so that the soil was the perfect level of dampness. Yet a mere week later, their leaves started to turn yellow and the petals wilted and sagged. How was this even possible when I had been so diligent?

Then, in a seemingly unrelated incident, the sink on our patio began to leak. We called a plumber, who came out to fix it.

"What in the world?" the plumber exclaimed as he lay under the sink. "Did you know that this sink is hooked up to the water softener line? No wonder this sink is rusted away and leaking—it's spewing pure salt water."

Lightbulb moment! I had been watering my plants with potent salt water for years. No wonder they were dying!

The plumber switched a few pipes around, and my flowers began to come back to life. Yellow leaves turned green, petals grew glossy and fragrant, stalks reached up toward the sun.

Two months later, my plants were still alive, thriving on clean, fresh saltless water.

> *Lord, shower me with clean, pure life-giving water today, so that I can grow and thrive under Your care. Amen.*
> —Erin MacPherson

Digging Deeper: Romans 5:2–6; Hebrews 5:12–14

Saturday, April 23

There is a time for everything... —Ecclesiastes 3:1 (NIV)

I pulled into my daughter's driveway to add items to the dumpster they were renting as they purged their house. That's when I saw it. On top of the heap was a child's desk, the kind I had used in elementary school—a metal chair attached to a wooden desktop that lifts, revealing a space to stash paper and pencils and books—and maybe even a snack to sneak when the teacher wasn't looking.

My mother had rescued it from a trash heap many years ago when my elementary school was being remodeled. It had lived in our playroom when our kids were growing up. Then my daughter Lindsay had it in their house when their kids were little. But they are no longer little.

"It hurts my heart to see the kids' desk in the trash heap," I told Lindsay, feeling more emotional than I would expect.

"I understand, Mom," she answered gently, "but it's broken."

I went home still thinking about the desk. Soon I got a text from Lindsay. "The desk had a great life with us. Many rounds of playing school. Many crafts born on its surface. Many supplies stored inside. The nostalgia is real. We loved it well."

Her words prove why she's good at purging. She's able to appreciate the life span of something and live with the good memory. Nostalgia is real but not a reason to keep something that's outlived its life span.

The next day I went back, dragged the broken desk off the pile, and took a picture of it to remind me of its life well-lived.

> *Lord, thank You that we have the capacity to store good memories in our souls forever.*
> —Carol Kuykendall

Digging Deeper: Proverbs 12:15; Ecclesiastes 3:2–15

Sunday, April 24

Even there your hand shall lead me, and your right hand shall hold me.
—Psalm 139:10 (ESV)

My oldest two sons were home for the weekend. Each lived hours away—one to the east and one to the west. The stopwatch in my chest started the moment they walked through our front door.

"What should we do this afternoon?" my husband, Lonny, asked on Sunday. Checkout time was close.

"Fly kites?" asked my youngest boy.

Sold!

One trip to the dollar store and a few miles later, all seven of us were at the park. The sun was gold and strong, and there was enough wind to lift our kites.

"Look at this," one son called. He ran over grass of deep green, his kite bobbing in the blue above him.

My own kite swirled and dove and arced back to the sky, as my boys covered most of the field. Sometimes they ran close and the strings threatened to tangle, but mostly they let their kites soar high. They laughed out loud, these living anchors of mine. Plastic diamonds of primary colors rose and twirled and swept low, each on a different trajectory. A different path. Together but separate. All held by the same sky.

It was true that good-bye is the other side of togetherness, and my sons were growing. But my boys-now-men were making an impact on the world. Following the Lord's lead. Helping others. Using their gifts. As it should be.

But we were still connected. These boys, their daddy, and I were family—tucked tenderly, lovingly, in the curve of our Father's hand.

Later in the day, when car engines started and the sidewalk at the end of the drive was evening-warm beneath my bare feet, I waved good-bye to two sons. It was okay. We were held.

Lord, thank You for holding my family close when we're apart. Amen.
—Shawnelle Eliasen

Digging Deeper: John 10:28

Monday, April 25

So don't be anxious about tomorrow. God will take care of your tomorrow too. Live one day at a time. —Matthew 6:34 (TLB)

I'd just come back from visiting two of my children in California and finally arrived at the airport at one in the morning. It was the first time I'd ever used the huge economy parking lot on the outskirts of the airport.

After gathering my bags, I made it up the four-story escalator to the tram that took me to the parking garage, then down the elevator onto the two-block-long moving sidewalk, and up another elevator to my floor, where I tried desperately to remember where I'd parked the car.

Luckily there was another couple with me on the first elevator. We struck up a conversation as we walked on the moving sidewalk and then into the second elevator. But once in the massive garage, they went left and I went right to look for our vehicles. I hated being alone in that giant garage that late at night. But I could still hear them talking, so I said a prayer and kept walking, knowing God would help me find my little blue car.

Suddenly, a car two rows ahead of me started beeping and the lights were flashing. And there, out of the corner of my eye, I saw the young couple. He'd hit the alarm button on his key so they could find their car. I walked toward them, hoping they would stay until I found my car. But when I reached them, there was my little blue beauty, right next to theirs.

It was a small thing, but in my heart I know that Jesus was protecting me in that garage.

Jesus, thank You for being my travel companion no matter where I am and for keeping me safe and in the care of others.
—Patricia Lorenz

Digging Deeper: Psalm 37:4–6; Matthew 6:30, 28:5–9; Philippians 4:4–7

Tuesday, April 26

"For I know the plans I have for you," declares the LORD, "plans to prosper you and not to harm you, plans to give you hope and a future."
—Jeremiah 29:11 (NIV)

"You're going to be late!" I hollered down the hall to my sixteen-year-old daughter.

A new semester, and this would be Micah's third tardy. Frustration weighed heavy on my shoulders. I punched the overhead garage-door button.

I shouldn't have been driving her to school at all, but last week she'd had a fender bender. Thankfully, the damage was minimal. My husband and I grounded her from driving for a month, hoping it would make her more careful.

Micah didn't think the wreck or being tardy was a big deal. I chalked it up to immaturity. But deep down, I worried. *Will she ever grow up? Be responsible?*

I backed my car out of the garage and pulled next to Micah's on the driveway. I gazed at the damage—cracked headlight, broken headlight cover, dented front bumper. Beneath the damage, I noticed a fuzzy caterpillar on the front tire. Reddish body, black head, long hairs that protruded. I hadn't seen a woolly caterpillar in years. But I knew that little guy needed to get off that tire if he was going to get strong enough to make a chrysalis and fulfill his destiny.

Getting out of my car, I picked him up and set him on a maple tree branch. A thought floated through my mind: *God is watching over my child just as tenderly as I am caring for this insect.* Like the caterpillar that would someday become a beautiful butterfly, Micah, too, would mature into who she was destined to be. All in God's time.

Lord, help me be patient and extend grace to my daughter as she makes mistakes and grows into who You've created her to be.
—Stephanie Thompson

Digging Deeper: 1 Corinthians 13:4–7; Galatians 6:9

Wednesday, April 27

Don't just pretend to love others. Really love them. —Romans 12:9 (NLT)

No! No!! No!!! NO!!!! I frantically clicked my computer's keyboard, trying to retrieve what was lost. But the words on the screen remained the same: "This message has no content." My heart sank. This was the last email I'd received from my lifelong friend Randy before he'd passed from this life onto the next. Now his final words had disappeared right along with him. I'd skimmed his email when it first arrived, but I had been headed out of town that day and had planned to reread the message more carefully when I returned. And then I never had the chance.

It wasn't Randy's farewell that I regretted losing most, even though those words were irreplaceable; it was his answer to my questions about his wife, Cindy, that I'd wanted to hold on to. After Randy's ALS diagnosis, it became obvious his wife would become a widow far too soon. I felt that one way I could continue to care for Randy was to care for Cindy after he was gone. But I didn't know her. So I'd asked Randy to tell me about her—to share her favorite flower, color, candy, books, and music. Now all of this information was gone.

That's when God gently reminded me that to love Cindy well, I needed to get to know her and not just know about her. So that's what I focused on doing over the next few months. By exchanging cards, emails, and texts with her across the miles, I got to know the beautiful woman that captured my dear friend's heart. In my loss of one friend, I unexpectedly gained another, and my life is richer for it.

Dear Lord, You've asked me to care for widows and orphans. Please show me how to love them in both personal and practical ways.
—Vicki Kuyper

Digging Deeper: Psalm 68:4–5; Romans 12:15; James 1:27

Thursday, April 28

He opens their ears to instruction and commands that they return from iniquity. —Job 36:10 (ESV)

Birds covered the road. The vehicle in front of me blazed forward, and a dark cloud billowed up from the ground—the frenzied motion of hundreds of escaping creatures somehow forming a graceful wave.

I hoped the birds would have the good sense not to return to the road, given I was only a few moments behind the first car. But they immediately dropped back down, blanketing the pavement with dark bodies I didn't want to crush.

As I neared the congested patch of road, they seemed reluctant to move. They finally lifted off again, rising in a dark, flowing shape—too close to my bumper. I pressed the brake, narrowly missing the slowest birds.

Why would the birds return to that same place? Hadn't they learned from the first car that they shouldn't be there? That it was dangerous? I breathed a sigh of relief that I hadn't hurt any of the foolish birds.

Realization smacked my conscience. I'm one of those birds. Nearly every day, I find myself returning to the same sinful behaviors. A bad attitude, a short temper, fear, or an idol of comfort.

Haven't I learned I shouldn't return to those sinful paths? That they're dangerous?

But better than headlights or a honking horn, my Father's voice calls to me, and He opens my ears to hear. He tells me to return to Him, away from those dangerous sins, and He lifts me on wings of safety.

Father, draw me away from the sins that lure me back today, and help me instead to return to Your loving and protective embrace.
—Jerusha Agen

Digging Deeper: Proverbs 26:11; Isaiah 44:22; 2 Peter 2:21–22

Friday, April 29

They have no speech, they use no words; no sound is heard from them. Yet their voice goes out into all the earth, their words to the ends of the world.
—Psalm 19:3–4 (NIV)

While I was sitting on a Waikiki beach, people-watching, my attention was snagged by a young mother and her small child who spoke another language. I wondered if my English-bound communication skills might hinder any attempt to interact with the lovely pair—the mother kneeling along the walkway with her camera, the toddler venturing into the sand. Back and forth he went, each time returning to savor his mother's approval. As the mother offered him praise, I joined in, laughing, nodding—simply unable to contain myself as his smile and clasped hands communicated to me, *I might not speak your language, but I'm so proud that you're pleased with me.*

While the writer of Psalm 19 extols the silent speech of the heavens, God's people are ever learning a language for the ages, daily taught by His Spirit: the language of love and servanthood. Just as God set the moon and stars in their courses, He set His Spirit in the hearts of believers to nudge us toward righteousness—guiding, instructing, and inspiring us as we learn to give Him free course. The Comforter Jesus sent to us is not simply a lofty-sounding description on a page in Scripture but a Person of the Godhead Who cares so much that He is grieved each time we fail to respond in love.

Whether it's volunteering to rock a sick baby or quietly handing a hot meal to an exhausted new neighbor, gestures of caring often outstrip the most eloquent sermons and the most jaw-dropping scenes in nature, and they speak as clearly as a toddler's smile.

Lord, like the heavens, help me to joyfully and consistently declare Your glory through the language of Your Spirit.
—Jacqueline F. Wheelock

Digging Deeper: Nehemiah 9:6; John 3:16

Saturday, April 30

Commit your way to the L ORD, *Trust also in Him, and He shall bring it to pass.* —Psalm 37:5 (NKJV)

As pollen dusted the cars outside and the sprigs of cherry blossoms sprouted on trees, I was bitten by the spring-cleaning bug. I bustled around the house with cleaning supplies and placed boxes in the hallway designated for items to throw away and donate.

My children, however, had an ongoing project in the corner of the guest room that was disrupting my routine. Legos were scattered about, and unfinished pieces of their work in progress were lined against the baseboard. It had been over a week since they'd touched them, and I was itching to scoop up all the colorful construction pieces and dump them in their designated bin. My youngest son must have sensed my impatience when he happened by the room and rushed in to stop my cleaning frenzy.

"Big things take time," my son pleaded. "We're working on it, little by little."

A few weeks later, I was frustrated and disappointed about the lack of progress on two of my business and ministry projects. What I'd planned on completing in one month had stretched out to six months and counting. It seemed that everything—and everyone—was screaming for my attention, so I couldn't devote the amount of focused attention to my projects that I'd anticipated. Then I thought of my son's words. *Big things take time.*

Noah worked on the ark for a hundred and twenty years before the flood. Nehemiah oversaw the rebuilding of walls in Jerusalem for fifty-two days. Sarah's desire to have children wasn't realized until she was ninety. I had to trust that when I was steadfast, disciplined, and committed, the works of my business, ministry, and legacy to the Lord would happen at His appointed time.

Lord, let the work that I do make a long-lasting difference.
Help me work in Your time and under Your grace.
—Tia McCollors

Digging Deeper: Proverbs 3:5–6, 16:9, 21:5; Luke 14:28

April

THE LORD IS NEAR

1 _____

2 _____

3 _____

4 _____

5 _____

6 _____

7 _____

8 _____

9 _____

10 _____

11 _____

12 _____

13 _____

14 _____

15 _____

April

16 ___

17 ___

18 ___

19 ___

20 ___

21 ___

22 ___

23 ___

24 ___

25 ___

26 ___

27 ___

28 ___

29 ___

30 ___

May

As the Father has loved me, so have I loved you. Abide in my love.

—John 15:9 (ESV)

Sunday, May 1

Call to me and I will answer you and tell you great and unsearchable things you do not know. —Jeremiah 33:3 (NIV)

My brother Howard had warned me it was coming. "We found some old files in Mom's garage," he'd said. "I'll send them to you."

They were files that Mom had kept on all of us "kids" over the years and the last things to be cleaned out of her house in California.

I was surprised at how big the box was. What could Mom have saved? She wasn't a hoarder. She'd always been practical like that. In the months since her death, I often reflected on her many good qualities, not only her practicality but also her generosity, humility, and curiosity, and how she always wanted to know about every detail of our lives. Even things I feared might bore others—some little accomplishment my boys might have made—she would be interested in.

I opened the box and was stunned. All these files. Not just on me but on each of our sons. A file for my wife, Carol. And files for different times of my life. Letters and postcards I had written home from camp or from other trips I had taken. Graduation announcements, class pictures, report cards, church programs, newspaper clippings. Cards, notes, articles I'd written, reviews of Carol's books.

If anyone wanted to do research on our lives, here was a source. But I was more touched about what it said about Mom. She cared. She remembered. She poured herself into us. She was proud of what we had accomplished. And she didn't want to forget a thing.

Love isn't something you just talk about. It's how you listen, how you invest yourself in others, how you give. Here it was in Mom's last gift.

God, show me how I can invest myself in others.
—Rick Hamlin

Digging Deeper: 1 Corinthians 13; 1 John 4:7–12

Monday, May 2

GOD'S FINGERPRINTS: The Gift of Knitting

For You created my inmost being; You knit me together in my mother's womb. —Psalm 139:13 (NIV)

Whenever I look for God's fingerprints in my life, all I need to do is remember my childhood. I never did well in school and feel fortunate to have graduated from high school. I'm dyslexic and didn't learn to read until the fifth grade. I was shamed, ridiculed, and often at the bottom of my class.

The summer I turned eleven, I longed to learn to knit. I have no clue why I found knitting appealing, as no one in my extended family had been a knitter. I pestered my poor mother until she agreed to take me to the local yarn store. There, I sat with ladies who patiently taught me. Little did I realize all the benefits that would come into my life as a result.

Because I was knitting from patterns, my comprehension skills improved as did my mathematical abilities. Once I completed my first project, I went onto knit another and then another, with a great deal of satisfaction and a sense of accomplishment. Knitting gave me a badly needed boost of positive self-esteem as I struggled through my education.

I have continued knitting all these years. My love of the craft has led to my writing stories that revolve around a yarn shop and to my position as the spokesperson for Knit for Kids, an initiative that started with Guideposts and was later moved to World Vision. Knitting took me to Kenya and Jordan, where I was able to personally distribute donated sweaters, blankets, and hats to children.

In retrospect, it's easy to see God's tender hand upon me as He gave me the gift of knitting. He brought this craft into my life at just the right time.

Lord, You knitted me together in my mother's womb and knew exactly what I needed to see me through life.
—Debbie Macomber

Digging Deeper: Psalm 139:16; 1 Peter 4:10

Tuesday, May 3

You keep him in perfect peace whose mind is stayed on you, because he trusts in you. —Isaiah 26:3 (ESV)

Our neighbors own emus.

They have a big field filled with wildflowers and bordered by a white picket fence. The emus live in the field, and when people walk by, the animals run over to the fence and stick their heads out. They are friendly and curious.

My dog, Zeke, loves those emus. Or at least he used to. Up until a few weeks ago, he would anxiously pull his leash to reach the field, then stand at the fence and stare at the giant birds, whimpering as if he wanted to go play with them.

Then something magical—or terrifying, depending on who you ask—happened. One day, as they ran toward the fence to greet us, we saw two tiny emus, fluffy and gray, trailing behind their parents. One of our emu friends had had babies!

I'm not sure whether it was the novelty of tiny fluffy birds running through a field or the surprise that his friends were no longer alone, but Zeke was completely terrified of the baby emus. As soon as he saw them, he jumped back, whined, and started shaking.

He gazed up at me wide-eyed, his eyes never leaving mine. Ever since, when we walk by that field, he averts his head to the side, his eyes never leaving mine until we pass the fence. It's ridiculous—the babies are adorable. But to him, keeping his eyes trained on what he can trust seems to be the only way to get through that long walk.

As funny as it is, I wonder if I can take the lead from Zeke and learn to do the same. When things are frightening, scary, or just new, I want to keep my eyes trained on the One I can trust.

Lord, keep my eyes focused on You as I walk through life. Amen
—Erin MacPherson

Digging Deeper: Proverbs 3:5; Romans 8:28

Wednesday, May 4

WISDOM'S DELIGHTS: Wisdom of Bearing God's Fruit

But the fruit of the Spirit is love, joy, peace, patience, kindness, goodness, faithfulness, gentleness, self-control; against such things there is no law.
—Galatians 5:22–23 (NASB)

I'm not much of a list maker—even my grocery list is hurriedly scrawled. But the one priority I try to accomplish is to answer yes to this question: Did I benefit someone today?

It could be a small thing—complimenting a parking attendant for her friendly greeting, telling her she's good at her job. Hearing her reply, "You just made my day." Or something bigger—bringing a recent widow home from surgery, checking in on her recovery, adjusting her leg wraps, delivering homemade soup.

The Galatians list is not so much a to-do list, though, as it is a way of being. In fact, the apostle Paul urged the church in Galatia to stop relying on legalistic requirements to be accepted by God. Instead, he told them to remember that Christ had set them free—that it was "faith working through love" (Galatians 5:6 NASB) that kept them right with God.

Paul then enumerated what a life lived in the presence and power of the Spirit of God looks like—and it is one list that does not make me nervous. It steadies me to know that I can grow in love and joy and peace. That kindness and goodness and faithfulness and gentleness can be my fruit. And that self-control (I do love my chocolate!) is not out of reach.

Paul concludes, "If we live by the Spirit, let's follow the Spirit as well." (Galatians 5:25 NASB) Jesus—through His life and death and resurrection—has made possible for me a Spirit-led life.

Holy Spirit, to live in Your fruit is to meet the highest goal.
—Carol Knapp

Digging Deeper: John 15:5, 8; Romans 14:17–19; James 3:17–18

Thursday, May 5

In her hand she holds the distaff and grasps the spindle with her fingers.
—Proverbs 31:19 (NIV)

I press the felting needle into the loose wool that slowly takes shape. The tiny barbs on the needle, too small to see, fuse the wool fibers together, and before you know it, a little felted owl ornament is born.

My sister in heaven had needle-felted, and I had inherited a plastic tub of her remnants and learned the craft from books and videos. When I first took on the hobby, I purchased my own wool and kept my sister's collection separate—it was special. Yet over time, that distinction has loosened, and the brightly colored wool she selected and purchased has all become one with mine.

Piercing a tiny of piece of raw wool again and again helps me work out my feelings as I silently talk to God. Right now, as this owl takes shape, I'm thinking about my oldest heading out to college and all the changes on the horizon.

"What are you making, Mom?" Henry asks.

"An owl ornament," I say. A beautiful owl born of felt—born of feelings.

It's a present for Solomon, who will graduate from high school in a few weeks. I'll fashion a tiny cap and gown on it, and it will grace our Christmas tree for years to come, to commemorate this milestone.

But felting isn't completely about the end creation; it's about the process—the beautiful letting go and working out of situations and worries, the healing that happens when I place the future in God's hands while creating something new with mine.

Dear Lord, thank You for the beautiful ways
You weave healing into my life.
—Sabra Ciancanelli

Digging Deeper: Psalm 121:1–2; Nahum 1:7–8

Friday, May 6

Show me the right path, O Lord; point out the road for me to follow.
—Psalm 25:4 (NLT)

"Let's walk down to the lake," I said to my husband, Kevin, after dinner. "Two pairs of Canada geese were there yesterday."

Kevin agreed, and we took off under ponderosa pines and scrub oak near our newly purchased cabin in northern Arizona. Hiking an elk path that led to the blacktop road, we passed the dipping blooms of Franciscan bluebells and the dainty white flowers of western spring beauty.

"I need hiking boots," I said, looking at my tennies that were more suited for an aerobics class at the gym than a jaunt over fist-sized rocks and fallen branches. "I'm feeling every rock through these thin soles."

The words had barely left my mouth when I slipped down a steep embankment. I fell hard on my shoulder in the soft mud at the edge of the highway.

"You okay?" Kevin asked.

I tested my shoulder and nodded, chagrined at my carelessness. The learning curve to cabin ownership had been steep. Wood-burning stove. Incinerator toilet. Well water. I mentally added *sturdy footgear* to the growing list of cabin needs.

Hundreds of frogs joined the ongoing evening song as we arrived at the lake. In the remaining light, we detected the silhouettes of the geese, partially hidden by the reeds in the shallows. The planet Venus peeked out from the clouds. And then I thought of another list I would write when we got back to the cabin: Honks of lifetime mates over the water. Pinks turning to violet on a sunset hike. A walking companion.

Even improper shoes would take me home.

In the new places my feet take me today, Jesus, help me see beyond the challenges to the beauty found there.
—Lynne Hartke

Digging Deeper: Psalm 119:26, 143:10

Saturday, May 7

Commit your way to the LORD; trust in him, and he will act.
—Psalm 37:5 (ESV)

Years ago, my little boys (now grown) and my dad planted lilacs near our Victorian so we'd enjoy their scent through the screens when the breeze blew. The spades were tall in my boys' hands and the ground needed Dad's strength to break. He placed the twiggy plants in the ground, and over time, they grew like wild, producing blooms deep purple and sweet.

Though we'd moved from the Victorian we loved, it still hadn't sold. The yard of the home we'd moved to was new-construction young. My ten-year-old, Isaiah, and I talked this over.

"We could plant lilacs, Mom," he said. "You love lilacs."

Off to the nursery we went. But as we headed to the register with three plants, I thought of the lilacs in our old yard. They were crowded close.

"Let's talk with someone about transplanting," I said. "About transplanting the bushes back home."

Soon we stood on familiar ground. We'd move every other lilac. Four would stay. Three would go. We trimmed branches as we'd been told.

Then Isaiah chipped at the ground.

To go deeper, I stepped on the spade. Soon we'd circled the lilac. I thought about our life and that yard that had brimmed with kids. Climbing the maple. Picnicking on blankets. Reading under the trees. The spade slipped under the bush and the roots broke. We heard them snap. My dad had been young when we planted these. And my oldest sons had grown to men. We pushed and pried until the lilac left the ground.

I looked at the young man beside me, dirt smudged over his brow. And the lilac all unearthed.

It was time for replanting.

I asked the Lord to go with us as our roots anchored anew.

Father, I trust You. I do. Amen.
—Shawnelle Eliasen

Digging Deeper: Proverbs 16:6

Mother's Day, Sunday, May 8

May she who gave you birth be joyful! —Proverbs 23:25 (NIV)

"Yesterday, I called my mom, crying," a young mom told me at MOPS (Mothers of Preschoolers), where I'm a mentor.

"Why?" I asked, curious because I learn lots from these moms living in a season different from mine.

"She always tells me how much she loved being a mom. She never talks about how hard mothering was. I asked her if she might have amnesia, because I've been having a hard time lately. My nine-month-old started crawling, which puts us in a dangerous new season. My three-year-old thinks he's a dinosaur, which he describes as the 'biggest, loudest, worst-listening dinosaur in the whole world.' So he runs and jumps and growls loudly at people, even in the grocery store. My sweet five-year-old daughter is having dramatic meltdowns."

"What did your mom say about having amnesia?" I asked.

"She said that mothering is both hard and full of joy. It is both fun and exhausting. She chooses to remember the good. Because it was."

"Did your phone call change anything for you?" I asked.

"Yes," she said, "I realize that mothering is *both...and*. I'm glad she recognized how hard mothering can be, and I'm starting a gratitude journal so I will remember all the good in this hard season."

As a mentor who wants to encourage moms of young children, I also need to remember the *"both...and"* of mothering, to both validate these moms' struggles and celebrate their joys. Mine too.

I'm thankful, Jesus, that You give moms enough amnesia to mostly remember the good, because there is so much good to remember.
—Carol Kuykendall

Digging Deeper: Song of Songs 8:7; Luke 2:19

Monday, May 9

*The L*ORD *is merciful and gracious, slow to anger, and plenteous in mercy.* —Psalm 103:8 (KJV)

I left my full-time faculty position at the University of Pittsburgh, but I still teach part-time. I love to teach but hate to grade. Evaluating student essays isn't like correcting math assignments. I have to judge the strange dance between writer and reader, the ways in which one human connects to another.

Worse, young people are often subject to wayward winds, which makes grading even more difficult. For instance, this term, I worked hard to parse the difference between a *B* and a *C* for Naomi's paper, knowing full well that Naomi had lost interest in the topic of "sustainability in Switzerland" about the same time she'd lost her job and the lease on her off-campus apartment. What grading rubric did I use for *that?*

The real irony is that *I* was not a stellar student at that age. I grappled with my own selfish interests, which did not include sustainability in Switzerland or school or virtually anything except finding something to dull the ever-growing anxiety about my life and where it was headed. So who was I to judge Naomi?

Truth is, my students are probably praying for the same thing that I am: grace and forgiveness—to receive a judgment more merciful than just, and to start anew.

Lord, Your mercy is not what we deserve, yet Your grace follows its own divine rubric.
—Mark Collins

Digging Deeper: 1 Chronicles 16:34; Romans 9:16

Tuesday, May 10

How great are his signs! —Daniel 4:3 (KJV)

God's directive floats through my head as I stand in this rural Zimbabwe landscape. Ahead, barefoot children line up quietly, holding their tin plates in anticipation of the meal that awaits.

We come here once a year to check on the progress at Village Hope, a project that God handed over to our family some years ago. We visit, enjoy the people, and assess the needs. Then we return home to Nashville and start raising money for the next year.

Village Hope started by providing food for the larger community through feeding programs at surrounding schools as well as through gardening and animal projects. Now we are also building a school and a library and supporting women's empowerment programs. Our list of new projects seems endless.

So His directive to me is a surprise: *Buy a piano.*

I shake my head as if my hair is wet or my ears are stopped up. My hand brushes across my face as if I'm swatting gnats.

Buy a piano, He says again.

"I'm sorry, this is the dumbest idea I've ever heard," I answer.

Buy a piano. He's not playing around!

"Paddington," I say to Village Hope's director, "buy a piano."

Paddington seems equally mystified. It's possible that he has never seen a piano. Certainly none of the children have.

I add, "Maybe the Presbyterian church in the city can help you find one."

Back in Nashville, the first photos arrive: a beautiful wooden piano loaded on the back of a pickup truck with a hoard of children crowded around. And later, ragged boys and girls lining up to touch the keys and hear the sounds.

So here's the place where I reveal the miracle. Except it hasn't yet happened.

God said, *Buy a piano.* His sign was clear. We moved forward, believing. I can't wait to see what happens next.

Father, sometimes, I guess, we just have to wait to see Your plans fulfilled.
—Pam Kidd

Digging Deeper: Romans 8:25

Wednesday, May 11

Do nothing from selfish ambition or conceit, but in humility count others more significant than yourselves. —Philippians 2:3 (ESV)

New York City dog runs are microcosms of the human population. You see friendly dogs and standoffish dogs, and the owners fall along the same divide. I'm somewhere in the middle. But not Gracie. As soon as we arrive at the dog run, Gracie immediately scouts for friends.

This morning she spotted a group trying to convince a Boston terrier named Barney to relinquish a tennis ball he had adamantly clamped down on. She joined them, her feathery tail swishing the air. It was quite a standoff, with the dogs in a semicircle in front of Barney, who was down on his haunches. Then all at once, he shot up, and the chase was on. Barney didn't get far before losing the ball. He skidded to a stop, but it was too late—a Lab had snatched it up. Soon it lost interest in the ball and abandoned it. Eventually, Gracie sauntered over and picked it up.

What she did next was remarkable: She trotted over to a man I recognized, who was sitting on a bench, reading the paper, his dog in his lap. The man usually kept to himself. So did his dog.

Politely as ever, and cautiously, Gracie approached. She dropped the ball at their feet, then sat. Another little standoff. Finally, the man lowered his *New York Times* and regarded Gracie. Then he smiled, picked up the ball, and gave it a little toss. Gracie bounded after it but ended up detouring to the entrance to check out a new canine arrival.

The man went back to his paper. His dog yawned and shifted in his lap. Gracie had greeted a new friend. She had done her good deed for the day. Had I?

> *Lord, in this city teeming with dogs and their humans, let me be more like Gracie and never hesitate to make a stranger a friend.*
> —Edward Grinnan

Digging Deeper: Romans 12:9–13; Colossians 3:12–14

Thursday, May 12

My child, never forget the things I have taught you. Store my commands in your heart. —Proverbs 3:1 (NLT)

I watch as a red-tailed hawk sweeps across the azure sky. Two dots follow its every move. It swoops. They swoop. It glides. They glide. Binoculars reveal the dots are its young. The hawk is teaching them the freedom of the sky. One dot veers away, then returns. The other does the same. This happens again and again, each veering wider and longer than its predecessor. At times, the little ones fly so far they disappear from my sight. The hawk doesn't follow. Eventually, its young return. But someday soon, they'll take to the open sky and won't come back.

Near our back woods, I see a mother pronghorn and its fawn. The baby's legs are splayed, its walk tentative. Gradually, it gains confidence, repeatedly trots circles around its mom, does a happy dance, tears away, then dashes back. Each leaving is a little longer, a little farther; each return is accompanied by a joyful fawn dance. The time of its venturing forth, never to reappear, will come soon.

Do these bird and animal parents find it as difficult as I did to let go, or do they just take it in stride? Perhaps they instinctively know and accept their role—to create, teach, say good-bye.

I think of my children. Each year of their lives, they, too, ventured farther from their dad and me, exploring and ultimately soaring on their own. But, thankfully, we have the blessing that, even as adults, they continue to circle back, returning often to dance at our side.

Dear Lord, Thank You for the gift of parenthood. It's hard letting go, but I know that it's all part of Your beautiful plan.
—Kim Taylor Henry

Digging Deeper: Deuteronomy 11:18–19; Proverbs 22:6

Friday, May 13

You will be like a well-watered garden, like a spring whose waters never fail. —Isaiah 58:11 (NIV)

Every year around the time my father passed away, I get a little nostalgic. I don't even notice it's coming. I find myself craving fried chicken, eyeing Diet Mountain Dew on the store shelves, and playing bluegrass gospel a little louder around the house. Then it hits me: it's almost May 19.

Each year, I try to think of something special I can do, something to show my kids, whom he never met, how special he was to me. But this year, the days were long and time was short and May 19 was—well, just about here.

I was trying to figure out what I could do when I got a message at work from my friend Matthew. He had dug up a bunch of daffodils. "Would your kids like to plant them in your yard?"

What Matthew couldn't have known is that my childhood home had been surrounded by woods that were dotted with—you guessed it—daffodils. I have so many happy memories of afternoons raking leaves while listening to Alabama football games or basketball scrimmages, all to the backdrop of those happy yellow buds.

That evening, we got right to work, digging holes along our front yard beds and dropping in the bulbs, taking care to leave their green stems pointing toward the sky. As we worked, memories flooded back, and I knew that even though I wouldn't see those yellow blooms this May, they'd be waiting for me next spring, ushering in a welcome return to May 19 with bright sunshine and joy.

Thank You, Lord, for gentle reminders that You are drawing near to us in times of joy and times of sorrow.
—Ashley Kappel

Digging Deeper: Psalm 34:18; Matthew 5:4; 2 Corinthians 5:8

Saturday, May 14

Love one another with mutual affection; outdo one another in showing honor. —Romans 12:10 (NRSV)

One day my two daughters and I were walking across the university campus near where we live, when we discovered a bird lying beside the sidewalk. The tiny creature was fully conscious, didn't look stunned or seriously injured, and yet was not using its wings. In fact, it showed no anxiety over our presence. And when my teenager knelt down and picked it up, the bird seemed happy to sit in her hands.

She, of course, then wanted to carry the bird home. We started to talk about how we could put it in a cardboard box, perhaps feed it something and call the humane society for help. Suddenly we had a plan. Our house is only about a ten-minute walk from the university, so we set off for home, the bird gently cupped in my daughter's hands.

About eight minutes later, the bird suddenly flapped its wings and flew thirty feet up into the trees. The three of us looked up at the bird and then at each other, stunned.

"Your work is done, I guess," I told my teenager.

It's interesting to imagine what happened. Did the warmth of my daughter's hands bring needed healing to subtly damaged wings? Was it just a little bit of loving care that was necessary to heal another creature? I imagine so.

Show me today, Lord, who needs my help or where even the warmth of my hands might bring healing.
—Jon M. Sweeney

Digging Deeper: 1 Peter 3:8–9; Colossians 4:5–6

Sunday, May 15

BLESSED BY ONE SWEET COOKIE: (Not?) the Boss of Me

Not every one that saith unto me, Lord, Lord, shall enter into the kingdom of heaven; but he that doeth the will of my Father which is in heaven. —Matthew 7:21 (KJV)

Awfully nice of your dog to take you for a walk!" a neighbor joked to me one day as Cookie dragged me along for the ride while she chased a squirrel. To Cookie, the word "heel" means—well—absolutely nothing.

When I was a kid growing up in the 1970s, they used to call the human the "master" of the dog. Most pet owners now prefer to call their pets "fur babies" or "companions." The newer terms describe our relationships to our pets much more accurately.

Cookie certainly never got the memo that I'm supposed to be the boss of her. When I think of how I jump up to let her in or out every time she scratches at the door, or how I always give her a little extra something to make her dog food more palatable to her refined tastes, or how I can't seem to resist those puppy dog eyes when she whines for me to come outside and throw her toy yet another dozen times. I suppose there's really little question about who trained whom.

All this makes me think of who Jesus is to me. Just because I use the term "Lord" for Him, does it really define our relationship? I can call Jesus "Master" all day long, but if I don't do what He says, it means nothing. If Jesus is my King, then I am His servant. I do what He says, regardless of whether it makes sense to me or whether I feel like doing it. Jesus is my Brother and the Best Friend I've ever had, but I must never forget that He sits on the throne—not me.

Lord, help me to be obedient to You.
—Ginger Rue

Digging Deeper: James 2:17; 1 John 3:18

Monday, May 16

SACRED SPACES: Basilica of Sacré-Coeur, Paris
Humble yourselves in the sight of the Lord. —James 4:10 (KJV)

The hot climb to this, the summit of Montmartre, had been worth the sweat and blisters. Now all of Paris spread before me. Behind me rose the majestic Basilica of Sacré-Coeur, brilliant white in the sunshine. Would the interior be as grand as its domed splendor?

I edged through the crowd and found myself in a packed church of staggering proportions. A service was just beginning. From my position far back in this sanctuary the size of a football field, I spied a seemingly endless procession winding through the standing worshippers.

Dozens upon dozens of celebrants in green vestments, some flashing gold trim, assembled on the altar. Dozens of choir members flanked them on either side. I tried to count. Were there sixty or eighty now on the altar? How many hundred worshippers? At least one thousand, maybe even two thousand. All these voices singing praise, plus the resounding organ, raised the hair on the back of my neck. Magnificent!

This pomp might have been my best take-home memory of Sacré-Coeur were it not for the elderly women seated on chairs in front of me. When the celebrant led the prayers and most of us sat with folded hands, these ladies eased themselves onto the floor. There they knelt on the cold marble, heads and hands raised in trembling supplication.

More than the pageantry within this grand edifice, their humble worship drew me closer to the divine.

Loving God, may I always approach You with a sincere heart.
—Gail Thorell Schilling

Digging Deeper: Psalm 95:6; Matthew 5:5; Romans 14:11

Tuesday, May 17

Teach us to number our days, that we may gain a heart of wisdom.
—Psalm 90:12 (NIV)

When my former work colleague, Rich, entered hospice care at home, he sent a moving note on social media, inviting friends to come visit. As Rich was very beloved, many people wanted to see him. His family created an online scheduling system to accommodate all the visitors at intervals that wouldn't overtire Rich.

I felt honored to be given one of the coveted after-work slots, but to be honest, I was a little afraid. Rich had been very ill for a while, and I wasn't sure what to expect: Would he be jovial or morose? Would he regale me with stories, like he always did, or would he be silent?

I walked in a little hesitantly, and Rich gave me his usual wide smile, lighting up his whole face, and invited me to pull up a chair. We talked about work, about how proud he was of his wife and daughters, and about his illness and how he was facing the end of his life.

Rich had always been wise, but his words that day were so inspiring that I wrote them down as soon as I returned to my car.

"I don't want to be known as a hero, and I'm not a warrior," Rich told me. "Cancer is going to do what it does, and you can't fight it. Rather, it's a test of endurance. I got some of the best care in the world, and I couldn't defeat it."

Rich passed away a few weeks later, but his positive and honest words have lived with me since. His calm wisdom showed me that he accepted what was to come and was at peace.

> *Father God, I thank You for the peace that You shower upon us in our most trying times, if we just turn our cares to You.*
> —Gayle T. Williams

Digging Deeper: Philippians 4:7; James 3:17

Wednesday, May 18

So do not fear, for I am with you; do not be dismayed, for I am your God. I will strengthen you and help you; I will uphold you with my righteous right hand. —Isaiah 41:10 (NIV)

During the months after my husband, Jack, died, I sometimes felt overwhelmed learning to live as a single woman again. I knew I had to start planning things with my friends. One day I organized a tour of some of the five-hundred-plus murals in downtown St. Petersburg with a dozen friends. It was a great day, but the idea of all that artwork painted on gigantic walls also seemed overwhelming.

Later I asked my daughter Jeanne, who teaches art at a college in California, how mural artists can keep the painting in perspective on such a gigantic canvas. Jeanne explained, "To begin a mural, you make a small painting that clearly describes the desired composition and color of the final work. Then you project the small work onto the desired wall using a small digital projector the size of your phone. Mural painting is actually easier than smaller painting because murals are created to be seen from a great distance and they are most often painted by people working collaboratively."

Collaboration. Perhaps that was the key to my single life as well. I needed to keep reaching out to find people to join me, not only socially but also in my various projects and chores.

Later, I was asked to organize a women's retreat at church. I collaborated with a whole committee of women, who met with me for weeks before the event. And it was only together that we made the day a success.

Collaboration. It's a wonderful word, isn't it?

> *Jesus, thank You for Your masterful help navigating the world as a single woman. Help me to reach out and pull others around me, just like You did on earth.*
> —Patricia Lorenz

Digging Deeper: Romans 16:1–4; 2 Timothy 4:17–18; James 1:2

Thursday, May 19

I give thanks to my God for every remembrance of you...I am sure of this, that he who started a good work in you will carry it on to completion....—Philippians 1:3, 6 (CSB)

Recently, eating macaroni and cheese at my table, a neighbor teen with special needs grew serious. "Just imagine." She paused. "What if I had never met you?"

For years now, I've been a mentor-friend—you might say a guiding hand—to her family. I've accompanied them to doctor appointments and school meetings. I witnessed her El Salvadoran mom's US citizenship ceremony. I've celebrated their birthdays. I spend hours every week with the teen, who comes over to cook or read or do homework.

"What if...?" Well, I'd taught her how to cut meat, cook eggs, wrap gifts, play "store," say mealtime grace, do puzzles, pronounce and understand new words, channel her anger, temper her fears...

But before I said a word, she lightheartedly supplied her own answer: "If I had never met you, you would never have tasted tamales or pupusas. You would never have eaten in my house." She smiled with pride—that she had given me a part of her heritage herself.

I smile, even now, days later. Her unexpected point of view—regarding how she had widened my horizons—inspires me to add to her list. She's expanded my community connections—new acquaintances with teachers and special-needs families. She's nudged me to be more flexible, generous, hopeful, and patient (though I've still a long way to go on that count). She's driven me to my knees in prayer. In short, she's allowed me to "just imagine" God's completed work.

Lord, give me and those I've come to love the grace to see Your good work in and through our relationships.
—Evelyn Bence

Digging Deeper: Psalm 20:1–5, 35:5–11

Friday, May 20

Search me, God, and know my heart; test me and know my anxious thoughts. See if there is any offensive way in me, and lead me in the way everlasting. —Psalm 139:23–24 (NIV)

I was seething that evening. I had needed to talk about something important—I can't recall now what it was—but Dave, my husband, had tuned me out, looking at the TV instead.

As I brushed my teeth, I imagined ways I could retaliate. ("Ha, I'll ignore *him* in the morning!") Not exactly cooling-down thoughts.

I knew better than to confront Dave right then. After forty-four years of marriage, we've learned to ignore that well-meant advice "Never go to bed angry." For us, an argument begun at bedtime, when we're both tired, never ends well. A small infraction tends to grow larger, and come morning, we have even more to resolve.

I prayed, *Dear Lord, I know what to do in the morning. What do I do now with my anger?*

I remembered my friend Eileen telling me about her wedding shower. Her female relatives had taken turns sharing their secrets of successful marriage. Her grandmother had spoken first: "I decided, early on, that I would automatically forgive him for ten things that make me angry. Then, when he did one of those, I'd think, 'Lucky for him, *that* was one of the ten!'"

The others loved the idea! Pens poised, they asked for her list of ten. Grandma gazed around the circle with a sweet smile, then said, "Hmmm, I never got around to writing them down."

With that reminder, I prayed for both of us. For Dave, who has forgiven me many more than ten times. And for myself, that I could forgive him this once.

By morning, I had completely lost my desire for revenge.

Thank You, Lord, for releasing my anger over a "one of the ten" infraction. Help me to be a forgiving person, every time.
—Leanne Jackson

Digging Deeper: Matthew 18:21–22; Luke 6:37; 1 Corinthians 13

Saturday, May 21

Give us this day our daily bread. —Matthew 6:11 (NRSV)

Today was one of those days when life seemed tenuous and uncertain. The world was ensnared in conflict and crisis. Over breakfast, my wife, Beth, and I discussed my approaching retirement from Mercer University and all we had left to prepare. Later, we sat at the same kitchen table and paid bills, seldom a comforting task. And as I looked at my calendar, I realized it was time for my annual physical examination. Something about this series of events and reminders set me on edge. I turned to my best friend—my young golden retriever, Lexi—and she gladly took me on a long walk.

As we rambled, I quietly grumbled and fought the clutch of anxiety. After a mile or two, sensibility and equilibrium slowly returned. I heard my own prayer voice quietly intone, "Give us this day our daily bread."

I think these seven words kept Jesus sane and balanced. He, too, learned that when you walk in partnership with God, you take life one day at a time. You focus on "this day." It may sound trite and elementary, but learning to live one good day at a time is foundational to happiness, contentment, and spiritual wholeness.

Sometimes we have to rediscover the same basic truths that have guided our lives for years, and this is one of those truths that make all the difference.

Father, may I hear Your voice whisper, "One day at a time. One day at a time. Simply one day at a time." Amen.
—Scott Walker

Digging Deeper: Matthew 6:34; Philippians 4:6

Sunday, May 22

Jesus said, "Let the little children come to me, and do not hinder them, for the kingdom of heaven belongs to such as these."
—Matthew 19:14 (NIV)

My grandchildren were always full of questions: *who, what, when, how,* and *why* seemed to be the most frequent words out of their little mouths. It could be exhausting trying to answer the barrage. Sometimes it was even annoying.

After reading a biography about author C. S. Lewis, however, I reevaluated my feelings on the matter. Lewis, who had no youngsters of his own, willingly opened his Oxford home to schoolchildren evacuated from bomb-shattered London during World War II. The experience—in part—inspired his popular children's book *The Lion, The Witch and The Wardrobe*—the first title in the Chronicles of Narnia series.

The book's publication resulted in a mountain of fan mail from around the world. Many of the letters were from children. Despite his fame and busy schedule, Lewis *personally* answered each letter. Some children wrote to him asking advice about pets, friends, and Sunday school classes. Others had spiritual questions about Jesus and heaven. He reassured many that heaven would indeed be better than Narnia.

Like Jesus, Lewis made time for youngsters. He considered it a moral obligation to answer their letters. That made me think long and hard about the way I take time to answer—or ignore—my demanding grandchildren. Patience, kindness, gentleness, and other fruits of the Holy Spirit could mature in my life if I would take the time to cultivate them. I know this is important. I know children are important too. After all, Jesus said so.

Heavenly Father, help me to patiently make time for children, just as You always make time for me.
—Shirley Raye Redmond

Digging Deeper: Psalm 127:3; Matthew 18:1–5, 18:10; Galatians 5:22–23

Monday, May 23

Martha, Martha, you are anxious and troubled about many things, but one thing is necessary... —Luke 10:41 (ESV)

"Mami, you're coming to my school for the show today, right?" my younger son asked as he ate his breakfast.

I was not eating breakfast. I was too busy packing lunch for my boys and thinking of my full day of work and errands.

"Mami!" he repeated, louder this time.

"What?" I snapped. "I already told you, I'm not sure if I can, but I'll try."

I've always made a point to attend my kids' performances at school, but this year, life was busier than ever. I stuffed the lunch bags into their backpacks and walked them to the bus stop. "Bye, guys," I said as the bus pulled up. My son looked at me with disdain and grumbled a barely audible good-bye.

I went back home and reshuffled my schedule, annoyed at how much it would set me back and add even more pressure to the rest of my week. But his disgruntled little face at the bus stop left me no choice.

I arrived at the school with a crowd of other families and took my seat as close to the front as I could. Minutes later, the children walked onstage, and I smiled when I saw Tyler.

He took his place and began to scan the audience, a look of worry on his face. I waved with both hands until he saw my face, the tension in his own instantly melting.

He performed with a giant smile on his face, and I was grateful for my decision to push away everything else crowding my day and to choose the one who mattered to me most.

Lord, remind me to look beyond the noise and worries that crowd my heart, and help me to focus on You and those You've given me to love.
—Karen Valentin

Digging Deeper: Ecclesiastes 3:1; Philippians 4:19

Tuesday, May 24

The eye is the lamp of the body. If your eyes are healthy, your whole body will be full of light. —Matthew 6:22 (NIV)

This year at my annual eye exam, I could barely read the big *E* at the top of the eye chart.

I was quickly referred to a corneal specialist at the Cleveland Clinic. After examining my eyes, the specialist said, "Well, the good news is we can fix the problem. You need to have corneal transplants in both eyes." He explained what to expect and asked if I had questions.

"How much improvement is likely?" I asked.

"It should be dramatic," the doctor said.

A few days after the surgery on my first eye, my vision was as sharp and as clear as crystal. I kept walking through the house and yard just to look at everything. It all looked new and distinct. The lines of objects were crisp and printed words bolder. I was fascinated seeing the before-and-after difference by alternately covering the repaired and unrepaired eye. The change was stunning.

Six weeks later, the second eye was done with similar results. I'd worn glasses since age thirteen, and now that both eyes were restored, the outcome was dramatic. My eyes were, perhaps, better than they ever had been.

Thrilled with the results, I began to notice another change: everything was brighter—the sun, the moon, stars, lamps, television screens, city lights, everything. And as my whole being was flooded with new light, I began to notice a difference in my spirit, attitude, enthusiasm, and even peace of mind—another surprise.

Yet even more dramatic is the indescribable gratitude I have for these gifts given to me!

Dear God, thank You beyond words for transplant donors who bring new life to others and for skillful surgeons and medical teams who do the delicate replacements. And most of all, God, thank You for guiding every step of the process and for Your healing grace. Amen.

—John Dilworth

Digging Deeper: Genesis 1:3–4; Luke 11:33–36

Wednesday, May 25

And you shall inscribe them on the doorposts of your house and on your gates. —Deuteronomy 6:9 (Tanakh)

Every door to my house has a mezuzah on its post. The one on the door to the side yard came from the synagogue gift shop. The one on the kitchen door to the backyard was a gift from a couple in our Los Angeles *havurah* (extended family). The one on the front door was given to us by our nun friend, Mother Miriam.

But the mezuzah I saw most often was one that had been made for us by our *rebbetzyn* (the rabbi's wife) as a gift for my husband, Keith, when he turned sixty. It hung on the door between the entry and the garage, and since I almost always left the house in my car, that one saw the most traffic. It was the one that kept me most aware of silently asking God, as I walked past, to be kind to us.

Ever since Keith died, I have touched that one and kissed my fingertips whenever I go to the car.

One day I was bringing groceries in from the garage, and I suddenly realized that I'd never kissed the mezuzah on my way *into* the house. Was it because my hands were usually full when I was coming in—if not with bags, then with my briefcase and books or with folders or the mail?

But the more I thought about it, the more I realized that wasn't the answer. Instead, it was because when I left the house, I wanted to be sure that God went with me and kept me safe. But when I went into the house, I was certain that God was already there, ensuring that I was always protected.

*Stay with me when I'm out and about, Lord,
and please keep welcoming me home.*
—Rhoda Blecker

Digging Deeper: Job 21:9, Psalm 36:8

Thursday, May 26

Whom have I in heaven but you? And earth has nothing I desire besides you. —Psalm 73:25 (NIV)

A mountain seems daunting when you're at the bottom looking up. But once you've climbed it and can gaze out from the top, you marvel at the view. And remember that first time you flew on an airplane and got lucky enough to sit by the window? Streets, cars, and houses took on a whole different appearance, while farms joined to form a kind of patchwork quilt.

The other day I was cleaning off a shelf when I discovered a small scrapbook of photos taken over two decades ago. Our younger son, Tim, then four, had broken his femur and had to be hospitalized in traction for twenty-six days. Can you imagine anything tougher than keeping a kid amused when he's immobilized in bed?

One of our good friends gave him a disposable camera, and the resulting scrapbook showed snapshots of family and friends looking down on him, smiling, waving, singing songs, and telling stories. It occurred to me that if someone picked up this scrapbook and didn't know what it was about, they'd be completely mystified. Why the odd assortment of characters, none seen in full? Why the background of a bland hospital ceiling?

It made me realize how little we know about a person until we consider their point of view. How are they seeing something? What is their vantage point? What would their scrapbook look like?

For twenty-six days, Tim had to see the world lying on his back. Today he's a seminary student studying to become a minister. I don't doubt that if he should ever visit a patient in the hospital, he'll know a lot about what they're seeing.

> *God, help me to see others as You see them. Let me understand and love. Help me know their point of view.*
> —Rick Hamlin

Digging Deeper: John 3:31; Colossians 3:2

Friday, May 27

Being strengthened with all power, according to his glorious might, for all endurance and patience with joy. —Colossians 1:11 (ESV)

BlueDog yawns and turns over. "Hang on, I'm almost done," I say, but he knows better. I'm putting the final touches on an illustration, which means I won't budge for hours. He sighs, but keeps a vigil of patient endurance nonetheless.

BlueDog started life as his breeding had intended—as a full-time cattle-herding dog. Putting his heart and soul into the job, he loved every moment. But after I suffered a career-altering back injury, BlueDog dedicated himself to protecting me instead of the herd. When I was forced to step away from full-time cattle ranching, my Plan B had turned into the less strenuous enterprise of illustrating children's books.

Today, BlueDog is still constantly by my side. Regardless of whether I'm checking the cow herd we summer or standing motionless for hours at a desk, he continues to do what he's been called to do.

I admired BlueDog's enthusiasm to serve in this new way. When God asked me to serve Him in a new way, I objected to the change. I didn't want to stop ranching. I rebelled, and I went through self-serving trials of denial, feelings of rejection, and deep depression. Years before that, when BlueDog had been a pup and wanted nothing more than to show me how much he wanted to obey me, I had longed to serve God as wholeheartedly as BlueDog wanted to serve me. But I had thought I would work only in my fields. I was to discover that God had a better plan.

I smile at BlueDog, content at my feet, going against his natural instincts but following his heart with the committed enthusiasm of a cattle dog. And I can only praise the Lord for taking my work and turning it into His.

Lord, let me ever serve You with patient endurance and unquestioningly throw my heart into anything You call me to do!
—Erika Bentsen

Digging Deeper: 2 Corinthians 1:6; 1 Thessalonians 1:3

Saturday, May 28

You keep him in perfect peace whose mind is stayed on you, because he trusts in you. —Isaiah 26:3 (ESV)

"Race you to the bridge!" one brother called to another. Then they bolted off like they had fire on their feet.

We were at our favorite park and the day was lush with green. My husband, Lonny, and I walked hand-in-hand as eleven-year-old Isaiah and thirteen-year-old Gabriel ran ahead. The bridge they ran toward had been built by the Civilian Conservation Corps in the 1930s. Constructed of cobblestone, it curved gently, the ends stretching out to each side of a ravine. The walls, waist high, were stone. Underneath, bramble grew thick and deep.

"Can we walk the edges?" Gabriel asked when we caught up. He sat on the wall, brown legs swinging.

"No," I said.

Lonny squeezed my hand.

"Please?" asked Isaiah.

Lonny looked at me and nodded. *Mama, they'll be okay.*

It was a place I find myself in often as I raise boys. They want to taste, feel, live, and breathe adventure; I want to hold them safe. That day it was boys and a bridge, but the lineup of similar scenarios had been long. One son desired a food sustainability research opportunity in Nepal. One worked in an inner-city hospital where a virus ran rampant. It went on and on. Life was a process of uncurling fisted fingers.

"Go ahead," I said.

And off they went. Two boys. Two sides of the bridge. Careful footsteps. One after another. As they got closer to the top, their strong legs moved faster.

Then there was sweet victory. Theirs. Mine. I know that adventure in a boy's life brings bold-hearted bravery to a world that needs it. My part, as Mama, is to trust in the Lord.

Lord, help me to trust You with what I hold dear. Amen.
—Shawnelle Eliasen

Digging Deeper: Psalm 28:7, 62:8

Sunday, May 29

I am reminded of your sincere faith, which first lived in your grandmother Lois and in your mother Eunice and, I am persuaded, now lives in you also. —2 Timothy 1:5 (NIV)

In Bible study, we were asked to tell how we became Christians. One man recounted the dramatic moment when his life did a U-turn. Someone else told of a gentle but memorable experience. I couldn't remember a time when I hadn't been a believer. *Have I missed something?*

A few days later, my brother Mike posted a picture on social media of a Bible our father had received when he was nine years old. It was inscribed by his Sunday school teacher, Mrs. Stutz, with the date "3/27/1921." The post was a vivid reminder of the faith heritage I'd received from grandparents, aunts, and parents, as well as from teachers such as Mrs. Stutz.

Aunt Annie Laurie had given me the beautifully illustrated *A Child's Book of Prayers* for my baptism. I still cherish it. She read Bible stories to me until I could read them myself. When I was five, Grandma Cue taught me the words and notes of the hymn "Wonderful Words of Life." My parents thought weekly attendance at Sunday school and church was as important as going to school. My music teacher asked me to play piano for worship when I was thirteen. The song was "I Surrender All," and I played so fast that I finished before the congregation reached the chorus.

At times I've questioned my relationship with God. My faith has changed, grown, and matured. And although I can't point to the day or hour I first trusted Christ as Lord and Savior, I am deeply thankful for the rich inheritance that has guided my walk with Him for a lifetime.

Precious Savior, keep me ready to pass on the faith at every opportunity.
—Penney Schwab

Digging Deeper: Proverbs 22:6; Ephesians 1:11–13; Hebrews 12:1

Memorial Day, Monday, May 30

Blessed is the nation whose God is the Lord....—Psalm 33:12 (NIV)

Most of the congregation wore red, white, and blue as we settled into our seats for the Memorial Day service. The choir began to sing "Mansions of the Lord," and I glanced at my husband to see tears running down his face.

My husband is a veteran, as are many in our community. Eglin Air Force Base borders the town on one side, and most of the residents here are either active-duty or retired military.

In this community, everyone relates to and understands each other based on their common experiences. They speak in acronyms like TDY, which means "temporary duty," an assignment away from home that can range from being days or weeks to being full deployments. They stay physically fit, whether retired or not. And they're deeply patriotic.

When jets fly over, people say, "That's the sound of freedom." If you're within earshot of the base at 5:00 p.m., you'll hear loudspeakers play the national anthem, and everyone pauses to salute or place their hands over their hearts until the last note sounds.

One of my favorite events is the church Memorial Day service, when patriotic songs are sung. As the armed forces salute is played, members of each service branch stand when they hear their anthem. Throughout the congregation, orchestra, and choir, men and women stand and are applauded. My husband stands at attention when the air force song is played, displaying pride for his own service as well as his father's.

How grateful I am for all of these men and women who have sacrificed their lives for the United States of America. And how grateful I am for Jesus, Who gave the most important sacrifice of all.

Lord, thank You for Your sacrifice and for this country where we can freely worship.
—Marilyn Turk

Digging Deeper: Psalm 33:12–22; John 15:13

Tuesday, May 31

There before me was a great multitude that no one could count, from every nation, tribe, people and language, standing before the throne and before the Lamb.... —Revelation 7:9 (NIV)

My children are growing up in a community very different from their parents'. While my husband and I grew up in a large metropolitan northern city, our four children are growing up in a small suburban southern town. So the racial and cultural diversity that my husband and I experienced is unfamiliar to our kids.

As African Americans, our children are often the only people of color in their classrooms, sports teams, and small-group Bible studies. They don't complain, but I complain plenty. I worry they will grow up without the racial pride my parents modeled for me and the African American history they taught me. I wonder if they feel unseen. I pray they learn to navigate being themselves and fitting in with the majority culture.

These concerns follow me daily. Yet one day, I studied a photo I had posted to social media. It included my daughter Jada's ten closest friends. These girls join us for a Bible club we recently formed—a monthly gathering for tween girls to play silly games, share their joys and struggles, and engage in a fifteen-minute Bible study that I teach. This Bible club has deepened friendships for my daughter and brought us both lots of joy.

Examining the photo revealed something to me: the girls in this group represent diverse backgrounds. They come from African American, Asian, Hispanic, and Caucasian cultures. Their parents were born in places all over the world—including Peru, Colombia, and Venezuela.

I smiled with this new revelation. The diversity I have wanted for my children is not only possible but is already a reality—in our home every month at Bible club!

God, help me to trust You to give my children everything they need.
—Carla Hendricks

Digging Deeper: 1 Corinthians 12:13–14;
Galatians 3:28; Revelation 5:9

May

THE LORD IS NEAR

1 _____

2 _____

3 _____

4 _____

5 _____

6 _____

7 _____

8 _____

9 _____

10 _____

11 _____

12 _____

13 _____

14 _____

15 _____

May

16 _____

17 _____

18 _____

19 _____

20 _____

21 _____

22 _____

23 _____

24 _____

25 _____

26 _____

27 _____

28 _____

29 _____

30 _____

31 _____

June

*Every word of God proves true.
He is a shield to all who
come to him for protection.*

—Proverbs 30:5 (NLT)

Wednesday, June 1

See what great love the Father has lavished on us, that we should be called children of God! And that is what we are! —1 John 3:1 (NIV)

I returned home after a brisk walk through the winding paths of my neighborhood, grateful for the cool shelter of my house. Not only was it hot and humid outside, but I had missed a thunderstorm by just minutes. As lightning struck and thunder rumbled, I hopped in the shower, eager to wash away the dust and sweat from my walk.

While showering, I thought, *Daddy would not approve of my showering during this thunderstorm.* Strange thought from a fifty-year-old woman who hasn't lived with her parents for nearly three decades. Even stranger for a woman whose father passed away several years ago.

Yet over the years, I have often had thoughts like these. While watching the Ravens play football on TV, I'll think, *Daddy would have loved this game.* Or, *He would have enjoyed this Civil War documentary.*

Sometimes I tear up thinking of the events he didn't live to experience. Oftentimes I chuckle thinking of situations he would have shared strong opinions about. Things like my taking a shower during a thunderstorm—an absolute no-no during my childhood. Due to my dad's cautious, sheltered upbringing, thunderstorms were occasions to sit still in a dark, quiet room, with all electronics powered down. And one should never, ever shower or bathe during a thunderstorm.

So as I showered, I washed away tears, along with the dirt and grime, grateful for the freedom to ride out a thunderstorm the way I wanted. And even more grateful for the sweet memories of the protective, loving father God blessed me with.

Lord, thank You for blessing me with a loving, protective father and for precious memories of him that bring me joy and tears.
—Carla Hendricks

Digging Deeper: John 1:9–13; 1 John 4:9–10

Thursday, June 2

The name of the LORD is a fortified tower; the righteous run to it and are safe. —Proverbs 18:10 (NIV)

There is nothing like the head-on view of the world children have. Beau, recently two and a half, is fully convinced he can ride his bicycle, which is actually a tricycle, but don't dare tell him that. He glosses over the pedals and uses his toes to zoom up and down our street with glee. Previously fearful of cars, he would now always repeat, "No cars gonna get me, Mama," a riff on my refrain of "I'm with you; the cars won't get you when I'm with you."

This time, though, he espoused, "No cars get me, Mama. I too fast. ZOOM!" and then "pedaled" off.

I took off after him, because tricycles don't come with brakes, not that he would've used them, and dragged him to the sidewalk. "Cars CAN get you, Beau," I said. "You're fast, but you're smaller than they are, and they might not see you."

I've always been one to feel like a touch of self-doubt or fear is a pretty healthy quality to possess. If I truly believed I was untouchable and all-powerful, what need would I have for God?

So that night, I reminded Beau that while he is super speedy, he's also still way smaller than a garbage truck, so we needed to pray for God's protection before our adventures—and also suit up in our helmet.

Now Beau knows that while he's not stronger than a truck, he has a copilot, even on his tricycle.

Lord, lead me as I teach my children in ways that won't break their spirits but rather bolster their confidence in You.
—Ashley Kappel

Digging Deeper: Psalm 91:1–16; Isaiah 41:10; 2 Thessalonians 3:3

Friday, June 3

O how abundant is your goodness that you have laid up for those who fear you, and accomplished for those who take refuge in you, in the sight of everyone! —Psalm 31:19 (NRSV)

"Are you kidding?" RJ said.

I glared at him. It was the first ice cream night of the season, and our godson was complaining because our usual spot was out of his favorite flavor.

"There are twenty-four other flavors," I said, trying to keep my voice even.

"I wanted the Chocolate Oreo Fudge," he groused as people in line grew restless. "Okay, how about the *Mocha* Oreo Fudge?" I asked.

"It's not the same!"

Someone behind us cleared his throat. "If you don't pick a flavor in ten seconds, I will pick one for you," I said.

Sighing dramatically, RJ selected Mocha Oreo Fudge, and we moved to a high table.

My husband saw me gearing up for a lecture on being grateful for what we have even if it's not perfect, but before I could start, he commented on how nice the barstools were. I closed my mouth and smiled ruefully.

For weeks I'd been making Charlie look at barstools online, determined to find ones exactly like the ones we currently had, which were disintegrating with age. Wayfair, Pier 1 Imports, Walmart, IKEA—I'd searched them all, complaining when I couldn't find exactly what I wanted: my old favorites.

Ice cream flavor or barstool. Money, career, or the perfect vacation. What's the difference when it comes to ingratitude? The Lord has given me, RJ, all of us so much more than we can even imagine, so much that we, indeed, take for granted as we yearn for our latest wish. Why was I expecting a child to count his blessings when I'd not learned to be grateful for mine?

Lord, forgive my ingratitude and accept
my humble thanks. For everything.
—Marci Alborghetti

Digging Deeper: Psalm 100; Luke 17:11–19

Saturday, June 4

WISDOM'S DELIGHTS: Wisdom of Joy
A joyful heart is good medicine, But a broken spirit dries up the bones.
—Proverbs 17:22 (NASB)

The literal meaning of "is good medicine" in this passage is "causes good healing." My mother—who had a mastectomy and completed cancer treatments at age sixty-nine— told me her doctor expressed enjoyment at having her as a patient. I'm sure it's because she exuded a quiet joy and confidence throughout her care, which came from the trust she had in her ultimate Caregiver.

Today's medicine understands the science behind joy and its effect on the body: dopamine and serotonin—the "feel good" neurotransmitters—are released from the brain into the body, and they positively affect other systems, including the immune system.

Even smiling can activate the flow of these important chemicals. Imagine what a spirit of joy and praise and thanksgiving can do!

Who wrote this ancient "prescription" for joy? "Solomon, son of David, King of Israel" (Proverbs 1:1 NASB), authored most of Proverbs—known as the Book of Wisdom. Earlier in Solomon's reign, God had appeared to him in a dream, saying, "Ask what you wish Me to give you." (1 Kings 3:5 NASB) Solomon asked for an "understanding heart" (1 Kings 3:9 NASB), and God responded, "Behold I have given you a wise and discerning heart...." (1 Kings 3:12 NASB)

Ultimately, however, Solomon was not able to hang on to his great wisdom. In his waning years, his heart "turned away from the Lord." (1 Kings 11:9) Trouble then came to him, and his joy was lost.

For me, the biggest joy-stealer is this very thing—turning away from God or allowing something to interfere with my closeness to Him. Communion with God—as it was for my mom—is the source of gladness in my life. It yields the "good medicine" of a joyful heart.

Lord God, help me to find my joy in You.
—Carol Knapp

Digging Deeper: Psalm 16:11; John 16:22; Philippians 4:8

Sunday, June 5

*Great is the L*ORD *and most worthy of praise; his greatness no one can fathom.* —Psalm 145:3 (NIV)

Today was youth Sunday at our church, and this year's theme was "How Great is our God?"

I always look forward to youth Sunday. I love hearing each high school senior connect their message to the worship theme in different ways. This year was even more stirring because of the theme's enormity.

Greg explained God's greatness through the development of music, Logan through a spectrum of colors, Sam through sports, and John through the universe and personal relationships. McKenzie described His greatness by contrasting stretches of dangerous rapids with pools of calm on a whitewater rafting trip, and Zoe through experiencing a fellow camper's changed heart after he confessed his sins and pleaded for God's forgiveness in the presence of his peers. Wow—so many paths describing the immensity of our God.

To hear each speaker talk about God's greatness stretched my mind to new frontiers of thinking. And even though I had heard six unique illustrations of His greatness, I had heard only six out of an infinite number of ways to describe how great our God is.

I left the service with a deeper awe of God and a hunger to explore, through other perspectives, the question of just how great He is. So now I pass onto you the same question I took away from youth Sunday to ponder: How do you describe the greatness of God?

Dear God, no matter how we explain Your greatness, we will never do it in a way that matches Your vastness! Help us to remember that You are so much greater than our biggest challenge and never too great for our tiniest need. Amen.
—John Dilworth

Digging Deeper: 2 Samuel 7:22; Job 36:26; Psalm 147:5

Monday, June 6

*L*ORD, *what are human beings that you care for them, mere mortals that you think of them? They are like a breath; their days are like a fleeting shadow.* —Psalm 144:3–4 (NIV)

A gentle breeze touched my cheeks as I sat cross-legged in the grass, watching my six-year-old blow bubbles. "Look, Mom!" she crowed as one left her wand and floated skyward. Suddenly— *pop!*—it was gone. *Just like people*, I thought with a heavy heart. *Here one second, gone the next.*

Last month, my dear grandfather had passed away. He was ninety-four and ready to join my grandmother in heaven, but the enormity of his loss was something I was struggling to absorb. I was chafing the part of God's creation that requires beautiful things and beautiful people to disappear. How could someone with such weighty presence in my life suddenly just be...gone? The void he left behind felt vast.

"Look, they're dancing!" Aurora called again. I followed her eyes and, sure enough, a cluster of glistening, rainbow-colored bubbles was twirling and bobbing in the wind. Tossed this way and that, the bubbles looked like they were dancing! It was beautiful.

True, each one did eventually pop. But then I realized, their popping wasn't the point, was it? Their point was their ephemeral dance heavenward and the glory they share with those left behind, watching them go.

Thank You, God, for helping me remember that I do not need to understand each facet of Your creation—like loss—to trust that You are at work within it.
—Erin Janoso

Digging Deeper: Job 42:3; Psalm 39:5

Tuesday, June 7

What man of you, having a hundred sheep, if he loses one of them, does not leave the ninety-nine...and go after the one which is lost...
—Luke 15:4 (NKJV)

I was entertaining my daughter, Natalie, with stories of my long teaching career at Central Christian College, but it made me sad. Most of my memories were about my failures: stupid things I'd said in lectures, methods I'd tried that fizzled, and students I could never reach.

"I did the best I knew how," I said. "I guess that's all anyone can do."

"You did great, Daddy, but you seem to be the only one who doesn't know that."

Shortly after that conversation, I received a letter from one of my first students, back in the 1970s. He told about how he came to Central as "a broken kid, with an alcoholic father and a suicidal mother. I didn't even know what a normal family looked like, until I saw Christian families like yours." He said that he'd had no clue what to do with his life but that, in my education classes, he decided that he just had to be a teacher.

He then told me about his long and fruitful career as a teacher of thousands, and he described his storybook family: a charming wife and five beautiful children.

As I reflect on his story, I have to ask myself, "How many successful students do I need to justify my years in the classroom?"

The answer: "One."

Thank You, Father, for showing me that I don't have to be a super achiever in order to be useful to You.
—Daniel Schantz

Digging Deeper: Luke 15:7; Hebrews 6:10

Wednesday, June 8

And of His fullness we have all received, and grace for grace.
—John 1:16 (NKJV)

The morning sun's rays filtered over the mountains. As I drove to my hayfield to start the task of irrigating, my mind wrestled over my Bible reading that morning about grace. Lately I'd been busier than normal, and my pace had pushed grace aside, often leaving impatience as my first response.

The engine labored as the road led up a steep hill. On my right, at the crest of the hill, rows of trees and old wooden fences led from the road to a historic ranch. A large herd of cows peacefully grazed the hillsides.

Suddenly, a small blue pickup raced from the ranch house toward the road I was on. I was only a few hundred feet from the driveway. Irritation rose inside me. *What is he doing? Doesn't he see me? If he doesn't slow down, he's going to T-bone me!* I received a small nudge: *Remember grace.* I slowed to a snail's pace.

The pickup barreled onto the pavement in front of me. The driver cranked the wheel and spun a right turn, squealing tires and leaving rubber. In a hundred feet, he wildly spun another right turn behind the thick row of trees and slammed on his brakes. A cloud of dust rose as he dashed out of the pickup.

Then as I crested the hill, I saw it: a herd of draft horses rushing toward a gate that opened onto the road. The driver swung it closed just in time.

Wow! But for him, they would have thundered in front of me. If I would have hit them, they are so tall, they would have gone through the windshield and crushed me!

I breathed deeply. Grace had opened the door for a miracle.

Lord, help me to respond in grace instead of impatience. Amen.
—Rebecca Ondov

Digging Deeper: Proverbs 19:11; Colossians 3:12

Thursday, June 9

She is clothed with strength and dignity; she can laugh at the days to come. —Proverbs 31:25 (NIV)

Madeline went to live with her daughter, Margherita, and my brother in Carmel, New York, after her husband died. In time, she developed a warm and loving friendship with my wife, Elba, and Elba and I and our two children became part of her family. Madeline attended our daughter's wedding ceremony and celebrated our family milestones. And at her ninetieth birthday, I offered the prayer of blessing for her.

Faith and church shaped Madeline's life and values. She never missed Mass on Sundays. So on the day when she was to go home to be with the Lord, the priest came to see her. He told Madeline that God loves her and then he served her Communion and gave her last rites. She was content and at peace.

Later that day, in early evening, Elba received a call from Madeline's daughter, who said, "It could be anytime." So we went to be with her. She recognized us and thanked us for coming to see her.

A few hours later, we got the call: she had passed away at the age of ninety-seven, surrounded by her family and caretaker.

I remembered how Madeline had loved to dance. When she'd become unable to walk and move around, I had held her hands, and we'd danced as she sat on the couch. She loved the moment and afterward she said, "When I get to heaven, I'm going to tell the Lord about you." I started laughing and replied, "Please let Him know all about me."

I miss Madeline's joyful spirit and love for the Lord. But I know she is up in heaven, dancing and telling the Lord all about her family—even her adopted one. Although no longer with us, she continues to inspire me to live with enthusiasm and to embrace others as family the way she did with us.

Lord, help us live a life filled with love, joy, and laughter.
—Pablo Diaz

Digging Deeper: Psalm 73:26; Matthew 5:8

Friday, June 10

Do nothing from selfish ambition or conceit, but in humility count others more significant than yourselves. —Philippians 2:3 (ESV)

On a recent Friday afternoon, I was looking forward to going home and relaxing after a long week.

While packing up to go home, I received a message from my friend and colleague Chrissa. "One of my military spouses from Fort Polk who just relocated there is having a very hard time," she said. It was Friday, so I knew she was off work, much like I was about to be.

In that moment, I had to make a decision—stay and figure it out (and sacrifice the start of my own weekend) or tell Chrissa I was on my way out of the office and would help on Monday.

Minutes later, I found myself on the phone, gathering information and resources to pass along to this military spouse who was struggling. As I glanced at the clock, I reminded myself that the privilege of serving military members is not bound by a schedule. Ultimately, the help that was needed didn't take much of my time. It was a small gesture.

I think of Chrissa's message every now and then, because it reminds me that the care and concern we bless others with have nominal cost but priceless meaning. One of the great blessings of living and working in a military community is to witness how intently care is shown to one another in both big and small ways.

On that particular Friday afternoon, Chrissa's outreach was God's message to me that we should all strive to serve with an open, generous heart and be willing to help others with extra effort.

Father, may my actions glorify You in the care, love, and understanding I show those around me in all ways. Amen.
—Jolynda Strandberg

Digging Deeper: 1 Samuel 9:4; Philippians 2; 1 Peter 2:12

Saturday, June 11

Love each other as I have loved you. —John 15:12 (NIV)

I was leaving a birthday party in a housing complex when I noticed a local television news crew setting up in the parking lot. I was curious, but they were focused on testing equipment, so I kept walking toward my car. That's when I noticed a young woman leaning against the back of a car, silently crying. I approached her hesitantly.

"Are you okay?" I asked. She shook her head.

I waited for her to say something, but her tears silently continued. I'm an instinctive hugger, but I didn't know this woman and didn't want to intrude.

"May I give you a hug?" I asked gently. She nodded, and I wrapped my arms around her while her body shook with the cries she now released.

"I can't believe that happened in the very next apartment," she finally muffled into my shoulder.

I waited. "I'm so sorry," I said, continuing to hold her.

More silence. Her crying slowly stopped and I found some tissues in my purse. I handed them to her and waited to see if she wanted to say more.

"May I pray for you?" I asked. She nodded. So I held her hands and prayed that she'd know God was with her, that she would feel His love and protection, and that she would know she was not alone.

"Can I do anything else for you?"

She shook her head. "Thanks," she said. "You gave me what I needed most."

Lord Jesus, thank You for giving me what I needed most.
—Carol Kuykendall

Digging Deeper: Isaiah 41:10; Romans 8:26–27

Sunday, June 12

You will show me the path of life; In Your presence is *fullness of joy; At Your right hand* are *pleasures forevermore.* —Psalm 16:11 (NKJV)

Late at night when the weather is good, I like to sit in the dark on my back porch, with Gracie at my side, and stare into the woods. The air is teeming with sounds and smells. Coyotes yip-howl on a distant hillside, and an owl hoots much closer. Night birds sing, quietly it seems to me, as befitting the hour. Crickets stridulate. I listen for creatures moving through the brush. Deer proceed stealthily with the caution of the hunted. Raccoons dart and stop. Chipmunks race. You can always tell a bear—they have no reason to conceal the heavy crunch of branches and leaves preceding them.

Smells wrap around the sounds. Night flowers and forest soil, the faint muddy scent of a flowing creek. The occasional passing skunk, not too close, I hope. They have their right to the woods too.

I glance at Gracie. Her nose twitches and her ears perk up. I envy her senses, so much more acute than mine. What story do they tell her? How much more does she perceive?

Finally, I still my mind, and the smells and sounds recede until there is a peaceful inner silence, a spiritual calm. I wait. I ask God if He can hear me. I wait. And I know. It's all I need to know. He is there.

By now, Gracie has fallen asleep. I scratch her head and she jumps up, ready for bed. So am I.

Thank You, God, for meeting me where I am in the world.
Your grace abounds and brings life everywhere.
—Edward Grinnan

Digging Deeper: Joshua 1:9; Job 36:11–12; Jeremiah 29:12–14; 2 Corinthians 9:8

Monday, June 13

BLESSED BY ONE SWEET COOKIE: Worthless Treasure
For where your treasure is, there will your heart be also.
—Matthew 6:21 (KJV)

Sometimes I think that instead of naming my dog Cookie, I should've named her after one of Santa's reindeer: Prancer. Whenever she gets ahold of anything new, Cookie prances around with it as though it were a bagful of diamonds. Occasionally it's a new toy I've bought her, but it can just as well be literal garbage.

The other day, I gave her a mostly empty syrup container. I thought she'd love it because she enjoys chewing so much, and I figured this way she could earn an occasional spot of sweetness for her efforts. But I found that her greatest delight came from making sure I could not retrieve the chewed-up container from her.

As soon as I walked outside, Cookie would come right up to me and dangle her prize close to my hands, only to snatch it back when I reached for it. She was so proud to be in possession of something she thought I wanted! She pranced around the yard proudly, taunting me. If she could talk, I'm sure she'd have said, "It's mine, and you can't have it!"

Later that evening, I joked to my family, "The way she brags, she ought to open a social media account!" After all, how many posts are essentially just photos of new toys? So often it seems that the joy we get from things is not so much from having the things themselves but from showing them off to others.

But my guess is that when God looks at our expensive cars and houses and whatever else, He sees those things pretty much the same way I see Cookie's empty plastic syrup bottle. And I bet we look just as silly prancing around.

Father, help me to remember to value what really matters.
—Ginger Rue

Digging Deeper: Galatians 6:14; 1 Timothy 6:7–8

Tuesday, June 14

I am the way, and the truth, and the life... —John 14:6 (ESV)

To be honest, it was a very little lie. It had slipped out after I'd been blamed for a solid week for a situation that was absolutely *not* my fault. Accused unjustly, I'd tweaked the truth ever so slightly as my frustration peaked. It was understandable, I thought, but it was also a lie—albeit one I assumed would have no repercussions.

My untruth did make the situation a tiny bit more complicated. Not a lot, but I writhed knowing I'd contributed to the mess. Still, I couldn't confess my tiny portion without having the other ninety-nine percent of the blame dumped on me by the person who was so eager to escape responsibility.

I turned to God and admitted my fault, asking Him how I could make it right. The answer I received was silence. I writhed some more.

The outer crisis soon passed. But my inner distress continued. Eventually, it began to seem unhealthy, so I asked the Lord to show me what else I needed to see. *You are being blessed with an understanding of how deeply untruth hurts Me,* came the reply.

Ah, yes! God is truth itself. Even the smallest dishonesty wounds the heart of Jesus.

Oh, Jesus! Thank You for allowing my heart to hurt like Yours. Grant me a healthy conscience, even if it hurts badly.
—Julia Attaway

Digging Deeper: John 8:1–11, 34–36, 14:15–17

Wednesday, June 15

I am with you always. —Matthew 28:20 (ESV)

I was sitting on the floor watching my seven-month-old granddaughter, Charley, play, when Jesus's words from Matthew 28:20 came to mind. For two weeks I'd had the gift of babysitting her while our daughter and son-in-law were at work. I wouldn't have traded that time for anything.

Yet I was feeling exhausted. It had been a long time since I'd had daily responsibility for an infant. I was gaining renewed insight into what the commitment "I am with you always" means.

I love Charley and would never leave her alone, even for a minute—so many dangerous temptations surrounded this delightful little girl, who could roll and pull herself across a room in a minute and who, if given the chance, would put anything and everything in her mouth.

Similarly, God's assurance of His constant presence has forever been my comfort. But had I ever thought about how deeply He must love me—and each of us—to willingly promise to care for us every hour of every day? It's not like He doesn't have anything else to do. He has the entire world under His care! Have I ever fully appreciated what God's promise—that He is always with each of us—means?

I choose to be with Charley. I want to protect her and meet her needs. And when she lets me know she wants me there and turns to me in joy, it makes my day. Isn't that how God must feel?

Dear Lord, the thought that You choose to be with me and each of Your children, every minute of every day, is astounding. May I continually turn to You, not only in need but also in joy, for that is what You give.
—Kim Taylor Henry

Digging Deeper: Deuteronomy 31:6; Joshua 1:9

Thursday, June 16

When you are praying, do not heap up empty phrases as the Gentiles do; for they think that they will be heard because of their many words.
—Matthew 6:7 (NRSV)

I was thrilled with our new apartment in downtown New London, Connecticut. Brand-new, it offered an amazing view of the city and the Thames River, right out into Long Island Sound. It was perfect, and I couldn't wait for summer so that I could start using the little porch. But we didn't make it out there once before the nightmare began.

It turned out that the street below was a motorcycle magnet. The combination of warm nights, city life, and a traffic light on the corner, where cyclists could idle and rev their engines, added up to the perfect summer storm. I didn't mind the other sounds of summer in the city—I actually enjoyed the sense of community—but the bikers were definitely a bridge too far.

For about the tenth time one evening, I asked Charlie in exasperation, "What is *wrong* with them? Do they really need to be so loud? Are they that desperate for attention?"

The next morning I realized that bikers aren't the only ones clamoring for attention. I was praying in our sunlit room, asking the Lord yet again to help me successfully complete a writing job I'd taken on. I realized I'd been pleading for the same thing, day after day, since I'd moved into the apartment. And I'd just read the passage where Jesus reminds us that the Father knows what we need without our asking.

Suddenly, for a change, it was blessedly quiet outside.

Lord, help me to be before You in silent, wordless love and trust.
—Marci Alborghetti

Digging Deeper: Luke 12:22–34; John 8:1–11

Friday, June 17

Therefore, as God's chosen people, holy and dearly loved, clothe yourselves with compassion, kindness, humility, gentleness, and patience.
—Colossians 3:12 (NIV)

I tossed a weed out of my flower bed. My underhanded throw reminded me of Dad's.

The last time we'd gardened together, he'd tossed my weeds with the same gesture. Then he began flinging my crocus bulbs aloft. I almost yelled, "No! Stop!" But it was the dementia, not him. After he went inside, I found most of my stray crocus bulbs and replanted them.

Throughout my childhood, gardening was Dad's respite from his desk job. I wasn't sure what electrical engineers did, but when I hugged him after work, I smelled his coworkers' cigarette smoke. I joined him outside whenever I could. Dad generously shared his gardening time with me, as he shared drawing and painting with my sister and woodworking with our brothers.

Dad tended all living things—tomatoes, blueberries, gladiolas, even me—with great care, attentive and unhurried. I soaked up our companionable silences and his quiet insights. Once, he taught me his method of trimming a shrub. I'd watched Dad cut branches individually, with handheld clippers, one bough at a time. I pointed out that our neighbors used electric hedge trimmers to make fast work and cleaner lines. Without criticizing anyone, he explained that new growth on a perfectly manicured cube or sphere is obvious; new growth on his bushes only adjusted the image slightly.

Dad has been gone twenty-two years, but I still think of him as I trim my shrubs to a soft profile with handheld clippers. And I smile when a stray crocus bulb blooms in my yard. It's like a jaunty wave from Dad!

Heavenly Father, thank You for loaning me my loving earthly father. How could I not picture You as kind, gentle, wise, and patient?
—Leanne Jackson

Digging Deeper: 1 Kings 3:3; Matthew 19:19

Saturday, June 18

Bear with each other and forgive one another if any of you has a grievance against someone. Forgive as the Lord forgave you. —Colossians 3:13 (NIV)

Moving forward in forgiveness looked like jars of jam. My sister had brought them for me.

Kerr jars clanked on Mom's kitchen counter. "It's homemade," she said. "Close to what Mom and Dad used to make."

There were two shiny pint-jars filled with red so deep and dark they seemed to hold secrets.

There had been silence between my sister and me for a long time. Things had happened. Choices were made. Words spilled. And trying to manage the mess had only made us messier. So it was easier to stay in our corners. Easier when her life didn't flow into mine.

But the Lord had been whispering. There are chairs at His table for those who need forgiveness. It's where the unmerited gather to receive the undeserved, unfathomable gift of grace.

I need that gift. I need that place at His table. One day I'll stand before a holy God, and the grace of Jesus will clothe me. It's pivotal. It's personal. It's the truth I base my life on.

And as I sit in my mother's kitchen, while she and my sons chat in the next room about school and their swim team and movies on TV, I know that forgiveness must flow forward. We can't receive without willingness to give. I see this understanding on my sister's face too. I see it in green eyes that are like mine. Maybe one day we'll talk about happened. Or maybe we'll never walk that ground again. But the Lord had brought us to a place of grace.

I wrapped my hand around a cool jar.

"Thank you," I said.

My sister nodded.

The jam did taste like our childhood. Mostly it tasted like sweet grace.

Lord, thank You for forgiving me. Help me to give and receive forgiveness. Amen.
—Shawnelle Eliasen

Digging Deeper: Ephesians 4:31–32

Juneteenth and Father's Day, Sunday, June 19

In Christ Jesus you are all children of God through faith.
—Galatians 3:26 (NIV)

My eyes scanned the crowd. There were probably a couple hundred people. Lines formed behind food trucks offering southern barbecue and organic fruit smoothies. Vendors displayed Afrocentric jewelry, graphic T-shirts donning poignant mantras and quotes, and children's books featuring multiethnic characters and themes.

My family had also left the cool comfort of home on this afternoon to venture downtown to celebrate. It was Juneteenth, a holiday commemorating the emancipation of enslaved people in America. For many years, African Americans have celebrated June 19, 1865, the day that enslaved people in Galveston, Texas, were notified of their freedom—freedom that had been granted two full years earlier by President Abraham Lincoln's signing of the Emancipation Proclamation.

After witnessing increased levels of racial tension in our community and the country, my husband and I have more intentionally exposed our children to racial discussions and teachings. They attend a biweekly gathering that my husband cofounded, which leads a community conversation on racial justice and unity. We have movie nights to view documentaries and movies that spotlight African American history and the fight for equality and justice. I encourage them to read books that highlight history that they have most likely missed in school. And this year, our local Juneteenth celebration served as an additional family learning experience.

As we listened to speakers share the significance of the holiday, I was grateful to witness a diverse group of people around me, celebrating in solidarity and honor of our past and in hope for a more just and equitable world, both for our children and our children's children.

Lord, help me teach my children to honor our past and grow in hope for the future.
—Carla Hendricks

Digging Deeper: Galatians 3:28; Philemon 1:12–16

Monday, June 20

But ask the beasts, and they will teach you; the birds of the heavens, and they will tell you. —Job 12:7 (ESV)

A cute picture on social media led me to the pet rescue website, looking at two teeny-tiny kittens. Their story was compelling: siblings, found barely alive in a box beside an interstate in Atlanta.

My heart went out to them, and for a second I thought about giving them a home, but worry stopped me. I'm a planner, and acting on a whim—especially when that meant taking on two more kittens—seemed crazy. Days went by, and I kept checking back, looking at their picture.

One morning their listing was gone. My heart sank. Just then the image loaded at the bottom of the page. I filled out the application and said a prayer, asking that the kittens find the right home.

In days, the kittens were bouncing around our house, bringing life to one of my favorite quotes from the classic movie *Harvey*: "In this world, you must be oh-so-smart or oh-so-pleasant." Of the two cats, Gillie is the pleasant one—he's long-haired and goofy, and he gets along with everyone. Sherry, on the other hand, is ornery but brilliant. She can open doors and will tear into any kitty treats she finds hidden in the cabinet.

A few minutes ago, Sherry chased Gillie down the stairs, onto the couch, and across the dog, before zooming back upstairs, making us all laugh. Now Gillie is perched in the top tier of a playhouse made out of old boxes, and I am reminded of how, the other day, my son Henry said, "Mom, it's hard to remember what it was like before we got them. They were a perfect find."

Dear Lord, thank You for the nudge from above that opened my heart to these brilliant and pleasant kitties and helped me recognize that, sometimes, my whims are Your will.
—Sabra Ciancanelli

Digging Deeper: Genesis 1:21; Proverbs 27:23

Tuesday, June 21

GOD'S FINGERPRINTS: The Blessing of My Husband

So they are no longer two, but one flesh. Therefore what God has joined together, let no one separate. —Matthew 19:6 (NIV)

God's fingerprints in my life have never been more apparent than when I met the man who would become my husband.

Shortly after graduating from high school, I'd moved to Seattle with a friend. Eight of us lived together in a large, rented house. Typically on a Saturday night, we'd all have dates lined up. I'd seen Gunther a couple of times and was dressed and ready to go when he called and canceled at the last minute. So after everyone else left for a night out, I sat in the house alone, feeling sorry for myself. Just as I was about to change clothes, the phone rang. It was Wayne Macomber. He asked for Neater. (I don't remember her actual name, but we called her Neater because she was neater than the rest of us.) When I explained that Neater was out for the evening, he asked if I would be interested in attending a movie with him instead.

Wayne was different than any man I'd dated. He was nearly five years older and something of a "bad boy." We were as different as night and day; he was unchurched and raised by a single mom. I came from a large extended family and had been to church every Sunday of my life. Despite our differences, Wayne was mature, caring, and gentle, and before long we fell in love.

If Gunther hadn't canceled our date, I would likely never have met Wayne. Later, when I decided to follow my dream of writing books, it was Wayne who encouraged and supported me.

Looking back, I see God's fingerprints all over our meeting and our life together. I have to believe Wayne was the man God had chosen for me.

Thank You, Father, for my husband, who has been a source of encouragement and love through the years. I am blessed by him.
—Debbie Macomber

Digging Deeper: Genesis 2:18; Psalm 37:4

Wednesday, June 22

Husbands, love your wives, just as Christ loved the church and gave himself up for her. —Ephesians 5:25 (NRSV)

Carol's napkin is still sitting on the table after dinner. After she's put her plate in the dishwasher and I have attempted to do the dishes. That's the deal we've had ever since our early years of marriage: She cooks dinner. I do the dishes. A division of labor. She's a better cook than I am, and I don't mind cleaning up.

But that napkin in its napkin ring. Why didn't she put it away in the drawer? I'd put mine away in the drawer, so that it's there, ready for dinner the next night and the next. What if I were to leave her napkin on the kitchen table all night? That way, she would have to look at it at breakfast, wondering why it was there. Wouldn't that teach her a lesson?

Wait, though, what lesson am I really wishing were taught? I turn back to the dishes in the sink. Remnants of the tomato pasta sauce she'd made from scratch and the fusilli in the colander that we can save for a next-day snack or lunch. And the salad in the big wooden bowl. She was the one who had bought the arugula and the endives and the romaine lettuce, which she had then washed and dried before dinner. Did I thank her for that?

I turn back to her napkin in its napkin ring. Isn't there lots she does for me, especially around the house? Wouldn't it be nice to do this favor for her? Gratitude can express itself in many ways.

I rinse the dishes, rinsing my own soul of its selfishness. Then I put the dishes in the drying rack and Carol's napkin ring in the drawer. The least I can do.

> *Let me be big, God, not small-minded, not petty.*
> *Let me love as You love.*
> —Rick Hamlin

Digging Deeper: Proverbs 17:9; 1 Corinthians 13:4; 1 Peter 4:8

Thursday, June 23

When the cares of my heart are many, your consolations cheer my soul.
—Psalm 94:19 (NRSV)

Every child says cute things—I know that. I don't share this with you because I think my child is more special than your child or grandchild. I share this because, this year, I am trying to learn from my eight-year-old daughter.

Last month, I was in a park not far from our house, pushing her on a tire swing.

"Push harder, Daddy!" she said, after a few minutes. I guess the velocity wasn't quite satisfying for her. But I had reasons for the pace of my pushing.

"I don't want to make you dizzy," I said. I was already, frankly, becoming dizzy just watching her go back and forth.

"I promise I won't get dizzy!" she yelled back, clearly wanting more excitement out of this routine activity.

"Okay, but I sure would," I said.

And then, "That's because you're old and need a vacation!"

Now, what would make her think that I'm either of those things? Kids see through us. She must be hearing me groan about aged creakiness and complain about too much work on my desk. But I don't want her thinking that's how I always feel, because I'm also thankful and grateful and energized.

> *God, help me to be upbeat today. Help me to show on my face, in my words, and in my actions that I'm excited for a new day.*
> —Jon M. Sweeney

Digging Deeper: Matthew 6:22; Mark 10:13–15

Friday, June 24

And my God shall supply all your need according to His riches in glory by Christ Jesus. —Philippians 4:19 (NKJV)

When my brother retired as a commercial airline pilot, I flew to Louisville for his last landing ceremony and retirement party. Because there were so many family members in town for the festive weekend, my son, grandson, and I stayed at the house of one of my sister-in-law's best friends. Barb was out of town for the weekend, and her home was better than a five-star hotel.

In the morning, as I enjoyed a cup of tea and raisin toast in the kitchen, I noticed a plaque on Barb's wall that read, "Life is a journey. Enjoy the ride." I pondered my own journey through life and decided that I am, indeed, enjoying the ride, even though sometimes it feels like the struggles outnumber the easy times. But another plaque in Barb's beautiful home said, "Don't worry about tomorrow. God is already there." Well, now, if that didn't take care of the struggles part of my life, I don't know what did.

It's such a simple truth, but one I often forget: God is already there, no matter where my journey is taking me. Whether it be through scary travels, sickness, the death of a loved one, health problems, financial struggles, or sad times with friends, God is already there to comfort me and lead me through the difficult times.

So now wherever I go in this world, I try to picture God Himself arriving there just ahead of me, welcoming me with open arms, with love, comfort, and compassion, and with a warm hand in mine, as we take the journey together.

Heavenly Father, never let me forget that You are the power beyond my comprehension—One Who is there for me every single minute and step of my journey.
—Patricia Lorenz

Digging Deeper: Matthew 6:8; Philippians 4:10–13; Hebrews 6:4–6; Revelation 21:23–25

Saturday, June 25

Then you can tell the next generation detail by detail the story of God, Our God forever, who guides us till the end of time. —Psalm 48:14 (MSG)

"Never abandon the dreams of your youth" was the fortune cookie message. My then-high-school-aged daughter, Jenn, and I had just finished our China King Buffet meal. Jenn asked me, "What were your dreams when you were a kid, Dad?"

With little hesitation, I told her about the pinewood apple-crate race car I made when I was nine years old. "I still remember the pleasure I felt painting red flames on it. My dream? When I grew up, I'd have a pickup truck with flames!"

As a result of this conversation, we began an artistic project, spraying blazing yellow and red fire on my bird's-egg blue 1979 Chevy Light Utility Vehicle (LUV). The flame truck served me well. It was a favorite, especially when we were later stationed at Fort Riley, Kansas. In fact, folks still ask about it, but alas, due to too much rust, the truck ended up in the junkyard. I miss it even today.

However, for my birthday last year, I received a long cardboard package from an unknown address. Inside were silver flame decals. Immediately I knew they were from Jenn. So on a sunny day, I transferred the shiny designs onto my 2013 Chrysler 200, which is deep-gray with a tungsten-metallic clear coat. The discreet flames added a touch of real "hot-rod class" to my otherwise staid vehicle.

The silver flames continue to bring great delight. To see them is to recognize how grateful I am. From the dreams of my youth, God has shown me the way. He shepherded me through paths of army chaplain service, including many enjoyable moments in my '79 Chevy LUV. Now our Lord continues to attend to, pilot, and guide my way. And for that, I am thankful.

Heavenly Father, thank You for Your detail-by-detail sustaining presence along these many roads of life. We go forward into a hope-filled future, assured by Your safeguarding hand.
—Kenneth Sampson

Digging Deeper: Romans 8:24, 12:12; 1 Peter 1:3

Sunday, June 26

If you pour yourself out for the hungry and satisfy the desire of the afflicted, then shall your light rise in the darkness.... —Isaiah 58:10 (ESV)

Volunteers from my church lead a weekly Sunday morning worship service at a nursing home. Several years ago, I signed onto the pianist rotation. I've grown accustomed to the dutiful routine: play three congregational songs, lead the liturgical responses, and then wander about, turning worship-book pages for physically compromised worshippers. *Ministry accomplished. Good-bye!*

But this week, the Spirit turned duty to delight. It started when I overheard an aide joking with a young resident who always sits soberly and silently in a back corner. "You're late for church," she said, knowing he was ten minutes early.

He laughed. "No, I'm not." *Who knew? He anticipates taking his place in the faith community.*

We sang. We read Scripture. I led the prayers. Amid the personal requests, I was heart-struck by a woman's most basic thanksgiving "that I was finally able to take a shower yesterday." *Lord, have mercy.*

After the leader said, "The peace of the Lord be always with you," I walked the room, touching the hands of every participant. Why was I surprised that all fifteen returned a godly greeting? *Peace.*

The leader whispered to me, "I'd appreciate your help distributing Communion." So instead of playing hymns, I held a chalice while approaching each congregant. I looked into the eyes of believers as they eagerly opened themselves to receive the blessed bread and wine. *Amen.*

Then as one voice, we sang "This Little Light of Mine." It wasn't my light shining on them—it was our lights shining on one another.

I walked to the car, inspired by a new view of ministry: "Everywhere I go...let it shine."

Holy Spirit, today, please turn a duty to delight.
—Evelyn Bence

Digging Deeper: Isaiah 58:11–14, 60:1

Monday, June 27

A friend loves at all times, and a brother is born for adversity.
—Proverbs 17:17 (ESV)

Upon my daughter-in-law's urging, I joined a social-media site. It was exciting to find so many friends and relatives, some new and many I had not seen or spoken to in years.

Soon, I was checking to see the latest "news" from my friends, sharing in their joys, disappointments, and life in general. I joined various groups with similar interests and felt connected to more people than ever. And on my birthday, I got more well-wishes than I'd ever had!

But then friend requests from people I didn't know arrived. At first, I was happy to be so popular, but when my account was hacked, I discovered some people wanted to cause me harm. I became wary and suspicious of anyone requesting to be my friend.

And that got me thinking, *What is a true friend? Who are my real friends?*

The first person I thought of was my friend Rosemary, whom I've known all my life. She's truly my closest friend—actually more like a sister, since we met in the church nursery as infants. Although our lives have gone different ways and we now live in separate states, we've stayed best friends over the years. Even after long periods without talking to each other, we can still pick up our conversations where we left off. Rosemary knows the whole story of my life and still loves me.

True friends are blessings—God's gifts to us—and I want to treasure the ones I have.

And so, as much as I enjoy the connections I've made on social media, I think I'll reach out to Rosemary today.

> *Lord, thank You for true friends. And thank You for being my real friend, who loves me at all times.*
> —Marilyn Turk

Digging Deeper: Proverbs 27:9; John 15:13–15

Tuesday, June 28

No discipline seems pleasant at the time, but painful. Later on, however, it produces a harvest of righteousness and peace.... —Hebrews 12:11 (NIV)

The sun's rays were relentless. Sweat trickled down my brow as I tried to ignore my pulse pounding in my ear. I slogged forward, one foot in front of the other, up the hill. It was a beautiful day, and—usually—jogging was one of my favorite ways to be outside. But it was June in Fairbanks, Alaska. The snow had only been gone for a month, and these sudden summertime temperatures felt hot indeed. Plus, this grade was besting me. *I should've taken the easier route*, I thought. *The one without hills.*

I ventured a glance toward the crest. *Ugh. Not even halfway there.* I worked to control my ragged breathing. *In, hold for a sec, out. In, hold, out.* Finally, I reached the top. As I paused to recover, my eyes wandered out over the valley below. An expanse of dazzling emerald green, dotted here and there with the deep pink of wild roses, stretched almost as far as I could see. Overhead, azure skies dazzled, interrupted only by a distant, dark cloud rimmed in gold by the sun. It was pouring a shimmery gray veil of rain onto the snow-white peaks of the Alaska Range far beneath it. My breath caught in my throat. The sight was stunning beyond words. And to think—if I'd taken the tempting, easy route, I would've missed it entirely.

As I resumed my jog, my feet felt lighter, my steps easier. And my heart was filled with gratitude. Sometimes the path God sets before me feels like an uphill battle, but the reward He has in store is worth it every time.

Lord, Jesus knew what awaited Him on top of Calvary's hill, yet He was not tempted away. The value of what He achieved there is beyond measure. Thank You.
—Erin Janoso

Digging Deeper: Psalm 37:5–6; Matthew 16:21–23

Wednesday, June 29

For I know that good itself does not dwell in me, that is, in my sinful nature. For I have the desire to do what is good, but I cannot carry it out. —Romans 7:18 (NIV)

News reports said one in four birds had disappeared since 1970. At first I thought they meant species, but they meant the actual number of birds—the world population. Soon after came news that the insect biomass—the world bug population, calculated by weight—had decreased even more rapidly.

Since birds eat bugs, both news items were horrifying to bird-watchers like me. I've gotten a flood of donation requests from conservation groups since then. I guess that many pleas for help must garner a response, right?

Well, the email deluge didn't work on me. While I sometimes donate in the form of membership fees, it's always to obtain new date guides for bird arrivals or some online birding tool. And although I do spend regularly to fill my feeders, I do it so I can see them eat. When it comes to being squeezed for unconditional donations, however, I'm the hardest rock out there: a diamond.

I wish I had the money to be more generous. After all, God cares about birds. In comparing people to sparrows—which many birders disparage as LBJs (Little Brown Jobs), hardly worth counting—Jesus says God doesn't forget a single one. The Bible even has bird conservation commands: If you find a nest, you're not to take the mother along with the eggs or chicks.

If I can't support beautiful disappearing creatures that I flat-out love, how will I ever embrace commands to love my neighbor—and my enemies!—anywhere as much as I love myself? I'd be lost without Jesus beside me, helping me carry out the good.

Father, open my heart to love according to Your greatest commands.
—Patty Kirk

Digging Deeper: Deuteronomy 22:6–7;
Matthew 6:25–33, 11:28–30; Luke 12:6–7

Thursday, June 30

Those who love me I love, and those who seek me will find me.
—Proverbs 8:17 (Tanakh)

In the past, whenever I was angry or anxious or if work was going badly or the news was upsetting or I was just plain worried, my husband, Keith, would point silently at the ceramic plaque on the wall of my office. It was a solidly beigy-cream color, with slightly raised letters that read, "Be still and know that I am God." Because there was little difference between the words and the background color, it was easy to glance past it without paying attention—and I often did.

After Keith died and wasn't here to point out the plaque to me, I forgot it was there at all. In fact, I had crowded my schedule with activities just to help me get through every day and to still feel needed.

In addition to all my teaching, I served on five committees at the synagogue. The synagogue community was very important to me. It had supported me through Keith's illness and held me together with understanding and compassion while I was grieving. So while I'd served on a couple of committees before, after Keith passed, I upped my volunteer hours significantly.

Soon, it seemed as if I was always running to one meeting or another, and the meetings usually involved a good bit of argument—we Jews are inveterate arguers.

Then one rare afternoon at home, I sat at my desk feeling exhausted, as if I'd somehow lost more than just Keith. I looked up and suddenly saw the plaque in sharp focus. I realized then that my constant activity had not only kept me from being still; it had kept me from being aware that all my synagogue service was not just for the community, precious as that was to me, but also for the One the synagogue existed to honor.

Thank You for always reminding me that You are there for me.
—Rhoda Blecker

Digging Deeper: Deuteronomy 12:28; 1 Chronicles 28:19

June

THE LORD IS NEAR

1 _____

2 _____

3 _____

4 _____

5 _____

6 _____

7 _____

8 _____

9 _____

10 _____

11 _____

12 _____

13 _____

14 _____

15 _____

June

16 _____

17 _____

18 _____

19 _____

20 _____

21 _____

22 _____

23 _____

24 _____

25 _____

26 _____

27 _____

28 _____

29 _____

30 _____

July

Let the message of Christ dwell among you richly as you teach and admonish one another with all wisdom through psalms, hymns, and songs from the Spirit, singing to God with gratitude in your hearts.

—Colossians 3:16 (NIV)

Friday, July 1

In the morning sow thy seed, and in the evening withhold not thine hand. —Ecclesiastes 11:6 (KJV)

As an investment adviser, I never tire of studying the world's great financial icons. There's Sir John Templeton, a fellow son of a Presbyterian minister, who was knighted by the queen of England for his expertise. There's Peter Lynch, of Fidelity Magellan, who achieved historic returns of a mutual fund during his tenure. And then there's the best of the best, our modern-day Warren Buffett. There are scores of storied investment successes from these kings of finance, but there's one more accomplished investor who is high on my list, and one a bit closer to home: my mom.

I entered the business just after college, and she embraced my decision hand over fist. Her knack for picking good stocks was an added surprise. Her method never changes: find companies who treat their employees fairly and make the world a better place. Period.

And why should I be surprised? She's only investing her savings the way she invests the rest of her life. She is an investor in people. She believes in them, and she funds them with her time and her love. From the expanding project in Zimbabwe that she and my father founded to her work with Nashvillians in need, her investments pay big dividends—for others.

Warren Buffett once said, "The incredible thing about love is that you can't get rid of it... people who just absolutely push it out, get it back tenfold."

Sounds just like something my mother would say.

Love. There's no better investment.

Lord, help me to be an investor in people—the greatest investment of all.
—Brock Kidd

Digging Deeper: Proverbs 11:9; Isaiah 58:10

Saturday, July 2

Thanks be to God for his indescribable gift! —2 Corinthians 9:15 (NIV)

It was the eighteenth anniversary of my father's death, and I still missed him terribly. I was doing okay until I wandered into an antiques mall and ran into Tom, one of Daddy's old horse-trading cronies.

When I was a little girl, the two of them had hawked their wares at weekend flea markets. Sometimes Tom dropped by our house to check out Daddy's latest find. I'd sneak to the top of the stairs to eavesdrop on their banter. Invariably, Daddy would counter Tom's offer, insisting he'd have to have something "to boot." That meant Tom needed to add more to the bargain.

Now Tom placed a frail hand on my arm and said, "I'll never forget when I tried to talk you out of your Shirley Temple doll, Roberta. I pulled out a crisp twenty dollar bill. Those big blue eyes of yours looked up at your dad, then checked me over, and you said, 'Okay. But I'd have to have a little something to boot.'"

Suddenly, I was that pigtailed kid again, the one who worshipped her daddy. Grief moved into every cell of my body. I could barely breathe.

"When I think of your father, I remember the things he gave *me* to boot," Tom said. "Stories he'd spin about growing up on the farm. The way he topped a saltine cracker with that sharp cheddar cheese he'd peeled off with his pocketknife..."

I added my own "to boot" moments to Tom's list. Then God seemed to whisper, *I've given you some things "to boot," too, Roberta.*

Not just a home in heaven where I'd be with my earthly father forever. But tools for today: His peace, joy, and love to help me through the hurting.

My "to boot," heavenly Father, is to thank You for Your great gifts to me.
—Roberta Messner

Digging Deeper: 1 Corinthians 12:7; Ephesians 2:8; James 1:17

Sunday, July 3

BLESSED BY ONE SWEET COOKIE:
Help in Times of Trouble

Do not let your hearts be troubled and do not be afraid. —John 14:27 (NIV)

Cookie has two least favorite days of the year: New Year's Eve and Fourth of July.

My usual fun-loving pup is, like many dogs, terrified of fireworks. Whenever revelers gather and make things go *kaboom*, Cookie loves me more than ever. Not only does she jump right into my arms, but she even curls her paws around my shoulders as though she is hanging on for dear life.

My heart goes out to her when she's fearful like this. Try as I might, I can't make her understand that I can protect her and that this will soon pass. Even as I hold her, she pants and shakes, but I know that she appreciates my being there. My presence doesn't take away her anxiety altogether, but at least I can offer some level of comfort.

On these occasions, I think of all the times in my life when God has held me and comforted me. I love God every day and am always happy to be in His presence, but when I'm most afraid, I suppose it is then that God feels the most near to me.

I guess that's the mystery of "the peace that passes all understanding" (Philippians 4:7)—that the Comforter's arms hold us ever more tightly when we are helpless. Nothing can separate us from God, and, in fact, the difficult times only draw us even nearer to His presence.

Lord, You alone can calm my fears and soothe my soul.
—Ginger Rue

Digging Deeper: Joshua 1:9; Psalm 23:4; Isaiah 43:1

Independence Day, Monday, July 4

Act as free men, and do not use your freedom as a covering for evil....
—1 Peter 2:16 (NASB)

I grew up in the Philippine islands, where my parents were missionaries. We moved there a decade after the end of World War II. The Philippines were the location of some of the fiercest land, sea, and air battles in that war. Military and civilian casualties were horrific. My parents lost many friends during that global conflict.

I remember, as a six-year-old boy, attending my first Independence Day celebration in the Philippines. Many shared out loud their vivid memories of the horrors of war and the cost of freedom. As a military band played national anthems, both the American and Filipino flags were raised.

What I most recall was looking up into my father's face as the flags fluttered. My father was a tough and burly cowboy from Colorado. He loved rodeos and bull-riding. He was as stout as a stump and as intense as a tornado. But on this day, tears flowed silently down his cheeks. It was the first time I saw my father weep. I instantly knew that we were experiencing a serious and poignant moment. Now when I think of patriotism and the cost of freedom, I always recall this Independence Day moment.

There is an old American folk saying that "Freedom isn't free!" Even a young boy could intuit this truth on that Independence Day in 1957.

Dear God, help us to live in responsible freedom. Amen.
—Scott Walker

Digging Deeper: 2 Corinthians 3:17; 1 Peter 2:16–17

Tuesday, July 5

She is not dead but asleep. —Luke 8:52 (NIV)

"Didn't you hear that Lydia passed away? It was weeks ago. It was in the paper."

I couldn't reply. My heart felt ripped from within. I had respected Lydia. We had collaborated on community projects, and hers was a friendly face at meetings.

All day I felt sick, imagining everything I wished I'd have said to her to let her know how much she had inspired me—her presence, wisdom, and sense of style; the neatness, precision, and professionalism she displayed in her career; and her business savvy and calm, commonsense leadership in our ranching community. She was, in a word, classy. The shock of hearing she'd contracted a sudden illness and passed away was tough to take. She wasn't even old.

The news was too abrupt. It wasn't fair. But it was too late.

Late that evening, I received word that it was someone else with the same name who had passed away; my friend was still very much alive. Although I was sad for that family's loss, I let out a joyful whoop as the cloud over my heart lifted. And in its wake came the determination to not let this moment, this precious gift of time, go to waste. My chance to tell her how much I'd like to be more like her was now.

I now know someone who died and was brought back to life; nothing as dramatic as it was with Jesus and Lazarus, but heartrending and joyous nonetheless. And it got me thinking of others who have inspired me with their special talents and personalities. Maybe this was the time to tell them too. What was I waiting for?

I praise You, Lord, for the inspirational people in my life.
Thank You for this unexpected second chance.
—Erika Bentsen

Digging Deeper: Philippians 3:17; James 5:10

Wednesday, July 6

The wind blows wherever it pleases. You hear its sound, but you cannot tell where it comes from or where it is going. So it is with everyone born of the Spirit. —John 3:8 (NIV)

Most times the Spirit of God is at work in our lives without our knowing which direction we are being led.

One afternoon I was at the office, writing my weekly blog. In the blog post, I was reflecting on a time when the Spirit had nudged me to resign my position at a nonprofit in California and return to New York to be a pastor. Then my cell phone rang. I didn't know anyone with a 727 area code from Clearwater, Florida, but then I heard a voice within say, *This could be a call from a church seeking a pastor.* Pressed for time, I decided not to answer the call.

Once my blog was finished, I checked the voice mail. "Hi, this is Dave. I'm the chair of the Interim Search Committee. We are wondering if you are interested in being a candidate for our church in Dunedin, Florida. If so, please give me a call back. Thanks." The first thing that came to my mind was the still, small voice that had been nudging me when the phone first rang.

I returned the call and agreed to be a candidate for the interim pastor position. The process took four months, and in the end, they selected me to be the transitional pastor at Saint Andrews Presbyterian Church. Looking back on that day, I realized the Spirit was moving and preparing me for my next place of ministry.

Lord, help us to hear and discern where Your Spirit is leading us.
—Pablo Diaz

Digging Deeper: Deuteronomy 4:12; Isaiah 30:21

Thursday, July 7

Mary has chosen what is better, and it will not be taken away from her.
—Luke 10:42 (NIV)

We went to the cardiologist today. When it was time to go in, Joan collapsed and her left side was limp," my father texted, "Fortunately, the emergency room was only fifty yards away."

Joan is my mom. She had had a stroke.

Granted, she'd had it in the most convenient location possible. She was taken for a scan, then admitted and taken to a different floor. Unfortunately, no one thought to tell my dad, who was waiting in the ER, where she had been taken. Doubly unfortunately, there was a no-visitors policy in effect at the hospital, so he didn't get to say goodbye before he went home that night. He didn't get to explain to staff that my mom has Alzheimer's, and he wasn't able to comfort her in her confusion. He drove home alone, not knowing if he would see his wife of sixty-three years again before she died.

It sounded pretty awful. I had to remind myself that feeling helpless is different than *being* helpless. While it was true that we couldn't visit, advocate in person for my mom's care, or hold her hand and tell her that we love her, we could still use the time God had given us faithfully.

We could call the nurses' station regularly, talk to my dad to offer support, and be thankful my mother had access to good medical care. It wasn't what I wanted, but it certainly focused my heart more fully on prayer than if I had been able to take action. The Martha in me was forced to be a Mary.

Fortunately, in a few days my mother could talk on the phone. A few days after that she was released. Giving thanks was substantially more intuitive than it had been.

Father, help me do what You ask instead of bemoaning my inability to serve in the way I desire.
—Julia Attaway

Digging Deeper: 1 Thessalonians 5:18; Hebrews 13:20–21

Friday, July 8

The LORD is close to the brokenhearted and saves those who are crushed in spirit. —Psalm 34:18 (NIV)

As I walked the dog under the treehouse that my nephew Jer built for my sons, I started thinking about how much I missed Jer and how much I wished he were here and not in heaven. I touched the nails on the treehouse ladder, thinking of his hands that had hammered them into the wood. He had been the one who wanted to build it so that part of the tree would come up through the floor and make a nice place to rest your drink while you played chess.

Soda nudged me closer to the edge of a property, and a single sad goose cried out. I'd never seen a single goose before, so I wondered if it was sick. It flew away to the neighbor's yard, where it once again wailed a lonely cry.

Back in the house, I researched what would cause a goose to be alone and discovered that if one goose falls ill and can't continue on with the flock, another goose will stay behind until the ill one gets better or passes. When you encounter a single goose, you are usually witnessing the goose that stayed behind, now on its journey to return to the group.

I went out to my front porch and scanned the neighbor's yard. I looked in the direction of the cry until I spotted the goose. Its call was something my heart already knew—a mournful cry of longing, of loss and missing, palpable across species. I felt myself well up, and I cried my loss as the goose cried his. And somehow when it took flight, I felt a tiny piece of my grief leave with him, carried up into the sky and out of sight.

Dear Lord, You comfort me in the most beautiful ways, showing me that I am never alone.
—Sabra Ciancanelli

Digging Deeper: Psalm 30:5, 55:22

Saturday, July 9

Do not boast about tomorrow, for you do not know what a day may bring. —Proverbs 27:1 (NIV)

What was I thinking?

My husband, Chuck, and I were the oldest on the parasailing boat. I looked at the young adults on board, in their tiny swimsuits with their tight abs, and then checked to make sure that my long swimsuit coverup hid my "mature" body. Boy, did I feel out of place! Why do this at our age?

Just a few weeks before, I'd attended my fiftieth high school reunion, when the realization hit me that I might be running out of time to check off all the items on my bucket list.

So when I thought about how to celebrate my upcoming sixty-eighth birthday, I decided to do something exciting instead of simply going out to eat and indulging in a sugar-laden dessert.

Parasailing. We live near the beach, so why not?

We strapped on our life vests and watched the others rise into the air like tiny kites, anxiously awaiting our turn. When it was time to take our place on the boat deck, I moved into position while harnesses were attached to the parachute. The captain asked if we were ready. Was it too late to change my mind? Chuck gave me a smile and a wink, so I nodded. He gave the captain a thumbs-up, the boat took off, and the parachute jerked us up, lifting us higher and higher.

At four hundred feet above the water, we entered a different world, a silent one. We floated above seagulls and the Gulf of Mexico's turquoise water, our boat becoming a tiny white toy. Chuck took a selfie of us and said, "Happy birthday!" as we drifted above the earth, thankful for the chance to have a new adventure. After all, you're only sixty-eight once.

Lord, thank You for every day You give me to enjoy.
—Marilyn Turk

Digging Deeper: Psalm 92:14; Isaiah 46:4

Sunday, July 10

But these are written that you may believe that Jesus is the Messiah, the Son of God, and that by believing you may have life in his name.
—John 20:31 (NIV)

Through the years I've received lots of feedback from *Daily Guideposts* readers.

Most comments are kind. One man called to say that his small church was facing the same struggles that mine was. "I read your devotional about keeping the faith to my Sunday school class," he said. "We decided if the few people in your church could keep serving Jesus, so could we."

Some responses are critical, however. A long, handwritten letter criticized an Advent series I wrote. I thanked the writer for his insights; they were correct for his faith tradition but not for mine.

Many messages are from people who have experienced loss and loneliness. A woman whose husband, sister, and only child had died wrote, "I hope you don't mind, but I pretend you are my sister. When I visit with you in my mind, I am less lonely." Through regular letters, we upheld and prayed for each other until her death twelve years later.

Another note read, "You have the same trials and troubles I have, and your devotions give me hope for a brighter future."

And the funniest comment came from a friend in Texas: "You are like a rock star to the over-seventy crowd!"

I've been praised, rebuked, misunderstood, and encouraged. But every message makes me aware of how deeply blessed I am to share with others my walk with Christ and how humbling it is to have others share their walks with me.

Lord Jesus, thank You for the written word and Your Word. Amen.
—Penney Schwab

Digging Deeper: Psalm 19:14; 2 Corinthians 3:2–5; Galatians 6:11

Monday, July 11

Your word is a lamp to my feet And a light to my path.
—Psalm 119:105 (NASB)

I grew up with Bible stories. There were the Sunday school ones. Then, later, the wooden-pew ones I struggled to keep my eyes open through. But the real impact for me came from listening to my grandpa pull tales from his old King James Bible.

The stories he told weren't about cartoon giraffes or smiling, perfect people. No, this was darker stuff. Battles and blood. Angels and devils in a great wrestling match over mankind. Here were lion killers, prostitutes, heroes, and liars. If it had been a drive-in theater, my mom would have shoved my head down behind the back seat and told me to stay there. In my grandpa's living room, I heard the Bible unfiltered. Men and women flawed to the core but loved wildly by their Creator and used for His glory.

When my grandpa passed, I was asked if there was anything of his I'd like to have. Without hesitation, I asked for that old King James Bible. Maybe in its pages, I could hear his voice again.

I did, and it impacted me deeply. You see, as I read the handwritten notes and prayers in the margins of those pages, something struck me. All those mornings my grandfather had gotten up before anyone else to study and read—that wasn't about knowing more. It wasn't about being better or even doing the right thing. It was simply because he wanted to spend as much time as he could with his Friend.

Through the years, I've met that Friend myself—heard His quiet voice, felt His arm around my shoulders. One day I pray I'll read His stories to my own grandchildren.

And one day I'll see my grandfather again. We'll sit together on cool summer evenings. And oh, what tales we'll tell.

Lord, thank You for Your nearness through the pages of this life.
—Buck Storm

Digging Deeper: Leviticus 26:12; Psalm 119:100–114; Romans 10:17

Tuesday, July 12

O Israel, hope in the LORD; For with the LORD there is mercy, And with Him is abundant redemption. —Psalm 130:7 (NKJV)

With all the streaming services I subscribe to, I still find myself tuning in to an old standby—TCM (Turner Classic Movies). Sometimes I watch an old film I've always wanted to see, but usually it's something I've seen a million times. Why is it that I'll sit up half the night watching *Citizen Kane, The Maltese Falcon,* or *The Empire Strikes Back* when I know every line by heart and I have to work in the morning?

The other night I was settling in to watch Stanley Kubrick's 1957 WWI drama *Paths of Glory* when Julee said, "How many times have you seen this?"

"Does it matter?"

"Well, I was just wondering…"

In fact, I think it does matter. A movie you watch over and over again for its entertainment value has proven its worth.

There are plenty of things like that in life—a beautiful view, a favorite dish, a great song, a sacred space—things you never tire of experiencing. My favorite movies impart a sense of comfort and familiarity and permanence. Plus, you never know when you're going to notice something you never noticed before.

My faith is not like an old movie, but it is an experience I seek over and over again. Whether it's through a church service, the Lord's Prayer, or an old hymn, I take refuge in the comfort and familiarity faith imparts and the ongoing recognition of God's plan for his people. I crave the continuity belief brings to my life and the rituals we practice over and over again. And every once in a while, I notice something I never noticed before.

Father, I turn to You over and over again. The redemptive message of faith never gets old.
—Edward Grinnan

Digging Deeper: 1 Corinthians 1:29–31; Galatians 6:9–10

Wednesday, July 13

But blessed are your eyes because they see, and your ears because they hear. For truly I tell you, many prophets and righteous people longed to see what you see but did not see it, and to hear what you hear but did not hear it. —Matthew 13:16–17 (NIV)

Decades ago, my father bought some stocks—and left them alone. "The market may go down," he said, "but it will always return."

When Dad died, I inherited his stockbroker. Anne is smart and generous with her time—especially with me, a somewhat disinterested player with a thin wallet. Several years ago, Anne suggested that I liquidate some of my stock. "My firm says to sit tight," she said, "but my advice is to sell. Obviously, it's up to you."

I chose to take her advice. But as Dad predicted, the market did return, and I lost some money. Time to find a new broker, right?

Nope. I'm still Anne's client. Yes, her forecast was wrong, but she took a stand and took the time to call me, and none of that for her benefit. She could've toed the company line and hid behind her firm's directive, but she didn't. She offered advice—but obviously it was up to me.

We have been blessed with free will to make decisions, right or wrong. "From the primal elements, You brought forth the human race and blessed us with memory, reason and skill," says the *Book of Common Prayer*. "But we turned against You...and we turned against one another...."

But I'm not turning against anyone. I'm sticking with Someone Who will challenge the prevailing opinion and Who has my best interest at heart, even if I don't realize it. I'll put my trust in that Someone even when—no, *especially* when—things go south.

Oh, and I'll stick with Anne too.

Lord, my fortunes may occasionally go down, but my true treasure will always return.
—Mark Collins

Digging Deeper: Matthew 6:21; Luke 12:21

Thursday, July 14

By faith Abraham, when called to go to a place he would later receive as his inheritance, obeyed and went, even though he did not know where he was going. —Hebrews 11:8 (NIV)

Summer doldrums. No classes to teach. No exercise classes to take. No writing projects due. Grandchildren in play care. I tried to fill my empty hours with knitting projects and crossword puzzles. I read dozens of books. I made and wrote notes to friends. What else? Didn't God need more from me than this?

So when the forecast promised fair weather and a low tide, I used my ample free time to drive to a small New Hampshire beach before 8:00 a.m. Only a few walkers and their ecstatic dogs dotted the mile of shore. A mild breeze across the twinkling Atlantic cleared my head and filled my soul as I rambled in the creaming surf.

Then I noticed erratic marks in the wet sand, some ten or twenty feet long. Tire tracks? Messages traced with sticks? Each long mark ended in a dark dot. I drew closer to investigate. Snails! When I squatted to observe, I saw a tiny creature about the size of an olive laboriously dragging its shell across three or four grains of sand at a time. How long had this tiny creature traveled to create this long trail? Did it have any idea where it was going? Or why? Nonetheless, it crept on.

So can I. Even now, when I don't seem to be accomplishing anything important, the tiny snail reminds me to trust the journey.

Know that our Creator watches over us all. And keep moving forward, even if only three grains of sand at a time.

Lord, You show me the path for my life, even when I can't find the landmarks. I trust You.
—Gail Thorell Schilling

Digging Deeper: Job 23:11; Proverbs 3:5–6; Isaiah 42:16; John 3:8

Friday, July 15

Carry each other's burdens, and in this way you will fulfill the law of Christ. —Galatians 6:2 (NIV)

As an adoptive mom, I have the privilege of supporting other families like mine through my staff role at church. When an adoptive or foster family finds themselves in crisis, or when they receive a new child placement, I recruit and train a team of volunteers to band around the family. This team becomes the family's advocates and cheerleaders—cooking meals, delivering diapers and formula, and providing respite care so that the parents can enjoy a date night or the mom can get a much-needed haircut.

Recently, a family announced that their two-year-old foster son would be leaving their home and moving in with his grandmother. They celebrated with this little guy, knowing that he would be placed in a safe, loving home. They were joyful for him, knowing the goal of reunification with his biological family would be achieved.

The day for him to move out came quickly. The family shared teary good-byes and bear hugs, knowing these would probably be their last. Then soon after he left, they had an idea. They wondered if the same support team that had rallied around them during this little guy's stay with them would be willing to rally around his grandmother too.

I thought the idea was genius and couldn't wait to share it with this family's support team. The team agreed, and for several months they delivered meals, took over clothing donations, and, perhaps most important, prayed for this sweet boy and his grandmother.

It has been a blessing to extend care for this family beyond their foster care placement and beyond our church family. This is caring for the vulnerable at its core. This is the church being the church.

Lord, help us to serve others inside and outside the church, seeing people as the treasured children of God they are.
—Carla Hendricks

Digging Deeper: Romans 15:1–6; Galatians 5:14

Saturday, July 16

The Spirit prays for us in ways that cannot be put into words.
—Romans 8:26 (CEV)

In a remote part of the Himalayas, in a muddy field, amid a herd of yak, I made a friend. Unfortunately, my yak-herder acquaintance and I lacked a common language, which limited how deeply we could connect. My Bhutanese only stretched as far as "Good morning!" and "Thank you." My newfound friend's English appeared to be comprised solely of "Hello," which she'd yelled repeatedly, beckoning me to join her as I took photos in a field near her home. It was an offer I couldn't refuse.

Carefully dodging yak patties, I half slid down a steep slope to my host's home—a tent fashioned from straw, a plastic tarp, and weathered Bhutanese textiles. The woman's easy smile and hearty laugh made me wish I could hang out and chew the yak fat with her all day, but our language barrier (and my travel schedule) meant it was soon time to go. After lots of pointing, shrugging, and smiling, we bid each other farewell with a warm hug and a wave. As I rejoined my tour group, I realized I didn't even know my new friend's name.

Language can be a bridge or a barrier—and I've always been a bridge-builder at heart. That's one reason I became a writer. But there are days, like this one, when I wish I'd followed the other career path I'd considered, mastering a handful of languages to become a translator for the UN. Sadly, I may not be able to communicate with everyone I meet, but at least there's no language barrier with God. Even when words fail me, God never fails to understand what I'm trying to say.

Dear Lord, the significance of calling Your Son "the Word" isn't lost on me. Thanks for caring enough to communicate with us and love us.
—Vicki Kuyper

Digging Deeper: Genesis 11:1–9; Psalm 139:1–4; Isaiah 65:24

Sunday, July 17

Through the praise of children and infants you have established a stronghold against your enemies.... —Psalm 8:2 (NIV)

My cell phone rang at nearly ten o'clock Sunday evening. It was my daughter Kendall.

"Mom, I'm in the ER with Genesee. We're okay, but I knew you'd want to know."

I could hardly breathe, waiting for more details about my six-year-old granddaughter. All I heard was something about getting a finger on her left hand caught in something and how it looked really bloody and bad.

"The bone in the top joint is badly broken. They've stitched up her cuts, but she'll need surgery in a few days. We're about to be released."

"How scary and painful!" I said, imagining the hysterics of that trauma for Genesee. "How is she?"

"I'll put you on FaceTime and you can ask her," Kendall said, "but she's been the bravest girl I know, even when it happened."

Soon I saw Genesee, lying on the big ER bed, smiling as she waved her fat hand wrapped in bandages. "Hi, Oma!"

"Genesee, tell me what happened!" I tried not to let my face reflect my pain as Genesee described the gory details.

"Know what, Oma?" She half whispered her last words, as if telling a secret. "I heard my daddy say a bad word when he saw my finger."

A few days later, she underwent a two-hour surgery and came home wearing a cast and sling. When I called to ask how she was, she gave me her Genesee-trademark response: "I'm good, Oma!"

I want that to be my trademark response in the next couple of weeks as I face a minor surgery I've been dreading. I want to be as brave as Genesee and tell everyone, "I'm good!"

Lord, I'm grateful for the youthfulness You give our children and grandchildren. Genesee's "I'm good" attitude is a gift to me.
—Carol Kuykendall

Digging Deeper: Matthew 11:25, 19:13–15

Monday, July 18

So neither the one who plants nor the one who waters is anything, but only God, who makes things grow. —1 Corinthians 3:7 (NIV)

I love hydrangeas and grow native species in my yard. But I couldn't resist the large lavender blooms of a new non-native variety I spotted at the local nursery, so I bought three bushes to add to my growing collection. After reading the planting instructions, I gave them premier semi-shady spots, enriched soil, the right dose of slow-release fertilizer, and extra water during the summer months. The following year, they leafed out but never developed blooms. And the year after that, only one bush survived, and it never bloomed.

Frustrated but refusing to give up, I moved the lone survivor to a sunnier location that fall and added extra mulch. In the spring I fed it special hydrangea fertilizer, and my summer reward was new growth and lavender blooms.

What was the problem? Regardless of what the planting instructions had said, the survival and growth of this non-native plant depended on something more. The new variety wasn't as hardy or adaptable as my native hydrangeas and required the perfect combination of sunlight, food, and water to flourish.

The journey of my lone survivor to thrive and bloom reminds me of my growth as a follower of Christ. Everything I've attempted on my own has failed. But everything I've done in God's will has succeeded. The difference is the light, food, and water source. Through experience, I've learned that only God produces lasting results.

Lord, thank You for being the Light of the World, our Living Water, and the Bread of Life Who enables us to grow and bear fruit that honors You.
—Jenny Lynn Keller

Digging Deeper: John 4:10–14, 6:35, 8:12; Colossians 1:9–12

Tuesday, July 19

Then Jesus came with them to a place called Gethsemane.... And taking with Him Peter and the two sons of Zebedee [James and John], He began to be grieved and greatly distressed. Then He said to them, "My soul is deeply grieved, so that I am almost dying of sorrow. Stay here and stay awake and keep watch with Me." —Matthew 26:36–38 (AMP)

A friend's two-month-old baby boy, who I cradled in my arms, looked up at me with wonder. I gazed back in my own amazement at how quickly his warmth and sweetness ushered me into undistracted peace. I was reminded of the ageless power of and need for human closeness.

The familiar passage of Jesus's struggle in the garden of Gethsemane strikes me as the supreme example of that need. As God's Son, Jesus could easily have gone there alone to commune confidentially and confidently with His Father, knowing all would be well in the end.

But perhaps with an eternal eye toward our future needs, He bore his own desire for the nearness of those whom He loved like brothers—men who had followed Him almost to the end of His destiny here on earth. He needed them close. When He could very well have decided to slip exclusively into His divinity and wait for the Father's will to be completed, He chose to express His need for comfort and familiarity by separating His closest friends from the other followers and asking them to stay nearby.

Literally or figuratively, the human touch—whether of a sweet infant snuggled to one's chest or of praying friends a few yards away—can be the arms of God for someone in pain. And if Jesus needed the nearness of others, can we ever question that need in us?

Jesus, help me discern and respond to the needs around me.
—Jacqueline F. Wheelock

Digging Deeper: Proverbs 18:24; John 15:15

Wednesday, July 20

I will not die but live, and will proclaim what the LORD has done.
—Psalm 118:17 (NIV)

I felt devastated seeing my twenty-three-year-old daughter paralyzed from her eyelids to her toes. She'd been diagnosed with Guillain-Barré syndrome, a rare disorder that damages the sensory nerve myelin. Doctors in the intensive care unit recommended a treatment of intravenous immune globulins. My husband and I called friends, urging them to activate the prayer chain on Bethany's behalf. We slept fitfully in chairs beside Bethany's bed.

The following morning, a nurse asked us to please send the people in the waiting room home. "There are just too many of them," she explained.

After taking the elevator down to the waiting room, we stood amazed at the crowd praying there. The sight of all those prayer warriors touched me. Tears stung my eyes. We soon learned that prayer chains had been activated in congregations all over town. We thanked everyone for their prayers on Bethany's behalf. We explained that doctors, having diagnosed her condition, estimated she would be in intensive care for three to six weeks, followed by months of physical therapy. We'd been warned that she might even be paralyzed, at least partially, for the rest of her life.

But God had other plans. Bethany walked again in less than a week! The doctors were astonished. So were we. As she had no residual paralysis, they didn't see any reason to keep our daughter hospitalized. Remembering the Bible verse about the prayers of the righteous accomplishing much, I could hardly wait to share the amazing news with our prayer warriors. The Lord had chosen to honor those earnest prayers with a miracle, and we are forever grateful.

Lord, may I never grow weary of thanking You for Your lovingkindness.
—Shirley Raye Redmond

Digging Deeper: John 5:8; 1 Thessalonians 5:16–18

Thursday, July 21

Therefore confess your sins to each other and pray for each other so that you may be healed. The prayer of a righteous person is powerful and effective. —James 5:16 (NIV)

We stood on the sidewalk behind our 1864 Victorian. We'd moved away from here a year ago, but this home—the home I still longed to live in—hadn't sold. In a week, renters would move in. My adult son, Logan, had come to help me say good-bye.

"Are you okay, Mom?" Logan asked. "Ready to go in?"

I was. And I wasn't.

My husband, Lonny, and I had moved our family across the Mississippi River to be near to where our boys would attend high school after years of homeschooling.

Some days I missed pirates sneaking down the stairwell in pursuit of treasured plastic gold. Other days I ached for shadow leaves in the sunbeams as they danced over old hardwood. I wanted to go home.

"We can come back tomorrow," Logan said. "If you don't want to do this today."

"No," I said.

We walked over the patio. As we opened the back door, the squeaky hinge welcomed us. We stepped over the threshold that held silent stories in layers of chipped paint. Sweetness from years of baking lingered.

My son took my hand as we prayed. Through our home. Through the memories of life, family, tears, and triumph. I reached out to feel the smooth, curved wood of the banister and the cool marble of the mantle. I watched light lavish on crystal and I let the doorbell chime. I wriggled the loose tiles on the fireplace where the boys had hidden their two-dollar bills.

I could almost hear my family there. But above it all, I heard my son's prayer. He thanked the Lord for our life there and asked that I'd be set free.

Lord, thank You for the prayers of the righteous.
—Shawnelle Eliasen

Digging Deeper: Jeremiah 29:12; 1 John 5:14

Friday, July 22

But I do not account my life of any value nor as precious to myself, if only I may finish my course and the ministry that I received from the Lord Jesus, to testify to the gospel of the grace of God. —Acts 20:24 (ESV)

My ten-year-old daughter, Jo-Ella, asked me, "You like Vacation Bible School, right?"

Seems like a simple question, but I struggled to answer. I thought about giving Jo-Ella the answer she wanted—"Yes." It most certainly would have been the easiest reply.

I had just finished facilitating a week of VBS for three hundred fifty children. Planning and logistics alone had taken six months. And as an introvert, I found the hustle and bustle of VBS week itself really draining. I was emotionally and physically exhausted, and to be honest, I wasn't filled with enthusiasm and joy about VBS in that moment. But I also didn't want to complain. So after a long pause, I settled with "It's a lot of work for me."

Jo-Ella's response took me by surprise: "But you like seeing all the kids learn about Jesus."

Indeed, I really, really did. And in that moment, I was blessed with perspective. Of course! The importance of "kids learning about Jesus" is why I do this work. I love watching our VBS volunteers pour their time and faith into the children. And the children's authentic responses to the Gospels is incredibly rewarding.

I know God has called me to this work, but when I grow weary, my focus can become clouded. So from time to time, I need to refocus, as we all do. And for this, perspective is a beautiful thing.

I am so thankful to those around me who continually call me to focus on His perspective, just as Jo-Ella did on that poignant summer day.

Dear Lord, help me to be attentive to the voices of others, which help me focus on Your perspective. May I continually heed Your hand in my life through my focus on Your will.
—Jolynda Strandberg

Digging Deeper: 1 Corinthians 4:1–3; 2 Corinthians 4; Romans 15:18–20

Saturday, July 23

I say to God my Rock, "Why have you forgotten me?" —Psalm 42:9 (NIV)

Have you ever stumbled upon something valuable? I once did.

On a summer afternoon, while walking in the woods with my dog Max, I came to a small forest of birch trees. The sun was shining brightly through the branches, which were thick with leaves.

Max saw a squirrel and bolted in pursuit. His leash flew out of my hand. Being nervous that Max might quickly vanish from sight, I ran a few steps, and suddenly my hair was caught on a low-hanging branch. It hurt! Also, I was stuck.

Stopping to set myself free, I looked up and saw a canvas bag hanging from the trunk of the tree. There was no one around. I looked inside the bag. There I found four small photo albums full of pictures of family gatherings, birthday parties, and scenes by a lake. I knew none of the people in the photographs.

For the next few months, I placed ads in our local newspaper: "Photo albums found in woods. Call me." No one ever responded.

I don't know what it means, but I suspect someone was very unhappy the day they cast out their happy photos. They didn't destroy them, but they sent them away.

I should place another ad in the paper: "God doesn't abandon us. When we are sad or depressed, God is there. In both our happy moments and when we're lonely, God is there."

Be my friend today, Lord.
—Jon M. Sweeney

Digging Deeper: Psalm 25:16, 42:10–11

Sunday, July 24

SACRED SPACES: Saint Katharine Drexel

The LORD your God will restore your fortunes and have compassion on you and gather you again.... —Deuteronomy 30:3 (NIV)

About two dozen of us stood in the drizzle that July afternoon, watching our pastor step on the shiny shovel and dig up a lump of earth. Somehow this clearing in the woods would become our new church home.

A year earlier, a fire had destroyed our St. Joan of Arc Church five miles south of here. All fall we'd worshipped in a tent, despite driving rain and puddles that created a hazard for the electronic keyboard and sound system. Once cold weather set in, we shared space in the local Congregational church. Then our parish merged permanently with St. Cecilia's about ten miles north—there were so many new faces in our congregation! The new church would be built halfway between the two old ones. But with so much change and so many new faces, could church ever again feel like home?

About a year later, on a glorious July afternoon, I arrived for the dedication of the new St. Katharine Drexel Church. As I stepped inside for the first time, I immediately recognized the old stained glass from St. Cecilia's behind the new altar.

Best of all, I recognized the faces of fellow parishioners—old friends in new pews—and the true body of the church.

Creator God, keep me mindful that those of us who love You are the church. The building is a bonus.
—Gail Thorell Schilling

Digging Deeper: Exodus 25:8; Ezekiel 37:27; 1 Corinthians 3:16

Monday, July 25

But everything should be done in a fitting and orderly way.
—1 Corinthians 14:40 (NIV)

I'm in the stage of life when every day is laundry day. Someone's sheets always need changing, the beach towels are needed to mop up big spills, and our clothes, especially during summer, get incredibly dirty.

Especially when the kids were younger, doing laundry was unrelenting, mostly because it was literally never finished. But when Olivia turned seven, I realized I needed to check my attitude. She was now old enough to take on my reactions as her own, and I wanted her to see that taking care of one's self and home is a blessing, not a burden.

One day, I taught her how to do the laundry. We talked about why we only use cold water (no sorting into stacks in this house!) and about what can and can't go in the dryer. We talked about saving energy, about when a load was too full or too empty, and about how to balance the washing machine so it wouldn't sound like it had a bowling ball inside.

How did Olivia react? In short, she beamed. "Mom, *thank you* for teaching me how to use the laundry machines," she said, "I can't wait to teach James and Beau when they get big."

Now, Olivia is only seven; she's not going to be tackling Mt. Washmore alone. But there was something in the moment of sharing how to do something with her that reminded me of the blessing of even dirty laundry. Too-small clothing? Thank You, God, that we're growing. Stains on the knees? What a fun day outside that was! And of course, ten minutes alone with my growing-too-fast firstborn? I may just start doing laundry twice a day.

Thank You, God, for showing me ways to be thankful for my home, my life, and my family in the most mundane daily chores.
—Ashley Kappel

Digging Deeper: Proverbs 22:6; Galatians 6:5; Philippians 2:14–15

Tuesday, July 26

*If you, O Lord, should mark iniquities, Lord, who could stand?
But there is forgiveness with you, so that you may be revered.*
—Psalm 130:3–4 (NRSV)

Do you count your steps? It seems to be all the rage, with various numbers being put forward as the ideal to strive for. For a while, the magical figure was ten thousand steps a day. Then others (more learned than I) pointed out that this was just an arbitrary figure. These others said science was showing that, as you went up in increments of four thousand, your health benefited—so then twelve thousand steps was some new marker. Like climbing Mount Everest, if you ask me.

I tried to ignore it all until I noticed that my phone counted my steps. Every day. And like a nagging teacher, it would comment, "You're taking fewer steps today." I'd frown at the app. But then, buying into it more than I'd like to admit, I found myself arguing with it: "You don't even make a difference between the steps I make running, versus going for a walk!" Or, "Why don't I get some extra credit for going *up* a flight of stairs instead coming down?" (Okay, maybe I need a better app.)

One day, while running a quick errand, I even found myself rushing back to the house to fetch my phone, because I wanted to make sure I got credit for *every step I took*. As though, if they weren't recorded on my phone, they didn't really happen.

Then I stopped myself. *God*, I thought, *You know how many steps I take, whether I've got my phone in my pocket or not*. It was the same way God knows about all my judgmental thoughts, my uncharitable impulses, and my efforts at loving my neighbor as myself.

"Thank You, God, for Your infinite forgiveness," I said.

Now I needed to forgive myself. And stop looking at the phone.

*Thank You, Lord, for keeping no record of all my wrongs.
Your own goodness is too rich to behold.*
—Rick Hamlin

Digging Deeper: Hebrews 8:12; Revelation 20:12

Wednesday, July 27

Behold, God is my salvation, I will trust and not be afraid....
—Isaiah 12:2 (NASB)

Life flies by, doesn't it? I was in the delivery room the day my daughter was born. And now she was having her own baby right on the other side of the door.

"You're gonna be a grandpa!" somebody said. I hardly heard them. That was my little girl in there.

Time crawled. I got a sandwich and coffee from the snack bar but didn't feel like eating. How much longer?

And then the nightmare.

They came from every direction. Doctor, nurses, staff—all running. Clearly something was seriously wrong.

Now, I'm a father. A problem-solver. It's what I do. Water heater, car, lawn mower, splinter in your hand...I'm your guy. I'll fix it. But in that awful moment, on the wrong side of that door, I felt more helpless than I ever had in my life.

Minutes ticked. They might as well have been hours. And no word. Man, I hated that door.

You know, there's only one place an earthly father can turn to when the world is spinning out of his control. And let me tell you, I turned there. I ran into the arms of the *heavenly* Father and gave Him my all. I'm not sure if I've ever prayed so hard.

Praise God, He stepped in that day and stepped in big. It was rough. And it was close. But that night, I was able to put my arms around both my daughter and my beautiful new granddaughter.

And the real Fix-It Guy, the True and Good Father, put His arms around us all.

Dear God, I thank You that You have the tools—love, grace, and mercy—to see me through this journey. Because my hands are empty.
—Buck Storm

Digging Deeper: Deuteronomy 33:26; Psalm 46:1–3, 63:7

Thursday, July 28

If my people...shall humble themselves, and pray...then will I hear from heaven... —2 Chronicles 7:14 (KJV)

Being tough is in my DNA. From being a high-school football offensive guard to riding horseback with my dad through treacherous mountains in blinding snow, I'm, well, tough.

I've certainly never been a yoga person—that is, until my wife, Corinne, announced, "Brock, I think you should try hot yoga. It's a great stress reliever."

Obedient husband that I am, I reluctantly signed up for a lesson.

It was humiliating.

The studio is kept at over ninety degrees. I felt like a discombobulated lumberjack stumbling through the poses, while much leaner and definitely more limber ladies and a few guys stretched athletically around me.

The pain of the yoga position "downward dog" (which stretches one's back, hamstrings, and calves) was downright excruciating, as the instructor fairly sang, "Doesn't this feel wonderful?" In lieu of strangling her in the middle of the class I resorted to a silent prayer: *Please, God, help me get through this!*

Maybe it was my stubbornness, or maybe it was the pride of simply surviving that first session, but I went back, and hot yoga was soon a part of my early morning routine.

Over time, the benefits surprised me. That first prayer, muttered out of pain, had opened up a new and much-needed dialogue with God, and yoga somehow became an unexpected prayer time for me. I was less stressed (and more limber) and also was growing closer to God.

"How was yoga this morning, Brock?" Corinne smiles as I walk through the front door, drenched in sweat.

I smile back. "Incredible."

Father, please help me to remember to fall back to prayer.
—Brock Kidd

Digging Deeper: Isaiah 55:6; Psalm 55:17

Friday, July 29

The LORD will guide you always; he will satisfy your needs in a sun-scorched land and will strengthen your frame. You will be like a well-watered garden, like a spring whose waters never fail.
—Isaiah 58:11 (NIV)

On any given summer morning, you can find my dad in his garden, picking a bounty of cucumbers, green beans, okra, tomatoes, and the like. As one of six children, Dad's green thumb was cultivated at an early age, under the watchful eye of his father. Amid dirt roads in Guilford County, North Carolina, in the early 1960s, he learned how to prepare soil and cultivate land, when to plant seeds and when to water, and how to prevent weeds from destroying what he's worked hard to procure. When properly tended, his crops have provided not only for him but for his family and friends, with whom he regularly shares baskets of overflow.

Recently, as my dad talked about preparations for an upcoming garden, he emphasized how his seeds only reach their full potential if he doesn't neglect them. His words made me think of the things I want to flourish in my life. That patience I needed for my son as he navigated through his teenage years needed to be watered with love. The roots of my marriage that I prayed would run strong and deep had to be strengthened with kindness. The peace that I wanted to shine over my life had to be cultivated with time in the word of God.

If my life is to flourish with long-lasting fruit, I must keep my soul cleared from the entanglement of sin and spend time in the Son-shine.

Lord, let my life flourish in abundance. May every great thing that You have planted in me spring forth richly.
—Tia McCollors

Digging Deeper: Psalm 92:12–14; Luke 8:15; Colossians 1:9–10; 2 Peter 1:5–8

Saturday, July 30

Not that I have already obtained this or am already perfect, but I press on to make it my own, because Christ Jesus has made me his own.
—Philippians 3:12 (ESV)

I was driving my fourteen-year-old son, Joey, to a birthday party when I heard five quick beeps coming from my steering column. I glanced down to see what was going on: out of gas.

There was a message flashing on my dashboard: "Range to empty: 0 miles." I asked my son to use Waze to determine the closest gas station. The options: 2.4 miles ahead of me, or 1.2 miles behind me.

I had a decision to make. Should I turn around and head to the closer gas station, or should I keep going forward, hoping that my momentum would carry me 2.4 miles?

My son chose for me. "Just keep going straight, Mom, you're already rolling pretty fast."

Looking straight ahead, I coasted along the rolling hills, watching the tenths of miles tick away. One mile in, the gas actually ran out (I must have been running on fumes up until that moment). In another half mile, I had slowed to half the speed limit.

By the time the gas station came into view, I was coasting along at about five miles per hour. Somehow I managed to steer my car up to the gas tank.

I took a deep breath and said a prayer of thanks that we had made it, grateful for my son's wisdom to just keep my eyes straight ahead and my car rolling. Because while I hadn't had the gas to make it to the station, I'd had the momentum to keep going forward.

Lord, remind me to keep my eyes on You, letting You pull me along even when I'm completely unable to move forward on my own. Amen.
—Erin MacPherson

Digging Deeper: Luke 9:62; Philippians 3:13

Sunday, July 31

Jesus answered and said to him, "Before Philip called you, when you were under the fig tree, I saw you." —John 1:48 (NASB)

I'm in love with benches. Their invitation to pause and rest. To take in a scenic view and contemplate the splendor of God. To sit with a journal or good book. To share space with a friend in quiet conversation.

For me a bench speaks of solace and peace—reminiscent of a child content on its mother's lap. When I need wisdom and guidance, or when I seek to calm down or be comforted, I go to my bench. It is a place of prayer and listening to God.

Never having owned a bench, I was dismayed to miss out on the spring yard sale at which my sister-in-law had sold her wrought-iron bench. Another sister-in-law had bought it—neither knowing my penchant for benches.

Soon after, my husband, Terry, and I traveled to Montana to visit friends. As we were standing outside with my friend Cathy, she pointed to an overturned bench against the garage and casually mentioned they were donating it.

"I'd like that bench!" I exclaimed.

It was a squeaky dark green iron glider—just right for two. It had a thick green-and-tan-striped cushion covering the back and seat. The cushion was singed along the seam, stuffing protruding, but I didn't care.

At home I found the perfect place for it—atop an embankment beneath the cherry trees, where a diamond-shaped "portal" through the leaves opened up onto our beautiful river valley. Terry oiled out the glider's squeaks. A friend sewed the cushion. I'd never had it so good!

And I had come by my bench in such a way there was no doubt the Lord provided it. Almost as if to say, "I would love to sit on that glider and spend time with you."

Thank You, Jesus, for knowing me so well—and for sharing my bench.
—Carol Knapp

Digging Deeper: Psalm 104:34, 105:3–4, 119:2, 139:1–2

July

THE LORD IS NEAR

1 _____

2 _____

3 _____

4 _____

5 _____

6 _____

7 _____

8 _____

9 _____

10 _____

11 _____

12 _____

13 _____

14 _____

15 _____

July

16 _____

17 _____

18 _____

19 _____

20 _____

21 _____

22 _____

23 _____

24 _____

25 _____

26 _____

27 _____

28 _____

29 _____

30 _____

31 _____

August

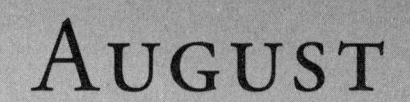

*You, Lord, are forgiving and good,
abounding in love to all who call to you.*

—Psalm 86:5 (NIV)

Monday, August 1

GOD'S FINGERPRINTS: His Hand Guides Us
See, I have written your name on the palms of my hands.
—Isaiah 49:16 (NLT)

If I have ever seen God's fingerprints in my life, it was during the sale of my first book. No moment in my life was more profound.

I'd been writing for five years and had completed four manuscripts. Rejections came so fast, I would joke that they'd hit me in the back of the head on my way home from the post office.

Then through a series of fortunate circumstances, I was able to attend a writers' conference and meet an editor. She read my book, looked me square in the eye, and told me the best I could do was toss it in the garbage. Sick at heart, I sat up all night, seeking God's wisdom. The reading for the day was John 14, which began with "Let not your heart be troubled." That was all the encouragement I needed. Refusing to accept the editor's brutal rejection, I sent a query letter to a different publisher, asking if they would like to review my story. Each day, as I waited for a reply, all the negative, ugly voices I'd heard in my childhood returned to haunt me.

One day I couldn't bear to listen to those voices any longer. Compulsively, I mailed the book to the publisher before hearing whether they were interested. Incidentally, when I returned from the post office and opened my mail, I discovered the answer to my query letter: "Do not mail us your book. We are not buying at this time."

Three weeks later, New York called and purchased my book. If I had waited a half hour, I would never have mailed off that manuscript.

All through the years, God has had His hand on my career and my success—especially when I needed encouragement the most.

Only You could have arranged these details, Lord, to prove to me once again Your love and guidance in my life.
—Debbie Macomber

Digging Deeper: 1 Peter 5:6–7; Psalm 116:1

Tuesday, August 2

At this they wept aloud again. Then Orpah kissed her mother-in-law goodbye, but Ruth clung to her. —Ruth 1:14 (NIV)

Good-byes are never easy, no matter how much you prepare or how far in advance you share with others the news that you are leaving.

I shared the news with my parents while driving them out of the city to my brother's home in Carmel. They were sitting in the back seat of the car when I said, "I was offered a position at a church in Florida. We will be moving in two months." There wasn't a word or sound out of them. I checked the rearview mirror to see their reactions. They looked sad and deep in thought. Finally, my mother said, "I am going to miss you. I'm sad that you are leaving."

A few days before our departure, we had a farewell dinner in the city with family and friends. After the gathering, I drove my parents home. We walked upstairs to their apartment, and when I hugged them good-bye, they began crying and then sobbing. The more we held each other, the more they cried.

This wasn't my first time moving away to another state. I'd moved out once to attend college and again—years later, with my young family—to go to seminary. But this was a different kind of departure. My parents were now in their eighties. Every moment with their children meant the world to them.

I promised to call them weekly. But words could not ease their pain. They were still crying as the door closed behind me.

Since that night, I have kept my word. Every Sunday evening, I faithfully call them. We talk about life, church, and family. We still miss each other, but our sadness has eased as we take joy and comfort in our weekly connection.

Lord, thank You for the love of family;
comfort those who are far from loved ones.
—Pablo Diaz

Digging Deeper: Luke 15:20; John 16:22

Wednesday, August 3

And the LORD said to Moses, "Why do you cry to Me? Tell the children of Israel to go forward." —Exodus 14:15 (NKJV)

It's midnight, and I can't sleep. I sit at my desk, despairing. I am scheduled for a difficult surgery, with a long recovery, and I just can't face it. But then I realize that I have been here many times before: At this desk. At midnight. In despair.

One time was when computers first came along. I knew I could never learn to use one. I am a poet, not a technician. It was hopeless. But I gave it my best shot, and here I am, typing this story on a computer.

Another time was after a couple of scary flying lessons in 1978. I decided that my dream of becoming a pilot was a terrible mistake, and I wanted to quit. Only my pride kept me going, but in six months, I had my wings.

Then there was the time my wife said, "We need to move to the country," and I cringed. Sitting at this desk, I had thought about leaving our beautiful downtown house, and I knew I would be wretchedly lonely and bored in the country. But here we are, and we are doing swimmingly.

In all those challenges, I just moved forward, one baby step at a time. And as I moved forward, obstacles receded and answers came forward.

When I do nothing, then nothing can be done. But when I take even one step forward, God steers me to the next.

Surgery will not be a party, but with God's help, I will survive it.

I thank You, Father, for all the times when You changed my despair into delight.
—Daniel Schantz

Digging Deeper: Isaiah 35:3–4; 2 Corinthians 4:8

Thursday, August 4

A friend loves at all times, and a brother is born for a time of adversity.
—Proverbs 17:17 (NIV)

I know a woman who, to my knowledge, has never said an unkind word about anyone in her life. I've wondered, *How on earth does she do it?* I, on the other hand, am guilty of not giving a few people I've met over the years even half a chance to grow a decent friendship with me. I simply decided early on that I would be cordial with these people but did not want to form real friendships with them because they were too different from me or were irritating in some way. Besides, I'd read and heard that it's best to surround yourself with happy, positive people. "Don't let the negative ones drag you down," the world says.

Then one Sunday my pastor talked about the importance of looking for the good in every person we meet. "Even the most negative people have some good qualities," he said. "Give them a chance." *Ouch.*

The next week a woman I'd been avoiding for years showed up at the pool. Remembering what my pastor had said, I smiled and said, "Good morning." A short conversation took place and gradually, over the next couple of months, I started to see her in a whole new light. There were reasons she was cranky. Her parents were both ill, her husband refused to help her with basic household tasks, and her best girlfriend had gradually dissolved their friendship.

That woman and I may never become close friends, but as we've gotten to know each other, the weight around my shoulders caused by my trying to avoid her has disappeared. I learned that it's not so hard to extend God's love and give everyone a chance.

> *Lord, sometimes I need a kick in the pants to reach out to a difficult person. Let me have it.*
> —Patricia Lorenz

Digging Deeper: 1 Samuel 18:1–5; 2 Samuel 16:17–19; Proverbs 18:24

Friday, August 5

But I trust in you, O Lord; I say, "You are my God." My times are in your hand.... —Psalm 31:14–15 (ESV)

The description of our rental house in Cape Cod said "four-wheel drive recommended," yet nothing could prepare us for the five-mile one-way rutted and shared road that required you to back up for several feet if an oncoming car approached.

When we finally reached the secluded house and turned off the engine, my mom got out of the car, bent down, and kissed the ground, announcing, "Good thing we have groceries, because we are never leaving."

The plus side to the terrible road was that the nearby private beach was stunning and empty. Every night my sons, nephews, and I took a sunset walk. One night, no one felt like going, so I decided to go alone.

When I reached the water's edge, it was high tide. I kicked off my sandals and put my toes in the water. The temperature was perfect—much warmer than usual, with gentle waves lapping the shore. I didn't have a suit on, just shorts and a tank top, but I couldn't help myself—the water was too welcoming, and I had never been in the ocean completely alone—so I went in.

It was glorious. I floated on my back and then went under. I was pretty far from the shore when I thought, *Maybe it isn't such a good idea to be out here alone.* Just then I felt someone looking at me, and I turned my head to see a seal, with wide watery eyes, dark as coal. I swam back to shore and kept the moment to myself—a secret between God and me.

Lord, I have faith that, with Your help, I am never alone.
With You, I see the world through blessed eyes.
—Sabra Ciancanelli

Digging Deeper: Psalm 37:5, 118:8

Saturday, August 6

WISDOM'S DELIGHTS: The Wisdom of Sacrifice

But Hannah...said to her husband, "I will not go until the child is weaned; then I will bring him, so that he may appear before the Lord and stay there for life." —1 Samuel 1:22 (NASB)

Hannah, wife of Elkanah, has no children in a culture where bearing children is expected. On their annual temple visit, she prays to the Lord in great distress, weeping bitterly. (1 Samuel 1:10 NASB) She asks for a son, vowing to give him to the Lord "all the days of his life." (1 Samuel NASB 1:11) The Lord answers Hannah's prayer, and the following year she gives birth to Samuel, meaning "God has heard."

She skips her temple visits the next few years until Samuel is weaned. Then she does as she promised and delivers him to the temple to live with Eli the priest, who will train him in the priesthood. Instead of returning home brokenhearted, she sings a song of thanksgiving for the greatness of God. (1 Samuel 2:1–10 NASB)

Every year she brings her boy a "little robe" she has made. (1 Samuel 2:19 NASB) In time, Samuel becomes a mighty prophet and leader in Israel.

Eli prays for more children for Hannah, and she has three more sons and two daughters. But she didn't know those children would be in her future when she boldly released her then-only child for God's larger purpose.

Hannah's story calls me to more—to God the Father sending His only Son, Jesus, "away" to live in the world—to open a path I can take, through faith in Him, to knowing God, now and forever.

The Bible says, "But as many as received Him, to them He gave the right to become children of God...." (John 1:12 NASB) When I think of the monumental sacrifice Father and Son made so I can be one more child in the family, I want to do as Hannah and Samuel did—serve God willingly from a grateful heart.

Thank You, Lord, for Your overwhelming gift!
—Carol Knapp

Digging Deeper: 1 Samuel 1, 2:1–11, 18–21; John 3:16;
Philippians 2:5–11; 1 John 3:1

Sunday, August 7

The Lord is a stronghold for the oppressed, a stronghold in times of trouble. And those who know your name put their trust in you, for you, O Lord, have not forsaken those who seek You.
—Psalm 9:9–10 (NRSVCE)

My husband, Charlie, is not known for his humility, and this is something I've noticed during prayer time. He prays in categories: first, for us; then for family and friends; and finally for those who are homeless, addicted, and in prison. And when he turns to praying for the world, he seems to feel that God needs a daily update.

"Lord," Charlie says conversationally, "the world is a really difficult place. There's a lot of violence, cruelty, war, and starvation."

Like He doesn't know that, I think.

"People are angry, violent, afraid, and confused," Charlie continues.

Big news flash to the Omniscient Creator.

"Many people, including leaders, don't know You or how to turn to You."

As if He hasn't noticed.

Charlie continues this dialogue with the Lord, often mentioning specific issues and events. I'm not proud to admit that sometimes I let my mind wander. But recently, feeling a bit guilty, I actually listened to the whole litany. After Charlie shared all the day's and the world's woes with God, he simply said, "Please help us to be kinder."

The next day, I paid attention again, and when Charlie finished his report, he concluded, "Lord, we're so sorry."

The day after that, he finished with "Show us the way."

By that point, I realized that it wasn't Charlie who needed to be more humble in our daily prayer.

When I speak with You, Father, help me to come to You as the child I know myself to be.
—Marci Alborghetti

Digging Deeper: Mark 9:33–37; Luke 11:9–13

Monday, August 8

We are the clay, and thou our potter; and we all are the work of thy hand. —Isaiah 64:8 (KJV)

I'm gloating.

One of the wealthiest men in the country has just left my office. I don't know how many financial advisers were vying for his business, but he has chosen me to manage his wealth. I think of the accolades that will surely come from my associates.

Yet even as I imagine myself at "the top of the heap," an inconvenient truth begins to dampen my euphoria: the "just noise" factor.

My friend Craig introduced me to the concept sometime back. For a time, Craig was known as the "Wonder of Wall Street," one who could ferret out what was crucial in an investment and what was "just noise." Later, after the Great Recession hit, he was able to see his losses as "just noise," when compared to the loving ways his family and his God came through for him.

"Just noise," I think, remembering why I entered this business in the first place. Growing up in a minister's home, I had been struck by how often those who spend their lives serving others had no one to serve them with their financial needs. I saw myself making life better for these people, helping them to create safety nets, plan for retirement, and achieve financial security.

I feel a bit sheepish now, as I recall my new client's future goals. Apart from providing for his family, he wants to create a huge trust to provide scholarships for minority students. He also plans to start a fund to reward innovations for renewable energy.

I look past my ego and see clearly. His net worth, his zip code, and all the usual trappings of wealth are "just noise."

My new client is just another child of God, looking for ways to serve.

Dear Lord, please keep me humble in the truth of knowing that there is a lot of noise around me, and I need only to listen for You.
—Brock Kidd

Digging Deeper: Proverbs 23; Psalm 43:3

Tuesday, August 9

Small is the gate and narrow the road that leads to life, and only a few find it. —Matthew 7:14 (NIV)

If hobbits were Greek, Monemvasia would surely be their shire. The rounded wooden doors on each hewn-stone home barely came up to my shoulder. Adding to the magical appeal of the medieval walled town was the fact that its residents all seemed to keep their house keys in the very same place—stuck in the exterior keyhole of their diminutive front doors. It felt like a friendly invitation: "Come on in and get acquainted! You're safe behind these walls."

Considering how limited the access was to get into town, even owning a front door key seemed a bit frivolous. After all, Monemvasia is located on a tiny remote island tenuously connected to the Peloponnese Peninsula by a narrow dirt causeway—no cars allowed. The arched entryway that leads through a narrow stone tunnel into town is barely wide enough for a donkey cart, let alone a tour bus. I had ventured in on foot and seemingly stepped back in time to a slower pace of life. I meandered cobblestone streets, hiked a serpentine trail to a clifftop Byzantine church, ate melt-in-my-mouth moussaka, and encountered more cats than people throughout the quiet, sun-drenched afternoon.

At day's end, as I exited Monemvasia (whose name means "single entrance"), I couldn't help but think of Matthew 7:14. I'd always viewed God's description of a "narrow road" leading to life as a restrictive one. But the restricted access into Monemvasia seemed to create a place of serenity and security for everyone who lived within its walls. Perhaps God's narrow way is simply an invitation into this same kind of life.

> *Father, I know Your grace, not my works, is what opens the narrow gate into Your presence. Today, please help me follow the path that leads directly to You.*
> —Vicki Kuyper

Digging Deeper: Psalm 16:11; Jeremiah 6:16; John 14:6

Wednesday, August 10

Now this is the confidence that we have in Him, that if we ask anything according to His will, He hears us. —1 John 5:14 (NKJV)

I rocked in my prayer chair and sipped my morning coffee as I reviewed the long list of things and people I had just prayed for. Although it didn't happen often, this morning I felt discouraged because it seemed I kept adding items to the list but not checking many off.

Lord, sometimes I feel like my prayers don't go above the ceiling. I could use some encouragement. I glanced at the clock. *Half an hour before I have to go to work. Maybe I should call Chuck.*

My brother answered with an excited voice. "You won't believe this!" He went on to share that someone had found his cell phone; the phone that he had lost in Flathead Lake while fishing nearly two years ago. In the 192-square-mile Montana lake (it's huge!), some guys were using a metal detector to locate lost lures, and they found the phone. They dried it out, and miraculously, after being underwater, it powered on!

Tears leaked out of the corner of my eyes as I heard him say in awe, "This doesn't just happen."

Nearly two years ago, I'd prayed that someone would find his phone and return it to him, that it would be a miracle to remind him how much God cares. Days passed. Then weeks. Then months. Then I forgot about it. But God didn't. And after all this time, the miracle was even sweeter for my brother—and for me.

Lord, help me to remember not to put a timeline on my prayer requests and to develop the confidence that You have heard all my prayers. Amen.
—Rebecca Ondov

Digging Deeper: Deuteronomy 4:7; Ephesians 1:15–22

Thursday, August 11

But let your communications be, Yea, yea; Nay, nay...
—Matthew 5:37 (KJV)

"I yam what I yam," that old cartoon character, Popeye the Sailor Man, would sing out in those Saturday morning cartoons. A patron saint to every mother's "Eat your vegetables" plea, Popeye ate his spinach, became super strong, and saved whatever day needed saving.

"I yam what I yam," he'd say, and "...I know who I am and I'm sticking to it!" My mother had an equally declarative statement. Looking straight at me, she'd say, "Pamela, you should always be a 'yay, yay' or a 'nay, nay' person."

Okay, I was often a bit slow at understanding my mother's words. But as the years flew by, I saw personal convenience eclipsing what we know is right, and her advice became auspicious in its meaning.

Feed the hungry, take care of the sick, visit the prisoner, welcome the stranger, Jesus said.

Oh, I can find excuses aplenty as I find myself saying, "Yay, yay" to Jesus's words but "Nay, nay" to what He asks of me.

Going back to my mother's admonition, I think of that old sailor Popeye, saying, "I yam what I yam."

Most of us learned who we were sitting in a little Sunday school chair or listening to a Bible story read at bedtime. We learned by seeing acts of kindness and generosity. We sang "Jesus loves the little children of the world" and believed, even then, what we were singing.

I wrap the memories around me like a warm blanket, and I remember who I am. I stand proud. I will try every day to be a "yay, yay" and not a "nay, nay." To *do* the words of Jesus and not just say them.

Father, yay to your truth; nay to what's easy and convenient.
Help me be strong.
—Pam Kidd

Digging Deeper: Psalm 1:1–2; 1 Thessalonians 5:21;
2 Thessalonians 2:15; 1 Peter 5:8

Friday, August 12

Beloved, let us love one another, for love is from God, and whoever loves has been born of God and knows God. —1 John 4:7 (ESV)

We don't have trash collection where I live part-time in rural Monterey, Massachusetts, so Gracie and I haul our garbage and recyclables to the town transfer station—aka the dump. Gracie loves dump day because Beth—of Beth and Dave, who preside over the facility—always comes over to the car and gives her a treat. Or two, if I'm not looking.

To get to the station, we pass by "the ladies" along Gould Road. The ladies are what everyone calls the magnificent dairy cows that belong to Gould Farm. Gould Farm is no ordinary farm, though. It is a farm where hope grows.

Founded in 1913 by Will and Agnes Gould, devout Christians and utopians, Gould Farm is a therapeutic community for people with mental illness. The Goulds believed that mental illness often robbed a person of a sense of purpose. So at Gould, staffers and guests live and work side by side, tending to the ladies, running the exceptional bakery, baling hay, and operating the legendary Roadside Café, which serves, hands down, the best breakfast in the Berkshires.

At a time when the intractably mentally ill were treated with almost sadistic cruelty by the medical establishment, the Goulds believed the sick should be treated the way Jesus would treat them—with love, kindness, respect, and empathy. I am struck by the irony that the transfer station, where we haul our disposables, abuts this pastoral sanctuary for those whom society so often discards.

That's why every time I pass by the ladies, I say a prayer for the staff and guests of Gould Farm. Especially the guests.

May I always embrace the outcast, give hope to the hopeless, love the unloved, reach out to the unreached. May I always reflect the love of Christ for those most in need.
—Edward Grinnan

Digging Deeper: Matthew 22:36–40; John 13:34–35

Saturday, August 13

The sweetness of a man's friend gives delight.... —Proverbs 27:9 (NKJV)

The S'mores Wars commenced a few years back with my friend Becky. We live half a state away but get together every year.

The wars started on a camping trip with our husbands. Becky had stayed in camp while the guys and I took a nearly disastrous fishing trip into an unexpected wind-chilled cloudburst. We returned hours later without any fish, soaked and shivering, with grizzly-sized appetites. After supper, we discovered Becky had eaten the chocolate bars we'd gotten for s'mores while we'd been out on the lake. She went to the campground store, but it was sold out of chocolate. We gave her plenty of flak while we ate graham crackers and marshmallows for dessert.

When we broke camp the following day, I hid a monster-sized chocolate bar in Becky's camper. She called as soon as she started unpacking, at which point my husband and I admitted to buying out the campground store's entire supply of one.

"Game on," Becky said, laughing.

Her first salvo: s'mores Christmas tree ornaments. My reprisal: s'mores cream pie. She mailed me a s'mores dog toy. I sent a recipe book. She sewed place mats with s'mores patterns. I scored big with Girl Scouts s'mores cookies. Our lines now firmly drawn, I await retaliation, armed with a s'mores fondue pot.

I give thanks for friends like Becky. When troubles arise, she's one of those friends you don't have to look for; she's already there. God knew what He was doing when He asked us to strengthen one another in fellowship and faith. Near and far, friends are the stitches that hold us together, all the while keeping us in stitches.

Lord, please bless these dear friends who light up our life with love.
—Erika Bentsen

Digging Deeper: Proverbs 17:17; John 15:12–14; Colossians 3:14

Sunday, August 14

But grow in the grace and knowledge of our Lord and Savior Jesus Christ. To him be the glory both now and to the day of eternity.
—2 Peter 3:18 (ESV)

On a best-of-summer afternoon, our family visited a historic village museum. We walked through Robert Frost's home, the Wright brothers' workshop, and the lab where Thomas Edison inspired and perspired to bring forth light. My youngest boys pushed steel to switch tracks for a train, and my mechanically minded son marveled over Model-T Fords. The highlight of the day, though, was a 1913 carousel. Hand-carved animals circled under bright lights while music played and an ornate canopy glittered gold.

We climbed up, chose figures, and held the reins. As we circled, I remembered long-ago little boys whose eyes went wide while we turned on other carousels. They'd grip the poles with summer-brown hands until knuckles paled white. How they'd giggle to express how their hearts felt free! I then recalled the sadness that came when the carousel stopped and glory stood still. They could've circled forever.

Spinning is good for a carnival ride, but not for my faith life. I'd been praying about how to use my gifts and talents to serve the Lord. Then He spoke to me through His Word. Trustworthy believers affirmed what he'd spoken, and opportunities appeared as sure as the sun. However, I was afraid to move ahead. Comfort was holding me back—a familiar path felt safer than traversing new ground.

But a faith walk is measured by forward movement. And when we walk with Jesus, He takes the lead.

My husband, Lonny, our boys, and I had fun that day. I saw my sons' little-boy faces in their smiles. When the carousel stopped, I saw the same sadness too. Not so with me. I was ready to move ahead.

Lord, give me forward-moving faith. Amen.
—Shawnelle Eliasen

Digging Deeper: Luke 17:5; Hebrews 6:1

Monday, August 15

BLESSED BY ONE SWEET COOKIE: Free at Last

He will wipe every tear from their eyes, and there will be no more death or sorrow or crying or pain.... —Revelation 21:4 (NLT)

Thanks to Cookie's confusion about who's walking whom, we bought her a harness. Not surprisingly, she's not a fan. I'm sure the contraption feels cumbersome and, by design, it prevents her from doing things she wants to do (like dragging me through the neighborhood behind her).

In fact, as much as she loves to go for a walk or to the dog park, Cookie dislikes the harness so much that she'd almost rather forgo the adventure than put it on. Once harnessed, she makes the best of it and runs for all she's worth, but when we get home...oh, what joy she feels as she shakes free of her shackles!

Each day after our outing, when I remove Cookie's harness, I think of my loved ones who've gone on to their reward: my dear friend Honey, who kept a smile on her face despite immobilizing joint pain; my grandmother, whose mind slipped away until she no longer recognized us; my daughter's sweet teacher, whose young body was destroyed by cancer.

I like to think of them shaking off these constraints in the presence of our Lord, never again having to feel pain or the betrayal of failing bodies or minds—and perhaps unable to remember what it meant to worry about anything at all.

Heavenly Father, what joy it will be to live with You forever, free of all burdens!
—Ginger Rue

Digging Deeper: Psalm 34:17, 68:19–20; Matthew 11:30; Galatians 5:1

Tuesday, August 16

Many are the plans in the mind of a man, but it is the purpose of the Lord that will stand. —Proverbs 19:21 (ESV)

I bought a jigsaw puzzle two weeks ago. It was an indulgence, but also a way to support a nonprofit I care about. I hadn't bought a puzzle in over a decade.

The thousand-piece puzzle of van Gogh's self-portrait arrived a week later. Oh my. *What had I been thinking?* We have six people in a New York apartment and one table. I was going to have to commandeer half of our familial eating space for a significant amount of time.

As I began to piece it together, I realized this was a *seriously* hard puzzle. There is not a straight line in the entire thing. The colors shift unexpectedly. The brushstrokes vary infinitely. I have luxuriated in looking at this self-portrait in the Metropolitan Museum of Art, but staring at it in pieces and trying to figure out how the colors and textures work together has brought me to a whole new appreciation of the genius of the piece.

It occurred to me that this is very much a metaphor for life. There is so much I can't understand, so much that doesn't make sense until after it all fits together. Once I can look back at the whole, the pattern and lines are clear. But in the moment of not knowing how things fit, it's all blotchy and incomprehensible.

And that's about me and my inability to see—not about God or van Gogh.

Lord, give me patience with not seeing and not understanding. Everything fits in the big picture, for it is Yours.
—Julia Attaway

Digging Deeper: 1 Corinthians 13:12

Wednesday, August 17

Instead of the thorn shall come up the cypress… —Isaiah 55:13 (ESV)

There were a lot of thorns popping up in my life, literally and figuratively.

First the literal ones: My son Will fell onto a rosebush and stood up with at least a hundred and fifty thorns all over his arm. I had to pick them out, one by one, with tweezers.

Then came the figurative thorns: Just as I'd put the final Band-Aid on my son, my boss called with some bad news. Layoffs companywide. One of my favorite coworkers had been let go, and no one's job was safe. Then my husband called. The AC on his truck was no longer working. Just then, the dryer started to make the most terrible clanging noise I had ever heard.

You've had days like that, too, haven't you? Thorny days, full of little tiny pricks, each one drawing blood. Days of discouragement and despair.

I've had many, but that day wasn't one of them. Because that day, Jesus showed up. He soothed my fears and He surrounded me with peace. Instead of the thorns that could have been—no, should have been—up came a beautiful, tranquil cypress.

My son healed quickly. My favorite coworker eventually got a job she loved and was able to move forward in her career. Our company stabilized. The AC on my husband's truck was fixed quickly and easily. And my dryer? That clanging was coming from twenty-seven arcade coins that somehow had made their way from my son's pockets into the drum. Noisy, yes, but not damaging.

We all have thorny days, but by trusting in Christ, we may find that while many of those days *seem* thorny, they might soon have us resting in the shade of a beautiful cypress.

Lord, give me the faith to trust in You on good days and bad, knowing that in all things, You are there. Amen.
—Erin MacPherson

Digging Deeper: Philippians 4:6–7; Isaiah 41:10

Thursday, August 18

But as for me, the nearness of God is my good.... —Psalm 73:28 (NASB)

It was a packed flight from Honduras to Houston, and due to an airline mix-up, my wife and I were seated several rows apart.

I'm an admitted introvert. So sitting with strangers for extended periods is never my favorite thing. But since I fly a lot, I've got the moves down: feigning sleep or opening a book usually wards off interaction. It's not that I don't enjoy people. I'm just a bit more comfortable at a distance.

I heard the woman before I saw her. And I knew—the way you always seem to know these things on planes—that she'd be my seat mate.

I dug for my book. Where was the thing? Too late.

She dropped down next to me with a sigh, all scarves and hats and fluffy things. Maybe I could try the sleep trick? She made eye contact—nope.

I tossed a silent petition to heaven for mercy. Heaven only smiled.

"So, what's your name, son?" the woman said. Heaven's smile turned into a laugh.

I told her and she introduced herself in turn. Then she leaned in. "Isn't it great?"

"Isn't what great?"

She grinned. "How much God loves us." So began a conversation that lasted the rest of the trip.

The thing is, no matter how many tricks we have, God will always find a way into the next seat. His nearness might not always be comfortable, but it's always good.

My new friend waited with me at the end of the jetway, just to give my wife a hug. Then she left us with a wave and a grin.

My wife smiled. "Wow. So...how was your flight?"

"You know what? I loved it."

Thank You, Lord, for pulling us out of ourselves. And into Your love.
—Buck Storm

Digging Deeper: 1 Chronicles 16:11; Romans 8:28; 2 Timothy 1:7

Friday, August 19

When I am afraid, I put my trust in you. —Psalm 56:3 (NIV)

"Mom," James, five, began at bedtime, "I'm gonna miss you when you die." This is not atypical behavior from James. He's my deep thinker, the one plotting on the map ten steps ahead of everyone else.

"I'm not going to die anytime soon, buddy," I told him.

"But," he started, "what if you get hit by a tree branch? From a surprise tornado? And you can't get away fast enough?" I decided maybe settling his heart would be better than dodging his questions.

"James," I said, "are you ever alone?"

James shook his head. "No, I have Jesus."

"That's right," I replied. "And if Mom did somehow die from a freak, surprise branch-throwing tornado, you would still have Jesus in your heart—plus Daddy, and your brother and sister, Nana, KK, Poppa. And I bet Auntie Kristi would even move here, at least for a week, to make sure you were okay."

His eyes grew big. "Really?" he asked. "And they'd all stay here?"

I nodded. "If that's what you wanted."

"If they all move in here," he said, "you can sleep in my room, Mom." For a moment, five-year-old logic had returned.

I pulled him in close, grateful that a mama's hug could still calm his churning heart, and safe in the knowledge that if anything ever did happen, he knew the One he could turn to first.

Lord, hear the prayers of our hearts. In times that we cannot voice our own fears, know them and calm us through Your love.
—Ashley Kappel

Digging Deeper: Psalm 27:1, 34:4; Isaiah 41:13–14

Saturday, August 20

Like a tree planted by streams of water, which yields its fruit in season...—Psalm 1:3 (NIV)

At the farmer's market, I beelined my way to my favorite vendor from the western slope in Colorado, home of the best peaches in the state. I was relieved to see a box still left.

"So glad you still have peaches!" I told the girl behind the table laden with the fresh vegetables of the season.

"There aren't many left on the trees," she admitted. "Eat your fill while you can."

"I like to stretch the season out," I said, searching for several just-right peaches, but I could only find a couple.

Once home, I washed them and stood over the kitchen sink, but one bite and I knew that peach season was almost over. I felt a sadness greater than one would normally feel from facing the loss of fresh peaches. Because I was reminded of the last time I had seen my father.

I had been pregnant with our second child, and we'd come from California to Boulder to see him. We knew he was nearing the end of his cancer journey. After a long weekend of family time, as we were getting ready to leave to go back to California, my mother was helping my dad into their car. They were going to drive to the western slope because he'd had a longing for fresh peaches, right off the trees.

"I'm glad you're going to get peaches," I said, closing his car door.

"Season's almost over." He smiled weakly. "Have to take advantage of what's left."

"I love you, Daddy." I reached through the window and held his bony hand.

He died two weeks later. Now every year I try to stretch out the peach season in his honor.

> *Lord, You tell us that for everything there is a season, which reminds me to make the most of every waning season.*
> —Carol Kuykendall

Digging Deeper: Ecclesiastes 3:1; 1 Corinthians 15:54–57

Sunday, August 21

In the same way, the Spirit helps us in our weakness. We do not know what we ought to pray for, but the Spirit himself intercedes for us through wordless groans. —Romans 8:26 (NIV)

This morning my pastor preached about an Old Testament story I didn't remember. As always when that happens, I scrolled through my Bible app behind the pew to check if the story's unfamiliar part had just been in the Bible version Mike was using.

Nope. Just my weak memory and lazy Scripture-reading habits.

In the story, Elisha's young servant walks outside one morning, sees that they're surrounded by enemies, and runs back inside, terrified. Elisha prays that his servant, despite his fear, will recognize the real story: that God's people outnumber the enemy in "chariots of fire." And the servant does. My pastor's message was that we need to see in the Spirit, as Elisha does, and not in our flesh. It was a good reminder.

But another message from my sneaky scroll-through electrified me: Here's this kid, terrified about the looming disaster, and the prophet prays not about the disaster but for the faith of this nameless, otherwise forgettable boy. In contrast, I'm a pitifully bad pray-er, too distracted by my to-do list, my phone, and the day's looming dangers to pray as well or as often as I should. At best, in the course of some dire conversation about houseguests, grades, a dying pet, or chemo, I'll suddenly worry about the faith of the person I'm talking to: my daughter, a student, or an atheist friend.

But in this biblical account of imminent disaster that never happens—followed by (as I learned in my scrolling) even worse disasters that actually do come to pass—God allowed me a glimpse of how He might be appropriating even my most distracted, fleeting worries as gainful prayers. Indeed, He's already busy answering them as the next disaster looms.

Father, transform my inattention into Your will for me and those around me.
—Patty Kirk

Digging Deeper: 2 Kings 6:8–23

Monday, August 22

He who is slow to anger has great understanding, But he who is quick-tempered exalts folly. —Proverbs 14:29 (NASB)

My wife, Beth, and I love animals. Recently, we adopted a golden retriever, Lexi, from an adoption organization. Lexi just had her first birthday, and she is a wonderful dog. However, like her new "parents," she has also inherited more than her share of stubbornness. I know this willful exuberance will diminish with maturity and training. But for now, we are having contests between her stubbornness and my patience.

Yesterday, Beth and I took Lexi for a walk. She gleefully refused to heel and almost pulled my arm out of its socket lunging for a squirrel. I was frustrated and pulled quickly on the leash to remind her who was walking whom! And then I heard Beth laugh and whisper, "Six months from now, you'll appreciate her strong will when she guards our house, retrieves our newspapers, and plays ball with you." I knew Beth was right.

Determination and passion are important in life. But it takes most of us repeated effort to find balance between maturity and assertiveness. Lexi is reminding me of important things as I try to teach her to be better behaved than I am!

Father of all creation, help me find my own healthy emotional balance each day. Amen.
—Scott Walker

Digging Deeper: 1 Corinthians 13:4; Ephesians 4:2

Tuesday, August 23

He was praying in a certain place, and after he had finished, one of his disciples said to him, "Lord, teach us to pray, as John taught his disciples."
—Luke 11:1 (NRSV)

Some prayers are so often quoted that we can forget how they came about. I was thinking about this the other day when someone mentioned how he liked that ancient prayer from Julian of Norwich, "All shall be well, all shall be well, all manner of thing shall be well...."

Born in Norwich, England, in the fourteenth century, Julian survived a devastating period of plague when as much as half of her town died of the disease. She herself was thirty when she suffered from some mysterious illness that was so serious she was given last rites. And someone brought her a crucifix. She gazed on it, and Jesus seemed to speak to her, giving her visions of God's redeeming love.

Redeeming love in a time of horror? It seems astounding, and yet she transcribed what she saw and heard, producing the first book in English written by a woman. She lived the rest of her life in a small cell attached to a church, praising God for His goodness and spreading word of His love.

As for her lovely prayer, I have often turned to it myself. Only recently, as I was reading about her, did I realize it wasn't exactly *her* prayer. Jesus gave her the words the way He gave the disciples the Lord's Prayer. The promise in them is God's: that even in the worst of times, "all shall be well, all shall be well, all manner of thing shall be well...."

I've never been to Norwich, but I've always loved the example of this woman who, in the midst of her suffering, saw that God's goodness always prevailed.

Lord, help me to know that, at all times, You are with me—and that all will be well.
—Rick Hamlin

Digging Deeper: Romans 8:26–28; Hebrews 13:8

Wednesday, August 24

Therefore do not worry about tomorrow, for tomorrow will worry about itself... —Matthew 6:34 (NIV)

People sometimes accuse me of being a worrier. I prefer to think of myself as a "concerner." But this evening, I couldn't silence the what-ifs inside my head. I had a furnace on the blink at my old log cabin and a sewage system that wouldn't cooperate. *What will go wrong tomorrow?* I asked God as sleep eluded me. *A year from now?*

Driving home on US Route 60, I tried to get a grip on things. Then just before the McDonald's, I noticed a familiar homeless man pushing a grocery cart stocked with his few earthly goods. We'd conversed on a number of occasions, and I tried to help him out whenever I could. Today his plight nagged at me, so I pulled off the road and rolled down my car window. "You need anything?" I asked. A slow smile worked its way across his bearded face as he shook his head.

"How about a nice juicy Big Mac?" When he didn't take me up on the offer, I added, "If you're not hungry now, it'll save till later." But he just gave me that same serene smile and kept going.

Finally, I could stand it no more. "What about *tomorrow*?" I fairly cried.

That stopped him in his tracks. "Tomorrow?" he said, turning from his cart to face me. Eyes filled with understanding—a knowing, really—met mine. He seemed to sense my angst about the future. He said nothing more, but his gentle gesture was so comforting, it guides me still: he cupped his hands and lifted them toward the sky, where his gaze was fixed.

Exactly where mine needed to be.

Dear Lord, You aren't my last resort. You are my first resource. Thank You for sending Your servant to show me.
—Roberta Messner

Digging Deeper: Job 38:41; Luke 12:24; 2 Corinthians 9:8

Thursday, August 25

Therefore we do not lose heart. Though outwardly we are wasting away, yet inwardly we are being renewed day by day. —2 Corinthians 4:16 (NIV)

On a recent cruise, we ate lunch with a couple we'd met on board. The wife was talkative. The husband, white-haired and older-appearing, was pleasant but spoke little.

That night my husband and I went to the ship's club for late-night music and dancing. The couple was there. The wife was on the dance floor with a female friend; the husband quietly watched from a chair. But as the band struck up a lively song that brought back my college memories, the husband jumped up, walked to the dance floor, and went to town. He waved his arms, shimmied to the floor and back, danced with a pole, took his jacket off, swung it around his head, then grabbed his wife, and the two danced and laughed like teenagers. After several songs of this, the husband sat down and resumed a dignified posture.

Watching them had made my night. It reminded me that no matter our age, inside us all is youthful joy just waiting to be released. As I joined the dance-floor crowd and looked around, I saw that joy on many faces and felt it on my own. Yes, on the outside we're an older group, but on the inside, we are still very much our younger selves.

Lord, thank You that although outwardly we're growing older, inside we can remain young. May we never be afraid to show it!
—Kim Taylor Henry

Digging Deeper: Psalm 92:14; Isaiah 46:4

Friday, August 26

I thank my God every time I remember you. —Philippians 1:3 (NIV)

As much as I try to appreciate the moment, birthdays for my kids are usually a stressful time for me.

For my son Tyler's tenth birthday, my stress was on another level. I promised more kids than I should have for a prebirthday sleepover, and my small apartment was now exploding with Nerf bullets flying everywhere. Little boys ran, climbed, and hid in unideal spaces with their play guns held to their chests.

Cleanup after dinner consumed me as they continued to scream and run. The dance party I'd planned, with glow necklaces, started off great but then turned into intense wrestling matches and balloon fights.

The next morning followed the same pattern—a loud breakfast, a trip to a virtual reality venue by subway, then pizza and cake back home.

After the last child left, I shut myself in my room and cried. I was tired and wound up, but mostly I regretted the feeling that I had not personally celebrated my son. He was now ten—double digits, and just a few years away from being a teenager. I looked at pictures on my phone of his past birthdays and cried some more. The first birthday, with his chubby cheeks and fistfuls of cake, then the second, third, fourth, and fifth. Each pictured a very different boy.

My son was alive and well in the next room, but knowing I could never go back and hold that baby again stung. I went into his bedroom and we snuggled. *Let me hold you now,* I thought, *hear your voice, kiss your face. Because year after year, someone else takes your place.*

> Lord, help me cherish the fleeting moments I share with loved ones and accept the changes that come with each passing year.
> —Karen Valentin

Digging Deeper: Luke 2:40; 1 Corinthians 13:11

Saturday, August 27

Those who consider themselves religious and yet do not keep a tight rein on their tongues deceive themselves, and their religion is worthless.
—James 1:26 (NIV)

"Hey, Chris," I said. "Can you give me a hand?"

I steadied the stack of boxes in my arms. Chris was supposed to be helping me take donations into the thrift shop. Instead, he was sitting in the passenger seat of my car, tapping at his phone.

"Chris?"

No response.

"Hey. Chris." I struggled to maintain a patient voice. "Please help me with these boxes."

"What's that?" Chris swiveled to face me. "Oh yeah. Just a minute." He returned to his phone.

I sighed. I had been mentoring Chris for six months. We had talked many times about the importance of serving others, so I was frustrated that he was unwilling to help me.

I walked to the other side of the car to get the rest of the boxes. Now with both of my arms full, I only had a few fingers to grasp at the door's handle. I reached and stretched. *Click.* The door swung open. Directly into the neighboring car. Leaving a gray scar on its red paint.

Sharp words burned at the back of my throat.

I wanted to call attention to Chris's laziness. I wanted to place blame on him. But if I lashed out at Chris, I would hurt him. And I would undermine the months I had spent with him.

So instead, I returned to the driver's side and took a scrap of paper from the dash. I wrote down my contact information and a note explaining the scratch. Then I placed the paper under the other car's wiper blade.

As I turned back, I noticed that Chris had set down his phone.

He was watching me instead.

Lord, help me to control my words. Let me use them only in ways that glorify You.
—Logan Eliasen

Digging Deeper: Psalm 19:14; Proverbs 21:23

Sunday, August 28

Come unto me, all ye that labour and are heavy laden, and I will give you rest. —Matthew 11:28 (KJV)

Despite its traditional role of being a startling sound-maker, I never thought an alarm clock should be so named or purposed. It seemed to me it should be designed to be a gentle reminder, not the conduit of a clanging, jarring sensation burrowing into a deep sleep like a fire threat. My idea of the word *alarm* was further altered after my pastor counseled me one day.

"The Lord sounds the alarm when it's time to rest," he admonished.

An alarm when it's time to rest? Interesting.

Mature Christians realize that our Savior has indeed set within us the Spirit, Who frequently notifies us of when we ought to do His bidding. But just as important, He lets us know when it's time to slow down and pay attention to the anxiety and sense of overwhelm we tend to repress. In fact, if we heed His whispers, we might discover that often when we ignore the rest God commands, the high productivity we achieve devolves into simply spinning our wheels.

Surely God does not need rest as we do, but in His far-reaching wisdom, He knew that humans—from the early tillers of the land to today's corporate executives—would become driven. So He modeled rest for us by creating a Sabbath, a time designated to do nothing categorized as work.

In a world where rest can seem only a costly dream, we sometimes feel compelled to ignore the bone-tiredness and imminent blown fuses that cause pain and regret. Might we all occasionally reconsider visiting the public park, planning a staycation, or taking a ride in the country? Might we allow the Holy Spirit's alarm to point us toward the rest we are commanded to take?

Lord, teach me to hear Your subtle alarm,
designed for my soul's much-needed rest.
—Jacqueline F. Wheelock

Digging Deeper: Mark 6:31; Hebrews 4:9–11

Monday, August 29

The soothing tongue is a tree of life, but a perverse tongue crushes the spirit. —Proverbs 15:4 (NIV)

My eleven-year-old son, Isaiah, longed for a ventriloquist puppet after he learned that I'd had one as a child. Imagine the joy when I found a vintage doll on eBay right before his birthday! It was just like the one I'd had. Right down to the plaid pants.

"Mom! Dad! I can't believe it," Isaiah cried when he pulled the doll from its box. Willie Talk wore a birthday hat, and his familiar smile was as big as my son's.

Isaiah worked diligently to practice the art of ventriloquism. Isaiah wrote dialogue and then he and Willie talked in front of mirrors. When the duo was ready to perform, family filled the living room.

"Hey there, Will. How are you?" Isaiah asked.

"Doing well." Willie turned his head. "I was made for this."

Isaiah's lips were nearly still when Willie spoke. The delivery of each word was intentional and deliberate, every syllable spoken with care.

As I sat there, I remembered how disciplined I'd been with my puppet's words too. But the next thing that came to mind wasn't as sweet to recall: I'd recently been much less disciplined with words. I'd been frustrated with a neighbor, and a fresh offense had pressed me hard. When I walked across the road to talk, angry words spilled fast.

Over the years, I've taught my boys what God's Word says about our words. They can be sweet like honeycomb or as refreshing as a brook. If fitly spoken, they're like golden apples in silver bowls. But careless, harsh words bring destruction. They're like slashing swords that bring folly and shame.

I knew what I had to do.

Willie and Isaiah continued their show that night. As they spoke, I was thankful that my heavenly Father had spoken too.

Lord, help my words to be gentle and life-giving. Amen.
—Shawnelle Eliasen

Digging Deeper: Proverbs 16:24, 18:4

Tuesday, August 30

In all your ways, acknowledge Him, and He will make your paths smooth. —Proverbs 3:6 (Tanakh)

This year, the anniversary of the death of my husband, Keith (the *Yahrzeit*), would fall on a day when the rabbi would be away. Because of this, the synagogue suggested that I say the Mourner's Kaddish—the prayer recited to honor God in the face of grief—the week before the proper time. I balked.

I felt strongly that I wanted to memorialize Keith at the right time. And the week before that right time was when I had to recite the prayer for my mother. I believed that both of them deserved their own times to be remembered.

I mentioned it to friends, and one of them said, "I'd be happy to set up a service in your home for the right time. Just tell me who you want to invite for the minyan prayer, and I'll take care of everything." I swallowed the thought that I'd be inconveniencing people and accepted her help. Because I didn't know how many people would be available or willing, I gave her twenty names, including my "here" family, hoping that no one would feel too put-upon.

On the night in question, I kept thanking everyone who arrived and apologizing for any disruption to their schedule. Everyone assured me they were happy to be there, but I was convinced that if I hadn't been so stubborn, the whole thing might have been unnecessary.

When we reached the point in the service for Kaddish to be said, I stood up. One of the men also stood and said, "I need to say Kaddish for my aunt." A woman stood, too, to say it for her father. They thanked me for giving them the opportunity to do it at the right time. Then we said the prayer together.

You always know what I'm supposed to do, God, and You always find ways to remind me of that.
—Rhoda Blecker

Digging Deeper: Lamentations 3:22; Psalm 70:5

Wednesday, August 31

SACRED SPACES: Merrymeeting Lake

My voice shalt thou hear in the morning, O LORD; in the morning will I direct my prayer unto thee, and will look up. —Psalm 5:3 (KJV)

It's 5 o'clock this August morning. My children and their grandparents are still asleep as I slip out the cabin's screen door and creep across the lawn to Merrymeeting Lake. My kayak hisses as I slide it across sand and into water so still it looks like polished chrome. As I ease myself inside, I bump the hull with a hollow *thunk. Shh! Don't wake anyone!* Gently I draw the paddle through the crystalline water. *Glide. Stroke. Glide.* Only two ripples mark my presence on the glassy surface.

About fifty yards from shore, I rest my paddle on the hull, and I drift. Even out here, the water is so clear, I can see a trout lurking in the bottle-green depths beneath me. It darts, pauses, then darts again. No one knows this fish is there but me. In fact, no one knows I am here either—except God. All is silence. All is peace on this lake so calm that a duck feather floats across it on the apex of its curl. I gaze toward the low mountains green with pines and the coming dawn, and I pray without words. In the tranquil sweetness of this morning, I have found a sacred place.

Perhaps fifteen minutes later, the sun inches over the mountaintops, and first light seeps into the sky. A solitary fisherman chugs into view. His wake sets my kayak gently rocking. Time to go.

Infused with enough of God's peace to last the day, maybe several days, I stroke and glide back to my family. I am blessed.

> *Creator God, thank You for the miracle of a fresh morning and the time to savor it.*
> —Gail Thorell Schilling

Digging Deeper: Psalm 46:10, 143:8; Proverbs 8:17; Mark 4:39

August

THE LORD IS NEAR

1 _____

2 _____

3 _____

4 _____

5 _____

6 _____

7 _____

8 _____

9 _____

10 _____

11 _____

12 _____

13 _____

14 _____

15 _____

August

16 _____

17 _____

18 _____

19 _____

20 _____

21 _____

22 _____

23 _____

24 _____

25 _____

26 _____

27 _____

28 _____

29 _____

30 _____

31 _____

September

Let us draw near to God with a sincere heart and with the full assurance that faith brings...

—Hebrews 10:22 (NIV)

Thursday, September 1

Have I not commanded you? Be strong and courageous. Do not be afraid; do not be discouraged, for the LORD your God will be with you wherever you go. —Joshua 1:9 (NIV)

I do not have fond memories of middle school. Violence in my Brooklyn school was common, with fights almost every day. Fear and loneliness sat so heavily on my chest during those preteen years, I even entertained the thought of suicide. Yet middle school did not define the rest of my life.

But when my oldest son moved onto middle school, those fears came back just as strong.

"You let me know how you feel there," I said multiple times before his first day. "If you don't feel comfortable, we can always do homeschool."

On his first day, parents led their kids into the cafeteria and Brandon happily found a table with some of his friends from last year.

That happiness, however, didn't last.

"They call me short," he confessed. Brandon was beginning to feel isolated and lonely, just as I had so many years ago.

"Do you feel like you're in danger?" I asked.

"No," he quickly answered, as if the question was ridiculous.

"Then you can do this," I said. "It's just a small part of your life."

For the first time I was happy to have experienced what I did as a preteen, so that I could help my son. Brandon and I talked for a long time about my middle school experiences. And all of the positive, life-giving ones that followed in high school and college.

As long as he felt safe, this would be a test of his strength, to know his worth and potential, despite what others said.

"I've got this," he said, with a new sense of confidence. With pride and heartache, I smiled at my son. "I know you do."

Lord, thank You for defining who I am and for being with me as I walk in my purpose.
—Karen Valentin

Digging Deeper: Isaiah 43:1–2; 1 Thessalonians 5:11

Friday, September 2

But the Lord is my haven; my God is my sheltering rock.
—Psalm 94:22 (Tanakh)

The synagogue's scholar in residence, here for a long weekend of learning, did not drive on Shabbat, so that ruled out his staying at any of the hotels in town. Our cantor asked me if he could stay in my guest room, since I live within walking distance of the synagogue and my guest facilities are on a different floor from the rest of my house.

I agreed to let him stay, but it had been a long time since anyone besides me was in the house overnight. And the first night he was there, even though he was comfortably removed from my living space, I was aware that something was unusual.

As I sometimes remembered to do when I was uneasy, I asked myself, "What is God trying to teach me?" Nothing I came up with seemed right until the next morning when I was up to my elbows in dishwater and the scholar came into the kitchen. "Where would I find the glasses?" he asked.

I couldn't get him one or point out the right place, so I said, "Put your hand on something." I'd learned long ago that giving verbal directions in a vacuum didn't work well, because everyone interpreted things like "the door over the canisters" differently, leading to "No, not that one." But once there was an agreed-on anchor spot, it was much easier. He put his hand on a cabinet door, and I told him to look in the cabinet directly to the left of the one he was touching.

As he poured himself some orange juice, I finally recognized God's lesson: when I don't know what's adrift in my life, I need to find an anchor point. And I reminded myself that the best anchor point for me in this changing world is always God.

Lord, You always provide an anchor to hold me steady when I am drifting.
—Rhoda Blecker

Digging Deeper: 1 Samuel 2:2; Psalm 61:3

Saturday, September 3

I will instruct you and teach you in the way you should go; I will counsel you with my loving eye on you. —Psalm 32:8 (NIV)

My children's earliest memories had been made in the house we were about to leave behind. Even though our newly built home was less than a fifteen-minute drive away—and they were excited about finally having their own rooms—they were sentimentally attached to what we had always described to others as our "house on the hill."

Tiny hands and feet that smudged the walls and spilled milk across the counters had grown into bigger hands that helped with dinner in our cramped kitchen. The space once overflowing with toys that had blinking lights and musical lullabies had been transformed into office space shared by me and my husband. We were overdue for a change.

With each packed box of our belongings, memories arose, and I began to feel wistful and sad. Birthday parties, family gatherings, movie nights, unfinished puzzles on the kitchen table, even sibling spats were precious. Yes, it was difficult to leave the place we'd made our home for ten years, but it would've been even more difficult to stay.

The feeling was familiar. Fourteen years earlier, I'd decided to leave the comfort and financial stability of a corporate position that I loved for the calling to be a full-time writer and stay-at-home mother to my firstborn. The decision was pivotal for my growth and a milestone in my faith and trust in God.

In my life, change has been a gift that allows to me to experience God in a new way. It's an opportunity to cling to His unchanging hand. When everything around me fluctuates, He stays the same.

Lord, when there is change in my life, I will trust in You. You've never left me before, and You never will.
—Tia McCollors

Digging Deeper: Deuteronomy 31:8; Isaiah 43:18–19; 2 Corinthians 5:17; Philippians 4:6; Hebrews 13:8

Sunday, September 4

WISDOM'S DELIGHTS: Wisdom in Obedience

Thus Noah did; according to all that God had commanded him, so he did. —Genesis 6:22 (NASB)

What catches my attention in this Genesis verse is that Noah did "all that God had commanded him." God had warned Noah a flood was coming and had given him divine instruction to build an ark of gopher wood to hold him and his family. It was also to carry a male and female from "every living thing of all flesh." (Genesis 6:19 NASB)

The ark would have three decks divided into rooms. It was to be covered inside and out with pitch. Its dimensions in cubits translated to 450 feet long, 75 feet wide, and 45 feet high. Floor space totaled over 101,000 square feet.

When all inhabitants had entered the ark, the Lord closed the door. (Genesis 6:16 NASB) This vessel—one hundred years in the building—kept Noah's family safe in the forty-day deluge.

God always has a good reason for His instructions.

Years ago I did not want to move to Alaska. It was my husband's dream, not mine. I knew all I had to do was say so, and we wouldn't go. I also knew God was telling me to give it a try. Unexpectedly, from this beginning, my writing career launched: how God changed my heart to embrace the move to Alaska became my first published story. Terry and I ended up living there fourteen years.

Listening to the voice of God—when my own is telling me something different—seems nearly impossible sometimes. I can't, or maybe am unwilling to, see why I should. But when I look at Noah, I see a man who didn't doubt God. Who persevered in doing "all God had commanded" when there seemed to be no real reason for it.

Obeying God is a choice. And that choice carries my future well-being.

Empower me, Lord, to choose obedience.
—Carol Knapp

Digging Deeper: Isaiah 48:17–18; Jeremiah 7:23;
Luke 6:46–49; James 1:25

Labor Day, Monday, September 5

Come to me, all of you who are weary and burdened, and I will give you rest. —Matthew 11:28 (CSB)

It's Labor Day. I spent the morning completing a jigsaw puzzle with a neighbor girl. "What's this holiday about?" she asked.

"Well, it honors the workers who build our cars and bake our bread and fix our streets. We have a day off. Let's enjoy." My heart was light, released from a burden I had carried for years.

I grew up on Bible admonitions: "redeem the time," "be as industrious as an ant," "work before the cosmic nightfall." I helped feed our large parsonage family—weeding carrots, shucking peas, peeling potatoes. At the church, I swept the sanctuary, collected trash, aligned chairs. I didn't catch the message about rest or play.

Early in my career, a much older boss had stopped by my Manhattan office and gently chastised me. "You haven't taken your vacation time."

"I just can't," I said. "I'm so busy." So indispensable, or so I thought—always a briefcase filled with manuscripts to read on the train and after dinner.

"Well, I can't *make* you schedule time off, but you *should*." *Get a life.*

Months later, after another mentor offhandedly said, "You take yourself too seriously," I listened. I stepped back and took a break. I went to a country cabin and prayed for wider horizons. I relaxed and crocheted. I read and wrote poetry. I memorized a hymn that shifted my long-term perspective: "Be thou my vision, O Lord." In Scripture, I looked for and now can see complementary guideposts: Redeem the time. Consider the ant. But rest in the Lord. Glide like an eagle and enjoy the holiday ride.

Lord, give us who labor too intensely the grace to slow down, look up, and relish Your promised rest.
—Evelyn Bence

Digging Deeper: Isaiah 40:31; Matthew 6:33

Tuesday, September 6

Do not forget to show hospitality to strangers, for by so doing some people have shown hospitality to angels without knowing it.
—Hebrews 13:2 (NIV)

The night before school started, I gathered the kids. "Let's say a special prayer for our year, for our teachers, and for friends who might be feeling a little nervous or shy about starting school tomorrow," I said.

"Dear God," I prayed, "help our teachers to be kind and wise, help us to have a great year learning interesting things and being with friends who might be shy. Help us look for them in the lunchroom and on the playground so that we can invite them to sit with us."

When I finished, James didn't lift his eyes. "Is it okay if shy kids do that stuff, too?" he asked.

"It's more than okay," I said, lifting his chin so his eyes would meet mine. "When I feel shy, I find the best way to feel better is to say a little prayer, then invite someone else to play. If you think about others around you, you tend to forget to worry about yourself."

The next day, he came home from school. "MOM," he said, climbing into the car, "we didn't get to pick our lunch spot, but we could pick our playground games, and I picked tricycles, and I invited a new boy—I think his name is Oliver—to come play, and Oliver has a big brother, and I think we're going to be good friends." He was beaming, and I was silently singing praises to God for knowing the prayer that my deep-thinking boy needed to hear from my lips.

> *Lord, make me less so that You may be more. Teach me to always look for Your sheep so that I may show them love.*
> —Ashley Kappel

Digging Deeper: Proverbs 29:25; Galatians 5:22–25; 2 Timothy 1:7

Wednesday, September 7

I thank my God upon every remembrance of you.
—Philippians 1:3 (NKJV)

Saying good-bye to an old friend is one of the hardest things I have ever done, whether that friend is a person, a beloved pet, or just a favorite house or car.

I can get very attached to an automobile, for example. So, when it was time to trade in our aging baby-blue Crown Victoria sedan, I truly mourned.

As I drove to the dealership, my mind replayed vacations in this blue steed: excursions to Galveston and Mackinac Island, Kitty Hawk and Savannah. Through all kinds of weather, this car was our "home away from home."

I love the Crown Victoria because it's kind of a "poor man's limousine." My granddaughter Hannah calls it "the smooth car." And yet it's rugged too, which is why it was used for taxis and police cars for many years. Above all, it was a practical car that I referred to as "my truck." I could haul a class of college students on a field trip or load the cavernous trunk with a quarter-ton of bagged sand and mulch for my garden.

I told my wife, "When I die, just bury me in my Crown Victoria. That would make me very happy."

As I handed the keys to the dealer, I thought of a line from Dr. Seuss: "Don't cry because it's over. Smile because it happened."

But when I say good-bye, I truly need to cry, and then to consolidate the memories that will enable me to smile for the rest of my life.

Thank You, my Creator, for giving me a memory that keeps alive precious things that have passed away.
—Daniel Schantz

Digging Deeper: Proverbs 10:7; Matthew 5:4

Thursday, September 8

You will hear about wars and stories of wars that are coming. But don't be afraid.... —Matthew 24:6 (ICB)

Pot of tea? Check. Plate of donuts? Check. Fully charged camera? Check. Curiosity? Check. Everything was ready for my eleven-hour journey. Thanks to the Suez Canal, all I had to do was sit on the balcony of my cruise ship and watch Egypt go by. The weight of how blessed I felt at this moment automatically sent prayers of thanksgiving sky-high.

As our ship passed the city of Suez on the south end of the canal, I responded in kind to waves from people on the shore—mothers hanging laundry, children heading out to play, fishermen mending their nets. Dolphins played alongside the ship. Blooms of jellyfish, abandoning their home in the Red Sea and heading toward the Mediterranean, periodically clouded the waters.

It wasn't until we passed a convoy of American military vessels headed the opposite direction that my lighthearted mood turned more somber. Recent conflict in the Middle East had warranted their journey through the canal. That realization fine-tuned my attention to the helicopters regularly passing overhead. Then I became aware of a slow-moving blue car traveling parallel to our ship, mile after mile along the shore. I snapped a photo and enlarged the image on my laptop. That little blue car was really an armored truck—a protective escort guarding our ship on its 102-mile journey.

War and terrorism are stories I see on the nightly news—or read about in the Bible. They don't often touch my daily life. But even if they do, I need not panic. God is like that little armored truck, always near, always alert, always prepared. Nothing can separate me from His love and care.

Lord, You remain in control, even when the world seems like it's spinning out of control. Thank You for the comfort of Your protection and presence.
—Vicki Kuyper

Digging Deeper: Deuteronomy 20:1; Psalm 112:6–8; John 16:33; Romans 8:35–38

Friday, September 9

Finally, all of you, be like-minded, be sympathetic, love one another, be compassionate and humble. —1 Peter 3:8 (NIV)

One September weekday, I attended an event for work that required me to catch a commuter train just after dawn, walk several New York City blocks, and then engage in cheery chitchat. All before 9:00 a.m.! I did it, but I can't say I was thrilled.

As I wended my way around the conference room, I noticed my colleague, Mariela, who had joined the company just a few months prior. I wanted to bring her into a conversation with another guest, but I could see tears brimming in her eyes. I didn't know what was wrong, but I sensed that idle chatter was not what she needed then. She was trying to force a smile, but she seemed pained.

When the event ended, I told her that she and I would walk to our office together while the others took the subway. I wanted her to have all the time she needed to release whatever was troubling her.

We walked, and she talked. For nearly two miles, she shared her concerns about a medical condition she had, which was not at all hopeless. As I'm not a doctor, I couldn't give advice, but I could offer a listening ear and a heart of compassion to Mariela.

As she talked, the tears fell. By the time we reached our office, she had come up with a new plan to deal with her condition, which included seeking additional medical opinions. She thanked me for helping her, when really, all I did was listen and show her love. It was our loving Father in heaven who intervened to see her through to a solution.

> *Heavenly Father, I thank You for being able to show Your kind of compassion and love to others. May they realize that they are seeing You and not me.*
> —Gayle T. Williams

Digging Deeper: Zechariah 7:9; 2 Corinthians 1:3–4

Saturday, September 10

Therefore put on the full armor of God, so that when the day of evil comes, you may be able to stand your ground, and after you have done everything, to stand. —Ephesians 6:13 (NIV)

Never again will I say the phrase "easy as riding a bike." A split-second event has erased it from my vocabulary forever. Although I'd ridden my mountain bike for years over rough terrain, the first time I pedaled my husband's road bike twenty yards on pavement, it started a chain of unforeseen consequences.

The lightweight frame and skinny tires glided over the road with little effort compared to my sturdy mud-loving mountain crawler. The brakes worked great—I squeezed the levers, the bike stopped. I moved my feet from the pedals to touch the ground, and both of us fell over. All I remember is seeing asphalt rush toward my eyes.

My spill gave me a bruised shoulder, a cut on my arm, and a scrape almost to the bone on my left shin. I limped away humiliated but thankful my head had come to rest less than an inch from disaster. In my haste to ride, I hadn't taken the time to put on my helmet. I should've also checked the seat height compared to my leg length. My injuries were the result of a lack of preparation.

Just as I didn't spare the time for these two essential safety steps, I also often skip my morning quiet time with God. My fall taught me several lessons, but the most important one was a reminder to put on my heart and mind the protective equipment God offers us daily.

Lord, thank You for protecting us when we don't realize we're in trouble and rescuing us when we cannot stand against the forces trying to defeat us.
—Jenny Lynn Keller

Digging Deeper: Psalm 68:20; Proverbs 2:8; Ephesians 6:14–17

Sunday, September 11

Fear not, for I am with you; be not dismayed, for I am your God; I will strengthen you, I will help you, I will uphold you with my righteous right hand. —Isaiah 41:10 (ESV)

Twenty-one years ago today, American Airlines Flight 11, out of Logan Airport in Boston, flew over my house in western Massachusetts, where Julee and the dogs were settling in for the Berkshire fall. Twenty-seven miles later, it made a left turn at the Hudson River and followed that ribbon of blue, flying nine blocks west of our Manhattan apartment before slamming murderously into the north tower of the World Trade Center. Just three miles downtown from there, I was working in my office at Guideposts.

Before long, we could see twin spires of smoke rising above the Financial District. Then came the men and women covered in ash, like a ghostly army in retreat, leaning on each other, faces streaked with tears and sweat.

Eventually, I went to my apartment and watched the coverage on TV, the towers collapsing over and over until I went for a walk through the deserted streets of my adopted hometown, wondering whether the city would ever be the same and praying to gain understanding.

The country has been through a lot in the twenty-one years since that infamous day. We have seen war and disease and economic hardship. Time and time again, I have heard the phrase "We live in uncertain times."

Indeed, humans have always lived in uncertain times. What could have been more uncertain than the time when a Savior was born in a region of the world that was in turmoil and revolt? Yet it was the birth of that Savior, at that time, that gave us the greatest certainty of all—the certainty of eternal life and of a peace that passes all understanding.

Help me to cling to You, Lord, when danger is close and my understanding falters.
—Edward Grinnan

Digging Deeper: Deuteronomy 31:6; Psalm 56:1–4; Romans 8:31–35

Monday, September 12

Seek the LORD and his strength; seek his presence continually!
—1 Chronicles 16:11 (ESV)

This morning on my drive to the grocery store, I took a shortcut through the local college campus. The sun was just rising, and there wasn't a student in sight. The trees held a hint of crimson and bright orange, and as I turned a corner, there was a deer, a beautiful doe, standing on the side of the road, waiting exactly in front of the crosswalk. I slowed to a stop, and the doe met my eye, then turned its head and walked safely over the painted pavement to the other side.

I watched, a little distracted, thinking that I should grab my purse, find my phone, and snap a photo or video, but I kept my eyes on the doe instead.

For the rest of the drive to the store, I second-guessed my decision not to take a photo. Would anyone believe what I had seen? Did it matter?

I went back and forth between wishing I'd taken a video on my phone and glad that I'd sat right where I was and taken in the moment without removing my eyes from the road. It's a weird struggle that social media and cell phones have created—this odd balancing between capturing experiences for others to see and fully experiencing them ourselves.

But then my mind went to that unbelievable, magical moment of connection, when the deer met my eyes and made sure I had seen her, and I knew I had made the right choice.

> *Dear Lord, it's easy to forget that this moment, right here, right now, is more important than anything else and that sometimes, most times, blessings are meant to be holy singular moments captured not on a screen but in our hearts.*
> —Sabra Ciancanelli

Digging Deeper: Psalm 16:11, 18:33

Tuesday, September 13

Take delight in the Lord, and he will give you the desires of your heart.
—Psalm 37:4 (NRSV)

Help me, please. I can't understand what happened. I've been pondering this for weeks.

One Tuesday afternoon, I went to lunch at a place where I've gone dozens of times before. Each time, I ordered the same tuna fish sandwich. It comes with homemade chips (*really* good ones) and a pickle. But en route to lunch this day, I was thinking for the first time, *I'm so hungry. Maybe I should order extra chips today!* The idea went over and over in my mind as I pedaled my bike the three miles to the market where the tuna fish lives.

However, by the time I got there, locked my bike, and walked to the counter, I ended up ordering the same as usual—not wanting to overdo a good thing. *I don't really need extra chips*, I said to myself.

A few minutes later, they handed me the bag with my food, and I took it upstairs to where there's open seating. I sat down and opened it. Inside, there were two bags of chips. What does this mean? "It's only chips," you may say. Yes, but it felt so unusual, unexpected, and special.

"Special blessings," a kind friend later said when I told him the story. I was uncomfortable with that answer.

"God testing you, to see if you'd pay for the extras," said another, piling on guilt.

Then my friend Mike said, "It's your guardian angel."

"Regarding potato chips?" I said.

"Yes," Mike said. "The angels sometimes give us what we want so that we'll learn to ask them for the things we need. And I never discount their sense of humor!"

You are my hope today, God, my protection and my comfort.
You hear the desires of my heart.
—Jon M. Sweeney

Digging Deeper: Proverbs 16:1–3; 1 Thessalonians 5:17–18

Wednesday, September 14

For we are God's handiwork, created in Christ Jesus to do good works, which God prepared in advance for us to do. —Ephesians 2:10 (NIV)

Balancing my plate of veggies, crackers, and cheese, I jostled for a spot to stand in the tiny band-hall kitchen. "Oh, sorry," I said as I bumped into another community band member. Rehearsal breaks always felt so awkward. The unstructured social time reminded me of my long-ago middle school cafeteria, where the truth of who belonged and who didn't played out each afternoon. I'd often been on the wrong side of that equation.

Perhaps that's why, when I looked around at the others crowding into the kitchen, I saw people that had been a part of the group longer than I had. People who played better, knew more people, and conversed more easily. People way more worthy of standing in my spot than me. I shifted, trying to make myself smaller so that a few more people could fit.

Then, when I'd just decided I should go sit back in the band room, "Relax, Erin," came the words of a fellow trumpet player. "Take up space."

I looked up at him, startled. Were my thoughts really that obvious? But his pointed, friendly remark loosened up something inside me. I did relax a little. I didn't go sit in the empty band room. This wasn't eighth grade anymore. The people here were good. I knew that.

What's more, how does wishing to make myself small value the sacrifice Jesus made for me? God made me in His image and prepared in advance a purpose for me. To fulfill that purpose, I must first remain in the room.

I need to relax. And I need to take up the space He made especially for me.

Thank You, God, for helping me remember my value, both in Your eyes and within this world in which You've placed me.
—Erin Janoso

Digging Deeper: Psalm 40:2, 100:3

Thursday, September 15

And we labor, working with our own hands. Being reviled, we bless; being persecuted, we endure.... —1 Corinthians 4:12 (NKJV)

Throughout the day, our landline rings, and it's often a telemarketer with a sales pitch. Usually, it's an aggressive fast-talker who intimidates me, and I hang up.

Today the phone rang, and the soft southern voice of an older woman spoke to me in a halting manner. She sounded as sincere and as vulnerable as a child, her voice filled with the hope of a sale: "I, uh, work for a company that, well, sir, we help people to understand the, uh, changes that are coming in...you know, Medicare?"

She struggled to make her presentation, but I just couldn't hang up on her.

At last she was done, and in a gentle voice I said, "Well, I thank you for calling and presenting your plan, but I don't think I am interested."

I braced myself for more pressure, but she simply said, "Okay, sir, I understand. But I want to thank you for not hanging up on me. You are a good man, and may God bless you."

As I hung up the phone, I felt my heart going out to her and to others who have hard jobs like telemarketing—a job that deals with hostile customers and constant rejection. I thought about people who have demanding bosses, terrible working conditions, and impossible quotas but who need the work, so they struggle on. I am thankful for their example of patience.

Lord, I do weary of sales pitches, but I also ask for courage for those who are forced to endure difficult and thankless jobs.
—Daniel Schantz

Digging Deeper: Deuteronomy 24:14; 2 Thessalonians 3:10–12

Friday, September 16

In their hearts humans plan their course, but the Lord establishes their steps. —Proverbs 16:9 (NIV)

We were leaving on a two-week trip the next day. I had more "must-dos" to complete than I could figure out how to get done.

A hiking experience popped into my mind. My wife, Pat, and I had been hiking in the Azores Islands, and we'd reached the mountaintop. As we snacked and enjoyed the magnificent ocean view, we realized there was no clear pathway down. The way we'd gotten there seemed too steep to safely descend. As we scanned the landscape, Pat spotted a partially hidden creek bed. When we were ready to head back, we made our way to the creek bed, which led us to a clearing, where we found a narrow path to a mountainside pasture. And from there, we found a path that took us the rest of the way down.

The experience taught me about the power of the next step. I still remember the sinking feeling we got when we didn't think we had a safe way down the Azorean mountainside. And how, once we spotted a possible solution and took the first step, the way back unfolded in good order.

So I started working the list that was overwhelming me by asking God to order my steps His way. New insights began filling my mind, silent whispers that nudged, "This next, not that." New tasks were added, others dropped off, a meeting was canceled. Step by step, the day unfolded, and by day's end, everything that had to be done was completed.

Some of my favorite days have sprung from ones that start with dread and end in gratitude for all God does through me once I yield to the power of His next step.

Thank You, God, for showing us Your way when there seems to be no way. Help us to trust You, step by step, through each day. Amen.
—John Dilworth

Digging Deeper: Exodus 3:1–22, 14:15; Psalm 37:23; Proverbs 16:3

Saturday, September 17

What man of you, having an hundred sheep, if he lose one of them, doth not leave the ninety and nine... and go after that which is lost....
—Luke 15:4–7 (KJV)

Our park was hosting a Highland Games Festival where a sheepdog herding demonstration was a hot item—until one naughty sheep escaped from the fold. Off into the woods went the sheep, with a gaggle of men in Scottish kilts in hot pursuit.

A search followed, but this one elusive sheep was not to be found. After the festival tents had been folded, only the sheep owner, who lived two hundred miles away, was left. I'd see him in the mornings, parked in his truck. He even created a sheep pen and put two other sheep in it, hoping they would attract the missing sheep.

When word got out, the community sprang into action. A Facebook page was created for Belle, the lost sheep. Hundreds of volunteers searched for her. And sightings were reported daily.

Neighbors took extraordinary measures. One friend posted notices on every street corner, while another rose early each morning and hiked through the park, calling for Belle.

Weeks went by. Then one morning, I spotted Belle's owner at the park, leaning on his truck and drinking coffee. I asked him, "Why haven't you given up on finding Belle?"

I expected something biblically profound.

"It's just the responsibility of owning an animal," he answered, with a rock-solid smile.

Belle was eventually captured and returned to her East Tennessee farm. She had quite a story to share with the herd.

From a sheep named Belle, we saw firsthand a Father Who never gives up on one lost child.

Lord, You are indeed our shepherd. We shall not want.
—Pam Kidd

Digging Deeper: Ezekiel 34:12; Psalm 23

Sunday, September 18

Humility is the fear of the LORD; its wages are riches and honor and life.
—Proverbs 22:4 (NIV)

The young woman walked hesitantly into our church service. She craned her neck as though looking for someone. It was my Sunday to sit at the back, to greet latecomers and help them to find a seat. When she caught my eye, I gave her a smile and made room for her on the pew. After the service, I introduced myself. She did the same. Her name was Brittany. She had come hoping to see Mrs. Amman, an elderly widow and a faithful member of our church family.

"She's not here today," I said, explaining that Sarah Amman was in the hospital recovering from pneumonia. Brittany appeared disappointed. She told me how Mrs. Amman had invited her to come to church many times over the years. She shared how the widow had made her grilled cheese sandwiches after school, when Brittany had been lonely waiting for her single mother to come home after working two jobs. She recalled handmade mittens at Christmas and a giant chocolate bunny at Easter.

I smiled as Brittany went on singing Sarah Amman's praises. The widow was humble in the truest sense of the word. She loved Jesus, and it showed. She always made time to think of others first.

I said, "I know a diner where they serve excellent grilled cheese sandwiches." When I offered to treat Brittany to lunch and then take her to the hospital to visit Sarah, her face lit up. I could hardly wait to see that same happiness on Sarah's face when her unexpected visitor arrived.

Lord, help me to think less often of myself and more often of others.
—Shirley Raye Redmond

Digging Deeper: 1 Corinthians 10:24; Philippians 2:3–4

Monday, September 19

And this is the record, that God hath given us eternal life, and this life is in his Son. —1 John 5:11 (KJV)

When my son emailed to say his father in hospice was slipping fast, I was volunteering on an island. I grabbed the next vessel to shore, and my daughters quickly found flights to travel three thousand miles to say good-bye. Though their dad and I had been apart for twenty-four years, the children and I were now gathered together at the nursing home.

Over the long weekend, kind words were spoken, apologies shared, and tears shed. I could not have dreamed of a more beautiful reconciliation.

Perhaps it was this pervasive spirit of forgiveness or the new medical treatment or the last rites that triggered the rebound, but Thad rallied to live another six weeks. By then, our daughters and I were home, but our sons were with him when he passed. They organized the celebration of life with a picnic in a park and, per his request, donated his body to a research institution. All details meshed for closure to a life on earth.

Nearly a year later, my son sent me a document from the institution that had included his father in research. This recorded a dignified goodbye with his burial at sea and included the precise latitude and longitude of the event, along with a small map. Strangely, the document included no year. The more I reflect upon this, the clearer it becomes to me: dates and numbers are meaningless in the infinity of eternal life.

Eternal Father, neither time nor space can separate Your love from us.
—Gail Thorell Schilling

Digging Deeper: John 10:28–30; Romans 8:37;
2 Corinthians 4:18; 1 Peter 5:10

Tuesday, September 20

My soul shall be satisfied as with marrow and fatness; and my mouth shall praise thee with joyful lips: When I remember thee upon my bed, and meditate on thee in the night watches. —Psalm 63:5–6 (KJV)

Night watches. That concept of a sole human being assuming guardianship over a specific domain in the dead of night can strike a note of larger-than-life loneliness, responsibility, and vulnerability. James Moore, a well-known African American gospel singer, spoke of the wee hours as one of the most difficult times for the person who lives alone, a time when there is no one to talk to—no one to numb the thoughts that attempt to steal the peace of God. These night-watch hours, he implies, are spaces where the mind is most susceptible to attack.

But the psalmist David suggests the night watch can also offer the priceless gift of solitude and an unparalleled opportunity to seek the presence of the Lord. When scriptures use the term "night watch," I love to imagine a person alone with the stars and moon in that time when we can shed all "fronting," all bluster and pretense. When we can, as my long-deceased father used to sing, "have a little talk with Jesus, tell Him all about our troubles. He will hear our faintest cry and answer by and by." Simply put, in our night watches, we have a choice: we can tense with negative expectations, or we can let go and let God's love swell our hearts and hopes.

Though it often requires effort to remember the Lord on our beds when the cares of the world try to drown us, it is well worth the effort when it yields that scriptural "peaceable fruit."

Lord, remind me consistently and often that I am never alone.
—Jacqueline F. Wheelock

Digging Deeper: Psalm 119:148; Lamentations 2:19; Luke 6:12

Wednesday, September 21

You armed me with strength for battle; you humbled my adversaries before me. —Psalm 18:39 (NIV)

Our gentle Labrador, Rugby, was attacked in our backyard. He had one wound on his shoulder and another on his back. It had happened at night where the grass gives way to woods.

"He'll be fine," our veterinarian said. "But I'm puzzled. A bite would be two punctures. Each site has just one."

My eleven-year-old Isaiah was listening, so I knew there'd be a mission. He'd find what had wounded his dog. A shake of his bank brought forth funds. A few days later, night-vision binoculars came via UPS.

"I'm ready," he said. "When Rugby goes outside, I'll wait for the attacker. I don't want my dog to be afraid." And for a week, Isaiah sat on the back porch when Rugby went out at night. He watched through binoculars that shot a ray of green. Beside him was a leather pouch of marbles and a slingshot carved like a bear.

Isaiah was armed and ready. He was fully prepared. What a way to live!

In the book of Matthew, Jesus tells us not to worry about tomorrow because each day holds trouble of its own. Some days, trouble comes in the form of circumstance. Or people. Trouble can also be our own schedule, thoughts, family, work, or situations that spin out of control.

We can't choose what comes against us. But we can be prepared.

When we spend time in His presence, His truth makes us strong. It changes our perceptions and reactions and how we persevere. He makes us bold. Unafraid. We become conquerors.

The Word is our weapon of war.

As for Isaiah, he never did find the mysterious creature lurking in the woods. But Rugby healed and eventually felt safe again.

The slingshot and marbles are still sitting on an old trunk on the covered part of our porch. They remind me to be prepared.

Lord, Your Word holds power! Amen.
—Shawnelle Eliasen

Digging Deeper: Psalm 46:1; Ephesians 6:10–18; Hebrews 4:12

Thursday, September 22

He who keeps Israel will neither slumber nor sleep. —Psalm 121:4 (NRSV)

Funny the way you can mute yourself and others on computers and phones. The conversation with our church study group on Zoom is wide-ranging, as always. But then there comes a moment where everybody is talking at once but only one ends up being heard—that person unwittingly holds us hostage by rambling on without knowing that their talking "mutes" us all.

It makes me think about my own capacity to mute or unmute myself or the world. Those anxious thoughts, those fearful meanderings, that inner list-making (adding or subtracting to stuff that might never get done). Yes, I turn to prayer and quiet meditation as a way to hover over the mute button on my mind. But sometimes, just at that very moment, the noise gets louder.

That's when it occurs to me how grateful I am that God doesn't have a mute button. He hears it all. On the flip side, God wants to hear what I'm thinking and feeling. So maybe I'm not supposed to mute myself in prayer.

Once, someone asked me if it was okay to tell God how angry he felt sometimes, even at God. I replied, "Don't you think God knows already?" In fact, when I keep myself unmuted, it gives us both a chance to work on the problem. I hear the anger, frustration, resentment, and irritation, and God hears it too.

Then I attempt to give it up. "You take it, God. You can help. And forgive me for my inability to love when that's all I really want to do."

We often say that God is immutable. Can I add that, in His hearing, we're "un-mute-able"?

Thank You, God, for listening. For hearing what I can't hear.
For discerning what I need better than I can.
—Rick Hamlin

Digging Deeper: Psalm 28:1; Isaiah 64:12

Friday, September 23

Do not be anxious about anything, but in every situation, by prayer and petition, with thanksgiving, present your requests to God. And the peace of God, which transcends all understanding, will guard your hearts and your minds in Christ Jesus. —Philippians 4:6–7 (NIV)

What was wrong with my dashboard? A trip to an out-of-state conference should've been easy after all the miles I'd driven in my life. I'd planned to arrive early to participate in all the activities, but on the way, my battery light started flashing. *A new battery should solve the problem*, I thought. But the battery checked out fine at the store. So I resumed my trip. Minutes later, my dashboard went haywire again. "God, help!" I prayed, when the car died again. Miraculously, the car made it off the highway and into a gas station.

I checked the time, realizing I'd miss the opening session. A nice man jump-started my car, but it died again. I prayed for help, and another sympathetic person dropped me off at a store where I could buy a battery. When I tried to purchase it, however, I discovered I'd left my wallet in my car. Another delay. Now I needed two more rides—one for my wallet, another for the battery. Things felt completely out of control.

I called a taxi service, which quickly sent a polite driver. For two hours, he drove me back and forth and even installed the battery for me.

Finally resuming my journey, I realized the futility of all the plans I had made. A Bible verse came to mind that said not to be anxious about anything. God was near. He was in control. I wasn't.

As the sun began to set, I prayed for God's continued protection and peace, knowing that no matter what time I arrived at the conference, it would be a blessed weekend.

Thank You, God, for being in control when I'm not.
—Marilyn Turk

Digging Deeper: Proverbs 5:21; Jeremiah 29:11

Saturday, September 24

How good and pleasant it is when God's people live together in unity!
—Psalm 133:1 (NIV)

When Charlie Miller, a pillar in my childhood church, died, I telephoned his daughter Karen to see what I could do. "Oh, Roberta!" she said. "I was just thinking, if the three of you girls could sing at Dad's funeral, I wouldn't ever ask for anything else in my life."

"The three of you girls" included my two younger sisters, twins Rachael and Rebekkah, and me. Karen's idea sounded lovely in theory. But the last time I'd seen Rachael, she'd said something that had just rubbed me the wrong way.

Still, Charlie Miller was special to us. So we worked up a few of his trio favorites like "I Will Serve Thee" and "The Longer I Serve Him." We practiced and practiced. Rachael sang the lead, Rebekkah added her middle part, and I put in my signature low alto. Although our appearance showed signs of the passage of forty years, we didn't sound too bad.

Many in the mortuary chapel that afternoon were from our old Seventh Avenue Baptist Church, and the memory of those dear days filled me with joy. Then something came over me. As our sister sounds joined in one voice with the words "Ruined lives are why you died on Calvary," I noticed an arm wrapping around Rachael. *It was mine!*

Amazingly, my resentment lifted, and I was filled with sweet forgiveness.

After the service, a knot of long-ago friends gathered. "You all blend like flour in a cake," one of them exclaimed. "You still have that close sister harmony," another said. "There's nothing like it."

She was so right: is there anything better than the harmony of relinquished resentment?

You came to restore harmony among Your children, Father! Thank You.
—Roberta Messner

Digging Deeper: John 17:23; 1 Corinthians 1:10;
Ephesians 4:3; Colossians 3:14

Sunday, September 25

The believers from there, when they heard of us, came as far as the Forum of Appius and Three Taverns to meet us. On seeing them, Paul thanked God and took courage. —Acts 28:15 (NRSV)

The worship center where I was hired to be a transitional pastor was filled with energy and joy. Friends were catching up with those they hadn't seen in a week. I was busy greeting church members. Worship was about to start when I saw a woman I didn't recognize talking with my wife. I walked over to say hi. The woman turned around, and to my surprise, it was Donna, a former colleague from the ministry division I had led at Guideposts. I hadn't seen her in years.

We hugged and exchanged a few words as worship was about to begin. I sat down and pondered, *How did Donna know we were in Dunedin?* I thought she had moved to the east coast of Florida, and we were not connected on Facebook. But it didn't make a difference. I was happy to see her.

After worship, I learned that Donna was living on the gulf side of Florida. "How did you know I was at Saint Andrews Church?" I asked. Donna shared that Lemuel, another former colleague, had told her that I had moved to Florida to be a transitional pastor.

I'm glad that Lemuel had shared my whereabouts with Donna, making it possible for us to reconnect. We were so happy to see each other. Elba took a picture of us to capture the moment of joy. I posted it on Facebook. We exchanged phone numbers and agreed to meet up again. Shortly after that visit, Elba, Donna, and I went out for lunch at a local restaurant.

And thanks to one friend reconnecting two old ones, we now remain in touch.

Lord, make ways for old friends to reconnect and to experience the joy of being with one another again.
—Pablo Diaz

Digging Deeper: Job 2:11

Monday, September 26

And in the time of their trouble, when they cried unto thee, thou heardest them from heaven.... —Nehemiah 9:27 (KJV)

Our dek-hockey team has given generously to the coffers of local orthopedists. The team's unofficial nickname is Twelve Guys, Seven Knees. It would be funny if it weren't true.

Recently, I added my contribution with not one but two tears in my meniscus. I knew the drill—get a referral from my primary care physician, get the MRI, get the surgery, complain about rehab and copays... and then reinjure it by going back too soon. How our species got this far is beyond me.

As expected, the MRI confirmed the damage.... "But other than that," said the doc, "your knees are in surprisingly good shape."

His assessment seemed insane to me—the orthopedic equivalent of "Other than that, Mrs. Lincoln, how did you like the play?" Was he looking at *my* knees? I can play Connect the Dots with all the suture marks.

As I left his office, I walked through the waiting room. I had to work my way around crutches and canes and wheelchairs and walkers and... *Oh, right. Now I get it.* My new meniscus tears paled in comparison to what this doctor saw every day: a litany of immobility and pain and suffering.

Sometimes God sends gentle reminders; sometimes God uses a sledgehammer. What I really need is an MRI of my heart, to catalog the multiple holes where perspective and compassion have leaked out.

I don't think they have a surgery for that. I'll have to rely on God.

Lord, restore my heart; have mercy on Your slow-to-learn pilgrim.
—Mark Collins

Digging Deeper: Job 9:28; James 5:13

Tuesday, September 27

But whose delight is in the law of the Lord, and who meditates on his law day and night. —Psalm 1:2 (NIV)

I was growing increasingly frustrated. We loved everything about our new preschool—the teachers, the curriculum, the toys—except the fact that it wasn't religious at all. Having come from a religious program, we were used to the kids praying before lunch, singing devotional songs during the day, and finding ways to weave the Bible into everyday lessons.

It was quite the tradeoff, but one we had to make for personal reasons. So I worried about how to layer in that teaching between the morning routine, two working parents, and an evening schedule that always felt a little rushed. Somehow premeal prayers and a bedtime-song routine didn't feel like enough. I prayed that God would show me how to include Him more in our daily moments so that my kids would naturally include Him in theirs.

A few days later, a friend casually mentioned a prayer her kids had said in the car that morning, and it was like a lightbulb went off in my head. Of course! I prayed every day on my drive into work; I'd even prayed about this specific problem, but it had never occurred to me to pray with my kids on their quick drive to school.

Now including prayer time in our drive has become a routine. We thank God for another day. We thank him for our health, friends, and school. We bring any fears or worries to Him about the coming day. And just like at meals, if I forget, they pipe up to get us started, which might be the best part of it all.

Lord, thank You for the found moments that I can use to spend with You. Help me teach my children to use those moments to go to You in prayer.
—Ashley Kappel

Digging Deeper: Psalm 62:1, 78:4; Proverbs 22:6

Wednesday, September 28

Clothe yourselves with compassion, kindness, humility, gentleness and patience. —Colossians 3:12 (NIV)

I pushed my overflowing cart toward checkout. The person behind me only had a few items, so I waved him ahead. His profuse thanks caught me off guard. It took me back to Scotland when I was seventeen.

From the age of twelve, I had saved money to go to Europe, and after graduating from high school, off I went with my aunts and uncles. We were taking a bus to a village to hike southern Scotland. We were alone on the bus with the driver, waiting for the departure time.

Obviously pleased to have an audience, he shared local tales with us in his thick brogue. And then, in mid sentence, he broke off. "Excuse me." He darted from the bus.

Through the window, we saw him hurry across the narrow road and hail a woman carrying parcels. He stooped to pick up something that had fallen from her bag and gave it to her with a tip of his cap. After returning to the bus, he started up where he'd left off with his story.

My aunt interrupted him. "That was awfully nice of you," she said.

The driver shrugged, as if surprised that it was even worth mentioning. "It costs nothin' to be kind."

That one simple act stayed with me through the years. Kindness had seemed as natural to him as breathing. Fred Rogers, of the children's TV show *Mister Rogers' Neighborhood*, encouraged his audience to "look for the helpers" in times of trouble, because we'll always find them. I don't want to look for them; I want to be one, just as Jesus commissioned us. How else can I serve someone today?

Dear Lord, shower me with opportunities to share kindness until it becomes as natural as breathing.
—Erika Bentsen

Digging Deeper: Galatians 5:22; Ephesians 2:7; 2 Peter 1:6–8

Thursday, September 29

O come, let us sing for joy to the Lord, Let us shout joyfully to the rock of our salvation. Let us come before His presence with [a]thanksgiving, Let us shout joyfully to Him with psalms. —Psalm 95:1–2 (NASB)

Yesterday I loaded my bike into the back of my truck and rode to my favorite biking route in middle Georgia. It is a safe, smooth country highway that stretches for miles through peach and pecan orchards.

Once there, I pedaled along on my bike, slowly embraced by a sense of gratitude. I entered into a natural conversation with God, expressing thanks for the many things in my life that have been so very good. Soon, I was filled with a euphoric sense of peace and a profound sense of gratitude, and the miles flashed by.

I am learning that there is a real connection between gratitude and attitude. I believe that a conscious sense of gratitude—even in the most severe and trying circumstances—has more to do with my health and happiness than any other emotion. Gratitude shapes and defines my attitude.

My aunt Fern was a single woman from Missouri who went to China and the Philippines as a missionary in the 1930s. She was stranded in the Philippines during World War II and placed in a prisoner of war camp for four years. Fear, hunger, disease, and death were always nearby. But she told me, when I was a child, that if you never lose your sense of thanksgiving, you will always find a sense of happiness. Gratitude will change your attitude for the better.

Dear Father, help me to consciously focus on thanksgiving.
May gratitude shape my attitude this day. Amen.
—Scott Walker

Digging Deeper: Philippians 2:1–18; 1 Timothy 4:4

Friday, September 30

I have called you by name, you are mine. —Isaiah 43:1 (ESV)

"Good to see you again." I approached the woman with confidence. Though she'd risen to success and fame since we'd last spoken, I was sure she'd remember me.

"Hi." She pasted on a smile that didn't hide the distant expression in her gaze.

I quickly explained who I was, but the lack of recognition in her eyes remained.

She turned away as I was speaking to her and rushed off to catch a friend who was passing by. Someone she apparently did remember.

I stood there for a few moments, stinging from her rejection and the feeling of insignificance that came from knowing she didn't remember our history together. From knowing she'd completely forgotten who I was.

A while later, I encountered the passage in the Bible where God says to His chosen people that He's called them by name. The statement struck me with wonder. Most of us forget individuals we've met out of only hundreds. Yet, even though God has countless people to track, He knows each one.

He knows me intimately, down to the number of hairs on my head. Better still, He knows my name. When I come to Him in prayer, He'll never fail to recall who I am or where we met. In fact, He will never forget a single word I've told Him.

This astounding truth covers the wounds from rejection and brush-offs in my past. I don't need an old acquaintance or famous person to remember me. I need only rest in the fact that the most notable Person in the cosmos knows me by name and loves me more than I can fathom.

Father, thank You that You know me and called me to You by name. Help me to grasp the wonder of Your loving care and knowledge of me.
—Jerusha Agen

Digging Deeper: Psalm 139:1–16; Isaiah 45:4

September

THE LORD IS NEAR

1 _____

2 _____

3 _____

4 _____

5 _____

6 _____

7 _____

8 _____

9 _____

10 _____

11 _____

12 _____

13 _____

14 _____

15 _____

September

16 _____

17 _____

18 _____

19 _____

20 _____

21 _____

22 _____

23 _____

24 _____

25 _____

26 _____

27 _____

28 _____

29 _____

30 _____

OCTOBER

Praise be to the God and Father of our Lord Jesus Christ, the Father of compassion and the God of all comfort, who comforts us in all our troubles...

—2 Corinthians 1:3–4 (NIV)

Saturday, October 1

Be of good courage, and he shall strengthen your heart....
—Psalm 31:24 (NKJV)

The light breeze rustled the golden leaves on the aspens that lined the banks of the Bitterroot River. My friend Mary and I lazily paddled our kayaks and watched an eagle high in a tree. We'd decided fall would be a perfect season to float the river because the water level wouldn't be too high, like it was in springtime. We didn't know that too low a water level could be more dangerous than one that was too high.

Soon our kayaks grated over rocks. The water funneled into one deep, narrow channel. My eyes widened, and I held my breath. Whitewater swept me into a bend. Deadfall limbs, which hung over the bank, reached for me. A crosscurrent hit the side of my kayak and spun it 180 degrees, so that I was going backward through a small rapid. When we reached a slow spot, Mary and I exchanged a wide-eyed glance and hoped we'd been through the worst. But we hadn't.

Although I prayed for safety, the farther we floated, the more fear paralyzed me. I couldn't even paddle. Then once again, water boiled underneath me. I felt the kayak lift and gain speed. In front of me were rapids and a series of bends. *God, what do I do?*

Don't shrink back. Paddle—hard.

It took all my courage to dig in my paddle, pull with all my strength, and believe that I would get through. As my kayak shot out of the rapids, a flood of confidence surged through me. *I did it!*

Although each bend after that got easier, Mary and I breathed a sigh of relief when we finally loaded the kayaks on the truck.

> *Lord, when life throws the unexpected at me, help me to remember to ask for Your help—and then to dig in with courage, believe, and get it done. Amen.*
> —Rebecca Ondov

Digging Deeper: Deuteronomy 31:6; Matthew 14:27

Sunday, October 2

From the breath of God ice is made, And the expanse of the waters is frozen. —Job 37:10 (NASB)

"We have an iceberg ahead. The captain will be pulling close."

It was what we'd all been waiting for. As beautiful as our cruise down the coast of Chile had been, it was Antarctica that was on everyone's mind.

My husband and I hurried out to the deck...and gasped. For several minutes, neither of us spoke. Tears streamed down my face. There, unbelievably near, was the iceberg. It was at least one hundred fifty feet tall and several football fields long, and it had an intriguing shape carved by the Master Sculptor. No other icebergs were in sight—just this one frozen expanse of magnificence in the midst of miles of navy-blue ocean. Azure-blue water splashed at its base and the same intense color sliced through arctic white in a large fissure near its top. The impact this sight had on us was also obviously felt by the rest of the hushed crowd that watched in wonder as our ship slowly circled the mammoth beauty. Tears streaked several faces.

What is it, when we view God's creations, that brings us to tears? Standing mesmerized by this experience for nearly an hour, I concluded that His creations connect us to Him in a profound way. Perhaps our tears are an overflow of the majesty that these creations speak to our souls.

Whatever the reason, the iceberg that stood before us that day, infused with His grandeur and power, is a sight I will never forget.

Thank You, Lord, for the splendor of Your handiwork and for the glimpse it gives us of You.
—Kim Taylor Henry

Digging Deeper: Psalm 65:8, 78:4

Monday, October 3

I will instruct you and teach you the way you should go....
—Psalm 32:8 (NRSV)

I was *so* lost one day in Italy. I was in Rome for work, and since I would be getting from one church to another via buses and trains, I thought I wouldn't need assistance. What a fool I was.

After a while, strangers were even offering to help, and I declined their offers. What an idiot I was.

Two hours after I was supposed to arrive at an appointment, my hosts sent out a search party. When they arrived at the bus station and found me about to board a bus that would have taken me the wrong direction, I even argued with them for a moment, saying that I knew where I was going. Sometimes it takes me a long time to learn a lesson.

I often imagine that the Lord is my shepherd, as is promised in Psalm 23, and that this means I rely only on God. I forget that God designed us to live together, to work together, to love each other, and to help each other along the way. My independence can be my downfall.

I hope not to make this sort of mistake again.

Show me the way, Lord, and please make me recognize the people You put in my way today who are there to help me along.
—Jon M. Sweeney

Digging Deeper: Psalm 133:1–4; Isaiah 41:10

Tuesday, October 4

WISDOM'S DELIGHTS: Wisdom in Humility

On the contrary, it is much truer that the members of the body which seem to be weaker are necessary.... —1 Corinthians 12:22 (NASB)

A stubbed toe. A sprained finger. A toothache. It doesn't take much to go wrong with one small part of the body to know how important it is. So when the apostle Paul writes to the church he founded in an ancient city in Greece called Corinth, regarding factions and rivalries among its people, he reminds them that they are members of one body—Christ. All valued. All needed.

In his day, Paul held status in ancestry and education and influence. Yet in Christ, he says he considers himself "the very least." (Ephesians 3:8 NASB)

An image of "the very least" presented itself some years ago while I was caring for my one-hundred-year-old aunt in California. We were visiting her daughter, my cousin, in her cabin up a canyon in West Hills. When I brought my aunt her morning cup of coffee, she looked up at me from her spot on the sofa and said, "You are a precious morsel in the Lord's hands."

Moments later I walked outside to my favorite perch on the rocks overlooking a valley. As I gazed out, a tiny hummingbird suddenly shot straight up, hovering in the sky just above me. It was backlit by the sun so that it seemed poised in the center of the circle of light.

My aunt's words returned to me. My heart wrapped around the vision of this little bird appearing in the magnificent flame of sun. I thought, *Lord, this is all I want to be. A precious morsel in Your hands.*

God can do much with a humble spirit—a humble life. Humility does not try to block the light with its own image. It is content to hover and be small and let God's light shine big and beautiful and bright.

Jesus, help me to keep a humble heart lit only by You.
—Carol Knapp

Digging Deeper: Psalm 25:9; Matthew 11:29; Philippians 2:3–4; James 4:10

Wednesday, October 5

Show hospitality to one another without grumbling. —1 Peter 4:9 (ESV)

I was running late to an appointment when the car in front of me slowed down. *What now?* I thought.

Ahead, a bright orange blob was in the middle of the road. Traffic came to a standstill. The blob approached, and I was able to make out what it was—a tall, lean dog. A greyhound mix, it had an orange coat that had come undone and was now flopping like a cape in the wind. The dog went to each car, weaving from side to side on the double yellow line. Car after car inched by.

Ahead I could see the dog nudge a pickup truck in the opposite lane. The driver rolled down his window and yelled, "Get out of the road!"

The car right in front of me put on its turn signal and moved to the shoulder. Then its driver's door opened and a woman got out. The dog ran to her. She checked its collar, opened her backseat door, and the dog jumped right in.

The woman was holding her phone as I was about to pass.

"Thank you!" I said. "Thank you for being such a good human!"

She held up her free hand and waved me forward, shrugging as if to say it was nothing. But I knew I had just witnessed something truly angelic.

Dear Lord, thank You for this beautiful moment of true kindness, when a stranger took the time to open the door and be an answer to a problem.
—Sabra Ciancanelli

Digging Deeper: Romans 12:10; Hebrews 13:1–2

Thursday, October 6

Call unto me, and I will answer thee, and show thee great and mighty things, which thou knowest not. —Jeremiah 33:3 (KJV)

For most of my life, cranberries had one purpose: to enhance the Thanksgiving turkey. And then the email came from my friend Julie: "Please pray for our cranberry crop. Dangerous storms are on the way!"

Cranberry crop? I had no idea that Julie's family were cranberry farmers. Pray for cranberries? Why not? So pray I did.

Later came a profuse note of thanks. I doubted that I had realistically saved a single cranberry, but credit was nice. Next, what should appear on my front porch but a huge box of beautiful "thank you" cranberries. And so began my cranberry romance.

"How do you grow these things?" I asked my friend.

Julie sent photos of berries on vines in low-lying fields. Later the fields are flooded, and the berries float to the surface, where they are easily harvested. Imagine! A lake of beautiful floating cranberries.

This is too cool, I think while googling "Are cranberries healthy?" Unbelievable! As a potent antioxidant, cranberries boost your immune system and help you stay healthy.

And next, the recipes. Cranberry sauce was only the beginning. Cranberry bread, cranberry bars, cranberry pancakes, and then the recipe shared by Julie: cranberry pie, now a new legend among family and friends.

God offers untold worlds, waiting to be known. And there are so many ways that we, as individuals, can discover their joys. For me, a simple prayer opened the door to a cranberry world.

And the beat goes on. Because recently I received a text from a friend who had lost his mother and was a bit lonely: "Came home late...and baked a cranberry pie. Thanks for the recipe."

I think God was pleased.

Father of cranberries, please keep showing us Your "mighty things."
—Pam Kidd

Digging Deeper: Numbers 14:21; Psalm 19:1; James 5:16

Friday, October 7

Mankind, he has told each of you what is good and what it is the Lord requires of you: to act justly, to love faithfulness, and to walk humbly with your God. —Micah 6:8 (CSB)

Six times a year for a decade, I've organized a potluck lunch and program at my church. I've engaged a speaker. I've hosted the event, welcoming guests, managing the kitchen and buffet line, leading grace, introducing and thanking the presenter, helping the impromptu cleanup crew. It's a vibrant ministry, especially for seniors.

But last week, things got complicated. First, a neighbor whose daughter I "grandmother" asked me to take her to—and attend—the teen's annual Education Plan school meeting. It was the same Thursday afternoon as the scheduled lunch. I said I'd be there and made arrangements to leave the church before the speaker's presentation.

Then on Wednesday, a seemingly insignificant car concern turned ominous. "It's not safe to drive," my mechanic said. "And it won't be ready before Friday."

Yeow. I considered round-trip taxis to church and school. Too much hassle. I phoned a church friend, explained my predicament, and begged for a morning ride to the church. "When I leave the lunch—early—I'll call a cab."

"Sure, I'll come for you," she said. "But it sounds stressful. Do you really need to be there?"

Her question shot through my surety. Later in the day, we talked again. "You're right," I told her. *Maybe I'm not indispensable.* "I've made some calls, and others will step up."

Thursday noon, my curiosity got the best of me. I called the church. "It's Evelyn—just hovering," I joked. "Any glitches with the lunch?"

"It's looking good. Not to worry."

Lord, when I think it "all depends on me," show me the resources at hand.
—Evelyn Bence

Digging Deeper: Galatians 6:2–10

Saturday, October 8

When anxiety was great within me, your consolation brought me joy.
—Psalm 94:19 (NIV)

James was having a hard day. Everything was too much: his room was too hard to clean, the stickers were not going on the right way, and his siblings were not playing the right games.

"Do you want to go for a drive, buddy?" I asked him. He peered up at me, his eyes red, and nodded.

We loaded up, just us, and drove the neighborhood. At first he was silent, then he bubbled over with everything he'd needed to tell me all day, about *Star Wars,* about dead bugs, everything. Then he fell silent again and asked if we could drive while we listened to his favorite songs.

"Sure, buddy," I replied. I didn't say much during the drive.

Finally, he piped up from the backseat. "I'm ready to go home now, Mom," he said.

As we walked toward the house, he snuggled against my side. "Thanks, Mom," he said. "I feel better."

"I'm glad," I told him. "You know, even grown-ups need to take time out for a few minutes every once in a while."

His eyes got big. "Really?"

"Yes," I said. "When I'm overwhelmed, I take a minute and say a prayer, do a dance, sing my favorite song, or just be silent. I find that if I ask God to help me calm down, and then I do something that makes me happy, I can reset my attitude and get back to my day."

We learn a lot in our days about how to care for others, but it's also important to learn how to take care of ourselves so that when things get dark, we can find the Light.

Lord, help me remember that I can always run to You, no matter how badly I feel about myself or my day. Let my hope always be in You.
—Ashley Kappel

Digging Deeper: Psalm 34:18; Proverbs 12:25; 1 Peter 5:7

Sunday, October 9

Always keep on praying. —1 Thessalonians 5:17 (TLB)

When I was in high school, the Girls Athletic Association organized a father-daughter dinner-dance. Knowing my dad wasn't crazy about dancing, I surprised him and took the money I'd saved for the dinner-dance and instead bought us two tickets to see the Harlem Globetrotters, who were in town that same night. As a big basketball fan, Dad was overjoyed—and the minute I saw those zany, theatrical, funny basketball wizards perform, so was I. Dad and I laughed together and enjoyed every minute. It's one of the only times I remember me and my dad being out together, just the two of us.

That night, over sixty years ago, I created my first memory with someone I loved deeply. Dad and I would talk about our Globetrotters adventure for years to come.

Now, as a grandparent, I want to create as many memories as I can for my nine grandchildren and their parents. That's why I've kept the condo owned by my late husband, Jack, so they have a place to stay and relax when they come to Florida to take in the sun, sand, and sea.

I also think going to church as a family when they visit helps create even more important memories. Snuggling close in the pew, reaching for a grandchild's hand, praying and singing together, and chatting with the priest and friends after Mass all combine to create an even more meaningful memory than anything I could ever create at the beach.

Father, help me create foundation-building memories for my family by encouraging them to attend church with me when they visit.
—Patricia Lorenz

Digging Deeper: Psalm 143:1–2; Isaiah 56:6–8; 1 Thessalonians 5:19–27

Monday, October 10

When I am afraid, I put my trust in you. —Psalm 56:3 (NIV)

A thirty-pound ball of fur landing on my blanket-covered legs was enough to wake me from a sound sleep.

"What's going on?" I scolded our rusty mutt, Mollie. I scratched behind her quivering ears. "You're not allowed on the bed."

Then I heard it. A rustling under the floorboards of this one-hundred-year-old cabin we had recently purchased in northern Arizona. I elbowed my husband.

"Kevin, listen!"

Dried leaves crunched under the wood planks in our bedroom. The day before, we had sealed multiple crevices in the foundation after discovering seven mice in the kitchen. But this sounded bigger than a mouse.

"Probably a squirrel," Kevin mumbled before turning over and going back to sleep.

I settled Mollie, a trembling mess of fear, back on her blanket. After eight years with us, she was usually confident, but faced with this new experience, she was reverting to her puppy days when she'd been alone and abandoned at the pound. With all the strange sounds and smells, her worry meter had been on overdrive. I wanted her to love the cabin, however, so I had been patient with her fear.

The next morning, a squirrel paraded across our deck. Mollie had been too afraid to challenge its intrusion on our property before, but apparently the squirrel's sleeping under the cabin was the last straw. Mollie bolted out the door, chasing the critter off with a growl and a bark. Then she pranced back to the cabin, her wagging tail like a victory banner behind her. She was acting, for the first time, like she owned the place.

Maybe she finally did.

Jesus, sometimes my anxiety parades around, rustling in the night. Give me courage to chase fear away, waving a victory banner when I return.
—Lynne Hartke

Digging Deeper: Isaiah 43:1; John 14:27

Tuesday, October 11

We saw him with our own eyes and touched him with our hands. He is the Word of life. —1 John 1:1 (NLT)

My wife and I were probably the last two people in the Western Hemisphere to have traded our old tube television for a large flat-screen.

For many years, our little twenty-one-inch tube television was good enough, but now our vision is slipping. So when some friends offered us their spare flat-screen TV for free, we eagerly took it. It was only about a foot larger, but what a difference it made! It was like seeing television for the first time.

Suddenly, we could see things we hadn't before, like the eye color of the actors and the facial expressions of people in quiz-show audiences. What we'd thought was the green backdrop of a garden show we liked to watch turned out to be banks of beautiful trees and shrubs. And during movies, we felt like we were inside the story and a part of the landscape.

In short, it was like we had moved ten feet closer to our TV.

Moving "closer" to people also improves vision, I am learning. For instance, I was somewhat intimidated by my new doctor. My first impression of him was that he was confident, aggressive, and blunt, but now that I have had time to get closer to him, I can see that he is a humble, dedicated healer.

There's an old saying: "Hold your friends close and your enemies closer." But as I have gotten closer to some of my "enemies," I can see that they are really friends in disguise.

*Thank You, God, for coming down to earth,
so that we can get a closer look at You.*
—Daniel Schantz

Digging Deeper: 2 Samuel 1:23–27; Proverbs 18:24

Wednesday, October 12

The Lord is my strength and my shield; my heart trusts in him, and he helps me. —Psalm 28:7 (NIV)

Julee came to breakfast. "I'm feeling a little down today," she said.

"Anything specific?" I asked, wondering how anyone could feel down on this perfect autumn day, when golden leaves stood out like cut glass against an immaculate sky.

"No, just blue."

I immediately went into fix-it mode. Had she slept well? Was it something I'd done? Should she check in with her doctor?

"No, just a little down. Think I'll take a walk."

"Take Gracie," I said, handing her our golden retriever's leash.

With Gracie outside, it would be a good time to vacuum. The ancient enmity between dog and vacuum had been well established in our house. Besides, it might take my mind off my wife's troubles. I grabbed the Dyson from the closet and fired it up. I'd have to be quick. They'd be home soon, which might be a problem. I confess I get a little obsessive when I vacuum. I can't stop until every molecule of dust and dog hair is vanquished. Sometimes an intervention has to be staged, the vacuum cleaner unplugged and taken out of my hands.

So I moved quickly, asking God to speed my labors, resisting the urge to go over the same spot on the same rug repeatedly. I couldn't make everything perfect. I had emptied the canister and returned the Dyson to its home just as the girls were returning.

Julee hung up Gracie's leash. "You vacuumed," she said, smiling. "I feel better already."

Julee gave me a hug, and Gracie wound around our legs. The day was looking brighter than ever, and I had learned a simple if obvious lesson.

Lord, help me to remember that it is the small things I do that usually make a difference. The bigger problems I must trust to You.
—Edward Grinnan

Digging Deeper: Ephesians 5:25–33; Philippians 2:2–5

Thursday, October 13

It is the Lord who goes before you. He will be with you; He will not leave you or forsake you. Do not fear or be dismayed. —Deuteronomy 31:8 (ESV)

Sheets of wind-driven rain pelted the airplane window next to my seat. Watching it come down, I felt a twinge of my familiar old fear of flying. I sighed, discouraged. I'd thought that monster was gone for good.

In recent years, I'd become so much better about not dwelling on potential catastrophes. Instead, with lots of help from God, I had learned (or so I'd thought) to say one prayer and then truly place my flight into His capable hands. But this weather wasn't helping. As we took off, bumping, jolting, and shuddering our way heavenward, a blanket of fear and anxiety settled over me, as heavy and dense as the cloud ceiling.

Suddenly, though, we broke through. The plane leveled off and steadied just as the cabin filled with a luminous golden light. I looked back out the window. It was a beautiful day. The rain was gone. Beneath us stretched a fluffy carpet of wispy-topped white clouds. And there, bathing everything it touched with its brilliant light, was the sun. It had been up here, shining all along—even while the rain clouds blocked it from my view.

Like God, I thought, as I relaxed back into my seat, my heart easy once again. Against the constancy of His light and love, the darkness of my inner turbulence doesn't stand a chance.

> *Thank You, God, for Your patience in the face of my most persistent and intractable fears, and for reminding me that, even when my eyes are clouded, You are there.*
> —Erin Janoso

Digging Deeper: Psalm 27:1; Luke 1:78–79

Friday, October 14

I am with you always, even to the end of the age.
—Matthew 28:20 (NASB)

What is God doing in your life right now?" Have you ever been in a small group where someone suggests sharing answers to that question? I have, and I confess, with embarrassment, that it usually fills me with fear rather than holy reflection. What if I can't quickly think of anything God is doing in my life at this moment? What if I don't have a good enough answer? Or I say something that sounds shallow? Am I more concerned about what others think than what I know? The more I let this fear grow, the more it paralyzes my brain.

So one recent morning, when I came across that question in a blog, I decided to deal with my unreasonable fear by talking to God about it, one on One. I began by praying and then going on a walk—two ways that I both talk and listen to God. And this is what I heard and now know:

God reveals Himself through my fears, so He allows this fear for His purposes.

He is in the midst of *everything* in my life, so I trust He is in the midst of my fear.

And He uses *everything* to draw me closer to Him.

No wonder I have nothing to say in answer to that question. When I focus only on my fear, it grows larger and becomes a barrier to seeing Him, not only in the midst of my fear but in everything else in my life.

But I also need to practice answering that question. So in my prayer time, I'm asking God, "What are You doing in my life right now?"

Lord, I know I can always step right through my fear and always find You at work in the midst of everything.
—Carol Kuykendall

Digging Deeper: Isaiah 28:16; Matthew 14:22–27; John 6:16–22

Saturday, October 15

How good and pleasant it is when God's people live together in unity!
—Psalm 133:1 (NIV)

I heard my father yelling in the living room and ran over to intervene. My mother had already beat me to it.

"Gene, leave them alone," she huffed. "They're not doing anything wrong!"

During this visit, my father's frustration with my ten- and twelve-year old sons had been frequent. He has moderate dementia, and any disruption to his usual routine is difficult for him to accept.

"Go watch TV," I said as my boys moaned about Papa.

When I was a child, my father had been the gentle one. He was the snuggle bug, the comedian who made us laugh till our bellies ached, and the one who never yelled. But for my boys, Papa was simply a grump.

The morning was beautiful, so I suggested we walk along the creek together. The boys didn't want to go, but I insisted. I wrapped my arm around my father and rested my head on his shoulder. The boys walked ahead. The division between them and my love for both made my heart ache.

As we continued to walk, my father spotted an orange golf ball on the other side of the creek. Collecting lost golf balls had become a hobby, as they lived so close to the community golf course.

I called the boys over, knowing they could get it for him. Excited by the challenge, they leaped over the creek and retrieved it. The boys and my father cheered. He complimented their athleticism, and the boys promised to get him some more.

As they continued to search for golf balls together along the creek, the tension lifted. No, they will never have the memories I have of my father, but they can still discover and collect a few sweet ones of their own.

Lord, thank You for the bond of family and the memories we make together, even when they're not picture-perfect.
—Karen Valentin

Digging Deeper: Psalm 103:17; Ephesians 4:3

Sunday, October 16

BLESSED BY ONE SWEET COOKIE: Settling In
He has made everything beautiful in his time… —Ecclesiastes 3:11 (KJV)

When we first got our dog Cookie, I wondered at times what I'd gotten myself into. She would wake me up several times a night, and she constantly required attention. She found something new to destroy nearly every day and was so hyper that I couldn't possibly keep up with her. For the first few months, I felt completely worn out. I asked my cousin who knew all about dogs how long this phase would last.

"Probably about three years," she said. Three years? I wondered if I could hang on that long! Good thing Cookie was so adorably cute!

But my cousin was right. Now at the three-year mark, I notice that Cookie, though still plenty energetic, seems finally able to enjoy a slower pace at times. As a puppy, she rarely wanted to curl up in my lap, preferring instead to tug or chase or almost-fetch (running after the ball but not giving it back to me!).

These days, Cookie enjoys long, luxurious naps in the sunshine by the window while I get some work done. When I walk by, she sometimes looks up at me, only to close her eyes again and return to her slumber. And best of all, she now likes to cuddle—an activity she barely tolerated as a wild and crazy pup. Oftentimes, we'll even pass the evenings together in a chair on the porch, Cookie sighing contentedly as I scratch her ears.

My young puppy was a cute little rascal, but my big girl is pretty charming in her own right too.

Father, thank You for making all phases of life sweet in their own way, from vibrant youth to the quiet, cozy settling down of age.
—Ginger Rue

Digging Deeper: Psalm 16:11; Ecclesiastes 3:1

Monday, October 17

Rise up in splendor and be radiant, for your light has dawned, and Yahweh's glory now streams from you! —Isaiah 60:1 (TPT)

It felt almost magical, like walking into another world. The workshop in rural Myanmar was brimming, floor to ceiling, with rows of exquisitely handcrafted lacquerware. But from across the overfilled showroom, a single black teacup caught my eye. A warm, golden glow was emanating from inside it. From across the room, it appeared the cup was home to its very own small sun. Never one to shun curiosity, I had to check it out.

I peeked inside. Empty. No candle. No light source of any kind. But the cup's interior was gilded with finely brushed gold. Its polished surface reflected the natural light around it with an intensity that burned inexplicably bright. I held the little cup in my hand, enchanted. Woven of bamboo and horsehair, then coated with ash and the sap of a lacquer tree, the cup was as light as the proverbial feather.

A saleswoman assured me it was not only affordable but watertight—the perfect vessel to hold my morning tea. I couldn't imagine pouring Earl Grey into this gilded work of art. But I could easily picture it in my humble little townhome, glowing with the warmth of an invisible flame.

Today, the cup sits on a shelf in my living room, catching the sunlight that streams in from my window and returning a vibrant glimmer of gold. It has become a daily reminder that I, too, am a vessel, one designed to reflect the light of God's love to others in a warm, invitingly beautiful way.

*Lord, polish me in whatever way best reflects Your light
into the lives of those around me.*
—Vicki Kuyper

Digging Deeper: Matthew 5:14–16; 2 Corinthians 4:6; Ephesians 5:8

Tuesday, October 18

Are not two sparrows sold for a penny? And not one of them will fall to the ground apart from your Father. —Matthew 10:29 (ESV)

I thought I had awakened to a normal day. I pressed play on my video exercise program and started the workout I'd done hundreds of times.

The sickening crunch when I landed a jump changed everything. Searing pain followed my ankle's awkward bend, later diagnosed as a severe sprain.

That day, in the second it took me to lift one leg and put it down in an exercise, my life changed, at least temporarily. I had to cancel plans and nurse my sprained limb long into the foreseeable future.

Six months later, I'd healed enough to attempt the same workout. But I stopped short of repeating that fateful move, fighting memories of the pain I'd felt the last time. I realized in that moment that the injury had caused more than physical damage—it had driven fear into my heart. My eyes were opened to vulnerability I hadn't seen before. How could I ever feel safe again?

Two truths seeped into my mind and then into my soul. Dangers always surround me. At any moment, I could stop breathing. My heart could cease to pump. I could contract a disease or be struck by a car.

Yet the most important truth is this: nothing will happen to me unless my sovereign Father wants it to. Even if He lets me fall, I can trust He'll use those falls for good and be with me every moment, comforting me. He'll use every step to grow me closer to Him.

I don't have to fear anything today or tomorrow, because there is no greater safety than resting in my loving Father's hands.

> *Father, help me to remember I'm not in control, but You are. And because of that, I am safe today and forever.*
> —Jerusha Agen

Digging Deeper: Job 38–39; Isaiah 41:10

Wednesday, October 19

Ask and it will be given to you; seek and you will find; knock and the door will be opened to you. —Matthew 7:7 (NIV)

One of the ministries of our small church is preparing funeral meals, either for members of our congregation or for families without a church who have lost loved ones. Last summer we were serving lunch at the senior center to accommodate a large crowd. I was the only helper who wasn't well acquainted with the grieving family, so I volunteered to do last-minute tasks while the other women attended the burial service.

I put salt and pepper shakers on the tables, cut the cakes, made coffee, and iced the water glasses, but finished with time to spare. I looked around for something to read, but there wasn't even a magazine. I decided to walk three doors down to the library for a book, then stopped short. Hadn't I asked God for extra prayer time earlier that morning? Wasn't "more time with God" one of the desires written down in my prayer journal? God's answer was staring me in the face: a quiet room and time alone. Jesus and I spent a precious uninterrupted fifteen minutes together before people starting arriving from the cemetery.

When the guests had gone and the last plate was washed, I headed home. I regretted the many opportunities I'd missed in my life, spending unexpected small bits of time flipping through magazines, looking at social media posts, or being impatient for the next activity, but I was deeply grateful for God's wake-up call that morning.

God is always delighted to spend time with me, I realized. All I have to do is accept the invitations into His presence.

Thank You, Jesus, for standing ready for a quick prayer chat as well as in-depth conversations.
—Penney Schwab

Digging Deeper: Isaiah 65:24; Romans 12:12; Ephesians 6:18

Thursday, October 20

The Jews had light and gladness, happiness and honor.
—Esther 8:16 (Tanakh)

At night, in the front of my house, there's a dark area between my porch light and the motion-detector light over the garage. To get from one to the other, you have to cross the deck and go down some steps. And the streetlights are far enough away that, on cloudy nights—or in fall, when darkness comes very early—it can be almost impossible to judge your footing when entering or leaving the house.

We tried to get a light installed over the steps when we moved into the house, but it was prohibitively expensive. So my visitors have learned to bring flashlights if they're planning to stay after sundown. I try to keep a small supply of flashlights on hand, too, to lend out to guests as needed.

But the lights I hand out usually vanish with the visitors. So when one of my guests was leaving after a meeting and said, "Oh, I forgot my flashlight," I discovered I had none left.

I was worried about my guest getting safely down the steps, because if she hurt herself, I would be liable, and I did not want to be sued. So as I let her out the front door, into the pool of light on the deck, I said, "I'll watch you until the light comes on." Of course, I meant the motion-detector light over the garage, but she didn't understand. She smiled and said, "I thought that's what you were already doing!"

After she left, I thought long and hard about how selfish I'd felt wanting not to get into a hassle. But she made me realize that's what God was always doing for me. And it was what He was always telling me to pass on to others—watch through the darkness, until the light comes on.

You bring me safely through the dark, Creator of Light,
and I am grateful beyond measure for it.
—Rhoda Blecker

Digging Deeper: Zechariah 14:6–7; Habakkuk 3:4

Friday, October 21

I can do all this through him who gives me strength.
—Philippians 4:13 (NIV)

My sciatica had reared its ugly head again, so my doctor recommended physical therapy. But I was recovering from a medication mishap that had left me anemic and weak, and my energy and endurance were nil. Physical therapy was the last place I wanted to be.

When I attempted the walking track for the first time, I didn't think I was going to make it through the first round. I was barely dragging when I passed a circle of patients conversing. To divert attention away from my pathetic effort, I said through labored breaths, "If you folks believe in the power of prayer, now might be a good time."

To my astonishment, those patients took me up on my half-hearted suggestion. Ronnie, the hip replacement who called me "Robert with an *A*," told me he was asking God to help me keep at it. Irene, the knee replacement, promised prayers when she was home alone at night. A guy with an arthritic knee assured me that we were all in this thing together and that God Himself would be the Source of our strength.

Even Mark my therapist sought the heavens as I struggled to stay on task with my back-strengthening regimen. "You can do this, Roberta," he said. "You are fearfully and wonderfully made. I promise, every session is going to get easier."

And it did. My sciatica decreased dramatically as well. Three weeks later when Mark told me I'd improved eightfold, I sought each one of my encouraging prayer partners, my unexpected community of caring, to thank them for their precious prayers. Miracle-working prayers that had buoyed me with a new strength that would surely see me through.

You show up whenever we do, Lord. Even in places we don't want to be.
—Roberta Messner

Digging Deeper: Psalm 139:14; Isaiah 40:31, 41:10; Ephesians 6:10

Saturday, October 22

Now faith is confidence in what we hope for and assurance about what we do not see. —Hebrews 11:1 (NIV)

Following in my footsteps, my daughter Jo-Ella has discovered a passion for horseback riding, but it took some time to get here.

We started slowly. Jo-Ella went to horse camp, then she took lessons for several months. I was waiting for her initiation into the world of horseback riding before we found a horse to call her very own. Initiation was tough. Jo-Ella fell off the towering horse she was riding and cried. It was hard to watch, and my heart sank. But soon, Jo-Ella marched up to the gate where I was standing to let me know she was okay. Then she proceeded to remount.

That bold act told me all I needed to know about Jo-Ella and horseback riding: she was committed. Not long after that inevitable first fall, my husband and I surprised Jo-Ella with her first horse, Snow Mist.

Jo-Ella's fall and subsequent remount reminded me of my own tumbles—tumbles from faith, from family, from friends. The challenging moments in life when I fell, then shook it off, confirming my commitment and priorities. Times when my beliefs and connections pulled me up off the ground, revealing my loyalties.

Everyone will fall at some point. Faith will be tested and relationships challenged. But the way we handle those moments in our lives—in areas like marriage, family, friendship, and faith—reveals what we feel is worth our effort and passion, what we value. And when we get back up and stick with it—well, that is commitment, loyalty, and passion!

Heavenly Father, create in me a loyalty and commitment to Your will. Guide me through my stumbles and help me focus on Your mercy and Your grace.
—Jolynda Strandberg

Digging Deeper: Psalm 37:24; Ephesians 6:17–19; Colossians 3:2

Sunday, October 23

I hereby command you: Be strong and courageous; do not be frightened or dismayed, for the Lord your God is with you wherever you go.
—Joshua 1:9 (NRSV)

I was out on my morning run when I came to the park in our neighborhood and noticed a sign—a paper taped to one of the lampposts. I didn't stop to read it, but one word popped out at me. It had three capital letters: F-B-I.

Oh, no, I thought, *there's been some terrible crime nearby, and the FBI are investigating.* A killing, a drug bust, maybe some international espionage situation gone wrong. Was nothing safe anymore? Would criminals with guns and knives come running around the corner at any minute? Should I not even go on these morning runs?

I stewed on it the rest of the day. It had me so worried that I carefully refrained from bringing it up to my wife at dinner or mentioning it at work. Why get others worried too? I was wary the next day when I went out running, and the next day too—so much so that I was unable to take in the view of the river or of the sun reflecting on the cliffs or of the birds rising on an updraft.

It was only that Friday that my worries were put to rest. More than that: they were skewered, ridiculed, pummeled. You see, that morning, as I came around to the entrance of the park, I noticed a big mobile trailer set up, electrical cords snaking around the sidewalk, lights rolled out from a truck, and a caterer cooking hot breakfast under an awning. FBI? They were shooting an episode for the TV series of that name.

An overactive imagination is not necessarily a bad thing. But as I remind myself, it's best used in faith and hope—not fear.

> *Thank You, Lord, for giving us imagination and vision.*
> *May we use it in love.*
> —Rick Hamlin

Digging Deeper: Psalm 56:3; Matthew 10:29–31; John 14:1

Monday, October 24

"If you consider me a believer in the Lord," she said, "come and stay at my house." —Acts 16:15 (NIV)

Negativity ruled as I sat in my rocking chair trying to shape my thinking into a posture of prayer and meditation. Only a few happy thoughts found purchase among the reports of violence, sickness, and politics, which stretched out before me like the proverbial forty miles of bad road.

I repeated a familiar scripture. "Whatsoever things are true, whatsoever things are honest…just…pure…lovely…of good report;…think on these things."

Still nothing.

I decided to take a more deliberate look at Paul's descriptors. The optimism in Philippians 4:8 could cause one to think Paul's experience as a missionary was all-encouraging, when, in fact, it was sometimes outrageous. (For example, see 1 Thessalonians 2:2 NIV.) How could he use an adjective like "lovely" after the terror handed him in Philippi? He was stripped, beaten, and imprisoned—unthinkable sacrifices for many modern-day Christians.

Paul *chose* to dwell on things that uplifted, perhaps even some of his experiences in Philippi: A wealthy seller of purple named Lydia who accepted his message and offered him shelter, saying, "If you consider me a believer in the Lord…come and stay at my house." And a jailer who tended Paul's wounds after a miraculous earthquake set him free from prison.

Like all Christians, Paul understood that, no matter the jolts of discouragement, there is a noneroding Rock to whom we cling—the eternal seat of glad tidings (good report), the Lion of Judah (our conqueror), the perfect Sacrificial Lamb (our salvation), and we consistently find Him worthy of praise when we search with our whole heart.

Help me, Jesus, to remember that You are always available to show me what is lovely.
—Jacqueline F. Wheelock

Digging Deeper: Psalm 3:3, 118:24; Philippians 4:5

Tuesday, October 25

To every thing there is a season, and a time to every purpose under the heaven.... A time to keep silence.... —Ecclesiastes 3:1, 7 (KJV)

I am in line at the pharmacy. A slight elderly woman is ahead of me, leaning on her walker.

Suddenly she turns and looks up at me with anxious eyes. In a tight voice, she says, "Have you ever had one of those days when everything goes wrong at once?"

"Oh, yes..."

"The handle on my microwave came off at breakfast," she begins, "then the wheel on my walker came off in the driveway." She goes on with a long list of problems.

I listen and nod sympathetically. "I am truly sorry," is all I can think to say.

After filling her order, she shuffles away. I move to the counter, but I am in turmoil about this woman's hardships. I know I could fix all the things she listed, but I don't know her or where she lives. I don't know what to do.

After my purchase, I've just started for the door when the little woman appears out of nowhere. She squeezes my hand and looks up at me with sparkling eyes.

"I just want to thank you for listening to my troubles. Sometimes all I need is for one person to know what I am going through, and then I am okay. My grandson will fix my stuff, but you have given me strength for this day."

She hobbles away, and I stand there reflecting on how easy it is to help people—just by keeping my mouth shut and my heart open.

*I thank You, Lord, for all my friends,
who listen to my woes and give me strength.*
—Daniel Schantz

Digging Deeper: Proverbs 17:28; James 1:19

Wednesday, October 26

*And He passed in front of Moses, proclaiming, "The L*ord*, the L*ord*, the compassionate and gracious God, slow to anger, abounding in love and faithfulness."* —Exodus 34:6 (NIV)

I pull into a parking spot at the optometrist's office. I'm ten minutes late. Yesterday a yoga session woke a wound in my back, and everything about the morning had been slow. Getting up. Getting dressed. Folding into the car. As I make my way up the sidewalk, I move like the Tin Man.

Truth is, it's not just my body that's rusty. My soul is worn. A couple of my sons are working through tough stuff, and I hurt for them. A dear friend just lost her job. My husband and I continue to feel the weight of the still-unsold Victorian we moved from two years ago. It's peace or panic, and today the latter ebbs close.

"Good morning," the optical assistant says from behind the front desk. She leads me to an exam room and explains the testing she'll conduct. I rest my forehead against a cool machine and find myself lulled by the cadence of her voice. It's familiar. She's from the South. This dark room feels brighter as she speaks.

I pull back. "Where are you from?" I ask.

"Alabama," she says.

I knew it.

"My dear friend is from Alabama," I say. "I hear her voice in yours."

I remember how Ginger encourages me. All the times she's spoken truth over tears and brought the Word to my worry. Suddenly I'm overwhelmed by the Lord's compassion. I just learned that the first way God describes Himself in the Old Testament is "compassionate," and now compassion covers me like an embrace.

My spirit breathes. Muscles in my back unclench. The Lord sees our soul condition, and He reaches for us.

Today, His compassion sounds like the voice of a friend.

Lord, Your compassion is the sweetest salve. Amen.
—Shawnelle Eliasen

Digging Deeper: Psalm 103:13; Romans 9:15

Thursday, October 27

Do not merely look out for your own personal interests, but also for the interests of others. —Philippians 2:4 (NASB)

I clipped down the hallway, my shoulders set and gaze level. I was on my way to meet a client. My first client.

I was both excited and terrified. What if the client recognized that I was a shiny, new lawyer? What if he asked me questions I didn't have answers to?

I breathed deeply before entering the conference room. Then I pushed my fears back and the door open.

Inside was a wiry, middle-aged man. I introduced myself. Then I set my briefcase in my lap, snapped it open, and removed a crisp stack of documents. I hoped I looked professional.

"Today I'm going to ask you background questions regarding your case," I said. "I need to better understand several events so we can decide how to proceed."

The client nodded.

I picked up my legal pad to review the list of questions I had formulated—questions about dates, times, and the wording of conversations. Then I looked up at the client.

And for the first time, I noticed his hands. They were trembling.

I had been so concerned about my image that I hadn't noticed this man's fear. I hadn't considered that this might be his first lawsuit. I hadn't thought about how intimidated he could feel sitting alone with an attorney.

So I set down the legal pad full of prepared questions. And I asked the man in front of me an unscripted one.

"How are you feeling?"

Father, draw my eyes away from myself and toward those around me.
—Logan Eliasen

Digging Deeper: Matthew 25:40; Romans 15:1–2

Friday, October 28

His purpose was for the nations to seek after God and perhaps feel their way toward him and find him —though he is not far from any one of us.
—Acts 17:27 (NLT)

Last year my husband and I bought a puppy from a guy playing with a gigantic dog family in a parking lot. Although Kris, my husband, believes pets should have other pet companions (and our beagle Sawyer's previous companion had died years before), we hadn't been looking for another dog. But when I saw those leaping puppies—Lab-coonhound mixes—I couldn't resist. Most of them were black, but some were a silvery purplish gray. I instantly loved a silver one with big bumbly paws. We named him Karl.

Now Karl's huge and rowdy in showing his love. When I open the door, he throws himself at me, the door, the entire front porch. Such is his enthusiasm. I worry he'll knock Kris or a visitor down our concrete steps, so I shout "Down!" which Karl seems to understand as "Again!"

Our daughter Charlotte, whose beagle is in fourth grade in dog school in California, recommends professional training, but dog schools don't exist in rural Oklahoma where we live. So I've been researching online.

Experts say jumping is a common complaint of dog owners, and they offer many "easy" cures. A knee in the chest didn't faze Karl, though. He thought I was joining in and stepped up his game. Giving him something to chew on—another tip—resulted in him leaping at me with something slobbery in his mouth. Not fun. Finally, I found the cure: pretending to ignore him until he sits, then lavishing him with love afterward.

That's how God trains me, too, I think—suffering my disobedience so silently that He seems absent. Eventually, I long for Him and obey, and I'm immediately aware of His loving presence, which was there all along.

Thank You, God, that even when I make You seem absent, You are there.
—Patty Kirk

Digging Deeper: James 4

Saturday, October 29

I am the resurrection and the life. Whoever believe in me, though he die, yet shall he live. —John 11:25 (ESV)

Gray skies hovered, appropriately gloomy and dark. Dear friends were burying their twenty-one-year-old son, and an army of supporters had filled the burlap blankets and wooden benches lined up for seating in the massive field they had chosen for his memorial service.

I sat on a red and beige blanket, feeling the earth's hardness beneath me. We waited in reverent quiet, the cool October air moving us to huddle together, hold hands, and link arms. The family began their march onto the field, a sea of black pouring in slowly, deliberately. Young men bore the exquisite but simple casket. And as if all of heaven and earth had stopped, there was silence among us. As the first speaker approached the podium, it seemed we all collectively exhaled.

The service was the most beautiful I have ever attended—honest and raw, captivating. His friends told funny stories about their good friend's antics and his heart for the marginalized. His siblings wept through tales of their hero. His parents shared accounts of the kid who broke bones climbing the tallest trees, the boy who spent his life thrill-seeking, and the young man who lost his way at times but loved Jesus passionately.

There was beautiful music and poetry. We sang along, laughed along, cried along, and near the end of the service, witnessed a miracle—gray skies that mirrored our sadness gave way to a glorious sun. I looked upward, feeling the warmth on my face, and praised God for showing up.

Through the sunshine, the Son reminded us that He was still present, still in control, and still in love with this young man, this family, and us all.

Lord, help us trust You with the loved ones that precede us in death, knowing that You love them and You love us.
—Carla Hendricks

Digging Deeper: Psalm 34:18; 1 Thessalonians 4:13; Revelation 21:4

Sunday, October 30

For I satisfy the weary ones and refresh everyone who languishes.
At this I awoke and looked, and my sleep was pleasant to me.
—Jeremiah 31:25–26 (NASB)

After I graduated from college, my first job was singing in a vocal music group sponsored by the Southern Baptist Convention. We were a young ensemble who performed college concerts and, through music, encouraged young adults to "live for a purpose and positively change the world." In one year, we sang on over one hundred college campuses.

Yes, it was a dream job for a young man. But it was also exhausting. The constant travel and energy required for quality concerts gradually took its toll on us. Though young, we all needed to learn the spiritual discipline of resting.

One day a wise veteran musician I respected talked with me. "Son," he said, "I will give you one piece of advice. You need to learn the art of taking a nap!" I thanked him for his advice and promptly dismissed it.

But I soon learned that his words were true and professionally important. In our busy world, we abuse our need for sleep and rest. And when we do, we pay a high price, which includes becoming less functional.

God created us to both work and rest. My older friend was correct—I did need to develop the art of taking a nap!

Dear God, may I remember that even You rested after creating our world. May I keep one day a week as a Sabbath and learn when to take a nap. Amen.
—Scott Walker

Digging Deeper: Genesis 2:2–3; Exodus 20:8–10; Matthew 11:28–30

Monday, October 31

You are worthy, our Lord and God, to receive glory and honor and power, for you created all things, and by your will they were created and have their being. —Revelation 4:11 (NIV)

As an artist, I have always relished creating my kids' Halloween costumes. I would plan weeks ahead, designing and painting the costumes they'd wear. Eventually, though, they preferred costumes with cheaply constructed fabric and plastic masks.

This year, however, they let me get creative again. Excitedly, I got out my glue gun, paints, brushes, fabric, and old clothes.

The day of Halloween, the boys put on my creations, and I went to work painting their faces and spraying color on their hair. They looked amazing!

Off we went, trick-or-treating in the neighborhood, and I beamed with pride as people smiled and commented on their costumes. Later in the evening, we attended a party with a contest. The top five costumes would get a big bag of candy. I was confident they'd place, and they did.

"We won!" they yelled, running toward me. We celebrated and hugged, until I reached for one of the prize bags to satisfy a craving for chocolate.

"Mami!" they protested, snatching back their treasure protectively. I was annoyed. It was my work and artistry that got them the prize in the first place, and now I had to beg for a Milk Dud?

But as I thought about my kids taking ownership of my work and enjoying the sweets of that labor, I realized I do the same thing. God has given me my artistic gifts, and yet I'm the one who is praised for that talent. Not only do I take sole ownership of that talent, a gift from God, but I also want to claim its sweet rewards without giving glory and honor to Him.

Lord, how often we take for granted all that You have created in our lives. Help us to be grateful and acknowledge that You have given us all we have.
—Karen Valentin

Digging Deeper: Genesis 1:26, 2:7

October

THE LORD IS NEAR

1 _____

2 _____

3 _____

4 _____

5 _____

6 _____

7 _____

8 _____

9 _____

10 _____

11 _____

12 _____

13 _____

14 _____

15 _____

October

16 _____

17 _____

18 _____

19 _____

20 _____

21 _____

22 _____

23 _____

24 _____

25 _____

26 _____

27 _____

28 _____

29 _____

30 _____

31 _____

November

The L<small>ORD</small> is good to all, and his mercy is over all that he has made.

—Psalm 145:9 (ESV)

Tuesday, November 1

And lo, I am with you always, even to the end of the age. Amen.
—Matthew 28:20 (NKJV)

"Days aren't long enough for everything I need to do," I complained to my brother.

"We are bound by time," Aaron said unexpectedly. "We're locked into now. We cannot step into the past. We cannot go into the future. But God is not constrained. What kind of God is a slave to time?"

My rant evaporated as he continued.

"God can go back to 1921 or jump ahead to 2293 at the same time. He's Master over Time. That means He had time to come to earth as Jesus and still be God in heaven." Aaron chuckled. "Can you tell? I've been reading about this lately."

I spent a sleepless night wrapping my head around it. God is right here beside me, right now. He is beside each one of us, every moment of our lives. He will judge us one day because He was right there when it happened! God makes this promise dozens of times in the Bible, and yet somehow it never sank in this way before. Immanuel, "God with us," became "God beside me."

My prayer life took on a new life as I understood this truth. He's right here. It's personal. It's tender. He's so close. He cares enough to spend every moment with us. Such immense love! Such immense protection!

For me, it's one thing to pray to an all-powerful Father Who Art in Heaven, knowing He can hear our prayers. But it's quite another to pray to the One right here beside me.

Lord beside me, Immanuel, every moment, You are here. I am never, ever alone. You never abandon us. How can You love us so much? Your ways are beyond our ways. Your love overwhelms me!
—Erika Bentsen

Digging Deeper: Joshua 1:9; Psalm 46:1; Matthew 1:23; Romans 8:38–39

Wednesday, November 2

And he said unto me, My grace is sufficient for thee: for my strength is made perfect in weakness.... —2 Corinthians 12:9 (KJV)

Aptly dubbed a "fair-weather fan" by my family, I've been known to exit the den when my basketball team gets into trouble. Through the years, however, I've sat still long enough to observe how arduously today's players work to build their bodies—doing what popular culture calls "strength training."

Understandably, athletes shun physical weakness. But more than ever, it seems, we live in a world where both physical and mental weaknesses are excessively frowned upon, while winning competitions and repressing vulnerabilities are set at a premium.

Occasionally, we, as believers in Christ, co-opt that stance, running the Christian race more as a competitor than a servant. And although God's Word admonishes us to be strong, it is strength in the power of *His* might that is key. As a Christian, I have admired the strengths and talents of other believers—their ability to quickly stanch the flow of tears, their seemingly unswerving faith that can instantly set aside life's tragedies, all in the name of strength. But is there not a place for transparency—acknowledging our weaknesses—in our walk with Christ?

Paul was open about the "thorn in [his] flesh." He reminds us that our imperfections can be God's way of revealing His perfect strength, prompting us toward repentant humility and spiritual maturity. His unsurpassed ability to carry us "is made perfect" through our weaknesses.

The Amplified Bible puts it this way: God's power "shows itself most effectively" through our frailties. What an unfathomable comfort when we find ourselves slumped in life's rooms of self-loathing! We can exit those places of failure, knowing Jesus can actually make good use of our weaknesses, for "when [we] are weak," then does His strength shine most brilliantly.

> *Dear Jesus, help me to more fully grasp that*
> *I have no strength except Yours.*
> —Jacqueline F. Wheelock

Digging Deeper: Psalm 27:1, 118:14

Thursday, November 3

There is nothing better for a man than to be happy and to enjoy himself as long as he can. —Ecclesiastes 3:12 (TLB)

I believe that we only need five things to be happy: someone to love, something to do, something to hope for, something to believe in, and something to laugh about. I believe in it so strongly that I even wrote a book about it a few years ago. During my research, I asked people what they needed for happiness. They said things like lots of money, good chocolate, the perfect figure, an expensive car, good health, or a cruise around the world. But I stick to my five things because, so far, they've kept me very happy.

I can even narrow it down to the two most important: something to believe in and something to laugh about.

If we believe in God and have faith that our lives will turn out okay with God's help, then we truly have nothing to worry about. Faith, believing in that which we cannot see or understand, is not only a blessing but also a gift, and not everyone has the gift of faith. Faith equals God— Father, Son, and Holy Spirit—a combination that takes care of us no matter what.

Laughter, the other most important ingredient for happiness, is so easy to spread. I send funny birthday cards to friends and family. I share funny cartoons and play silly jokes on friends. Sometimes, on game day, I post a photo of myself on Facebook wearing my Green Bay Packers cheese head. Other times, I wear my Groucho Marx glasses, with the bushy eyebrows and big nose, in the car when running errands. Then I wave to people just to enjoy their laughs.

> *Lord Jesus, thank You for being the rock that keeps me anchored and happy. And God bless my rubber chickens, for they, too, shall reduce stress and spread mirth.*
> —Patricia Lorenz

Digging Deeper: Matthew 17:20–21; Romans 10:9–12; Ephesians 1:6–8

Friday, November 4

Give, and it will be given to you. A good measure, pressed down, shaken together and running over, will be poured into your lap....
—Luke 6:38 (NIV)

I recently did something I've wanted to do for a long time. It was a very little thing but had a big impact on me.

I was in a dollar store, standing in the checkout line. Behind me was a girl, about eleven years old, with her mother. In her arms were four small teddy bears. When I purchased my items, I said to the clerk, "Put her teddy bears on mine too." It was only four dollars, but the looks on the faces of that girl and her mother were priceless. Their mouths gaped. The mother talked about there still being good people in this world. Those behind her in line nodded in agreement. The daughter thanked me and said she was giving the bears to girls who don't have much. She was keeping only one for herself and would name her "Peaches."

The delight that this tiny bit of giving generated in my heart was way out of proportion to the size of the gift, but that's how God works. He made giving more blessed than receiving (Acts 20:35). Certainly that's not ever the reason we should give—so we'll get back. But interestingly, it's something we can't avoid.

As a well-known quote says, "Those who bring sunshine to the lives of others cannot keep it from themselves" (James Matthew Barrie). Through a young girl and her teddy bears this was confirmed to me as true.

Holy Father, Thank You for big lessons learned in small ways.
—Kim Taylor Henry

Digging Deeper: Proverbs 11:24–25; Matthew 10:42

Saturday, November 5

By wisdom a house is built, And by understanding it is established.
—Proverbs 24:3 (NASB)

My garage is one of the universe's great mysteries. I clean it and organize it, but no matter what, a few short months later it looks a lot like a trailer park after a tornado. I don't remember it happening, but it does.

One of the great blessings in my life is that my wife and I share our property with our two kids, their spouses, and our first grandchild. The garage, actually a big shop, is also shared. And I'll just come out and say it—my children are a whole lot more organized than I am.

And so it was a few days ago I found myself standing smack-dab in the middle of tornado alley for a family cleanup day. I looked around me. Three families' worth of stuff piled high. The prospect felt overwhelming. But we were all there, even my baby granddaughter in a playpen. And we dug in.

You know, our God created the universe with a thought. He imagined stars, and they *were*. He holds them all together in His hands. But the thing that continually amazes me most about our Creator is His insistence on showing up in the most mundane moments. He rarely comes with thunder and lightning and fanfare, but He always comes. I felt His arms around me, around us. I felt *joy*.

Because, gathered with the people I love and the God Who holds my days in His hands, I was, and am, a rich man.

My daughter-in-law put some music on.

My granddaughter gave me one of the world's greatest gifts—her toothless smile.

And I heard God's voice say, *Isn't it good?*

It was—and still is.

> *Lord, thank You for Your presence. Thank You for Your love.*
> —Buck Storm

Digging Deeper: Psalm 16:11

Sunday, November 6

...from whom every family in heaven and on earth derives its name.
—Ephesians 3:15 (NIV)

"Exciting news!" read the email from my uncle. "I was watching this history series on television, about war, and they had footage of the end of World War II. My father, your grandfather—I saw him. It was him. I'm sure of it. It was amazing but only lasted a second or two. We don't have any movies of him. Only still photographs. Do you think you can help find the footage, so you can see it?" he asked.

I love a challenge—especially a research project. And I know very little about my grandfather because he died when my dad was only ten. So I couldn't wait to jump on it. By lunchtime, I'd found the footage. For the first time in my life, I saw my grandfather, on the USS *Missouri,* in his navy uniform, smiling and waving.

"Hello!" he seemed to say through the black-and-white footage, "I am here! I'm your grandfather."

"Grandpa!"

It was amazing. He was only on the screen for three seconds of the three-hour special, and he was among a sea of other sailors. So how had my uncle seen him? What's more, why did I feel such a tremendous recognition of love and family?

As I shared the footage with my siblings and their children, I realized that we have people we've never met—people who were here before us, family who love us and are in heaven now— waving and cheering us on.

Dear Lord, thank You for this gift—this amazing blessing that helped me recognize I have more heavenly support than I ever imagined.
—Sabra Ciancanelli

Digging Deeper: Genesis 10:32; 1 John 3:2

Monday, November 7

But it was you, my intimate friend—one like a brother to me. It was you, my advisor, the companion I walked with and worked with.
—Psalm 55:13 (TPB)

After the birth of our second child, my husband, Wayne, and I were bursting out of the seams in our tiny two-bedroom home. We badly needed more room and went in search of a house that would meet the needs of our growing family.

After viewing several homes, Wayne was strongly attracted to a corner house in a quiet neighborhood. I liked it as well, although it only had two bedrooms on the main floor and another in the basement. The yard and garden area made up for what we lacked in bedrooms and so we made an offer, which was accepted.

Shortly after we moved in, Marilyn, a close neighbor, stopped by to welcome us. She was warm and friendly and was raising a young family herself. After we got to know each other, Marilyn invited me to attend a Bible study, and I accepted. That decision forever changed the course of my life and that of our family. It was through this Bible study that I invited Christ into my life.

Only later did I learn that Marilyn had walked down our street with an open Bible in her hand, praying for each family. Seeing that our home was up for sale, she prayed for the family who would move there and for the opportunity to share Christ. That family was Wayne, me, and our two little girls.

In retrospect, the house didn't really suit our needs; nevertheless, it was the house God planned because it was the one that would lead us to Him.

May I be the kind of neighbor Marilyn was to me, Lord, willing to share my faith and be not only a good neighbor, but a good friend.
—Debbie Macomber

Digging Deeper: Romans 1:16; 1 Peter 1:22

Tuesday, November 8

And this is the boldness we have in him, that if we ask anything according to his will, he hears us. And if we know that he hears us in whatever we ask, we know that we have obtained the requests made of him. —1 John 5:14–15 (NRSV)

When I first arrived at the church in Florida, a member named Lisa told me she knew about me from reading *Daily Guideposts* for many years. We got to talking about how the devotionals are an integral part of her spiritual development and journey. She also told me that she journals in her *Daily Guideposts* book, listing prayer requests and answered prayers.

One of her prayer requests had been about changing her job. Lisa had been with the same employer for fourteen years but had felt a nudge to move on. As an older adult, she thought the idea of moving to another job was exciting—yet it was daunting. So she prayed many times about the matter, hoping God would hear and answer her request for guidance.

But after a few months and several phone interviews with various companies, she became a bit frustrated. Lisa was disappointed that the positions she was interviewing for didn't meet all that she really wanted from a job.

Soon she sensed God placing in her heart the desire to be more specific about the job she wanted and to seek it boldly. She journaled in her *Daily Guideposts*, "I ask in Jesus's name for the most perfect job, with a great salary, great benefits, awesome people to work for and with, and something close to my home."

Three months later, she was blessed with everything she had asked for in a job and more! She has been at the job for several years now, and every day, she feels God's hand guiding and leading her.

Lisa is a firm believer that prayer can change everything.

Lord, teach us to pray with boldness and confidence.
—Pablo Diaz

Digging Deeper: Isaiah 38:5; James 1:6

Wednesday, November 9

Jesus replied: "'Love the Lord your God with all your heart and with all your soul and with all your mind.' This is the first and greatest commandment. And the second is like it: 'Love your neighbor as yourself.'" —Matthew 22:37–39 (NIV)

The great African American writer Toni Morrison once said, "There is no such thing as race. None. There is just a human race." And while we may indeed be all the same children under God, the construct of race is very real. It's a reality we've been grappling with since our birth as a nation.

My first conscious encounter with racism came when I was very young, maybe six years old. My mother and father took me with them on a trip down South, to Virginia, where my dad attended a business convention. We stayed in a grand old hotel near Old Point Comfort.

That first night, my parents had to attend an event, so they arranged for a babysitter through the hotel. The babysitter was an older African American woman who was to take me downstairs to the lobby restaurant for dinner. I figured she'd sit with me while I ate, but instead she left me at the host stand after telling the maître d' what I was to have. I was shown to a huge table, where I practically disappeared into a giant chair while I ate my favorite dinner—fried chicken with extra honey. My babysitter kept a watchful vigil from a corner of the lobby.

Years later, I learned that Old Point Comfort was where the first slave ship had made landfall in 1619.

Today, segregation laws may be long gone, but we still struggle with the toxic legacy of racism, the plague that was brought to these shores by that first ship. The process we continue to go through is painful but ultimately freeing. And if we are ever able to achieve Toni Morrison's one human race, we must go through it.

God of love, under You we are all one people. Help us to find understanding and reconciliation, to love our neighbor as You have commanded.
—Edward Grinnan

Digging Deeper: John 13:34; Acts 10:34–35; 1 John 2:8–11

Thursday, November 10

The Lord has done it this very day; let us rejoice today and be glad.
—Psalm 118:24 (NIV)

Turning five is a big deal to a four-year-old, so when James realized his birthday fell on a day we'd be gone on an extended family vacation, he voiced his concerns. Would they have cake in Colorado? Would he get to have pizza? How would all of his friends make it there?

The first two questions I could handle, but the third made me worry. James had changed schools that fall, and friendships were coveted more than ever. I prayed to God that James would enjoy his special day, even if his friends couldn't be there.

Packing for the trip, I stashed a few presents I knew he'd like, plus a few decorations for the vacation house. He woke on his birthday to red streamers and balloons in his bedroom, presents for breakfast, and a party attended by his loving aunt and uncles, who sang loudly and mostly on key.

Still, I worried. There was no bounce house, no friends, no party besides our cake and ice cream after dinner. For my boy who had been through so much change, all I wanted was for him to get what he wanted, if only for a day.

That night, as I tucked him into bed, he hugged me and said, "Mom, this was my best birthday ever." In that moment, I thanked God for James, but even more, I thanked Him for being a God Who cared about a little boy's birthday and a prayerful mama's hopeful heart.

Lord, thank You for caring about the details of my life.
In You, I find my joy.
—Ashley Kappel

Digging Deeper: 1 Corinthians 10:31; Philippians 4:4

Veterans Day, Friday, November 11

Therefore encourage one another and build each other up....
—1 Thessalonians 5:11 (NIV)

"Here comes another veteran," a friend said to me as I entered the office. Then he told me that he and another colleague had just been thanked for their military service earlier that morning.

The conversation moved on to an exchange of favorite memories from their military years. With beaming faces, they described their separate experiences, and for a while, their hearts and minds were filled with the special friendships of those they had served with. It felt good to be drawn into their joy—a joy that came because two people had simply said, "Thank you for your service."

In recent years, I've noticed an upward trend of expressions of gratitude for veterans by individuals, businesses, organizations, and communities. Changing planes a couple of years ago in Dallas, I came upon a line forming on both sides of the concourse to welcome a military unit home from Afghanistan; the thunderous applause was heartwarming. And this year, driving through Florida, I was passed by a pickup truck wrapped with the emblems of each military branch, along with a tribute: "To The Brave Who Served."

Even though some veterans may feel uncomfortable being recognized, your gratitude can certainly lift their spirits. Just think of my two friends, who were still talking about their experiences hours later!

So today, I encourage you to look for the veterans in your life. Thank them and remember that, regardless of their role, they each pledged their life to defend our freedom. Your appreciation will give the veteran a lift of encouragement that he or she can recall throughout the day, and it may even spark another conversation!

Dear Lord, thank You for the freedoms we have because of the brave who served. May we always look for ways to build them up in gratitude. Amen.
—John Dilworth

Digging Deeper: Matthew 20:28; Romans 16:4; 1 Peter 4:10

Saturday, November 12

I will refresh those who are weary.... —Jeremiah 31:25 (GNT)

I know I am pushing myself too hard, because I am getting irritable, but I enjoy planting trees so much that I resist anything that interrupts my momentum.

So when my wife calls from the garage to say, "We need to go to the farm and get some pecans," I go, but inwardly I am kicking and spitting.

We cruise slowly west out of Moberly, and soon the pecan groves appear on the left: rows and rows of pretty, vase-shaped trees, casting a dappled shade on the soft grass below. *A perfect place for a picnic,* I think.

Today the harvest machines are shaking the trees, causing the nuts to fall to the ground. Then the nuts are loaded into trucks that will haul them to the processing center at Shepherd Farms. When we enter the sales room, there is a wonderful nutty fragrance in the air, and I breathe in deeply. Then I peer through the visitors' viewing window, entranced by the ingenious machine that cracks the pecans, spitting the shells into one vat and the nutmeats into another.

While Sharon bargains with the clerk, I browse the other offerings: walnuts and macadamias, sorghum molasses and butter pecan syrup, jams and jellies. All goodies that bring back memories of Thanksgiving dinners past.

Back on the road, I feel wonderfully refreshed. My irritation is gone, my joints feel good, and my heart is beating musically. Oh, and I have decided to plant a pecan tree.

I nibble on fresh pecans and pray:

Thank You, Father, for a good wife, who always knows just when to interrupt me—before I hurt myself.
—Daniel Schantz

Digging Deeper: Psalm 23:2–3, 127:2

Sunday, November 13

According to the kindness that I have done unto thee, thou shalt do unto me..... —Genesis 21:23 (KJV)

"Daddy, why is that man standing outside in this cold?" my daughter Ella Grace asks from the back seat.

I had already spotted him standing on the corner. He had a sign that said, "Anything helps. God Bless."

I swallowed hard and prayed. *God, how do I answer?*

"We can't really know why some people have so little while we have so much, Ella Grace," I say, "but what we know is that God expects us to reach out with kindness and share what we have."

I could tell Ella Grace wanted a better explanation, but I didn't know what else to say. That night I ended our dinner blessing with "God, give us opportunities to help others."

After I finished the blessing, Ella Grace asked, "Mama, will you take me to the store tomorrow? God showed me an opportunity today."

The next evening, I found Ella Grace and her older sister, Mary Katherine, organizing piles of socks, scarves, gloves, and assorted snacks. "What in the world?" I asked.

My wife, Corinne, smiled. "It's Ella Grace's idea. We're making 'love bags' to hand out to those we see on the street who seem to need them."

Soon our car trunk is filled with the love bags, deliveries are made, and there are extras to share with others who want to join Ella Grace's project.

I can't help but believe that every bag contained a breath of kindness and that God was well pleased with each offering.

God, open our eyes to the opportunities You offer
to spread kindness and show Your love.
—Brock Kidd

Digging Deeper: Isaiah 54:8; 1 Corinthians 13:4

Monday, November 14

Happy are those whose help is the God of Jacob... who executes justice for the oppressed; who gives food to the hungry. The Lord sets the prisoners free. —Psalm 146:5–7 (NRSV)

I could hear the clanging of the iron-bar gate as we were escorted across the open exercise yard. Four of us from the Protestant Men of the Chapel group were going to our Monday evening Bible study, which is held in the United States Disciplinary Barracks (nicknamed "the DB"), a massive, forbidding prison at Fort Leavenworth, Kansas.

A friend noticed my tattered Bible, with its ripped and taped vinyl cover and its torn pages ready to fall out. "You know, there's a leather shop here in the stockade. Maybe you can get a new cover for your Bible."

Days later I visited the DB's upholstery/cobbler shop. I observed the room's off-white paint, dingy from too many recoats. The atmosphere seemed oppressive, with a funky odor and air a couple of degrees too warm. I left my Bible for repair.

Ten days later, I returned for pickup. I can still see the smile of healthy pride as a soldier-inmate-craftsperson returned the chaplain's Bible to me. His sense of satisfaction beams in my mind to this day.

I still use the thick, black leather-bound Bible, due in part to the careful notes inscribed on so many pages. But I also just like to place my hands on its smooth, stiff cover. Just feeling the now well-worn binding reminds me that God wants to have each one of us as His friend. He's excited to love and care for us all.

Compassionate God, I take to heart Your words "Regard prisoners as if you were in prison with them." (Hebrews 13:3 MSG) Be especially close to those in penitentiaries, stockades, and jails around our globe this day.
—Kenneth Sampson

Digging Deeper: Psalm 9:9; Isaiah 42:5–7; Matthew 25:36–40

Tuesday, November 15

Therefore encourage one another and build each other up, just as in fact you are doing. —1 Thessalonians 5:11 (NIV)

When my friend's daughter calls to tell me her mama's gone to heaven, I cannot even speak. Everything stops. The words, my feelings, are stuck solid. Losing this beautiful woman was not a part of our plan. We'd been friends for years.

Later I weep separately with five different sons.

Jalois made us feel like something beautiful was beating in our own chests. She made us believe we were extraordinary. Her love was consistent and strong. She gave hugs that went from the outside in. She was generous with all she had. Her eyes shone with love. Her own soul had been salvaged and saved, and unbridled joy was the outflow.

What I'd miss the most, though, was my friend's encouragement. Times had been tough, but she never let me brush against despair. Jalois reminded me that we were held in holy hands. "The Lord has this. You are loved," she'd say. "It will be okay."

As I get dressed for Jalois's funeral days later, my hands shake. All of this is surreal, and I'm suddenly afraid. Afraid to be without this positive, affirming friendship. Afraid of where my thoughts will sometimes stray without it. As I root through the closet for a long-lost black shoe, I'm so full of missing that my chest feels tight.

And my phone rings. It's my grown son, Logan. He lives hours away and can't make it to the service.

"How are you, Mom?" he asks.

"I'll miss her, Logan."

There's a silence. Then words that are salve to my soul: "I know," he says. "And I just want you to hear this today. God has this. You are loved, and things will be okay."

Thank You, Lord, that encouragement reaches forward and that hearts can hold encouraging words forever. Amen.
—Shawnelle Eliasen

Digging Deeper: Proverbs 12:25; Colossians 3:16; 1 Thessalonians 5:14

Wednesday, November 16

But when you are tempted, he will also provide a way out so that you can endure it. —1 Corinthians 10:13 (NIV)

"Guess what I brought for snacks today?" I asked my friend Jerri as I placed my pan on the table before our meeting. "Brookies!"

"Oh, no!" she moaned, because we share an out-of-control response to brookies. They are a yummy cross between chocolate brownies and peanut butter cookies that we discovered in our grocery store bakery. What's not to love about that combination?

At the end of the meeting, Jerri looked longingly at the leftover brookies in the pan. "You take them home," I told her.

"I can't have a pan of brookies around," she confessed. "I just keep straightening the edges."

That might sound confusing, but I knew exactly what she meant. I do the same thing! Instead of cutting myself a normal piece, I slyly slice along the jagged edges, eating the small bits, as if I'm fooling myself about how much I'm eating.

I took the leftover brookies home and set them on the counter. Immediately, I felt the temptation building, and without even thinking, I reached for a knife and started to stealthily slice across the edges. Then something stopped me. This wasn't so much about whether or not to eat a brookie. It was about feeling guilty because I was giving into temptation and covering my tracks by straightening the edges.

I paused long enough to remember that God said, when we are tempted, He provides a way out. His "way" this time was to walk out of the kitchen.

Lord, I don't know why food issues often reveal faith issues for me. But surely You know why. That's why You nudge me and strengthen me to make one small right choice at a time.
—Carol Kuykendall

Digging Deeper: 2 Samuel 11:2–5; Matthew 6:5–13; James 1:13

Thursday, November 17

BLESSED BY ONE SWEET COOKIE: Poetry in Motion

I praise you, for I am fearfully and wonderfully made....
—Psalm 139:14 (ESV)

My dog, Cookie, is a mutt we rescued from the pound. Our best guess is that she's part pit bull and part Labrador. To most eyes, she's probably not the most majestic of creatures, but sometimes when I watch her, I can't help but wax poetic!

I remember studying the poet Gerard Manley Hopkins in college. I loved his work because of his skill in poetic form and because, as a Jesuit priest, Hopkins loved to show readers the beauty of God's world. A major theme in Hopkins's poetry is that God created each creature for a purpose, and when we fulfill the purpose God designed us for, we are offering praise to our Maker.

That's why, when I take Cookie to the dog park and let her off the leash, I marvel at how she takes off and runs for all she's worth. She's the fastest dog at the park most days, and just watching her muscles contract and release reminds me of the awesomeness of the One Who made her. And the joy she gets from running like that? I can feel it in my own soul. Often, I can't help but laugh out loud just to see the unbridled happiness in my sweet pup.

Obviously, Cookie isn't a student of poetry, but I think that on some level, she understands perfectly what Hopkins meant. I like to think that when she runs with such speed and agility, it's her own little offering of praise to the loving God who made her.

God, Your handiwork takes my breath away!
—Ginger Rue

Digging Deeper: Isaiah 64:8; Ephesians 2:10

Friday, November 18

Who of you by worrying can add a single hour to your life?
—Luke 12:25 (NIV)

I pulled the scarf around my neck and zipped my jacket while walking through the field with Sunrise, my golden retriever. The November breeze waved the long stems of grass and rustled Sunrise's feathery coat. Normally, I shave off the long hair on her legs and belly so that it doesn't get tangled and matted, but I'd been too busy this year.

I groaned. *Another thing to add to my list! How am I going to get everything done?*

Throughout this past year, I'd had a cottage being built on my farm, but delay after delay kept holding things up. By now, the lease on the place where I was currently living would be up in three weeks.

Sunrise chased mice through the thickets as I trudged through the field of worry. *How was I, a single woman, going to move a lifetime's worth of stuff in three weeks?* I'd hired a crew to put up a fence for the horses and, even though I'd pestered them, it still wasn't done. *What am I going to do with the horses?* My heart raced.

When I turned homeward, Sunrise bounded toward me. My mouth dropped in horror. The long feathers of her coat were matted with burs. "Oh, Sunrise, what did you do?" Nothing less than I'd done to my mind by trudging through the field of worry, allowing it to become matted with the cockleburs of impossibilities.

I took a deep breath. *Lord, I can't do this by myself. Please help.*

Miraculously, over the next couple of weeks, the crew finished the fence and nearly thirty people *asked me* if there was anything they could do to help.

Remind me, Lord, to shave off worry before it starts
by first asking You for help. Amen.
—Rebecca Ondov

Digging Deeper: Proverbs 12:25; Matthew 6:25

Saturday, November 19

My soul yearns for You in the night, my spirit within me earnestly seeks You. For when Your judgments are in the earth, the inhabitants of the earth learn righteousness. —Isaiah 26:9 (NRSVCE)

The crossword clue was "Everything's okay." My husband had filled in "The end."

Charlie and I work on crosswords together but not always at the same time. When I picked up this particular puzzle, he'd completed half the blanks, but this one—"The end"—wasn't working with any cross words. I finally figured out the actual answer: "I'm fine."

I smiled. The perfect nickname for my husband would be "Everything's Okay Charlie." It wouldn't occur to him that the clue "Everything's okay" would refer to a single person, as in "*I'm* fine." For Charlie, "Everything's okay" is how life should be, and end, for *everyone*.

And he tries to make it that way—whether it's getting up quietly to avoid waking me, buying a friend morning coffee, helping a first-time offender enter a treatment program, or sitting on a panel about affordable housing. Charlie hopes to fix everything for everyone until everything's okay.

In this, he's my greatest teacher. It's not that he always succeeds but that he never gives up; he always believes there's a way to make things better.

I find it all too easy to feel overwhelmed by all that's wrong. Sometimes I use faith to hide from how complicated life is or from how many problems I, and others, face. I retreat into waiting for the Lord to fix things. Charlie never forgets that we are as often called to serve, or to wait *on*, the Lord as we are to wait *for* Him.

Father, give me the courage to do Your work.
—Marci Alborghetti

Digging Deeper: Psalm 71:1–12, 17–23; Mark 1:14–20, 29–31

Sunday, November 20

And let us not neglect our meeting together, as some people do, but encourage one another.... —Hebrews 10:25 (NLT)

The phone rang Saturday evening. Friends who had moved away were unexpectedly in town. They offered sketchy details: their daughter—hospitalized for a mental breakdown; their grandchild—placed in foster care. Then, "We'd like to go to church with you tomorrow." Yes, sure, wondering how an hour in church would ease their crisis.

When Margaret and her husband arrived, I whispered, "The pastor's away; it's a guest preacher," meaning I wasn't sure what to expect. Here's what we got: a gospel story of healing. Provided with resources beyond himself, a man with crippling disabilities stood up and walked.

After the sermon, I showed Margaret a line in the bulletin: "Prayer for Healing." "It should be scheduled next Sunday," I said. "Not sure why, but here it is today. Do you want to go up front, for anointing prayer?" Yes.

Touched by grace, she returned to her seat, weeping hopefully.

Hemmed in, I whispered to a fellow worshipper. "Monica, could you find a cup of water for my friend?" Yes. Delivered and sipped.

After the closing "thanks be to God," the visiting priest—a trained counselor—spent quality time with the parents, listening and making helpful suggestions. Margaret effusively thanked me, though I had played a minor role in the morning's mercies.

"Get this," she said. "Someone advised the priest not to include the misscheduled anointing prayers, but he followed the script anyway. Providential or what?"

As I sent them on their way, they still faced hardship but were heartened.

I thanked Monica for bringing water. She replied, "It was a pleasure to help. Just a little thing may nudge someone into a better state. I hope the church helped your friends find the grounding they needed."

Lord, as we gather for worship, reveal Your presence and meet our needs.
—Evelyn Bence

Digging Deeper: Psalm 122; Matthew 10:42

Monday, November 21

Even in laughter the heart may ache, and the end of joy may be grief.
—Proverbs 14:13 (ESV)

Since my PawPaw's passing this past year, grief has seemed to sneak up on me at the most inopportune moments. Most recently, it was at a church service at my children's school. As I sat there, the choir started to sing one of the songs my PawPaw used to loved—in fact, the very one he had asked to be played at his funeral. I couldn't control the love rolling down my cheeks, so I had to leave the service.

I have even been caught off guard by grief that has crept into daily life. I have found myself trying to hide tears at seemingly mundane moments: at the grocery store, in the car, at church. I had thought I'd already grieved my grandfather, long before his body left this earth, because his mind had been slowly leaving us for many years.

After some regular recurrence of these moments of grief, I started to search within myself. I found that since I can no longer see him, hug him, or ask about how he is feeling, I am grieving his physical absence immensely. This soul-searching has caused me to change how I react to the overwhelming moments when love and longing run down my cheeks.

Now whenever I feel grief at seemingly ordinary moments, I take the opportunity to thank God that I was blessed with great love and a godly grandfather. I find that thanking God for the blessing that was my grandfather reminds me that, while he is no longer physically here, his love and influence are eternal. I still carry within me his lessons of presence, family, and faith.

> *Father God, bring comfort and peace to those who mourn. May Your eternal love wrap those who are in the depths of grief with mercy and care.*
> —Jolynda Strandberg

Digging Deeper: Jeremiah 8:17–19; Lamentations 3:31–33; 2 Corinthians 7:9–11

Tuesday, November 22

First of all, then, I urge that supplications, prayers, intercessions, and thanksgivings be made for all people. —1 Timothy 2:1 (ESV)

It's one of the last things I like to do before I fall asleep. You've heard of people counting sheep; well, I like to go through the alphabet and remember the people I want to pray for.

A is almost always for my niece Addie; *B* is for Barry, my nephew-in-law; *C* is usually for my wife, Carol; *D* is invariably for my sister Diane; *E* is (well, you don't have to tell him) for editor extraordinaire Edward Grinnan; and *F* is for a dear friend who suffers from chronic pain.

The names change from night to night, as do the needs. Occasionally I have more than one name for a letter. You'd think I might get stuck at letters like *X*. Who would that be? (I don't happen to know any Xaviers.) But then I found myself remembering an X-ray technician at the hospital one night and all those other hospital workers—the nurses and doctors and techs. They could use some prayers. Or sometimes *X* is that person I don't really want to pray for at all—I don't even want to remember their name—but there it is—*X* marks the spot. Time for forgiveness.

Our sons come up toward the end of the alphabet. *T* is for Tim and *W* is for William, his older brother. *Y* means don't forget to pray for yourself; there's always something. And then *Z*. That makes me think of sleep, lots of zzzzzz's for the rest that God can give me when I know that the worries I've had in my heart are now in His hands.

Lights out. Time for bed.

You know what's in my heart and head, Lord. It's all Yours, from A to Z.
—Rick Hamlin

Digging Deeper: Ephesians 6:18; James 5:13–16

Wednesday, November 23

You shall love your neighbor as yourself. —Matthew 22:39 (NASB)

Gas up, climb on, start mowing.

Almost two acres, so it takes a while. The engine noise blocks out the world. Get in the rhythm. Time to relax, time to think.

Unless you bring the world with you.

And, that day, how could I not? Everything had become a relentless press. News, social media, every conversation—the very air tense with turmoil. Neighbor raged against neighbor, family against family.

Hate was having a field day in the heart of man.

I didn't need to ask God where He was in it all. I knew. His heart was with the ones He loves—everyone. He wasn't absent. Not up there somewhere, biting His nails. He was *here*—loving, pressing, offering hope to the least of these.

Even so, as I started my first pass of the mower, I had to ask Him to calm my own inner storm. Because, alone with my thoughts, I began to slip under the waves.

I caught a movement to my right. I did a double take. Another mower in my yard. My neighbor buzzed by me with a nod, leaving behind him a wide swath of cut grass. I started to say something, but he kept going.

This went on until we'd tag-teamed my whole two acres.

No explanation, no expectation of anything in return. Just a smile and a wave as he made his way home.

Imagine that. I asked for peace, and the God Who made the universe answered with a simple wordless act of neighborly kindness.

As I put my mower away, the inner storm was gone, receded to flat seas and a calm breeze.

"Thank you," I whispered to the blue.

And I felt a heavenly arm across my shoulder as I walked toward the house.

Thank You, Lord, for Who you are—a marvelous mystery and a constant, beautiful surprise.
—Buck Storm

Digging Deeper: John 16:33; Colossians 3:13

Thanksgiving, Thursday, November 24

It is God who arms me with strength, and makes my way perfect.
—Psalm 18:32 (NKJV)

"I'll go start the car," my husband called as he grabbed his jacket. I looked with dismay at the clock. How had it gotten so late? I pulled a hot pan of winter squash from the oven and poked it with a fork. Not even close to done! This was terrible.

Friends had generously invited our family to join them for Thanksgiving dinner, since they knew we'd be spending the holiday far from family. All morning, I'd been fretting and stressing over making the perfect dish to bring along—a token of our gratitude for being included. But half-done was about as far from perfect as one could get. Some friend I was. What would everyone think? Yet we couldn't show up empty-handed, so—cringing—I covered the pan with aluminum foil and dashed with it out the door.

A rush of deliciously fragrant, warm air steamed out into the cold Fairbanks night as our friends opened their door to greet us. Shame-faced, I explained my squash debacle. Our host shrugged, unconcerned. "The oven's still hot. We'll pop the squash in, and it'll be done in no time." And it was. All that stress, worry, and self-condemnation I'd put myself through—for nothing. I should've known better.

Later, as we all joined hands to bless our Thanksgiving meal, I smiled, my heart full. There's only ever been one perfect person: Jesus. I am so thankful I have friends that, like God, do not require or expect perfection in order to be included at their table.

Thank You, Lord, for the reminder that my perfectionism is a trap, a distraction that focuses only on what is missing and wrong. It is the opposite of the abundant life You wish me to live.
—Erin Janoso

Digging Deeper: Luke 10:41–42; Romans 8:1; 1 John 4:18

Friday, November 25

Every good and perfect gift is from above, coming down from the Father of the heavenly lights.... —James 1:17 (NIV)

"We're going on a shopping spree," my mother-in-law exclaimed over the phone. "Just pick a day, and I'm taking you out to the stores!"

My ex-husband's mother had always called us, usually either to check in or to plan a weekend to take the boys, but this took me completely by surprise.

Reluctantly, I picked a day after work, and we met up at Macy's on Thirty-fourth Street.

"Pick out whatever you want!" she said, helping me look through the racks. "What do you think of this?"

I went straight for the price tag and told her it was too expensive.

"What do you care about expensive?" she chastised. "Are you buying it or am I?"

She made me try it on, along with a dozen other garments, but we left that department with only two shirts. That wasn't enough for her.

"Excuse me, ma'am," she said to one of the saleswomen on the next floor. "This is my beautiful daughter-in-law. I just want her to pick out as much as she wants and make her feel special. Can you help her do that?"

Several shopping bags later, she took me out to dinner. I thanked her profusely, still feeling guilty for how much money she spent.

"Karen," she assured me, "you deserve all of this and so much more!" She continued to praise me for the mother I was to her "grandbabies" and told me how proud she was of the woman I'd become.

"You will always be my daughter-in-law," she said, a loving phrase she began telling me after my divorce from her son.

Yet sitting with her that evening, I no longer felt like her daughter-in-law. I was simply her daughter.

Lord, thank You for Your constant love that never changes and for calling me Your child.
—Karen Valentin

Digging Deeper: 2 Corinthians 9:8; 1 John 3:1

Saturday, November 26

Come no closer! Remove the sandals from your feet, for the place on which you are standing is holy ground. —Exodus 3:5 (NRSV)

Our eight-year-old floored us this morning. We were hosting a Bible study in our living room, and the topic had turned to the question *What is a "sacred place" for you?* The conversation went on for about twenty minutes among fifteen people while my eight-year-old came and went, paying no attention. Or so we thought.

About an hour after all of the guests had left, our daughter turned to my wife and me and said, "I was thinking about what you were talking about, and I was thinking... my sacred space is between my parents."

Wow! Out of the minds and hearts of babes, right? I wasn't surprised at the thoughtfulness of what she said or the love in the sentiment. She's a lovable, thoughtful kid. But I was amazed that she seemed to easily grasp the idea of sacred space, as well as her place in a world of sacred spaces.

I am determined to live more consciously in a world that is sacred—to see, touch, and hear the sacredness of what's around me. I'm also determined to make my life more of that place where my daughter might experience the sacredness of God.

Lord, make me aware today of how my presence should reflect Your presence.
—Jon M. Sweeney

Digging Deeper: Jeremiah 29:11; Matthew 18:19–21

First Sunday of Advent, November 27

WE BEHELD HIS GLORY: Experiencing Jesus's Presence

For he knows how we are formed, he remembers that we are dust.
—Psalm 103:14 (NIV)

A freeway sign flashed a warning: Blowing Dust. Low Visibility. With no measurable rain since August, there was plenty of dust to blow around. More than a hundred days of dust. And without rain to pack it down, dust along the freeway was hazardous. Thankfully, I had only a few miles to drive before parking at a trailhead on South Mountain in Phoenix.

Mollie, my four-legged hiking companion, and I set out. We were aiming for the desert wash, a meandering arroyo hedged by packed soil walls, rough from centuries of rinsing during the monsoon season. I longed for my own rinsing, my own blowing away of dusty thoughts as I prepared for Advent, the celebration of His coming. My heart felt dry. Lacking.

In contrast to my sober thoughts, Mollie bounded through the dirt, her eyes laughing at the freedom found in the short escape. She buried her nose in the scent of crushed mountains and was not content until she did it again. And again.

Around us, the November desert was unclothed. Naked. No blossoms. Just the stripped, bare, brown earth, interrupted by broken bits of plants. My feet slid and twisted in the collected dirt and pebbles from the surrounding mountains. I knew if I hiked to the ridgeline, I would see Camelback Mountain and the surrounding peaks, but there in the wash, we trudged through a giant dustbin.

Shuffling my feet, I was thankful God has a thing for dust. After all, He sent Jesus to walk a dirt-covered Earth, to stir up dust in places where it had collected for too long.

This Advent season, may I step into the winds of
Your presence as You blow away the dust in my life.
—Lynne Hartke

Digging Deeper: Ezekiel 37:27; Philippians 2:5–8

Monday, November 28

She oversees the activities of her household and never eats the bread of idleness. —Proverbs 31:27 (Tanakh)

I have always been a better housekeeper than cook. The best evidence for this is that I've never set fire to the living room or bedroom, whereas in the kitchen, I have three fires to my credit. I have even been known to set off the smoke detector by making toast. So saying that "I'm a better housekeeper" is, I believe, the equivalent of saying that I'm a faster turtle.

When my husband, Keith, was alive, he did all the cooking, laundry, and housecleaning, so I got used to being able to ignore those things. After he died, I was on my own. I took on the laundry first and was encouraged when I figured out the washing machine. I didn't have to learn to cook, because there were frozen dinners and takeout orders. I resented cleaning chores and settled into a kind of neglectful routine.

Then friends from Los Angeles came to visit, so I worked hard to overcome my distaste for things like dusting and sweeping to make my house presentable. When Janet and Howard arrived, I was really happy to see them, but I was startled when Janet asked me, "Do you know how blessed you are to have such a beautiful home?"

It took me hours to process the question and really look around at the place I was living in. Of course, I loved it. But I had only been seeing what God had taken away—and not seeing that the place where I lived was a gift. Yet that's exactly what it was. I knew from that moment on that I would have to take better care of that gift. I bought a DustBuster.

I'm sorry I didn't recognize, Lord, that Your gift needs care, and that I need to maintain it.
—Rhoda Blecker

Digging Deeper: Ecclesiastes 10:18; Lamentations 3:32

Tuesday, November 29

I will give to the Lord the thanks due to his righteousness, and I will sing praise to the name of the Lord, the Most High. —Psalm 7:17 (ESV)

My friend Allison invited me, along with several other women, over for dinner.

Once we arrived, she delighted us with a six-course tasting menu.

We started with tiny toasts with goat cheese, fig jam, and Granny Smith apples. Next came smoked salmon on cucumber, with dill crema. After that we had ravioli with roasted red-pepper sauce, then chorizo-stuffed mushrooms, then a bacon-wrapped filet with horseradish and blue cheese. We finished with a three-layer dessert—pistachio cookies with homemade whipped cream and raspberries, stacked into beautiful towers.

As we enjoyed the wonderful meal, we all raved to Allison about her amazing cooking skills.

"Your kids are so fortunate to have you cooking for them!"

Allison shrugged. "Oh, I don't cook for them. If I made my kids these foods, they would just complain and pick them apart."

Oh, how convicting.

Jesus often lays out an elaborate, beautiful, extraordinary meal for us. Yet we complain. We pick His gifts apart. We aren't grateful for His incredible faithfulness and kindness and mercy.

Still, He doesn't stop cooking things up for us. Instead, He just keeps giving, whipping up elaborate gifts that we don't deserve.

Father God, I want to be cognizant of Your gifts each day, not overlooking them or complaining about what doesn't go right. Thank You for Your faithfulness. Amen.
—Erin MacPherson

Digging Deeper: Psalm 9:1, 69:30

Wednesday, November 30

Love each other with brotherly affection and take delight in honoring each other. —Romans 12:10 (TLB)

My grandfather, William Porter Knapp, was a grade-school teacher in the early 1900s. After he retired from teaching, he was a rural mail carrier in his tiny hometown of Blandinsville, Illinois, from 1918 to 1945. For the first twenty years, he drove a small wooden mail buggy pulled by a horse on the gravel and dirt roads of his country route. Often his patrons had to help him dig that buggy out of soggy, muddy ruts in the road during the rainy season.

In the late 1940s, Grandpa's buggy was sold at auction and bought by a woman who kept it in her barn until it rotted. In 1997 my uncle Jim retrieved what was left of the buggy and gave it to his daughter and son-in-law, who had it restored by an Amish woodworker. Finally in 2019, my family and I took the buggy back to Illinois and presented it to the Blandin House Museum as a gift to the town. It was the star attraction at the annual Farmers Picnic parade that year, riding high on a flatbed truck for all to see.

The presentation ceremony made me think about what my legacy will be after I'm long gone from this earth. Will something I've written be read years after my death? Will one of my painted jars or alcohol-ink paintings make it into a museum someday? I doubt it. But that's okay, because the greatest legacy I can hope for is that I will be remembered as a mother of four, a grandmother of nine, and a faith-filled woman with a sense of humor. And without a doubt, the faith-filled part is the most important.

Father, thank You for letting me be born into a family of kind, hardworking souls with generous spirits. Help me to grow those qualities and pass on that legacy.
—Patricia Lorenz

Digging Deeper: Psalm 34:14–15; Proverbs 31:25–31; 2 Peter 1:5–9

November

THE LORD IS NEAR

1 _____

2 _____

3 _____

4 _____

5 _____

6 _____

7 _____

8 _____

9 _____

10 _____

11 _____

12 _____

13 _____

14 _____

15 _____

November

16 _____

17 _____

18 _____

19 _____

20 _____

21 _____

22 _____

23 _____

24 _____

25 _____

26 _____

27 _____

28 _____

29 _____

30 _____

December

*I have set the L*ORD *always before me:*
because he is at my right hand,
I shall not be moved.

—Psalm 16:8 (KJV)

Thursday, December 1

He restores my soul; He guides me in paths of righteousness For His name's sake. —Psalm 23:3 (NASB)

As I review my life, I realize that many of the pivotal events that occurred were moments I had little to do with. When I was twenty years old, I had no money to return to college my junior year. As I grumbled and groaned, my mother asked me to drive a friend to Mercer University to begin her freshman year. While unloading her baggage, I met a Mercer professor who told me about a scholarship that Mercer offered. I immediately visited the admissions office, and one week later I was a Mercer student. Now, fifty years later, I am retiring as senior lecturer and director of the Institute of Life Purpose at Mercer University.

Also, during my senior year at Mercer, I applied for a student missions program to teach school in Liberia, West Africa. Later, while being interviewed for the position by a student panel, I was riveted by a beautiful young woman I had not met. Two years later we were married, and Beth and I have now shared our lives together for forty-five wonderful years.

These two events have shaped and fulfilled my life, but in a sense, I had very little to do with them. So often the things we plan are not as important as the "God-breathed surprises" we encounter. God is always one step ahead of us, providing for our needs.

Father, thank You for Your joyful surprises! Amen.
—Scott Walker

Digging Deeper: Genesis 2:7; Proverbs 16:9; Isaiah 58:11

Friday, December 2

In vain you rise early and stay up late, toiling for food to eat—for he grants sleep to those he loves. —Psalm 127:2 (NIV)

The tiny café, brightened by vibrant artwork and colorful linens, was abuzz with conversation. One woman nearby was sharing about how she'd tried a new dance class. An elderly gentleman at the table next to us announced he was reading Plutarch. But I was focused on listening to Natalie, who was sitting across from me. Over bowls of fresh berries drenched in heavy cream, I watched my friend's face light up as she discussed her upcoming move to Ecuador. I promised we'd talk again before she left.

After bidding Natalie good-bye, I headed to another café to meet my mother. We talked, and she was frail and a bit fearful about the future, but I cherished each moment we had together. As a heavy rain began to fall, I called her a cab and waited with her in the parking lot until it arrived.

In a similar parking lot, a few weeks earlier, I'd happened upon a friend I hadn't seen in over a decade. Randy had been ill and was so thin that when I hugged him, I could feel his bones just beneath the skin. But our hug was warm and wonderful as we expressed to each other how grateful we were for our years of friendship.

Though I cherish each of these encounters, not one of them was real. Each took place in a dream. But that didn't make them any less sweet. Natalie will soon be in South America. My mother passed away more than two years ago. Randy died last fall, without my ever having the chance to hug him good-bye. But lately, while I sleep, God seems to be extending my time with the people I love. It's no wonder I wake up with a smile.

> *Lord, thank You for the dreams You've given to me and others. Thank You for making even the time that I sleep a precious gift.*
> —Vicki Kuyper

Digging Deeper: Psalm 3:5, 4:8, 121:3–4; Proverbs 3:24

Saturday, December 3

And what do you benefit if you gain the whole world but lose your own soul? —Matthew 16:26 (NLT)

I'm rarely bored enough to watch TV, but I sat through a documentary of a famous rock band. Beginning with their meteoric rise to stardom and worldly glory, their experience was soon followed by the cataclysmic mental free fall from the pressures of celebrity and public demand. Trapped by fame, the group's members each spiraled lower and lower. The band eventually broke up, but the soul damage was already done. Divorce, suicide, drug abuse, alcoholism—plus real danger from psychotic fans—all dogged them continuously until their untimely demises. Unfortunately, theirs is not a unique story.

It struck me that so often, people sacrifice all to achieve fame, only to discover they are too human to cope with that much earthly worship. I kept thinking, *What if they'd given God the glory for their success instead of claiming it all for themselves? What if they'd acknowledged they had been gifted especially to echo God's amazing grace, instead of trying to shoulder the burden of talent alone?* We aren't designed to compete with His glory; we're made to reflect His grace.

Through my own, much humbler experiences, I know that not a single talent I possess is mine alone. Rather, they were given to me for His specific purpose. God opens the doors He wants opened and closes the ones He wants closed. I don't know His plans. I do know I will give my utmost for what is asked of me and leave the rest up to Him.

And whether or not my words or deeds achieve much attention by earthly standards, having Him work through me is beyond meteoric!

Lord, to YOU be the glory, forever and ever. Amen.
—Erika Bentsen

Digging Deeper: Joshua 7:19; Psalm 63:11; 1 Corinthians 10:31

Second Sunday of Advent, December 4

WE BEHELD HIS GLORY: The Word became Flesh

And the Word became flesh, and dwelt among us, and we saw His glory, glory as of the only begotten from the Father, full of grace and truth.
—John 1:14 (NASB)

I stared at my December calendar filled with commitments. There was no room to breathe. Parties. Shopping. Bills. Baking. I struggled with a sense of impending stress and looming anxiety. What had happened to the joyful anticipation of Christmas?

When I was a young girl, my family had used a paper Advent calendar—a winter scene in blue, covered in white glitter. Mom had purchased it at the department store for less than a dollar.

Each morning, my three siblings and I would race downstairs to open a calendar window while we warmed up next to the heat register and ate Cream of Wheat. Then we'd cram our feet into snow boots and race to the bus. I'm sure Mom and Dad had hoped it would be a time for memories and religious instruction, but more often than not, we argued over whose turn it was to open the window—and we did it in the age-old language of children seeking to be noticed in a life-is-not-fair-to-me world.

Rather than the typical stable scene, woodland animals and birds had waited behind each window of that advent calendar. On the twenty-fourth day, Mary, Joseph, and baby Jesus completed the landscape as "the Word became flesh and dwelt among us."

The people in Christ's time had needed a residing Jesus. My siblings and I needed Him too. I still need Him.

I need Jesus at home with me in the planning of parties. Jesus hanging out as I shop. Jesus with me as I pay bills. Jesus lingering in the kitchen during Christmas baking. Jesus breathing peace into all of the details of an overloaded calendar. Jesus, God with us. With me.

Jesus, I am opening wide the window. Come be at home with me.
—Lynne Hartke

Digging Deeper: Isaiah 9:6; Matthew 1:23

Monday, December 5

So with you: Now is your time of grief, but I will see you again and you will rejoice, and no one will take away your joy. —John 16:22 (NIV)

As I waited in the checkout line with a carton of milk in my hands, the woman in front of me turned and said, "Harold did the shopping. I haven't been alone in fifty years. He loved to shop. Prices. I can't believe the prices."

I smiled at her.

"He died three days ago," she continued. "Three days. Feels like a lifetime already." She started to cry, and the cashier looked away.

"It's okay," I said. The woman looked embarrassed. I nodded and told her, "Grocery stores can be overwhelming. I don't really like them, either."

"Me too!" the cashier said. "I hate grocery stores."

I looked at the cashier and laughed. And then the older woman laughed. She wiped her face with a tissue from her pocket and nodded. "Thank you," she said. She touched my arm. "Thank you."

"It's okay," I said.

"Is it?" she asked. "Is it going to be okay?"

I nodded and she nodded back.

I watched her walk out the automatic doors, looking lost and confused and yet doing everything she could to keep going forward—to shop, to cry, and to laugh.

Heavenly Father, please help all those feeling the weight of grief. Comfort them and guide their hearts to know that You are with them and that it will be okay.
—Sabra Ciancanelli

Digging Deeper: Psalm 34:18, 73:26; Matthew 5:4

Tuesday, December 6

You need to stick it out, staying with God's plan so you'll be there for the promised completion. —Hebrews 10:36 (MSG)

I was feeling smug, self-satisfied. Nineteen brand-new *Daily Guideposts* books, in individual cardboard boxes, were ready for mailing. They'd surely arrive in plenty of time for Christmas.

What was more, I found that my 5¾-inch by 8¾-inch holiday greeting card envelopes fit perfectly on the mailing boxes I was using for the books. With super-strong clear strapping tape, I carefully affixed a card to each box. A two-for-one—book and card going out together.

With confidence, I hauled a supersized grocery bag overflowing with nineteen boxed books to the post office. Rachel, our always neighborly post office official, greeted me.

"Anything liquid, fragile, or perishable?" Rachel asked as I placed a box on the scale. I pressed hard on the red NO button on the screen.

"What about these envelopes? Do you have a letter in them? If so, it's going to cost you four times the amount to send each one."

"Oh," I mumbled. Quadruple the price, just to satisfy my two-for-one wizardry? I took a deep breath and told her I'd send the cards alone and readdress the boxes.

"Sweetheart, I'm always looking out for you" were Rachel's final words as I departed.

Once home, I took up the task again, and did so in a more restrained manner. A mood of quiet perseverance reframed my thinking. I readdressed each box.

In the process, a spirit of calmness, composure, and stability graced my day. Thankfully, the remainder of the holiday season was, likewise, grace-filled.

Gracious Lord, too often I get wrapped up in schemes of my own making, ready to forge ahead on my own. Empower me with Your patience and staying power, that I may truly enjoy Your presence and people this day.
—Kenneth Sampson

Digging Deeper: Psalm 130:5; Ecclesiastes 7:8; James 1:4

Wednesday, December 7

Enoch walked with God.... —Genesis 5:24 (NASB)

"I was thirteen when it started," Ray said.

This took me by surprise. Not the statement itself, but the fact that Ray had spoken at all. All the time I'd spent facilitating the senior-living Bible study, and I could probably count on my fingers the times I'd heard from Ray. Today's study was over, but Ray had lingered.

"When what started, Ray?"

"The conversation." He scratched his neck, cheeks a little red. "See, we didn't have much money, so my pop made a deal with a farmer in the next county for me to come work for the summer. He handed me a sack of food and water, put me on my bike, and told me to ride straight down the road for a hundred miles until I got there. A hundred miles! Different times then. Took me a few days. I started talking to God on that ride. And we've been having our conversation ever since."

I've come to realize that those moments when God presses in and speaks—those defining moments—are never when I expect them. I know I didn't expect one that day. I'm sure Ray never expected to have the impact he had. But his simple story spoke. For Ray, God wasn't just the One he ran to in distress or visited on Sunday. No, his God was an everyday, every-minute necessity. A confidant and traveling Partner—a constant and beautiful Presence.

Ray's pedaled on out of this world now. But I know the conversation echoes through the heavens louder than ever.

As for me, I'll hop on my bike and head down the road.

Maybe you will too.

The wind at our back, sun on our face, and God by our side—this is one ride that will never end.

Thank You, Lord, for Your faithful insistence.
—Buck Storm

Digging Deeper: Deuteronomy 31:6; Matthew 28:20; Hebrews 11:5

Thursday, December 8

And my spirit rejoices in God my Savior, because he has looked with favor on the humble condition of his servant.... —Luke 1:47–48 (CSB)

For several years I've periodically taken two young neighbor girls, accompanied by their Spanish-speaking grandmother, to a medical lab. The sisters' overwhelming fear stresses out everyone involved. On one visit, a frazzled technician dismissed the younger girl. "I don't have time for this!" Her colleague accepted the challenge, and, together, we coaxed and calmed. As always, I came home emotionally depleted. The girls' quick "Thank you, bye" never satisfied my desire for appreciation.

That same patient technician welcomed us again last week. She clearly remembered us: maybe it was the older sister thrashing to ward off a needle or the younger one gagging on a medicinal potion; maybe she connected my wispy halo-white hair with my determined coaching and singing.

Unfazed, she was ready. The girls had matured, but still I restrained hands, prayed for courage, and grasped for engaging songs, settling on an alphabet singalong.

Then, "We're done!" And out the door, sweet relief.

The technician followed us to the parking lot. She spoke boldly to the girls and their grandma but wanted me to overhear. "God sometimes sends us an angel. Do you see?" She nodded toward me. "*She* is your angel, helping you learn, showing you ways to be brave." She'd seen other assimilating families. "Most people don't have someone like this. Thank God for her. Be good to her. Appreciate her."

Startled, I hugged her good-bye.

In the car, the girls translated for Grandma, then suddenly asked, "Miss Evelyn, why are you crying?"

I didn't answer. Their grandma said something and they explained: "Grandma says you're crying because the woman broke your heart."

My heart—broken open by a stranger's proclamation of grace. Maybe so. God sometimes sends a messenger to encourage His servants.

Lord God, my blessed spirit rejoices in You with thanksgiving.
—Evelyn Bence

Digging Deeper: Hebrews 13:2; 1 John 4:7–16

Friday, December 9

A time to cry and a time to laugh. A time to grieve and a time to dance.
—Ecclesiastes 3:4 (NLT)

As a pastor I have walked with people and families battling against drugs or alcohol in both their best and worst times.

When I met Joe, we immediately bonded. Over lunch he disclosed to me how he had struggled with alcohol as a younger man. Where he grew up, drinking was a way of life at home and in the community. His grandpappy, father, and other members of his family drank. He followed in their footsteps starting in his early teens.

In his late thirties Joe realized that if he kept drinking, it would kill him. Tired of his life, Joe committed himself into a rehab program. After thirty days, he began faithfully attending the AA meetings. He rekindled his faith and joined a church. I now rejoiced with him over his sobriety of thirty-plus years. He had overcome a horrific addiction.

Unfortunately, the disease had not ended with him. His daughter and grandson were now both battling addiction. The last time he heard from his grandson was on Facebook, and he asked, "Papa, how did you get sober?" Joe shared the steps he took to become a whole person again, but he was still deeply worried about his grandson and asked me to pray for him.

A few weeks after our lunch meeting, I received a text. "Pastor, my twenty-nine-year-old grandson passed away sometime last night of apparent overdose. This alcohol and drug abuse is cunning, baffling, and powerful. Please pray for his mother, grandmother, and the rest of our immediate family. If not for the grace of God, there I go."

My heart sank. All I could do was mourn and pray for him.

*Lord, we rejoice with those who have overcome addiction
and pray for those still in need of wholeness.*
—Pablo Diaz

Digging Deeper: Job 2:11; Romans 12:15

Saturday, December 10

When the cares of my heart are many, your consolations cheer my soul.
—Psalm 94:19 (ESV)

Every December, I get a sudden urge to be festively busy. I suddenly feel like if I'm not baking cookies, planning events, doing holiday crafts, or decorating—well, everything—then my kids will struggle to have a merry holiday season.

But sometimes the best-laid plans fail. Like that Sunday night I was going to create an elaborate hot-chocolate bar for our family's Advent celebration. My Crock-Pot failed to work properly. The chocolate burned. I couldn't find the marshmallows. The candy canes were crushed. And by the time I sorted out the mess, I had nothing festive to serve during our family Advent time.

Guess what? We still had a wonderful time. We sang songs, we read the Bible together, we talked, we snuggled in blankets under the Christmas lights, and we had a truly memorable night.

No cocoa. No cookies. No Christmas ornament crafts to align with the theme.

I want to encourage you this holiday season: Yes, the cookies and crafts and parties and hot cocoa bars are a ton of fun. But they aren't necessary for a meaningful Christmas season.

What's necessary is Him. Jesus. Just Him.

So when you're getting the urge to bake more cookies, plan more parties, do more crafts, and do and be more, just stop. Pause. And focus on Him.

Jesus, You are the reason for this season, so help me to press into what really matters, even as I am festively busy. Amen.
—Erin MacPherson

Digging Deeper: Proverbs 3:5–6; Philippians 4:6

Third Sunday of Advent, December 11

WE BEHELD HIS GLORY: Daily Mercies
Because of God's tender mercy, the morning light from heaven is about to break upon us. —Luke 1:78 (NLT)

"What were you doing outside?" my husband, Kevin, asked as I came in the back door. "It's only sixteen degrees."

"I wanted a picture of the sunlight coming through the icicle."

"What icicle?"

I pointed out the picture window. A three-foot icicle hung from the edge of our cabin in northern Arizona, the frozen tip ending right above the patio table covered in twelve inches of December snow.

Eyes wide, Kevin grabbed his camera. As we stepped outside, two stellar jays darted back and forth among the branches of the towering ponderosa pines, playing a game of tag above us. Snow cascaded like a promise, the white shower landing on our shoulders. A gray squirrel ventured out, seeking a forgotten seed under the abandoned bird feeder. He chattered his displeasure when he came up empty. The horizon above the frozen lake was stained tangerine as a mountain chickadee hopped on the porch railing, joining the morning menagerie.

Suddenly, the birds and squirrel stilled, as if obeying an unspoken cue. Breathless, we joined the rest of creation in wordless testimony as the first rays of dawn hit our faces. The icicle beside us blazed as shafts of light refracted in all directions, striking the diamonds in the snow with golden color.

Our cameras captured the moment of God's daily mercy still breaking forth in a new day. The birds trilled the morning song as the squirrel dove once more in the snow and came up with a forgotten seed.

Daybreak had come.

Jesus, may Your tender mercy that brought You to this earth break out of my heart and refract in all directions.
—Lynne Hartke

Digging Deeper: Luke 1:77–79; John 1:1–4

Monday, December 12

Now faith is the substance of things hoped for, the evidence of things not seen. —Hebrews 11:1 (KJV)

Struck by the kindness we found in an Alabama Waffle House, I was once nudged to write a devotion about the restaurant and the gracious woman who met us at the door. I meant to share the published article with the restaurant but kept procrastinating. What if it made the restaurant staff uncomfortable? Or worse, what if they thought I was presumptuous?

Then one morning as we were headed out the door, on our way to the Waffle House, the book seemed to appear on the kitchen counter out of nowhere.

I grabbed it and, a few minutes later, was mumbling about marking a page as I thrust it into the hands of the same greeter. She disappeared into the back of the restaurant, and then came to stand before us as we sipped our coffee. She had tears in her eyes.

"That was me you wrote about," she said.

I noticed that the waitresses and cooks were taking turns visiting the back room. They would come out smiling, wiping a tear, thanking me.

So that was that. Or so it seemed.

A few days later, a woman rushed up to me in the grocery store.

"You are the one who brought the book," she said. She began to cry. "We were trying to find you. Two days after you gave us the book, the lady you wrote about suddenly died. "You made her so happy and we wanted to ask permission to read your words at her funeral."

Coincidence? A book appearing suddenly? An unknown woman in a grocery store?

Might this instead be "evidence of things not seen"?

> *God, I find myself unwittingly in the midst of Your plan. It seems You have Your finger in every pie: even the Waffle House Southern Pecan Special. Thanks for choosing me to be a player.*
> —Pam Kidd

Digging Deeper: Psalm 107:8, 119:18

Tuesday, December 13

But from everlasting to everlasting the Lord's love is with those who fear him, and his righteousness with their children's children.... —Psalm 103:17 (NIV)

The other day I was flipping through the cable channels looking for something to distract me from a couple of deadlines I was procrastinating on. I landed on an old familiar show that I'd never really gotten into, even when it had been a network hit: *The Waltons*.

My mom loved *The Waltons*. She didn't otherwise care much for television, but she rarely missed an episode of her favorite show about a tight-knit family living through the Depression and World War II in small-town Virginia. Mom came from a strong-willed Irish-Catholic clan in Philadelphia, but something about the Walton family and their bygone world brought out her latent sentimentality...and an occasional tear. I never quite got it. It was a generational thing, I concluded. Mom and her family had lived through those twin cataclysms.

It was Mom's battle with Alzheimer's that made me reconsider *The Waltons*. The disease stripped away Mom's memories layer by layer, and what can be crueler than a disease that severs our connection to the past? Once, when my wife, Julee, and I were visiting her at the memory-care facility where she lived her last years, Mom kept referring to Julee as my sister. How could she be confused about that? She'd known Julee for years.

Julee was more understanding. "She knows I'm family," she explained. "That's all that matters."

Now I finally understood the connection that Mom felt with the fictional Waltons. It was their devotion to each other that drove the story line of every episode and motivated the characters. I was no John-Boy, but in the resilient Waltons, Mom recognized her own family, past and present, and the love that held us together, no matter what.

Father, You plant us in families so that we may grow in love. Mom never forgot that. Neither will I.
—Edward Grinnan

Digging Deeper: Psalm 103:11–18; 1 Corinthians 13:13

Wednesday, December 14

My feet have closely followed his steps; I have kept to his way without turning aside. —Job 23:11 (NIV)

"Did you use the original or adapted lefse recipe?" I asked my sister Renae as I rolled out the thin, traditional Norwegian flatbread on a floured surface.

"Original."

"Ah, that explains it." I added more flour to the sticky dough. The original recipe—given to Mom from her mother—used less flour, about eight cups, in a giant recipe we rolled out every year for Christmas festivities. Mom had always fussed with ingredients, experimenting and trying different versions, until she had settled on a recipe with ten cups of flour.

"I like the elasticity of this recipe," Renae explained as she turned a circle of dough on the hot griddle. "The dough just needs to be ice-cold."

"With lots of flour for rolling," I added.

Renae nodded as she used the long wooden turning stick with Norwegian rosemaling painted on one end, a stick used by my mother and grandmother before her. Despite our efforts of containment, soon flour dust was everywhere. We "skated" on the tile floor as we rolled and flipped lefse after lefse.

"There's even flour on the carpet," Renae said, pointing at the outlines of footprints leading into the living room. "You can tell where we have been."

I laughed and grabbed another circle of dough. And I thought of the footprints of the women before us who had celebrated faith and family with this tradition, whom we were now following.

Jesus, may I be intentional in the footprints I leave this Christmas season while celebrating old and new traditions.
—Lynne Hartke

Digging Deeper: Deuteronomy 6:7–8; John 5:19

Thursday, December 15

Be of good courage, and he shall strengthen your heart, all ye that hope in the Lord. —Psalm 31:24 (KJV)

It was a week before Christmas and the holiday spirit was nowhere to be found.

I had been raised in a home of hope. But I was worn out from work and the world seemed to be tilting toward a sort of hopelessness I hadn't seen before. Around the world, boundaries separated us. At home it seemed the same, with neighbor against neighbor.

"Santa's on his way, Daddy," three-year-old David suddenly informed me as we sat in a booth waiting for breakfast.

For a moment, I enjoyed his sweetness. "Yep, and Jesus's birthday is coming soon," I answered.

Sadly, my statement came not from hope or any joyful anticipation I was feeling, but from obligation.

As David finished his chocolate chip pancakes, our waitress appeared, grinning widely.

"Well...you might not believe this." Her eyes glistened. "But these people I've never seen here before wanted to pay for your breakfast."

I was stunned. I looked around the restaurant, expecting to see a client or a family friend.

"Oh, they didn't know you," the waitress explained. "I guess they just wanted to do something nice for someone before Christmas. They've made my day." She brushed a tear away.

I felt a rush of warmth and looked at David, whose face was covered with chocolate and syrup. It was then I remembered hope.

"Mine too," I smiled back. "I'd like to pass it on and buy someone's breakfast."

She nodded. "I thought you might say that."

God, thank You for the hope that You give us so often and so unexpectedly; help us hold onto it and to pass it on.
—Brock Kidd

Digging Deeper: Proverbs 13:12; Lamentations 3:26

Friday, December 16

Put on the whole armour of God, that ye may be able to stand against the wiles of the devil. —Ephesians 6:11 (KJV)

I was delivering a Christmas present to a friend's home in secret, so I parked in a neighbor's driveway. Turns out that in the dark, it only appeared to be a driveway. My SUV nearly went over an embankment and into a creek. When the tow truck rumbled up, I learned there had already been ten such incidents that month in the same spot.

No good deed goes unpunished, Roberta, I inwardly grumbled. *Why did this have to happen at Christmastime?*

After I was back on the road, I noticed a scraping sound coming from underneath my vehicle. Later, a mechanic checked everything out and brought me the crumpled culprit. Strangely, he was smiling.

"Your little mishap destroyed your skid plate," he told me. "This baby here is your auto's armor. So none of the important parts are damaged. There's not a scratch on anything."

My SUV could have been totaled had that skid plate not faithfully done its job. And something else, or should I say Someone Else, had shielded *me* from harm as well. Because *I* could have been badly hurt too.

Because I am a believer, my life is designed to have God's armor as my protection. I just need to secure my shield of faith—my Spirit's skid plate—and remember that though I may be inconvenienced for a couple of hours from time to time, I am never out of God's care.

Thank You for Your powerful protection, Lord. Every hour of every day.
—Roberta Messner

Digging Deeper: Ephesians 6:13, 16; 1 Thessalonians 5:8

Saturday, December 17

Dear friends, let us love one another, for love comes from God.
—1 John 4:7 (NIV)

One of the last times I saw my friend Jaynie, she was welcoming me at the door in her wheelchair.

"Come in," she said, with an enthusiasm that denied her waning journey with aggressive cancer. "I have something for you!"

I followed her into the kitchen where she had several pieces of silver on the counter. I smiled because we'd recently had a conversation about the many silver pieces we'd gotten as wedding gifts that were now tarnished and stashed away because they were too much trouble to polish. That pasty polish makes such a flaky mess.

"Here's the gift," she said, opening up a small, round plastic container and pulling out a damp wipe. Then, with total satisfaction, she whisked it around a tarnished silver bowl, instantly transforming it back into its brand-new sparkling condition.

"That's magic, Jaynie!" I exclaimed. "What fun!"

"It's yours!" she said, handing me the container of magic wipes.

That was so Jaynie! She loved sharing her insights and discoveries, especially when she believed they might make someone's life easier.

Jaynie died a couple of months later.

At Christmastime, I wrapped up jars of those magic wipes for friends who, like me, had pieces of tarnished silver stashed away. After they opened their gifts at our festive gathering, I demonstrated how one wipe easily transformed a small silver bowl. Then I told them about my friend Jaynie and how she had loved discoveries that she could pass on to others.

Within days, they sent pictures of the ways the magic wipes prompted them to dig out and use more of their stashed away treasures. Just like Jaynie.

Lord, one of the best ways I can honor a loved one's memory is to pass on her legacies.
—Carol Kuykendall

Digging Deeper: Romans 12:10; Philippians 1:3–6

Fourth Sunday of Advent, December 18

WE BEHELD HIS GLORY:
The Light Shining in the Darkness

The Light shines in the darkness, and the darkness has not overcome it.
—John 1:5 (NIV)

"I do *not* have a lighthouse collection."

My husband, Kevin, uttered the phrase every time he opened another present at Christmastime to find a lighthouse. The collection had been started by a church secretary who gifted him with several lighthouses after Kevin preached a series on being a light in a dark world. As other people visited his office, they saw the unofficial collection and, when given the chance, added to it. Now after thirty-five years of pastoring, Kevin declared the lighthouse collection would not move with him into a new office.

"This one could go on the Christmas tree," I said as I helped him pack. I lifted a small wind chime from the giveaway box. The lantern pane glowed with bright yellow paint above a black-and-white tapered tower. From the foundation swung four metal chimes. It was the ugly duckling of lighthouses compared to its elaborate neighbors.

"Take what you want."

At home, I hung the lighthouse on the lowest branch of our Christmas tree. Our year-old granddaughter, Juniper, watched with interest as the chimes swayed with movement, tinkling out their melody.

Throughout the rest of the Christmas season—whenever I turned my back—Juniper crawled over to the tree and jostled the branches so the lighthouse would jingle. She ignored the wrapped presents, bright lights, and shiny ornaments, focusing on a simple wooden lighthouse that did not belong in a collection but had finally found its way home on our tree.

Light of the World, help me shine with Your light this Christmas, even in places I feel I don't belong.
—Lynne Hartke

Digging Deeper: Matthew 5:14; John 8:12

Monday, December 19

But when you give to the needy, do not let your left hand know what your right hand is doing, so that your giving may be in secret.
—Matthew 6:3–4 (ESV)

Sure, our kids believed in Santa when they were young. We believed too. We believed that there could be a power of goodness outside of ourselves and of generosity and gift-giving. Santa was never a character in the church Christmas pageant. But honoring the birth of Jesus is something worth celebrating. Carol-singing, lighting the Advent candles, saying prayers every night, asking for your heart's content, and then, always on the night before Christmas, leaving a glass of milk out for Santa, in case he wanted it.

There were moments when we didn't quite cover our tracks. A seven-year-old William observed one Christmas morning that Santa seemed to have the same wrapping paper that we used. Interesting indeed.

But the exchange that sticks in my mind most was when our son Tim was four. We'd gone to church the evening before, and on Christmas morning, after opening the presents, I was taking the trash down to the basement. With Tim.

"Daddy," he said with great thoughtfulness, "I know that you and Mom are Santa." A long pause. "Is that true?"

I gazed into his inquiring eyes. I wasn't going to lie. "Yes," I said. "That's true."

He took it in, then stopped. "You're teasing me," he said, not quite ready to give up the myth. We left it there. For another year or two.

Santa is named for a real saint, St. Nicholas, who lived in the late third and early fourth centuries. He is said to have rescued girls from human trafficking and miraculously calming a storm at sea. He also was famous for gift-giving in secret. Like we do every Christmas in honor of God's gift to us all. No lie.

Just between us, God, I will give. No one else should ever have to know.
—Rick Hamlin

Digging Deeper: Proverbs 18:16; 2 Corinthians 9:7

Tuesday, December 20

As the Father has loved me, so have I loved you. Abide in my love.
—John 15:9 (ESV)

I held the baby against my chest as my rocker arced to and fro, but he continued to cry—not a whimper but a red-faced, real-tears, all-out wail. This little one was comfortable with me. I mentored his mama. I'd been in his life since his beginning. But he wasn't feeling well.

Mama would be back soon, but every moment was one moment too long. I stood. Moved him to my shoulder. Swayed. No help for this little mister. Until Mama returned. Once he was in her arms, the crying ceased. He rested, tiny face pressed into the curve of her. His fists unclenched. Cheeks stained red returned to pink. Her presence brought peace.

It reminded me of the time in God's Word when two sisters waited for the peace of Jesus's presence when their brother, Lazarus, was ill. But Jesus didn't arrive until Lazarus was in the grave.

Martha met him with anguish. "Jesus," she said, "if You'd been here, he wouldn't have died."

The sisters had longed for a healing. But Jesus called Lazarus from the grave, and they received a resurrection. The presence of Jesus is like that—always more powerful than we can imagine. It changes circumstance and soul.

I often succumb to worry over my loved ones or over a tough circumstance I can't see the end of. My soul cries like a babe needing comfort. When I'm so disturbed that I'm distraught, I can be sure that I've not practiced being in the presence of Jesus.

He brings hope. He works in ways I cannot fathom. Trusting the presence of Jesus is training myself to receive peace.

With the little one lost in sweet slumber, his mama and I sat and visited. The rocker creaked as soft and gently as our words.

Presence changes everything.

Jesus, Your Presence quiets me. Amen.
—Shawnelle Eliasen

Digging Deeper: John 11:21, 32, 44

Wednesday, December 21

A generous person will prosper; whoever refreshes others will be refreshed.
—Proverbs 11:25 (NIV)

As a child, I loved Christmas completely. Family fun, gifts, and decorations made the day magical and memorable. For years, I tried to create the same feelings for my own family's Christmas celebrations, but something always seemed to be missing.

About seven years ago, my neighbor James gathered up a group of children and their fathers on Christmas morning, and they began visiting the homes of local senior citizens to sing carols. It was casually planned but perfectly executed, and it brought joy not only to the seniors but also to the children and dads. Our family—including me, a mom—eventually joined the group, and later even more kids and moms joined us. Last Christmas, our group had expanded to more than twenty people, and we traveled by a caravan of cars to seniors' homes and to a local nursing home.

Going caroling with our neighbors means that we have less time to open gifts and a shortened window to make dinner. But that doesn't matter much to our family, because singing carols—out of tune, without practice, but with so much enthusiasm—brings us almost as much joy as it brings to those we sing to. My sons, now in their twenties, have grown up realizing that Christmas is not only about giving and getting presents; it's also about giving of your time and your talents.

Our family's Christmas celebration is far different from what I experienced as a child, but it's so very fulfilling and inspiring. And I wouldn't have it any other way.

Father God, thank You that we are able to celebrate the true spirit of our Savior's birth by sharing and showing love to others. It brings us closer to others while drawing us closer to You.
—Gayle T. Williams

Digging Deeper: Hebrews 10:24, 13:16

Thursday, December 22

He will yet fill your mouth with laughter and your lips with shouts of joy.
—Job 8:21 (NIV)

"Dave, we have a problem up here!"

It was December 22. We were expecting a houseful for Christmas. As I got ready for bed, I'd heard a soft *drip…drip…drip*. Following the sound, I discovered a drenched carpet under a cracked toilet tank.

I ran for our stash of old towels. Dave turned off the water. We mopped up together, grumbling. Gradually, mercifully, our mood changed, and we began trading encouragements in shorthand:

"It's only water!" (An earlier leak in our basement had been a sewage backup.)

"This is *not* a crisis; just an inconvenience." (Dave's cancer had taught us the difference.)

Suddenly I remembered the room below us. "The dining room!"

Clutching old bath towels, we ran down the stairs. Water dripped from the ceiling onto our china cupboard. I spread towels while Dave retrieved our ladder. He climbed up and touched the drip. Then like the legendary Dutch boy, Dave shoved his finger in the dike. He gasped, "Grab a bucket!" We caught two gallons before it slowed to a trickle.

The next day, our daughter Emily arrived to help us decorate for Christmas. We played Christmas music and brought the boxes in from the garage. But our eyes kept wandering to that ragged hole in the ceiling and the blue plastic bucket underneath, on top of the cabinet.

Emily said playfully, "We need to decorate the Christmas bucket!" She drove to the dollar store.

Upon her return, while grinning, she dropped the bucket into a huge red and green gift bag. And that Christmas, Rudolph pranced festively above our china cupboard.

Precious Lord, thank You for Your gifts of perspective and laughter.
—Leanne Jackson

Digging Deeper: Psalm 46:1; Romans 12:12

Friday, December 23

You know about the kindness of our Lord Jesus Christ. He was rich, yet for your sake he became poor in order to make you rich through his poverty. —2 Corinthians 8:9 (GW)

This Christmas, our daughters' and their boyfriends' schedules threatened to make celebrating as a family impossible. So, Kris (my husband) and I splurged on a holiday in Yucatán for us all.

We stayed at my friend Donald's gloriously dilapidated mansion: cracked plaster walls in faded colors, unbelievably high ceilings, tall double doors opening from every room onto an overgrown courtyard. In the courtyard, iridescent grackles dipped their bills into an icy blue pool. And from everywhere in the house you could smell flowers, hear birds calling, and see the glittery green jungle.

It was paradise—minus modern plumbing, refrigeration, electricity, and navigable sidewalks. So first thing, Donald demonstrated for us how to use the tiny bathroom's pump toilet and trickle of a shower.

On our day trips through vast Mayan ruins, I limped most of the way, because early on I had stepped wrong. We ate little—mostly eggs and fruit—and spent our days outside, watching birds, joking around, reading. At night we huddled under the main room's single bulb, playing backgammon.

On Christmas Eve, we attended midnight Mass at the neighborhood church, which was rowdy with crying babies and shushing grandparents. The highlight of the service was a radiant couple in shorts and flip-flops carrying their newborn to the creche at the altar.

Although Kris and I explicitly believed in the Jesus their baby symbolized, this may have been the holiest Christmas I've ever shared. The unembellished joy of that service made Christmas rich.

Father, help me pare away the commerce and gaudiness of my worship to see only You.
—Patty Kirk

Digging Deeper: Matthew 16:19–24

Christmas Eve, Saturday, December 24

WE BEHELD HIS GLORY: The True Gift of Christmas

And she brought forth her firstborn Son, and wrapped Him in swaddling cloths, and laid Him in a manger, because there was no room for them in the inn. —Luke 2:7 (NKJV)

"Sorry we're late," Jessica said as she entered my home in a rush with her two boys.

Two hours late! Didn't she realize I had no room in my busy schedule for this? Jessica had agreed to wrap presents to earn extra cash.

"My neighbor was fixing my brakes," Jessica explained as she reached for a roll of silver snowman paper. My ill humor vanished. Each Sunday, the young family had walked to our church from a nearby women's shelter, until Jessica had been able to purchase a dilapidated car with a damaged windshield, no brakes, and missing side mirrors. Now her simple explanation for their tardiness shifted something crowded inside me, making room for compassion.

"Would you like cookies and cocoa?" I asked the boys.

The boys nodded and settled in to watch a Christmas video. As she wrapped, Jessica shared the challenges of living in a shelter. The noise. The lack of privacy. How they locked all their belongings in the car trunk for safekeeping.

After the presents were stacked neatly under our tree, Jessica refused the money I tried to press into her hands, explaining that a peaceful evening in my home was enough of a gift.

As Jessica edged the beat-up car away from the curb with her greatest treasures buckled in the backseat, I thought of another family seeking shelter in an inn and finding no room. The gift of that night, like this one, was hidden in humble circumstances, waiting to be seen.

Jesus, sometimes the gift of Christmas arrives in unexpected ways. This Christmas Eve, help me open the door and invite You in.
—Lynne Hartke

Digging Deeper: John 3:16; James 1:17

Christmas, Sunday, December 25

WE BEHELD HIS GLORY: The Savior Is Born

And she will have a son, and you are to name him Jesus, for he will save his people from their sins. —Matthew 1:21 (NLT)

Even if our grandson is a city boy, he needs a play barn," my parents explained when I called to thank them for the farm set they had given our two-year-old son, Nate. My parents were in Wisconsin, along with aunts, uncles, and cousins from all over the Midwest, for food, laughter, and milking the cows while celebrating Christmas at the farmstead that had been in our family for a hundred years.

Meanwhile, my husband, Kevin, Nate, and I were spending Christmas in our new home near the Phoenix metropolis—there were plenty of buildings and plastic snowmen but not a farm animal or relative in sight. We made our own joy, adding tamales to our traditional menu and playing carols while we opened gifts, including Nate's favorite, "Away in a Manger." With toddler enthusiasm, he always shouted the line where Jesus was "asleep on the hay!"

Nate played with his new barn under the Christmas tree while I picked up wrapping paper and bits of ribbon. When I went to straighten the nativity set by the fireplace, though, I realized baby Jesus was missing. I checked under the furniture and even sorted through the trash can.

"Nate, where is baby Jesus?" I asked.

"Asleep on the hay," he said, pointing to his red barn. Sure enough, baby Jesus was resting next to the feeding trough, surrounded by the animals.

Even as a city boy, our son knew where Jesus belonged on Christmas Day—in a plastic barn of new beginnings.

Dear Jesus, fill my heart with a child's wonder this Christmas so that I know where to look for You.
—Lynne Hartke

Digging Deeper: Luke 2:1–20; 2 Corinthians 9:15

Monday, December 26

From the creation of the world, God's invisible qualities, his eternal power and divine nature, have been clearly observed in what he made. As a result, people have no excuse. —Romans 1:20 (NOG)

In Mexico this Christmas break, we visited Coba, the least touristy of the Mayan ruins, spread out in a jungle so vast we had to rent bicycles to view them. With my sprained ankle, I could hardly walk, much less ride a bike, so I sent the kids on ahead while my husband and I tried to photograph the invisible birds we heard everywhere.

Somehow, in the process of renting bikes, our daughters had a fight, and Lulu, trailed by her boyfriend, sped off on her bike, away from Charlotte, leaving me to fret. Having grown up in a dysfunctional household characterized by rage fits and broken relationships, I've always wanted more than anything else for my girls to love each other. Their mildest disagreement undoes me.

Soon, though, a trio of green jays with magnificent blue heads, black faces, and bright yellow eyes distracted me. Then Kris took off after something with his camera just as something else large bustled above me. I peered, breathless, into the greenness, to see not the huge bird I was expecting but a family of monkeys, one clearly the mom with a baby clinging to her. They were moving arm-by-arm through the branches.

Moments later, Charlotte appeared from one direction, Lulu and Seho from the other. All three stopped, leaning in on their bikes to crowd around the rock I was sitting on.

"Did you see the coatis? Those raccoon things?" and "What about the turquoise and red bird we saw? Did you get a picture of one of those?" I showed them the jays and the one photo I'd managed to get of the monkeys.

Truly, nature—tangible proof of our divine Parent's character and abiding presence—heals us.

Father, help my loved ones notice You. Heal them. Heal me.
—Patty Kirk

Digging Deeper: Job 12:7–12

Tuesday, December 27

God was kind and decided that Christ would choose us to be God's own adopted children. —Ephesians 1:5 (CEV)

For a good portion of my life, I assumed I had Jewish roots. Both my maiden name and that of my mother sound Jewish. Even some of the recipes handed down from one generation to another have distinctive Jewish overtones. Christmas wouldn't be Christmas without halva.

All four of my grandparents had emigrated from a German settlement inside the Ukraine, where many Jews had settled. They'd all left to come to the United States around the same time as the story *Fiddler on the Roof*. The idea of being one of God's chosen people excited me. What a heritage. What a privilege.

Then I took one of those DNA tests. To my disappointment, I discovered that not only was I not Jewish, but I have no defining country of origin. With blood ties that bounce all over Europe—German, French, English, and Welsh—I had not a drop of anything Jewish. To say I was disappointed would discount my feelings. I was so sure I was one of God's chosen people.

But shortly after receiving the DNA test results, I read the verse from Ephesians that reminded me I had been chosen—and not only chosen but adopted into God's family. I am His child, adopted in love. I am His chosen one. What a heritage. What a privilege.

Dear Jesus, because of You, I have been adopted into the family of God, and that is exactly where I want to be no matter what my DNA says.
—Debbie Macomber

Digging Deeper: Romans 8:15; Ephesians 1:5; 1 John 3:1

Wednesday, December 28

But he said to me, "My grace is sufficient for you, for my power is made perfect in weakness." Therefore I will boast all the more gladly of my weaknesses, so that the power of Christ may rest upon me.
—2 Corinthians 12:9 (ESV)

Every time I looked at the Christmas tree, I saw a reminder that this year would be an imperfect Christmas. The top quarter of the lights on the tree had gone out weeks before, and in the hustle and bustle of the season I never had time to put up a new set.

I never managed to decorate our wreath with lights, either. And I didn't mail Christmas cards until after the holiday. To an extreme perfectionist, these details felt like major failures. It didn't help that relationship crises had also timed with the holidays to make a messy, imperfect kind of season. But it was a fitting finish to what had been a messy, imperfect kind of year.

No matter how hard I tried, I couldn't make the year go smoothly—I couldn't fix problems or avoid troubles. I couldn't be perfect or make things perfect for others. Too much was out of my control.

As I began to anticipate a new year coming, I reflected on the imperfection that weighs me down with a sense of failure. But in the midst of that reflection, I caught a glimmer of something I'd forgotten: as we walk with Christ, He sanctifies us daily, redeeming our imperfections for a beautiful purpose. Only in my weakness do I realize how much I need God's grace.

In my messy, imperfect days, His power is made perfect. Ultimately, that's the only perfection I need in order to call each day a success.

Lord, thank You that You are perfect so that I don't have to be.
—Jerusha Agen

Digging Deeper: Psalm 18:30, 19:7; Matthew 19:21

Thursday, December 29

Therefore, as God's chosen people, holy and dearly loved, clothe yourselves with compassion, kindness, humility, gentleness and patience.
—Colossians 3:12 (NIV)

The day I'd been dreading dawned at last. Duncan, our twelve-year-old Scottish terrier, could barely lift his grizzled head from the cushion in his dog bed. Nor was he interested when I tried to tempt his failing appetite with a bit of deli turkey. It broke my heart to see him struggle to his feet to make his way to the doggie door. He was so clearly in pain, and I couldn't stand his suffering any longer.

With a heavy heart, I called the vet. Her assistant met us at the door of the clinic and gently carried Duncan into the office. The teenage girl who regularly helped in the kennel brought a soft blanket to wrap around Duncan as he was gently lifted onto the examination table. No one rushed me as I hugged my dear pet for the last time. Silently, I thanked God for the blessing of this loyal canine companion, who had so often been a visual reminder to me of the Lord's lovingkindness, which endures forever.

Later, while I was trying to write a check for the vet's services, my vision blurred with tears. The receptionist kindly told me to make the payment at another time. A few days later, I received a sympathy card signed by the vet and her staff, along with a keepsake: Duncan's little pawprints memorialized in ink on a card. The tears flowed, but my heart was warmed by their kindness—a precious gift in my time of loss.

Thank You, Lord, for those who brighten our days with gentleness and kindness.
—Shirley Raye Redmond

Digging Deeper: Galatians 5:22; 1 Peter 3:4

Friday, December 30

Watch, therefore, for you know neither the day nor the hour.
—Matthew 25:13 (RSV)

Last night I had the world's most boring dream. I was trying to get lunch in a Manhattan cafeteria, waiting in a ridiculously long line. That was the bulk of my dream: waiting in line, in real time. Finally, the line started moving and moving quickly. No, actually, as it turned out, the line was dispersing—because the lunch counter had closed up for the day.

That was it. I woke up angry and confused. I could've dreamt about my Nobel Prize acceptance speech (*"I'd like to thank the committee..."*) or about flying with two oversized time cards as wings (an actual dream). But no, I dreamed about waiting—literally waiting for nothing. Even Sigmund Freud would've said, "Wow, bud. You're, like, really dull."

Truth is, it's a boring but accurate dream. I've spent much of my life waiting—in lines, in traffic, on hold. I could take some solace in the many biblical tales of waiting (forty years in the desert comes to mind), but it's not much comfort. There was just nothing to learn from such a dream.

Unless... maybe it's a subconscious reminder of what a little slice of time we have left, a reminder that my endless waiting is often the result of my own poor planning—and that I have the choice to do something *other* than waiting, like praying. Or helping. Something (anything) to overcome my own willful inertia and to trust the voice inside me that sounds mysteriously like Yoda from *Star Wars*: "Do or do not—there is no try."

Time to act. But first, lunch. I'm still waiting to eat.

Lord, my dreams are small, and my will is often weak. Teach me to find strength in Your will and walk in Your ways.
—Mark Collins

Digging Deeper: Psalm 69:3; Luke 12:36

New Year's Eve, Saturday, December 31

Be strong and courageous. Do not be afraid or terrified because of them, for the LORD *your God goes with you; he will never leave you nor forsake you.* —Deuteronomy 31:6 (NIV)

It was ten o'clock at night, and I still didn't know what to do. Should I leave the comfort and safety of my parents' home or take a car service with my boys to have New Year's Eve at the beach?

"I don't know," I said, debating the idea with my mother. "We should ring in the new year with a bang!"

Her mind was already set. She'd stay home with my father in her pajamas, watching the ball drop in Times Square.

"Florida drivers are crazy," she reminded me. "Especially on New Year's Eve. Do you really want to risk being on the road with the kids?"

I shrugged and sat on the couch deflated. I watched the crowds in New York City on my mother's TV, remembering the time I rang in the new year at Times Square. I'd been reluctant to go, but I went anyway to accompany a friend visiting from out of town. As much as I'd dreaded the crowds, cold, and lack of bathroom access, it turned out to be one of the best New Year's Eve celebrations of my life.

I shot up from the couch. "Boys! Get dressed! We're going to the beach!"

A quick drive later, we were eating ice cream and strolling on the sand. Music played, people danced, and the boys lit up the night sky with sparklers in their hands. As I watched them having fun, I was grateful we'd taken the chance, despite the what-ifs.

Soon, fireworks were exploding over the ocean, and we were shouting in excitement with everyone else who hadn't stayed home in their pajamas.

Lord, help me not to live life in fear. Let me celebrate this life You've given me with faith and courage.
—Karen Valentin

Digging Deeper: Psalm 16:11

December

THE LORD IS NEAR

1 _____

2 _____

3 _____

4 _____

5 _____

6 _____

7 _____

8 _____

9 _____

10 _____

11 _____

12 _____

13 _____

14 _____

15 _____

December

16 _____

17 _____

18 _____

19 _____

20 _____

21 _____

22 _____

23 _____

24 _____

25 _____

26 _____

27 _____

28 _____

29 _____

30 _____

31 _____

Fellowship Corner

As a teacher and student of God's Word, **Jerusha Agen** is awed by the letters of love the Father writes into every moment of our lives. Writing devotionals is a special opportunity to sit down and focus her attention on these evidences of God at work.

With a BA in English and a background in screenwriting, Jerusha is a speaker, suspense writer, and the author of the *Fear Warrior* blog, where she writes about fighting against fear in our everyday lives. Jerusha also teaches as an industry professional in Tricia Goyer's "Write That Book" subscription group.

You'll often find Jerusha sharing irresistibly adorable photos of her furry fear warriors (three big dogs and two little cats) on social media. Visit Jerusha at JerushaAgen.com and connect with her on Facebook, Instagram, Pinterest, and Twitter.

"I have a friend who frequently repeats the adage 'Getting old is not for sissies,' and I have to admit I'm starting to see what she means," says **Marci Alborghetti**. "I'm gaining a better understanding of what aging means as my parents, my friends, Charlie, and yes, I, face more of the health and mobility challenges of getting older. But I think the real challenge in aging is in the spiritual and emotional realms. It is in understanding and accepting that the Lord is indeed nearer to us in a different way than when we were younger. That's a little scary, but I've also found it a deep comfort. My work now is not only to recognize that the Lord is near to me but to open myself up to that nearness and draw nearer to Him."

"This year has been all about how moving forward incrementally is the way to go," writes **Julia Attaway** of New York City. "My fourth child will graduate from high school and has a full nursing scholarship to college, a possibility that was incomprehensible four years ago." Her conclusion: God doesn't always expect us to see the way through hardship. He expects us to love Him in difficulty as much as we love Him in pleasant times and to make each simple decision based on that love. "Making

Fellowship Corner

the choice to love God regardless of how things work out in this life is pivotal," Julia says. Faithfulness is everything.

Evelyn Bence of Arlington, Virginia, writes, "Four years ago, to memorialize a friend, I planted a hydrangea in the front yard. Its greenery flourished, but nary a blossom—until this spring, when it was covered with blue beauties that made me smile.

"For nearly ten years, I've been like an extra grandmother to a girl in the neighborhood—now a maturing teen. Many evenings she calls, and together we say a short form of Compline, a liturgical type of bedtime prayers. These few moments help to assure us both that God is near."

Erika Bentsen celebrated the fourth anniversary of her miracle back surgery this year. "I know my back is completely restored," she says, "when Mom gets me a chain saw for Christmas!" It's battery operated and small enough to tie to the saddle or tote around on the four-wheeler. "I absolutely love it. It's so handy."

The first two books she illustrated found their way into a Disney movie. "They're used as stage props; isn't that the craziest thing ever? At first I thought it was a joke. How in the world—out of the millions of books out there—did ours get chosen?" She chalks that up to a nudge from God that she's on the path He's chosen for her. "God is good, all the time! And I love His sense of humor."

"You know that saying that you can't teach an old dog new tricks? Well, this year I was the old dog," says **Rhoda Blecker**, "and my new trick is (to my amazement) working. I have never been a cook. Those three kitchen fires were more than proof of that. Keith did all the cooking in our marriage; indeed, he used to ask me what I ever did for food before I met him. But the advice of friends—that I couldn't mess anything up if I got a slow cooker—made me curious, and when my twin, Nell, told me that it did the cooking for you, I was sold. I got a decent slow cooker

Fellowship Corner

and started experimenting. By the fourth meal, the food was not just edible like the first three, but good! I think Keith would be proud of this old dog."

Sabra Ciancanelli of Tivoli, New York, writes, "Our dog Soda lost his sight this spring. It happened quickly without warning, and it broke my heart to watch his world go dark—to know that he wouldn't see my face or a special treat or any of the things he loves. Amazingly, he adapted quickly, learning how to climb the stairs and navigate the house without bumping into doorways. The first time after his blindness that he rolled on the rug and showed his belly, a sign of utter joy, I cried to know he was happy.

"Change isn't easy. Especially accepting the challenges that come with age and time. As I write this, Soda is sitting on the window seat and looking out, just like he did when he could see. I send up a prayer of thanks for the blessing he is to me and the lessons God teaches through the love we share."

"I did the math," says **Mark Collins** of Pittsburgh, Pennsylvania. "I have been writing for *Daily Guideposts* for twenty-five years. This is the perfect opportunity to thank all of the loyal readers who have written to me—so much so that I rarely catch up in my responses. I am sorry I'm such a lousy correspondent; please know that I am deeply grateful for your invisible company every day. And a quick shout-out to the *DGP* editors and production team. After a quarter century, you'd think I'd be able to hit at least one deadline. Maybe next year?"

When not missing deadlines, Mark and his wife, Sandee, are the still-proud parents of their still-odd grown daughters, Faith, Hope, and Grace.

This past year, **Pablo Diaz** and his wife, Elba, moved to Florida, where Pablo became the transitional pastor of a church. They love the weather, the lifestyle, and the west coast of the state. Although they miss their family, they stay connected through regular FaceTime calls.

Fellowship Corner

"I'm back preaching weekly, leading church staff, and caring for the spiritual well-being of the members of Saint Andrews Presbyterian Church in Dunedin," says Pablo. "One of the many blessings is meeting members who read *Daily Guideposts* and *Walking in Grace*. I'm so thankful for all of our readers."

This year Elba and Pablo will celebrate their fortieth wedding anniversary. "We're so grateful to God for His blessings and keeping us together," Pablo says. "We look forward to many more."

"The most significant event this year for me is having my vision fully restored through successful corneal transplants, for which I am so grateful and blessed!" says **John Dilworth** of Massillon, Ohio. This year, John and his wife, Pat, have also enjoyed discovering the many things they love about living in their downsized home, including meeting new neighbors and taking walks with their dog, Skipper.

Their travels included a road trip down the East Coast to Florida and spending time with family and friends along the way. They also took a land and river excursion that started in Prague and ended in Paris. "We visited the Guggenheim Museum in Mainz, Germany, where we saw one of the original printed Bibles," says John. "Prior to the printing press, it took a person three or four years to hand-scribe one copy of the Bible. What a difference the printing press made in spreading God's Word!"

"Over the past few years, I have learned how to rely on God in times of change," says **Logan Eliasen**. "This year, I have learned to seek Him in times of consistency. This has been a year of settling in. I decided to make Des Moines, Iowa, my home. I began a permanent position as an attorney at a law firm. And I deepened and strengthened already formed friendships. The steadiness of normal life has, at times, felt strange to me, but through it I have learned to trust God in new ways. He has been worthy of that trust. He truly is the one who both moves mountains and settles souls."

Fellowship Corner

"For me, this has been a year of reaching," says **Shawnelle Eliasen** of LeClaire, Iowa. "Reaching to the Lord for contentment, peace, joy, and the ability to trust Him when life changes. I'm still adjusting to our new home, and I'm still missing our old one. And my boys—they're growing so fast."

Shawnelle has found that while her family is growing and changing, the Lord is growing and changing her too. She's moving into a mentoring role with younger women, some of them mothers of small children. "The good and grace-filled thing about reaching for the Lord, though, is that we don't have to reach far. He's reaching back. And when we open our fists, He's faithful to fill our hands."

"Last year in my bio, I mentioned that Julee was about to have long-awaited spinal surgery," says **Edward Grinnan** of New York, New York. "The procedure was successful, but she landed back in the hospital with a post-operative infection that required IV antibiotics three times a day for seven weeks. They inserted a PICC (catheter) line so we could manage the infusions at home. I got pretty good at administering the medicine, though Julee will admit she is not the most patient patient. Still, it was a blessing to be part of her healing process."

Edward is working on a new book for Guideposts, where he is vice president of Strategic Content Development. "The book delves into my family's history of Alzheimer's and especially my mother's battle with dementia and how it affected my brother, sister, and me." This will be his third memoir for Guideposts, following *The Promise of Hope* and *Always By My Side*.

One benefit of finishing a book: more time at his cabin in the Berkshires with golden retriever Gracie, who gets a daily walk in the Massachusetts woods. "That's where God always feels closest to me," Edward says.

Rick Hamlin and his wife, Carol, are pleased to have their son, Timothy, and his wife, Henley, living much closer to them: the couple has taken residence in New York City while Tim attends seminary to become an ordained minister. Rick's older son, William, and his wife, Karen, continue

Fellowship Corner

to stay in San Francisco, where Will works for Pinterest. Both Rick and Carol have new books. Rick's short volume on contemplative prayer, *Even Silence Is Praise*, will be released in February 2022 (published by W, a division of HarperCollins); Carol's historical novel, set in Gilded Age New York, *Our Kind of People*, came out in fall 2021. Rick's attitude about prayer is that it's something everyone can do. "It's one of the few things I can think of," he says, "where trying to do it is doing it."

Lynne Hartke says she struggled to adapt to the nonsnowy Christmases of the Sonoran Desert, where she now lives, after moving from the forests of northern Minnesota. But after three decades of exploring desert trails with her husband, Kevin, and their rust-colored mutt Mollie, Lynne has encountered the beauty found in barren places—a beauty also enjoyed by the couples' grown children and grandchildren, who all live in Arizona. She is the author of *Under a Desert Sky: Redefining Hope, Beauty, and Faith in the Hardest Places*.

As a breast cancer survivor, Lynne receives inspiration from other survivors at the cancer organizations where she volunteers. Connect with her at lynnehartke.com.

"In times of joy and in days of uncertainty, the Lord continues to prove Himself to be faithful and true," says **Carla Hendricks** of Franklin, Tennessee. "I see His faithfulness in my family, which includes my husband, Anthony, and our four kids, Kalin, Christian, Joelle, and Jada. Now ages fourteen to twenty-five, they are no longer little kids, but teen girls and young men.

"As I continue to serve my church's care ministry, I also see His faithfulness to His people—those walking through adoption, foster care, single parenting, divorce, recovery, and financial hardships.

"In addition to being involved in ministry, I continue to enjoy writing, losing myself in amazing books, and enjoying fun movie nights with my family. By the way, movie night is serious business for the Hendricks family, with plenty of popcorn, LaCroix sparkling water, and everyone's favorite theater-size candy. Mine happens to be dark-chocolate Raisinets!"

Fellowship Corner

"Oh, normal day, what a treasure you are!" describes how **Kim Taylor Henry** continues to feel about life. "Just enjoying good health, family, and the joys of each day, be they big or small, is a thrill to me," she says. "One of our big joys was welcoming our daughter Rachel's fiancé, David, into our family and watching as they exchanged vows on a mountaintop, with majestic Mt. Hood as their backdrop. Spending time with our three grown children, their spouses, and our six grandchildren continues to be our greatest delight. We had the added blessing of experiencing the beauty of South America and the breathtaking magnificence of Antarctica. But the best gift of all was knowing God is near, every minute of every day.

"I'd love to hear from you; visit me at kimtaylorhenry.com."

Leanne Jackson of Fishers, Indiana, says, "I know the Lord is as near as my breath. Even, or especially, when I'm too weary to pray." At those times, she feels God's presence through the steady prayers of friends. They sustained her as she drove nearly nonstop from Indiana to Virginia, after her mother fell and required brain surgery. They continue to support her during oncology appointments with her husband, Dave. Leanne savors texts and emails from local and long-distance friends.

God regularly places new friends in her path—other dementia caregivers, other writers for Guideposts, other volunteers at her church and food pantry, and now you, dear readers of *Walking in Grace*. "I am thankful for friends, near and far, who pray for us and we for them," Leanne says. "The Lord is near!"

Erin Janoso, her husband, Jim, and daughter, Aurora, continue to live in both Alaska and Montana. Aurora's black cat, Schwarz Stiefel, also joins the family when they travel back and forth. "'His name means Black Boots in German!" Aurora would insist on telling you.

"Our family loves both states," says Erin, "and I am very glad that, for the time being, we do not have to choose between the two."

Erin keeps busy as a freelance writer and continues to play her trumpet in the Billings, Montana, and Fairbanks, Alaska, community bands. "I am so

Fellowship Corner

happy music is a part of my life once again!" says Erin. Aurora is enjoying her first grade year of homeschool, as well as theater classes, choir, and many other activities. "I am immensely grateful for the many blessings that exist in my life!"

Ashley Kappel lives in Alabama with her husband, three kids, and golden retriever rescue. This year has been a blur of dance recitals, dinosaur museums, and baby milestones, and she's savoring every minute. She asks for your prayers that God would renew her patience and strength as she mothers three adorable souls and continues her walk with Jesus.

Jenny Lynn Keller was raised in the South and loves her Appalachian mountain heritage and the family she discovered growing up there. Her passion is transforming their rowdy adventures into stories filled with hope, humor, romance, and a touch of suspense. She is an award-winning author and frequent speaker on the history, culture, and beauty of the Great Smoky Mountains and surrounding area. Southern folklore and places of interest are highlighted on her website, jennylynnkeller.com. Each week she posts a down-home update on Facebook.com/jennylynnkeller and on her website blog. Her story "A Pinto for Pennies" appears in Callie Smith Grant's *The Horse of My Dreams*, a compilation of true horse stories.

"Time flies when you're having fun!" reports **Brock Kidd** from his hometown of Nashville, Tennessee. "My wife, Corinne, and I stay amazed daily with our two daughters, Mary Katherine and Ella Grace, and little David is a source of constant comic relief. When our oldest son, Harrison, recently came home from college to visit, David insisted on doing the prayer over dinner that night. David's prayer was short and sweet: 'Dear God, thank you for Harrison being home. Daddy and I need more boys around here!'"

In addition to a joyous gig as a dad, Brock continues to find happiness and a way to a serve through his career in wealth management.

Fellowship Corner

"How fortunate we are to have all our family near," says **Pam Kidd** of Nashville, Tennessee. Son Brock and his family, along with daughter Keri and her family, live just ten minutes away from Pam, in opposite directions. "And to add icing to the nearness cake, we live right across the street from a twenty-six-hundred-acre park, where David and I walk most days. Although God is ever near, there's something extra nice about sharing time with Him in a place of trees, streams, and birdsong."

Pam is equally grateful that her partnership with God and her family extends into efforts to improve life for a little community in rural Zimbabwe. "Each of us heads special projects there," Pam says. "We dream and scheme, travel together, and plan lots of get-togethers to celebrate this good life we have been given."

Patty Kirk's year started out rocky but ended up peaceful. In January, she returned from a family trip to Yucatán with a sprained ankle that ended her nearly twenty-year practice of jogging twenty-one miles per week. Her husband, Kris, had surgery—a carotid endarterectomy—followed by a hematoma on his hip that took months to heal.

They managed to hobble through the snowy leap-day wedding of their daughter Charlotte to longtime boyfriend Reuben Britto. In the Tamil language of Reuben's parents and extended family, the Britto and Kirk families are now *sambandi*, which means "all one family." The newly enlarged family, spread over the United States, joins up regularly for Zoom game nights.

Patty says because she hasn't been able to jog, she is spending time cultivating the best garden she's ever had.

Carol Knapp, of Priest River, Idaho, says, "My husband, Terry, and I praise God for a peripheral-nerve stimulation system Terry has had permanently installed in his back to help alleviate his chronic pain. This opens a whole new world for us. So much so that we invested in an 'oldie but goodie' travel trailer. I also have a request in with the oldest of our twenty grandchildren to ride along in his semitruck at some point when he transports big loads in the Pacific Northwest.

Fellowship Corner

"It was such a pleasure taking the train last winter to California to visit my ninety-three-year-old uncle Bob. He got so excited about riding the rails, he booked a sleeper car and came to see me in the spring! All this travel talk reminds me how present and faithful God has been in my life's journey. He is the bedrock of my and Terry's fifty years together."

"We live our lives in seasons, and I like my season," says **Carol Kuykendall** of Boulder, Colorado. "I'm enjoying our three adult children and ten grandchildren. Like Mary, who stored ponderings in her heart (Luke 2:19), I've gathered ponderings from many seasons, which helps me recognize moments that need to be added. Moments when the Lord is near. Like painting rocks to look like Easter eggs with a grandchild and hiding them in plain sight in the neighborhood. Like driving my husband, Lynn, "anywhere his heart desires" on his birthday, which usually involves exploring small towns in Colorado. Like taking our dog, Zeke, to a new trail, where he jumps in every muddy stream with pure joy, even though it means I have to wash him when he gets home.

"In this season, my world is smaller but deeper. I lead a team of mentors in our church's Mothers of Preschoolers group and cherish the deep relationships formed between moms and mentors as we encourage each other in different seasons." For more, visit Carol's website, carolkuykendall.com

"For more than thirty years, when people asked me, 'What do you do?' I'd reply that I was a writer," says **Vicki Kuyper** of Colorado Springs, Colorado. An author of more than fifty books, including *Wonderlust: A Spiritual Travelogue for the Adventurous Soul* and *A Tale of Two Biddies (A New Wrinkle on Aging with Grace),* Vicki considers writing to be a true joy in her life. But seasons change—and so has Vicki's job title!

As she says, "With the birth of my fifth grandchild, I will become an official granny nanny. Since I will spend several days a week caring for a newborn, I will spend less time writing and more time snuggling. Of course, writing for *Walking in Grace* will continue to be part of my abbreviated

WALKING IN GRACE 411

Fellowship Corner

freelance schedule. I so enjoy putting into words the ways I see God working in my life throughout the year. Having the opportunity to share my firsthand experiences with other members of the Guideposts family serves as a daily reminder to keep my eyes and heart open, expectantly ready to catch a glimpse of God's presence."

"When my four children were teenagers, I thought it would be great if they all lived in four different parts of the country so I would have fun visiting them," says **Patricia Lorenz** of Largo, Florida. "Unfortunately, that's exactly what happened! Jeanne and Andrew and their families are over an hour away from each other in California, Michael is in Nevada, and his three children are in Ohio. Julia and her three live in Wisconsin. Since they all scattered, I moved to Florida in 2004. I love my adopted state, but I sure do miss my kids and nine grandchildren.

"I've had to adopt a whole new family of friends in Florida—my neighborhood friends, acquaintances, and members of my water aerobics class and church are the people I depend on as I wing my way through my seventies. My children and grandchildren may be far away, but the Lord is near and so is my extended family. I feel blessed, indeed."

Debbie Macomber is a #1 *New York Times* bestselling author and one of today's most popular writers, with more than 200 million copies of her books in print worldwide. In addition to fiction, Debbie has published three bestselling cookbooks, an adult coloring book, numerous inspirational and nonfiction works, and two acclaimed children's books. Celebrated as "the official storyteller of Christmas," Debbie has Christmas books published annually, five of which have been crafted into original Hallmark Channel movies.

She serves on the Guideposts National Advisory Cabinet, is a Youth for Christ national ambassador, and is the international spokesperson for World Vision's Knit for Kids charity initiative. A devoted grandmother, Debbie and her husband, Wayne, live in Port Orchard, Washington, the town that inspired the Cedar Cove series.

Fellowship Corner

"I keep my Bible and my prayer journal close to my bed," says **Erin MacPherson** of Austin, Texas, "because the assurance that comes from knowing that my God has it all under control brings peace . . . and sleep. Things get a bit frantic with kids running from school to soccer practice to art class, a garden to tend to, writing to do, and a golden retriever to snuggle. But that fast-paced busyness is always replaced with peace when I pause, pray, and realize that He is there, right in the middle of my crazy. He is there, and He is good."

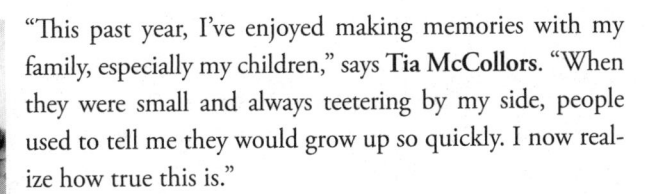

"This past year, I've enjoyed making memories with my family, especially my children," says **Tia McCollors**. "When they were small and always teetering by my side, people used to tell me they would grow up so quickly. I now realize how true this is."

One of the things Tia has relished most since joining the Guideposts family is the encouraging emails from devoted readers. "Many of the readers who've reached out to me were introduced to *Daily Guideposts* by their parents, and they, in turn, are sharing it with their children. Guideposts has been a generational blessing to many families, and I'm honored to be part of the legacy."

Tia expresses her creative side through writing, speaking, and—her newfound interest—using her husband as a guinea pig to taste-test her recipes. So far, they've all met with his approval.

You can connect with Tia online at TiaMcCollors.com or through her Fans of Tia Facebook page. Or follow her on Instagram @TMcCollors.

The Lord has never seemed nearer to **Roberta Messner** than during this past year. Her total pain relief from neurofibromatosis continues and is one of God's unbelievable gifts of grace, she says. Roberta credits the care and prayers of her beloved *Guideposts, Daily Guideposts,* and *Walking in Grace* family with helping her to hold on to hope. She chuckles about the adjustments she's had to make after spending half a century in a prison of pain. "I can no longer tell someone I can't do something because I have a headache!" she says with a smile.

WALKING IN GRACE 413

Fellowship Corner

On the serious side, Roberta also finds that she can no longer squander a second of her time. "I've been the recipient of such mercy and miracles," she says. "I have a joy and contentment I have never known, and I find I want few things that I don't already possess." Her deepest desire is to tell stories of God's redemption and healing . . . gifts available to all of us at any stage of life.

Rebecca Ondov of Hamilton, Montana, constantly called on God—much of the time in desperation—while having a cottage built on her farm. "It was hard being a single woman and the general contractor on the project," she says, "and doing some of the labor, too, while also working a regular job. Nearly every night, I knelt at my bedside, totally exhausted, and prayed for wisdom and safety for the crews I'd hired. So much of the time, I felt enveloped by His presence and peace as He guided me though this exciting and tumultuous time." This year she's looking forward to landscaping her new home and planting fruit trees and a garden.

On weekends you'll find her in the mountains on hikes, horseback rides, kayak trips, and camping adventures with friends. She invites you to connect with her on Facebook and on her website, rebeccaondov.com

Shirley Raye Redmond has written for *Focus on the Family* magazine, *Home Life*, the *Christian Standard*, and Chicken Soup for the Soul's *Touched by an Angel*. Her devotions have appeared in multiple volumes of Guideposts's *All God's Creatures* devotionals. Her most recent children's book is *Courageous World Changers: 50 True Stories of Daring Women of God*. Her *Pigeon Hero!* won a national Oppenheim Toy Portfolio Gold Book Award, and *Lewis & Clark: A Prairie Dog for the President* was a Children's Book of the Month Club selection.

She has been married for forty-five years to her college sweetheart, Bill. They are blessed with two adult children and their spouses, plus four adorable grandchildren. She joyfully serves as prayer chairman for her Community Bible Study class in Los Alamos, New Mexico.

Fellowship Corner

Ginger Rue is being phased out of a job. "The goal of parenting, I'm told, is to work yourself out of your job: to prepare your children not to need you," she says. "It's a weird feeling, being proud of the adults they're becoming while also missing those days when they relied on me for everything." By the end of 2022, Ginger and her husband will have one college graduate and one high school graduate, with another close on their heels. "I dropped our son off somewhere the other day and watched until he was safely inside. Then I laughed. He's over six feet tall and is much more likely to protect me at this point than I am to protect him!" No matter how old they get, though, Ginger says, "They're always going to be at the top of my prayer list every single day."

Chaplain Kenneth Sampson is a retired army chaplain and lives with his wife, Kate, a spiritual director, in Cornwall-on-Hudson, New York. Ken continues fulfilling part-time service as military liaison for Guideposts. He takes much joy and delight in life's blessings, which include granddaughter Chanel and the patient, love-filled parenting she receives from son Michael and son-in-law Steven; Kate's successful recovery and healing from recent major heart surgery; daughter Jenn's callings toward art, editing, and graphic design; his new ten-inch Delta table saw purchased to honor a recent birthday; and the many take-your-breath-away moments he's experienced while living in the Hudson Highlands. He enjoys inhaling fresh air while taking in Storm King Mountain views from his front steps and experiencing camaraderie in the Cornwall Presbyterian Church kitchen while drying dishes for Newburgh Ministries benefits.

Daniel Schantz and his wife, Sharon, of Moberly, Missouri, took a time machine back to the 1950s, visiting the places where Sharon grew up in Joplin and Carthage. For the first time, Daniel saw the little house where Sharon lived during her teens and the beautiful marble high school she attended. He took photos of everything, including the

Fellowship Corner

Fairview Christian Church, which her father started, and Ozark Christian College, where he was a professor.

Daniel feels the nearness of God most when he is out under the heavens. "I'm an early riser," he explains, "and I like to stand outdoors, facing the east to catch the first hint of daylight. I ask God to provide the light I need all day to find my way safely through this complicated world."

With little grandsons on opposite coasts—Jace on the West and Leo on the East—**Gail Thorell Schilling** of Concord, New Hampshire, finds reassurance in knowing that the Lord is near them even when she is not. "I did enjoy a lengthy stay with Leo recently. I taught him a lot of the spring flowers blooming in his Maryland neighborhood—and he taught me some Turkish!" Nana Gail also escaped a few days of winter when she visited a friend and some family in Florida, where she met her grand-nephew in person and grand-niece by video chat.

Gail is delighted to report that, after nine attempts, she finished her "feather and fan" stitch scarf. Her next challenges? Learning to play the kalimba, an African finger piano—and learning more Turkish!

"It's been a year of loss and learning," writes **Penney Schwab** of Copeland, Kansas. "On August 18, after months of deteriorating health and two hospitalizations, my husband, Don, died. We were blessed to have kind, generous support from family and friends as I cared for him at home during his final five weeks. He was visited in person or via FaceTime by all of the grandchildren and died surrounded by his children, a grandson, and a dear friend. He was at peace as we read Scripture and sang him home to Jesus; his eyes were already fixed on heavenly scenes the rest of us couldn't see.

As I face the challenges of living alone, settling the estate, and managing the farm business without the one who was truly my better half, I rely more and more on God's promise in Psalm 145:18: "The Lord is near to all who call upon him, to all who call upon him in truth."

Fellowship Corner

"I didn't exactly tell the truth on the Los Angeles apartment application I filled out when my wife and I married back in 1989," says **Buck Storm**. "I listed my profession as 'writer.' Figured it wasn't much of a stretch. After all, I wrote songs, and I'd get to books eventually. But life often sidetracks. Those songs wound up taking Michelle and me around the globe. It took me twenty-five years and a lot of miles to become a novelist, but several books in now, I made good on that application.

"I know this—I'm blessed beyond words to be surrounded daily by everything and everyone I love. Thank you, Jesus, for breathing life into these dry bones. I feel Your arm around my shoulder. You are *good*. And the best part is knowing the journey will never end!"

Buck Storm is a critically acclaimed literary-fiction author, musician, and traveler. His books and songs have made him friends around the world.

Jolynda Strandberg serves as a director of religious education for the US Army at Fort Campbell, Kentucky. She has spent twenty-three years as a civilian with the military. She and her family reside in Clarksville, Tennessee. She is a proud wife and mom to three children, ages twenty-seven, ten, and six. Blessings received this past year include a new family member—an older horse named Snow Mist.

Jon M. Sweeney is grateful to have stayed put in the same home for three years running. "That hasn't happened for us in a while," he says. "We have moved around too much." Jon and his wife, Michal, live in Milwaukee, Wisconsin, where they are raising two daughters. Jon is also enjoying watching his two grown children flourish: one now in graduate school (librarianship) and the other working in business.

The fourth book in Jon's children's fiction series, *The Pope's Cat*, was recently published.

Fellowship Corner

"This year's *Walking in Grace* theme, 'The Lord is near,' is close to my heart," says **Stephanie Thompson**. "Our sweet little pug dog crossed over the rainbow bridge in September. When I dropped her off at the groomer, I never imagined I wouldn't be picking her up. It's been six months, and our family still misses and morns Princess the Pug."

When Princess passed, Stephanie posted a pictorial memorial of her dog's twelve-year life on Facebook. "Friends and acquaintances offered heartfelt condolences in the Facebook comments. Several made donations to animal-related charities in Princess's name, some sent sympathy cards, and we even received an oil painting of our adored pup. All these expressions of kindness encouraged our family in our time of grief."

Stephanie and her husband, Michael, live in an Oklahoma City suburb with their teenage daughter, Micah; a schweenie (shih tzu/dachshund mix) named Missy that they inherited from Michael's grandparents; and the "stray that stayed," Mr. Whiskers, a tuxedo cat that appeared on the driveway one cold December day to adopt them.

"This year, we made some changes to our busy family schedule. Instead of being stressed out from commitments, I let go of several," says **Marilyn Turk** of Niceville, Florida. "Our grandson Logan was ten this year, and his father moved in with us awhile, allowing Logan to spend more time with him. The Lord was certainly near as we adapted to a new family situation.

"My husband, Chuck, and I were able to take a short trip by ourselves to visit friends in the mountains. Thank God, He was near, because traveling hairpin mountain roads scared me to death. Logan went with us on another trip in our RV, during which we enjoyed whitewater rafting—another exhilarating yet frightening adventure that I wouldn't have attempted without knowing God would be with us!"

Marilyn has been blessed to have three more inspirational historical fiction books published, including her first Christmas book. She has enjoyed getting to know readers and becoming prayer partners with them.

Fellowship Corner

"'You're an amazing mother!' is something I see a lot on my social media posts," says **Karen Valentin** of New York, New York. "Friends and family see the positive side of my mothering there—taking fun adventures with my boys, watching them compete or train in their sports, filling with pride when they do something impressive. I post about the parts that are not so positive, as well, but it's usually brimming with humor.

"But my social media posts don't show the times when I yell or hurt my kids with my words. People don't see the arguments that are really about maintaining my position of power instead of bending my will to do what's best for them. But as often as I remind my kids that I am human, I have to remind myself as well. As often as I ask them to forgive me, I must forgive myself. I am an imperfect mother because I am an imperfect person. We all are. But with everything that I do right as a mom, I have to agree that I'm an amazing mother too!"

"As I write these words, this is a significant week for me," says **Scott Walker** of Macon, Georgia. "I have just officially retired from Mercer University as I near my seventieth birthday. How this will change my life, I do not know. I will continue to teach one course each semester. And I will enjoy sharing many cups of coffee with young adults as we discuss their lives, their hopes, and their dreams.

"You can retire from a job or even a vocation. But you cannot retire from the basic dream of your life. I want to love God and His children: this is a dream that is eternal. And I intend to write, create, explore, and enjoy beauty all the way into that new dimension of eternity. Some dreams never die. They just grow better and clearer with age!

"Forty-five years ago, when Beth and I were married, we were graduate students living off of the exuberance of love and dreams. Most of these dreams are still alive and blend youth with age. We have learned that in all stages of growth and challenge, God has provided."

Fellowship Corner

Jacqueline F. Wheelock has never known life outside of Christian influence. The image of her father reading Scripture aloud around a wood-burning heater at the close of the day is one of her dearest memories, especially given that his formal education ended at second grade. The youngest of six girls, Jacqueline always enjoyed the coziness produced by the oak logs their father chopped, but it was his passion as he labored to sound out the words of the Bible, as well as the compassion in the Word itself, that helped produce in Jacqueline a lingering love for God and an ensured eternal rest.

Now a writer of fiction, she is a former English teacher who loves to play word games—usually after deciding she will do nothing else practical for the day—and enjoys retirement with her husband, Donald. She is the mother of two adult children and the grandmother of two girls.

Gayle T. Williams is a native New Yorker, now living in the city's suburbs with her husband and two sons. She is a faithful member of New York Covenant Church in New Rochelle and has been a reporter, writer, and editor for magazines and newspapers over the past thirty years. She currently works as a writer and editor for an academic medical center.

In addition to being a news junkie, she enjoys a good game of Scrabble and a wide variety of music, ranging from forties jazz (thanks to her parents) to today's hip-hop. She is honored to be able to share God's blessings upon her life with the readers of *Walking in Grace*.

SCRIPTURE REFERENCE INDEX

ACTS
2:44–45, 18
16:15, 325
17:27, 329
20:24, 222
20:35, 339
28:15, 293

CHRONICLES 1
16:9, 51
16:11, 280
28:20, 89
29:13, 105

CHRONICLES 2
7:14, 228

COLOSSIANS
1:11, 160
3:7, 218
3:12, 76, 184, 296, 397
3:13, 185
3:16, 200

CORINTHIANS 1
4:12, 283
10:13, 351
12:22, 305
14:15, 10
14:40, 225

CORINTHIANS 2
1:3–4, 63, 301
4:16, 259
8:9, 391
9:15, 202
12:9, 337, 396

DANIEL
4:3, 143

DEUTERONOMY
6:9, 158
28:2, 109
30:3, 224
31:6, 399
31:8, 314

ECCLESIASTES
3:1, 67, 75, 123, 326
3:4, 377
3:7, 326
3:11, 93, 317
3:12, 338
4:12, 49

11:6, 201
12:7, 90

EPHESIANS
1:5, 74, 395
2:10, 94, 282
3:8, 305
3:15, 341
4:16, 92
5:25, 189
6:11, 384
6:13, 278

ESTHER
8:16, 321

EXODUS
3:5, 361
12:26–27, 108
14:15, 237
34:6, 327

EZEKIEL
36:26, 97

GALATIANS
3:26, 186
5:6, 137
5:22–23, 137
5:25, 137
6:2, 215
6:9, 56, 77

GENESIS
1:11, 111
1:14, 46
2:7, 43
5:24, 375
6:16, 272
6:22, 272
8:16, 101
21:23, 348

HEBREWS
1:14, 38
10:22, 268
10:25, 355
10:36, 374
11:1, 323, 380
11:8, 214
11:16, 11
12:11, 195
13:2, 274
13:3, 349
13:5, 86

HOSEA
2:20, 53

ISAIAH
12:2, 227
26:3, 136, 161
26:9, 354
40:31, 22
41:10, 151, 279
42:6, 32
43:1, 298
43:19, 2, 9
49:16, 235
55:13, 251
58:10, 193
58:11, 146, 229
60:1, 318
64:8, 242

JAMES
1:17, 360
1:26, 261
4:6, 30
4:8, 35
4:10, 149
5:16, 221

JEREMIAH
9:24, 83
29:11, 60, 82, 126
29:13, 72
31:25, 347
31:25–26, 331
33:3, 134, 307

JOB
8:21, 390
12:7, 187
23:11, 382
29:19–20, 122
36:10, 128
37:10, 303

JOHN
1:5, 386
1:12, 240
1:14, 372
1:16, 175
1:48, 231
3:8, 206
8:12, 24
11:25, 330
13:9, 114
13:15, 4
14:6, 181

14:27, 203
15:9, 133, 388
15:12, 178
16:22, 373
20:3–4, 117
20:31, 210

JOHN 1
1:1, 312
1:9, 110
3:1, 168
3:17–18, 295
4:7, 246, 385
5:3, 49
5:11, 287
5:14, 244
5:14–15, 343
14:1, 235
14:3, 260

JOSHUA
1:9, 55, 269, 324

KINGS 1
3:5, 171
3:9, 171
3:12, 171
11:9, 171
17:24, 28

LAMENTATIONS
3:22–23, 8
3:23, 61
3:56, 40

LUKE
1:47–48, 376
1:78, 379
2:7, 392
3:11, 23
6:38, 339
8:52, 205
10:22, 5
10:27, 48
10:41, 156
10:42, 207
11:1, 257
11:13, 26
12:20, 106
12:21, 106
12:22, 106
12:25, 353
15:4, 174
15:4–7, 285
16:10, 54

WALKING IN GRACE   421

Scripture Reference Index

19:35, 110
19:39–40, 112
23:34, 70
23:41, 115
23:55–56, 116
24:39, 90
24:46–47, 118

MARK
6:31, 104
10:8, 103

MATTHEW
1:21, 393
5:37, 245
6:3–4, 81, 387
6:7, 183
6:11, 154
6:19, 107
6:21, 180
6:22, 157
6:33, 41
6:34, 125, 258
7:7, 42, 320
7:14, 243
7:21, 148
9:37–38, 14
10:29, 50, 319
11:28, 262, 273
13:16, 213
16:26, 371
18:19, 17
18:22, 70
19:6, 188
19:14, 155
22:37–39, 344
22:39, 358
24:6, 276
25:13, 398
25:35, 13
26:36–38, 219
28:20, 182, 315, 336

MICAH
6:8, 308

NEHEMIAH
9:27, 294

PETER 1
1:3, 79
2:16, 204
3:8, 277
4:8, 21
4:9, 306
5:7, 102

PETER 2
3:18, 248

PHILIPPIANS
1:3, 152, 260, 275
1:6, 152
1:9, 25
2:3, 12, 144, 177
2:4, 328
3:12, 120, 230
4:6–7, 80, 291
4:7, 203
4:8, 325
4:13, 322
4:19, 91, 191

PROVERBS
1:1, 171
3:1, 145
3:6, 71, 264
3:24, 44
8:17, 197
11:25, 389
14:13, 356
14:29, 256
15:4, 263
16:9, 284
17:17, 194, 238
17:22, 171
18:10, 169
19:21, 62, 250
22:4, 286
22:6, 47, 73
23:25, 141
24:3, 340
27:1, 209
27:9, 247
29:25, 19
30:5, 167
31:19, 138
31:25, 176
31:27, 363

PSALMS
1:2, 295
1:3, 254
4:4, 78
5:3, 265
7:17, 364
8:2, 217
9:2, 59
9:9–10, 241
16:6, 121
16:8, 368
16:11, 85, 179
18:32, 359
18:39, 289
19:3, 129
23:1, 52
23:3, 369
23:4, 39
25:4, 139
25:4–5, 37
27:4, 3
28:7, 57, 313
31:14–15, 239
31:15, 32
31:19, 100, 170
31:24, 302, 383
32:8, 271, 304
33:12, 163
34:4, 119
34:18, 208
36:6–7, 45
37:4, 281
37:5, 130, 140
42:9, 223
48:14, 192
50:15, 6
51:1, 68
55:13, 342
56:3, 253, 311
63:5–6, 288
68:4, 55
72:12, 96
73:16–17, 69
73:25, 159
73:28, 66, 252
86:5, 234
90:12, 150
94:19, 190, 309, 378
94:22, 270
95:1–2, 297
103:8, 142
103:14, 362
103:17, 381
104:34, 95
118:17, 220
118:24, 345
119:105, 211
119:151, 1
121:4, 290
127:2, 370
127:4–5, 20
130:3–4, 226
130:7, 212
133:1, 292, 316
139:10, 124
139:13, 135
139:13–14, 15

139:14, 88, 352
139:23–24, 153
144:3–4, 173
145:3, 172
145:9, 335
145:18, iii, 416
146:5–7, 349

REVELATION
4:8, 7
4:11, 332
7:9, 164
21:4, 249

ROMANS
1:20, 27, 394
2:11, 58
7:18, 196
8:26, 36, 216, 255
12:9, 127
12:10, 84, 147, 365
14:19, 16
15:7, 87

RUTH
1:14, 236

SAMUEL 1
1:10, 240
1:11, 240
1:22, 240
2:1–10, 240
2:19, 240

SONG OF SOLOMON
6:3, 29

THESSALONIANS 1
2:2, 325
5:11, 346, 350
5:14, 31
5:17, 310

TIMOTHY 1
2:1, 357

TIMOTHY 2
1:5, 162

TITUS
3:1, 113

AUTHORS, TITLES, AND SUBJECTS INDEX

Adam and Eve, 110
Advent, 7, 69, 210, 362, 372, 378–379, 386–387
Aegean Sea, 54
Afghanistan, 346
Africa, 369; Liberia, 369; Kenya, 135; Zimbabwe, 143, 201
African American culture, 164
African American history, 164, 186
African Americans, 18, 186, 344, 288
Agen, Jerusha, 27, 94, 128, 298, 319, 396
Alabama, 146, 327, 380
Alaska, 13, 195, 272; Fairbanks, 195, 359
Alaska Range, 195
Alborghetti, Marci, 14, 81, 119, 170, 183, 241, 354, 402
Alcoholics Anonymous (AA), 377
"A Living Hope" series, 110, 112, 114–118
Alzheimer's disease, 207, 381
American Airlines Flight 11, 279
American flag, 204
American history, 9
American military vessels, 276
Americans, 56
Amish, 365
Amyotrophic lateral sclerosis (ALS), 127
Angels, 30, 38, 211, 281, 376
Antarctica, 303
Anxiety, 25, 31, 36, 80, 142, 147, 154, 203, 262, 314, 372
Arizona, 139, 311, 379; Phoenix, 46, 362, 393
Armed Forces Salute, 163
Army chaplain, 192
Ash Wednesday, 68, 75, 79
Asian culture, 164
Atlantic Ocean, 214
Attaway, Julia, 40, 68, 181, 207, 250, 402–403
Awana, 47
"Away in a Manger" (carol), 393
Azores, 284

Band-Aid, 250
Barrie, James Matthew (author), 339
Basilica Cattedrale de Nostra Signora dell'Orto, 10
Basilica of Sacré-Coeur, 149
Béchamel sauce, 111
Bence, Evelyn, 32, 61, 78, 113, 152, 193, 273, 308, 355, 376, 403
Bentsen, Erika, 57, 103, 160, 205, 247, 296, 336, 371, 403
Bhutanese language, 216

Bible, 5, 95, 110, 195–196, 211, 220, 240, 245, 255, 273, 276, 291, 295, 298, 336, 342, 378; Amplified (AMP), 337; King James version (KJV), 113, 211
Bible Belt, 11
Bible study, 41, 94, 162, 183, 342, 349, 361, 375
Birds, 13, 105, 121, 128, 136, 179, 196, 324, 372, 379, 391, 394
Birthdays, 32, 56, 152, 176, 178, 192, 194, 209, 223, 230, 256, 260, 263, 271, 338, 345, 383
Bitterroot River, 302
Blandinsville Farmers Picnic, 365
Blandin House Museum, 365
Blecker, Rhoda, 52, 108, 158, 197, 264, 270, 321, 363, 403–404
"Blessed by One Sweet Cookie" series, 16, 84, 148, 180, 203, 249, 317, 352
Bluegrass gospel, 146
Book of Common Prayer, 213
Boston Logan International Airport, 279
Bucket lists, 52, 209
Buffett, Warren (investor), 201
Byzantine church, 243

California, 22, 111, 125, 134, 151, 206, 254, 305, 329; Laguna Beach, 111; Los Angeles, 158, 363; West Hills, 305
Calvary, 195, 292
Camelback Mountain, 362
Canada geese, 55, 139
Caribbean cruise, 96
Caucasian culture, 164
"Celtic Alleluia" (hymn), 10
Cemetery Land Reclamation Project, 69
Central Christian College, 174
Central Park, 68
Charity, 19, 107
Chevrolet (Chevy), 192
A Child's Book of Prayers, 162
China, 297
Christian communities, 10
Christians, 10, 14, 68, 77, 162, 174, 246, 262, 325, 337
Christmas, 7, 15, 138, 247, 286, 372, 374, 378, 382–387, 389–396
Christmas Eve, 391–392
The Chronicles of Narnia: The Lion, the Witch and the Wardrobe (book), 155
Chrysler, 192
Church of Panagia Evangelistria, 54

Ciancanelli, Sabra, 6, 39, 73, 101, 138, 187, 208, 239, 280, 306, 341, 373, 404
Citizen Kane (movie), 212
Civilian Conservation Corps, 161
Civil War, 168
Cleveland Clinic, 157
"Climb Ev'ry Mountain" (song), 59
Collaboration, 151
Collins, Mark, 20, 75, 142, 213, 294, 398, 404
Colorado, 46, 112, 117–118, 204, 254, 345; Boulder, 254; Denver, 112, 115; Estes Park, 115
Communion, 32, 176, 193
Compassion, 18, 191, 197, 277, 294, 327, 392
Connecticut, 11, 119, 183; New Haven, 11; New London, 119, 183
Cornwall Presbyterian Church, 69
Courage, 8, 14, 17, 28, 30, 56, 101, 302, 376
Cross, 18, 68, 70, 79, 110
Crossword puzzles, 61, 214, 354

Daily Guideposts (book), 15, 95, 210, 343, 374
David (king of Israel), 171, 288
Diaz, Pablo, 176, 206, 236, 293, 343, 377, 404–405
Dignity, 12
Dilworth, John, 48, 95, 157, 172, 284, 346, 405
Discernment, 56
Disciples, 70, 106, 117, 257
Disney World, 102
DNA tests, 395
"Do-Re-Mi" (song), 59
Douglas, Michael (actor), 24
Dutch boy (fictional character), 390

Earl Grey tea, 318
Easter, 75, 79, 109, 117–119, 286
"Easter Parade" (song), 75
eBay, 263
Edison, Thomas (inventor), 248
Eglin Air Force Base, 163
Egypt, 113, 276
Eli (biblical priest), 240
Eliasen, Logan, 110, 112, 114–118, 261, 328, 405
Eliasen, Shawnelle, 21, 105, 124, 140, 161, 185, 221, 248, 263, 289, 327, 350, 388, 406
Elisha (biblical prophet), 255
Elkanah (father of Samuel), 240
Emancipation Proclamation, 186

Authors, Titles, and Subjects Index

EMBRACE ministry (Encouraging Multitudes by Raising Affection, Concern, and Empathy), 87
Empathy, 246
The Empire Strikes Back (movie), 212
Encouragement, 48, 235, 244, 346, 350, 390
England, 201, 257; London, 155; Norwich, 257; Oxford, 155
English heritage, 395
English language, 10, 129, 216, 257
Europe, 296, 395
"Every Day with Jesus" (hymn), 51
Examen, 61

Facebook, 49, 55, 285, 293, 338, 377
FaceTime app, 217
Faith, 11, 28, 40, 48, 57, 72, 91–92, 95, 102, 117, 162, 176, 210, 212, 222, 240, 247–248, 255, 271, 323–324, 337–338, 354, 356, 365, 377, 382, 384
Father's Day, 186
Feast of the Epiphany, 7
Federal Bureau of Investigation (FBI), 324
Fiddler on the Roof (musical), 395
Filipino flag, 204
Financial District, Manhattan, 279
Flathead Lake, 244
Florida, 74, 96, 206, 236, 293, 310, 343, 346, 399; Clearwater, 206; Dunedin, 206, 293; Keys, 74; St. Petersburg, 151; Tampa, 96
Ford, 248; Model T, 248; Crown Victoria, 275
Ford, Mary (vocalist), 57
Forgiveness, 21, 68, 70, 142, 172, 185, 226, 287, 292, 357
Fort Polk, 177
France, 10; Paris, 52, 149
Franciscan bluebells, 139
French heritage, 395
Freud, Sigmund (neurologist), 398
Friendship, 8, 29, 164, 176, 238, 323, 345–346, 350, 370
Frost, Robert (poet), 248

Galapagos Islands, 52
Galatia, 137
Generosity, 134, 245, 387
Georgia, 9, 297; Atlanta, 187; Macon, 9; Savannah, 275
German heritage, 395
Gethsemane, 219
Girls Athletic Association, 309
Girl Scouts, 113, 247

Glory, 27, 112, 173, 211, 248, 332, 371
God, 5, 9, 11, 13–15, 17, 20, 22–27, 30, 32, 37–38, 41–43, 46, 48–49, 52, 55, 58, 60–63, 67, 70–72, 74, 79–82, 86, 88, 90–91, 93–95, 97, 104, 106, 109–110, 112–117, 119–121, 125–127, 129, 135, 137–138, 143, 152, 154, 158, 160, 162, 168–169, 171–173, 176–182, 185, 188, 191–192, 195–197, 202–203, 206–207, 212, 214, 216, 218–220, 222–223, 225–229, 231, 235, 237–244, 247, 250, 252, 255, 257–258, 262–265, 270–272, 274, 276, 278, 281–284, 288, 290–291, 294–295, 297–298, 302–305, 307, 309, 313–315, 318, 320–322, 327, 329–332, 336–340, 342, 343, 344–345, 348–352, 355–359, 361–363, 369–372, 375–376, 379, 395–397
"God's Fingerprints" series, 60, 135, 188, 235
Goethe, Johann Wolfgang von (author), 20
Gould Farm, 246
Grace, 30, 32, 56, 63, 72, 80, 94, 138, 142, 152, 175, 185, 308, 355, 371, 374, 376–377, 396
Gratitude, 32, 52, 105, 120, 141, 157, 170, 189, 195, 284, 297, 346, 359
Great Depression, 381
Great Recession, 11, 242
Greece, 54, 243, 305; Corinth, 305; Monemvasia, 243; Nafplio, 54; Peloponnese, 54, 243; Philippi, 325; Tinos, 54
Grief, 31, 63, 96, 202, 208, 264, 356
Grinnan, Edward, 11, 50, 80, 107, 144, 179, 212, 246, 279, 313, 344, 357, 381, 406
Guideposts ministry, 293
Guideposts office, 279
Guillain-Barré syndrome, 220
Gulf of Mexico, 96, 209

Halloween, 332
Hamlin, Rick, 22, 59, 79, 134, 159, 189, 226, 257, 290, 324, 357, 387, 406–407
Hannah (wife of Elkanah), 240
Harding, Vincent (historian), 18
Harlem Globetrotters, 310
Hartke, Lynne, 139, 311, 362, 372, 379, 382, 386, 392–393, 407

Harvey (movie), 187
Havura (extended family), 158
Health, 22–23, 75, 191, 226, 295, 297, 338
Heaven, 14, 19, 25, 44, 77, 83, 104, 138, 155, 173, 176, 202, 208, 252, 277, 330, 336, 341, 350
Hendricks, Carla, 63, 91, 164, 168, 186, 215, 330, 407
Henry, Kim Taylor, 88, 145, 182, 259, 303, 339, 408
Highland games, 285
Himalayas, 216
Hispanic culture, 164
Hobbits (fictional characters), 243
Holy Spirit, 16, 18, 36, 61, 93, 129, 137, 155, 193, 206, 255, 262, 338, 384
Honduras, 252
Hope, 29, 32, 37, 60, 72, 90–91, 93–94, 101, 186, 210, 246, 283, 324, 358, 383, 388
Hopkins, Gerard Manley (poet), 352
"How Great Thou Art" (hymn), 51
Hudson River, 279
Humane Society, 147
Humility, 110, 134, 241, 305, 337
Hurricane Irma, 74
Hurricane Sandy, 11

"I Have a Dream" speech, 18
Illinois, 365; Blandinsville, 365
Immanuel ("God is with us"), 336
Independence Day (Fourth of July), 203–204
Instagram, 111
Intensive care unit (ICU), 43, 220
Iowa, 112, 118
Ireland, 83
Irish-Catholic family, 381
Irish heritage, 75
Irish step dancing, 83
"I Surrender All" (hymn), 162
Italian language, 10
Italy, 10, 304; Chiavari, 10; Rome, 304
"Itsy Bitsy Spider" (song), 51
"I Will Serve Thee" (hymn), 292

Jackson, Leanne, 23, 153, 184, 390, 408
Janoso, Erin, 13 82, 104, 120, 173, 195, 282, 314, 359, 408–409
Jeep, 112, 118
Jerusalem, 18, 110, 130
Jesuit priest, 352

424   WALKING IN GRACE

Authors, Titles, and Subjects Index

Jesus Christ, 4–5, 7, 13, 18, 21, 24, 28, 40–41, 44, 47–48, 70, 83, 86, 106, 110, 114–115, 117–118, 125, 129, 137, 148, 154–155, 162–163, 181–183, 185, 196, 205, 210, 218–219, 222, 240, 245–246, 248, 251, 253, 257, 282, 286, 288–289, 296, 305, 320, 330, 336–337, 342, 359, 362, 364, 372, 378, 383, 387–388, 391, 393, 396
"Jesus Loves Me" (hymn), 51
"Jesus Loves the Little Children" (hymn), 51, 245
Jewish heritage, 395
Jews, 197, 395
Joseph (father of Jesus), 372
Joseph (Hebrew patriarch), 113
Joy, 5, 84, 90, 137, 141, 146, 164, 171, 180, 182, 202, 222, 236, 249, 259, 263, 292–293, 340, 346, 350, 352, 389, 391, 393
Judea, 117
Julian of Norwich, 257
Juneteenth, 186

Kansas, 192, 349; Fort Leavenworth, 349; Fort Riley, 192; Garden City, 76
Kappel, Ashley, 44, 71, 102, 146, 169, 225, 253, 274, 295, 309, 345, 409
Keller, Jenny Lynn, 37, 74, 218, 278, 409
Kentucky, Louisville, 191
Kidd, Brock, 24, 201, 228, 242, 348, 383, 409
Kidd, Pam, 19, 90, 97, 143, 245, 285, 307, 380, 410
Kindness, 48, 70, 90, 137, 155, 229, 245–246, 296, 348, 358, 364, 380, 397
King Jr., Reverend Dr. Martin Luther, 18
Kirk, Patty, 15, 38, 111, 196, 255, 329, 391, 394, 410
Knapp, Carol, 5, 55, 70, 106, 137, 171, 231, 240, 272, 305, 410–411
Knit for Kids, 135
Knitting, 135, 214
Kubrick, Stanley (film director), 212
Kuykendall, Carol, 46, 89, 123, 141, 178, 217, 254, 315, 351, 385, 411
Kuyper, Vicki, 26, 58, 127, 216, 243, 276, 318, 370, 411–412

Labor Day, 273
Lazarus (of Bethany), 388

Legos, 78, 130
Lent, 69, 75, 79, 119
Lewis, C. S. (author), 155
Lincoln, President Abraham, 56, 186
Lion of Judah, 325
"The Longer I Serve Him" (hymn), 292
Long Island Sound, 183
Lord's Prayer (Our Father), 154, 212, 257, 336
Lorenz, Patricia, 4, 53, 96, 125, 151, 191, 238, 310, 338, 365, 412
Love, 21–22, 26, 29, 37, 41, 47–49, 53, 55, 58–59, 74, 80, 83, 88, 108, 117–118, 129, 134, 137, 176, 178, 188, 191, 196, 201–202, 229, 238, 246, 257, 276–277, 288, 314, 316, 318, 329–330, 336, 341, 350, 356, 361, 381, 395
"Love bags," 348
Lynch, Peter (investor), 201

Machu Picchu, 52
Macomber, Debbie, 60, 135, 188, 235, 342, 395, 412
MacPherson, Erin, 12, 83, 122, 136, 230, 251, 364, 378, 413
Magnetic resonance imaging (MRI), 294
The Maltese Falcon (movie), 212
"Mansions of the Lord" (hymn), 163
Martha (biblical sister), 207, 388
Martin Luther King Jr. Day, 18
Marx, Groucho (comedian), 338
Mary (biblical sister), 207
Mary (mother of Jesus), 372
Mass, 72, 176, 310, 391
Massachusetts, 72, 246, 279; Berkshires, 246, 279; Boston, 10, 279; Cambridge, 72; Cape Cod, 239; Monterey, 246
Matthew, book of, 289
Mayan ruins, 391, 394
McCollors, Tia, 29, 92, 109, 130, 229, 271, 413
Medicare, 283
Meditation, 290, 325
Mediterranean Sea, 52, 276
Memorial Day, 163
Mercer University, 154, 369; Institute of Life Purpose, 369
Mercy, 70, 193, 252, 364, 379
Merrymeeting Lake, 265
Messner, Roberta, 30, 47, 86, 202, 258, 292, 322, 384, 413–414
Mexico, 394; Coba, 394; Yucatán, 391

Michigan, 11; Mackinac Island, 275
Middle East, 276; Jordan, 135
Military, 163, 177, 204, 276, 346
Miracles, 18, 97, 143, 175, 220, 244, 322, 330
Mississippi, 18
Mississippi River, 221, 105
Missouri, 297; Moberly, 347
Mister Rogers' Neighborhood (TV series), 296
"Mockin' Bird Hill" (song), 57
Monkeys, 394
Montana, 57, 231, 244
Montmartre, 149
Moore, James (gospel singer), 288
Morrison, Toni (author), 344
Mother's Day, 141
Mothers of Preschoolers (MOPS), 89, 141
Mourner's Kaddish, 264
Myanmar, 318

NFL (National Football League), 41, 168, 338
Nature, 129, 394
Nebraska, 112
Nehemiah (governor of Judea), 130
Neighbors, 7, 16, 23, 32, 78, 129, 136, 148, 152, 196, 208, 226, 263, 273, 285, 308, 342, 358, 376, 383, 389, 392
Neitch, Dr. Shirley, 86
New Hampshire, 10, 119, 214
New Jersey, 11
New Mexico, 11
New Year's Day, 2–3
New Year's Eve, 203, 399
New Year's resolutions, 2–3, 17
New York, 11, 176, 206, 235, 250; Brooklyn, 269; Carmel, 176, 236; Chelsea, 11; Manhattan, 11, 273, 279, 398; New York City, 40, 144, 277, 399
The New York Times, 144
Noah (biblical patriarch), 101, 113, 130, 272
Nobel Prize, 398
"No Other Love" (song), 59
North Carolina, 229; Guilford County, 229; Kitty Hawk, 275
Norwegian tradition, 382

Oklahoma, 111, 329
Old Testament, 255, 327
Ondov, Rebecca, 43, 121, 175, 244, 302, 353, 414
Oscar (Academy Award), 24
OxyContin, 30

Authors, Titles, and Subjects Index

Paine, Thomas (politician), 18
Palm Sunday, 79, 110
Passion Week, 110
Passover (Pesach), 108
Paths of Glory (movie), 212
Patience, 58, 101, 155, 229, 256, 283
Paul (apostle), 135, 305, 325, 337
Peace, 83, 104, 137, 150, 157, 176, 193, 202–203, 219, 229, 231, 251, 265, 279, 288, 291, 297, 327, 358, 372, 388
Pennsylvania, 11; Havertown, 11; Philadelphia, 381
Peter (apostle), 70, 117
Pets, 6, 45, 148, 155, 187, 255, 275, 329, 397; Boston terrier, 144; chow chow, 45; golden retriever, 50, 80, 144, 154, 179, 246, 256, 313, 353; Labrador-coonhound, 329; Labrador retriever, 144, 289, 352; Scottish terrier, 397
Philippines, 204, 297
Philips Brooks House, 72
Plutarch (philosopher), 370
Pneumonia, 22, 286
Ponderosa pines, 139, 379
Popeye the Sailor (fictional character), 245
Post-traumatic stress disorder (PTSD), 15
Prayer, 3, 5, 22, 26, 29–30, 36, 40, 42, 49, 51–52, 56, 67, 71–72, 75, 87, 89, 91, 95, 102–103, 114, 125, 149, 152, 154, 176, 187, 193, 207, 211–212, 220–221, 228, 230–231, 240–241, 244, 246, 255, 257, 264, 274, 276, 290, 295, 298, 307, 309, 314–315, 320, 322, 325, 336, 343, 355, 357, 387
"Praying Together" series, 2–3, 17, 25, 36, 42, 49
Presbyterian ministry, 69, 143, 201, 206
Presidents' Day, 56
Protestant Men of the Chapel, 349

Queen of England, 201

Rebbetzyn (rabbi's wife), 158
Redmond, Shirley Raye, 155, 220, 286, 397, 414
Red Sea, 276
Resurrection, 137, 388
Roadside shrines, 54
Rocky Mountains (Rockies), 112, 114, 118
Rodgers and Hammerstein (composers), 59

Rogers, Fred (TV host), 296
Rudolph (fictional reindeer), 390
Rue, Ginger, 16, 84, 148, 180, 203, 249, 317, 352, 415

Sabbath (Shabbat), 52, 262, 331, 270
Sacred spaces, 361
"Sacred Spaces" series, 10, 54, 72, 149, 224, 265
Sacrificial Lamb, 325
Saint Nicholas, 387
Salvadoran, 152
Salvation, 93, 325
Sampson, Chaplain Kenneth, 69, 192, 349, 374, 415
Samuel (biblical prophet), 240
Santa Claus, 180, 383, 387
Sarah (Abraham's wife), 130
Schantz, Daniel, 31, 174, 237, 275, 283, 312, 326, 347, 415–416
Schilling, Gail Thorell, 10, 54, 72, 149, 214, 224, 265, 287, 416
Schwab, Penney, 41, 45, 76, 162, 210, 320, 416
Scotland, 296
Scottish kilts, 285
Seder, 108
September 11 terrorist attacks, 11, 113, 279
Seuss Geisel, Dr. Theodor (author), 275
Seventh Avenue Baptist Church (West Virginia), 292
Sharpie marker, 105
Shepherd Farms, 347
Solomon (son of David), 93, 171
The Sound of Music (musical), 59
The South, 327, 344
South America, 370; Chile, 303; Colombia, 164; Ecuador, 370; Peru, 164; Venezuela, 164
Southern Baptist Convention, 331
Southern barbeque, 186
South Mountain Park and Preserve, 362
Spanish language, 376
Sport utility vehicle (SUV), 384
St. Andrews Presbyterian Church (Florida), 206, 293
Starbucks, 47
Star Wars (movie franchise), 309, 398
St. Cecilia Church (New Hampshire), 224
St. Joan of Arc Church (New Hampshire), 224
St. Katharine Drexel Parish (New Hampshire), 224

Storm, Buck, 62, 211, 227, 252, 340, 358, 375, 417
St. Patrick's Day, 83
Strandberg, Jolynda, 28, 56, 177, 222, 323, 356, 417
Strength training, 337
Subaru, 120
Suez Canal, 276
Sunday school, 155, 162, 210–211, 245
Superstorm Sandy, 11
Switzerland, 142
Sweeney, Jon M., 7, 77, 147, 190, 223, 281, 304, 361, 417

Taizé, 69, 72
Temple, Shirley (actress), 202
Templeton, Sir John (investor), 201
Tennessee, 285; Nashville, 143, 201
Texas, 41, 186, 210; Dallas, 346; Galveston, 186, 275; Houston, 252
Thames River (Connecticut), 183
Thanksgiving Day, 307, 347, 359
"This Little Light of Mine" (hymn), 193
Thompson, Stephanie, 2–3, 17, 25, 36, 42, 49, 126, 418
Tin Man (fictional character), 327
Trick-or-treating, 332
Turk, Marilyn, 51, 67, 163, 194, 209, 291, 418
Turner Classic Movies (TCM), 212

Ukraine, 395
United Nations (UN), 216
United Parcel Service (UPS), 289
United States Disciplinary Barracks, 349
United States of America, 56, 163, 395
United States Postal Service (USPS), 374
University of Pittsburgh, 142
US Army Corps of Engineers, 69
US citizenship, 152
US Route 60, 258
USS *Missouri*, 341

Vacation Bible School (VBS), 47, 222
Vacuum cleaner, 313; DustBuster, 363; Dyson, 313
Valentin, Karen, 85, 156, 260, 269, 316, 332, 360, 399, 419
Valentine's Day, 47
Van Gogh, Vincent (painter), 250
Venus (planet), 139
Veterans Day, 346

Authors, Titles, and Subjects Index

Victorian home, 105, 140, 221, 327
Village Hope, 143
Virginia, 344, 381; Old Point Comfort, 344

Waffle House, 380
Waikiki Beach, 129
Walker, Scott, 9, 154, 204, 256, 297, 331, 369, 419
Wall Street, 11, 242
Wall Street (movie), 24
The Waltons (TV series), 381
Washington, President George, 56
Washington, Seattle, 188
"We Beheld His Glory" series, 362, 372, 379, 386, 392–393

Wedding anniversary, 41, 53
Welsh heritage, 395
Wesley, John (theologian), 95
Western Hemisphere, 312
West Point (US Military Academy), 69
Wheelock, Jacqueline F., 18, 93, 129, 219, 262, 288, 325, 337, 420
Where Do We Go from Here: Chaos or Community? (book), 18
White, Jim (songwriter), 75
Williams, Gayle T., 8, 87, 150, 277, 389, 420
Wisconsin, 393
"Wisdom's Delights" series, 5, 70, 106, 137, 171, 240, 272, 305

"Wonderful Words of Life" (hymn), 162
Wordsworth, William (poet), 93
World Trade Center, 11, 279
World Vision, 135
World War I, 212
World War II, 155, 204, 297, 341, 381
Wright brothers (aviators), 248
Wyoming, 10

Yahrzeit (anniversary of a death), 264
Yoda (fictional character), 398

Zoom app, 290

A NOTE FROM THE EDITORS

We hope you enjoyed *Walking in Grace 2022,* published by Guideposts. For over 75 years, Guideposts, a nonprofit organization, has been driven by a vision of a world filled with hope. We aspire to be the voice of a trusted friend, a friend who makes you feel more hopeful and connected.

By making a purchase from Guideposts, you join our community in touching millions of lives, inspiring them to believe that all things are possible through faith, hope, and prayer. Your continued support allows us to provide uplifting resources to those in need. Whether through our communities, websites, apps, or publications, we inspire our audiences, bring them together, and comfort, uplift, entertain, and guide them.

To learn more, please go to guideposts.org.

We would love to hear from you:

To make a purchase or view our many publications, please go to shopguideposts.org.
To call us, please dial (800) 932-2145
Or write us at Guideposts, P.O. Box 5815, Harlan, Iowa 51593